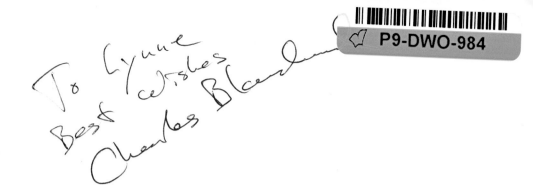

POSITIVE PIANO

HISTORY'S GREATEST PIANISTS
ON HOW TO SUCCEED WILDLY IN LIFE

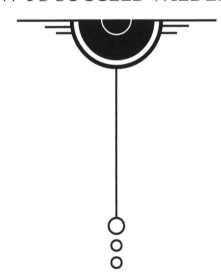

Charles Blanchard
© 2015

ISBN 978-1-944294-00-7   Paper

Library of Congress Cataloging - in - Publication Data pending

Contact : www.positivepiano.com
Cover and internal design : Julian Williams
First Edition: October 2015

o

For my parents, Joseph and Frances Blanchard,

I miss you guys, thanks for your love…and the piano lessons

CONTENTS

Everything must be possible.
JOHANN SEBASTIAN BACH

*Take it for granted from the beginning
that everything's possible on the piano,
even when it seems impossible to you, or
really is so.*
FERRUCCIO BUSONI

*The vexation of an obstacle begins when
one imagines that it is insurmountable.*
MORIZ ROSENTHAL

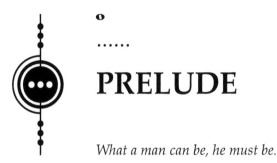

PRELUDE

What a man can be, he must be.

—ABRAHAM MASLOW

Inside each one of us is an astounding wealth of creative potential. Our entire life represents a unique opportunity to realize this birthright, a dynamic process psychologists call self-actualization. Besides physical growth, the process includes our mental development and all multi-faceted life experience, both joy and suffering. The challenge is to make the most of the unique gifts we're blessed with, to actualize our potential, achieve happiness and contribute greatly.

Self-actualization. Although associated with Maslow, the 19th century neurologist Kurt Goldstein (1878-1965) coined the term - in active tense. It's all in the doing; the choices and the actions. What we do and how we do it eventually define our unique identity or 'self'.

We are what we repeatedly do.
ARISTOTLE

There's infinitely more to it than snapping a selfie. Humans innately yearn to express the creativity within their inner selves. Sometimes perceived practical concerns win out and we get side-tracked in activities that stifle and frustrate our higher purpose. Adversity is an unfortunate fact of life (Latin: *adversitatem* or opposition). How we deal with that opposition to our desires can either wear us down, or make us stronger.

Humans first seek to fulfill basic physiological and social needs: food, water, shelter, and sexual gratification. Next comes the need for friendship, love, and self-esteem. Given a modest success in attaining these, the highest stage of self-actualization and personal fulfillment is defined by moral and ethical behavior, spirituality, and artistic creativity.

Like everyone else I've often wondered about my purpose in life, questioning how best to go about developing my talents. I've worried about how to earn a living and still be true to my inner nature. And I've asked myself why the world is the way it is, and how to make it a better place.

One thing's for sure: we're in this together. Everything we do affects others, just as their actions affect us. I wish you and I could sit down together and share our experiences, ideas, and dreams; commiserate on our frustrations and setbacks; and somehow pool our strengths in collaboration. We could help each other accomplish our goals, and become happier and more fulfilled in the process.

We can benefit greatly from the experience of accomplished persons, past and present. Valuable wisdom from the past may be found in letters and diaries, and anecdotes recorded by eye-witnesses. When these involve the most successful people of an era, this wisdom can be truly transformative – if a person is ready and willing to learn from it and proactively implement beneficial changes.

A large body of such material from the 19th century music world is increasingly relevant today. Ever since I was a kid I've loved the great pianists and composers and their artistic legacy. I believe that their wisdom as human beings has value for all. Their experience and insights can be a real education. Along with invaluable practical information about music technique, there are references to virtually all the important philosophical issues in life.

The indispensables in pianistic success? Are they not very much the same in all successes?
JOSEF HOFMANN

The reverse sentiment holds as well. The indispensables underlying any success are very much like mastering the art of playing the piano. Everyone can benefit from this book because these proven principles for success in piano playing are directly applicable to overcoming challenges and acquiring mastery in every field of endeavor.

You may be surprised by some of the deeply profound perspectives of the 19th century. Far from the clichéd 'secrets' touted by shallow contemporary self-help books, this is genuine classical wisdom, all readily accessible by studying this brilliant group of men and women who in the course of their lives profoundly self-actualized to an astonishing degree and bequeathed to us that priceless artistic legacy.

A common denominator of truly great people is the desire to assist others. They progressed way beyond personal ego and recognized that the striving is about greatness for humanity. They always had kind and encouraging words for those struggling to realize the artist within.

They told me it was a common saying at Weimar - "Liszt always helps whenever he can".
BETTINA WALKER

So many musicians gained recognition through the assistance of Liszt, and owe it to the publicity he gave them. He loved to discover talent and those who wished to make serious progress in music always found him encouraging.
COUNT ALBERT APPONYI

Gottschalk loved talent, but loved more to encourage it. "Unselfish as Gottschalk" became a proverb among a certain musical coterie in New York, and to this day it is quoted when any truly great artists (too few of them, alas!) give their services as quietly and unostentatiously as he ever gave his.
OCTAVIA HENSEL

If Leschetizky believed in a pupil, he did everything in his power to help him. He never pretended that the road to success was simple or easy; on the contrary, he pointed out and emphasized the difficulties.
ETHEL NEWCOMB

If you're not yet familiar with the names Franz Liszt, Louis Moreau Gottschalk, and Theodor Leschetizky, you will be shortly. These super achievers of the 19th century, and many more, are going to reach out from the past and help you succeed in a big way.

There's a huge amount of material on 19th century piano playing and the volume of related information in all fields has since grown tremendously and is still multiplying. How can one be expected to sort it all out? These days our typical reaction is to specialize, as epitomized by university academic departments and corporate management hierarchies with their increasingly narrow job descriptions - and that's part of the problem. We're occupied more and more with less and less and few are putting it all together, systematically and wholistically, with the big picture in mind.

You're probably used to seeing that word spelled 'holistic'. That reminds me of a hole in the ground, with something missing. The spelling should reflect thinking and acting in the context of the whole, so I'm changing it to *wholistic*.

Positive Piano takes a comprehensive look at the success strategies of great pianists and composers of the 19th century and presents a wholistic synthesis of this treasure trove of wisdom. It highlights their most powerful ideas and advice in many areas, explores how and why they excelled, and integrates this with the latest relevant information in the areas of health, psychology, and management.

True wisdom is timeless so we'll also dig into some musty ancient philosophical and religious tomes, the same ones the great 19th century pianists and composers read and greatly benefited from. Beethoven loved Plutarch and Homer; Liszt avidly read Marcus Aurelius, Dante, and Goethe and was inspired by the example of St. Francis. Robert Schumann often refers to the novelist Jean Paul. Curiously, Chopin was not a reader, but a patriotic love of his Polish homeland powerfully impelled his creative muse. One of his earliest compositions as a child of eight was a *Polonaise*, and his final one, literally composed on his deathbed was a *Mazurka*.

Virtually everyone on the forthcoming list of hugely talented pianists and composers weighs in with hard-earned experiential advice on what does (and doesn't) work for success. And they'll virtually cheer you on with pep talks to keep you going when you temporarily lose heart. In fact, the most important component of this book is the collected quotations from these masters.

I have gathered a posie of other men's flowers, and nothing but the thread

that binds them is mine own.
JOHN BARTLETT

The unique creative synthesis of this book stems from my personal interpretation of these quotes and my own life experience and education. How you interpret this synthesis will be a function of your own experience and education to date.

The result becomes a powerful procedural and motivational blueprint for your as yet unimagined potential success; because to actualize it you must first start imagining success and believing in yourself. Please, get comfortable and read on; but very soon you'll need to roll up your sleeves, and begin working for your success.

A prelude is much more than a simple introduction; it's a meaningful creation in itself. Consider your life up to this point as a prelude to what remains in store for you. Wherever you are at this moment in your life's journey, you've acquired valuable skills and experience and have racked up many significant accomplishments. Well and good; but the process of self-actualization doesn't end until you do. An individual vision of what's possible can and should evolve and expand with time; it's that new, greater vision that leads to greater accomplishment. As long as you're breathing you can always do more, and the best is yet to come.

The German saying *"Wer schreibt, der bleibt"* insinuates that written words have more staying power than spoken ones. Pianists and composers who wrote a lot tend to be disproportionately represented here, but that doesn't necessarily mean that those who didn't leave a lengthy written record aren't as important. Poets know that the most meaningful message is often compactly expressed in the fewest words.

No age has ever been 'perfect' and the 19th century is no exception. We find material in the vast music literature that is inconsistent and not always 'positive'. Guided by my title, a lot of this stuff didn't make the cut. The main point is that each generation is confronted with the same fundamental life issues and it behooves us to conserve, and learn from, the best of our common heritage.

Learning and personal growth are unending, mastery is a lifelong process – or should be. No single book contains sufficient wisdom and knowledge to answer all your questions and guide you through all of life. Since every life is different you will in effect write your own book of life. Complementary sources, both old and new, will be recommended for further reading and it's important to follow up on them for best results, not just perfunctorily, but really thinking about what you read.

Reading furnishes the mind only with materials of knowledge; it is thinking that makes what we read ours.
JOHN LOCKE

It's not just a question of information, with computers there's an over-abundance of that these days and our world is still far from perfect, to say the least. And now we have the eloquent prophecy of imminent salvation by artificial intelligence. The tech-lords of Silicon Valley want to save us from ourselves, or at least line their pocketbooks so they can buy not one but two apartments in San Francisco. C'mon – we can't even get people to use a century old analog device called the turn-signal.

We've had virtual reality ever since we moved out of the forests and into houses. The early adobe, wattle and daub, or thatched grass weren't too far removed from nature but today's steel, glass, and concrete in effect hermetically seals us off from it. And the new 'virtual reality' is going to be really great … we're told. I used to be into numismatics and was initially puzzled by a pristine uncirculated coin being labelled a 'virtual gem' until one particularly honest dealer explained: 'virtual' means 'not'.

As individuals we must acquire qualities of critical thinking, flexibility of thought, open-mindedness, self-reliance, maturity and wisdom. Progress requires the ability to imagine something better and the courage to risk trying it.

Reading is really just a prelude to thinking, but transformative growth depends on psychological readiness to embrace change through decisive action. So get ready to read, think, and act.

To read without thinking is like accumulating building materials without building anything.
RABINDRANATH TAGORE

And things may not always sink in the first time around. An individual's ability to absorb and understand intellectual concepts via language varies greatly. Often one has to read, then experience life a bit, then go back and re-read to become aware of truths previously only superficially understood or barely perceived at all.

Books must be read as deliberately and reservedly as they were written.
HENRY DAVID THOREAU

I wish someone else had written this book years ago; it would have made my study of the piano a lot easier. Well, it's making it easier now; but more importantly, if you truly think deeply, and act on this amalgam of powerful, proven wisdom it will vastly improve not only your piano-playing but your life.

And speaking of books on music - let me advise you to read them but not to believe them unless they support every statement with an argument that succeeds in convincing you.
JOSEF HOFMANN

Oh, oh … the pressure's on; I'll do my best.

Those 19th century masters knew a thing or two about creating and playing beautiful piano music. They succeeded in life on a scale that evokes admiration centuries later. You can count on it – they were passionately engaged in life for the long-haul, trading immediate gratification for patience and perseverance. They evolved an integrity and work ethic capable of accommodating a magnificent vision.

The chapters ahead explore their life experiences and reveal the fundamentals behind their great success. This legacy can potentially inform and motivate, but it bears repeating: everything remains theoretical until you choose to act. If you're expecting some magical secret to success, without lifting a finger except to tap on a glass screen or press a button on a remote control … you'll be disappointed. The first step towards your success hasn't changed in centuries – you must consciously accept responsibility for your own destiny.

I will take fate by the throat; it will never completely bend me to its will.
BEETHOVEN

A note to the reader: you may have noticed the publisher's legal disclaimer in the front matter affirming that nothing in this book should be construed as medical or legal advice. Given the nature of this book let's hope that's sufficiently cautioning and entertaining as it stands.

Though now deceased, all the persons quoted in this book were once very much alive. Any resemblance to them by living individuals is highly recommended.

But remember, most of this information is over a century old and is the opinion of pianists or composers; you know, the kind of people you wouldn't want your daughter going out with, much less marrying. Also, they in turn were often influenced by Greek and Roman philosophers who have been dead for two thousand years.

Remember that all is opinion.
MARCUS AURELIUS, EMPEROR OF ROME

And heaven forbid, even the Bible is quoted. So no guarantees, okay? Reader, beware. *Caveat Lector*

Let me also say right up front that we'll spend some time analyzing various theories about 'success' from the contemporary worlds of business and psychology. We're going to take some of their most precious sacred cows and grind them into hamburger meat (no offense to the great religion of Hinduism is intended). I've discovered that some piano players who lived over a hundred years ago offer a wealth of advice that's infinitely wiser and more practical than the current wave of purported 'self-help'.

Your author also promises to spare you the all too common self-congratulatory hyperbole about me, me, me - if you've been reading any of those recent business and psychology books you deserve a break from that.

Nothing has so bad an effect as to praise oneself.
CHRISTOPH W. von GLUCK

How disagreeable the man who is always dragging conversation round to his personal affairs, and calling attention to his wonderful qualities and his distinguished achievements and the things which he can do so much better than anyone else. We infinitely prefer the man who lets us find out his greatness for ourselves to the person who is always hustling us into acknowledging it.
SIR HUBERT PARRY

I sincerely hope *Positive Piano* will be a fun, informative, and stimulating experience for you. And may you be inspired and compelled to act, persevere, and magnificently manifest your creative life dream.

Charles Blanchard

Chapter 1

......

THE GOLD STANDARD

Always play as if a master were present.

—ROBERT SCHUMANN

It seems to be human nature for every generation to feel superior to previous ones. But civilization is more of a continuum with crests and troughs, good times and bad, progressive periods of enlightenment, followed by periods of relative ignorance. Every generation, and every individual, has a window of opportunity in which to make a contribution. Maybe we're smarter today, maybe not; smart and wise are not necessarily the same thing.

We've come a long way in some categories, take technology for example. Our relatively advanced knowledge provides us with potentially better utilization of natural resources, more efficient and profitable business, virtually instantaneous communications, and improved healthcare (well, kind of - more on that later). Science and engineering technology has even taken us to the moon, something 19th century author H. G. Wells was writing sci-fi novels about. Of course, envisioning a thing is the first step.

Thanks to the computer and Internet we have much greater access to information ... and misinformation. And we've also gained deeper insights into human psychology. It seems as though we're smarter in almost everything and yet we're still confronted with the same fundamental challenges, only more intensely and on a larger scale.

Positive Piano

Everything has been figured out, except how to live.
JEAN-PAUL SARTRE

As far as playing the piano goes, they definitely did it better in the 19th century. The greatest musical artists of that era composed some of the most beautiful and expressive piano music ever, and by all accounts their inspired performances were uniquely breathtaking, marvelous, and magical. They set an incomparable artistic standard that remains unmatched today despite all our current advantages.

Why was that particular era so conducive to pianistic greatness and how did they do it? Of course there was keyboard genius and innovation earlier, for example, J.S. Bach and sons, Domenico Scarlatti and Handel. Five of the greatest musical artists of all time were born in the 18th century: Haydn (1732-1809), Mozart (1756-1791), Beethoven (1770-1827), Hummel (1778-1837) and Schubert (1797-1828). All except Mozart lived into the early 19th century.

In hindsight, momentum was building. Contributing to the mix on the eve of the new century was Carl Czerny (1791-1857). This unique man combined aesthetic vision, work ethic, and amazing perseverance to become perhaps the ultimate music pedagogue and 'achievement' coach. Even as a ten-year old, Czerny so impressed Beethoven that he was taken on as a pupil of that great man.

Czerny learned and matured tremendously under Beethoven, and went on to teach another ten year old boy who subsequently became the greatest of all pianists - Franz Liszt. Czerny has also indirectly influenced legions of pianists over the years through his many volumes of études or study pieces.

Arbitrary points on a timeline don't tell the whole story but they offer perspective. In retrospect, it seems that nature had been gradually setting the stage, preparing to achieve a high-density critical mass of piano talent. Then, at the dawn of the 19th century a musical floodgate was unleashed, followed by a legendary flourishing of the musical arts led by the piano.

1800 Joseph Kessler
1803 Henri Herz
1809 Felix Mendelssohn
1810 Robert Schumann, Frederic Chopin
1811 Franz Liszt, Ferdinand Hiller, Marie Pleyel
1812 Sigismond Thalberg
1813 Charles-Valentin Alkan, Stephen Heller, Richard Wagner
1814 Adolph Henselt
1816 William Sterndale Bennett
1817 Émile Prudent
1818 Henri Litolff, Theodor Kullak, Alexander Dreyschock
1819 Clara Schumann née Wieck, Charles Hanon, Karol Mikuli
1822 Joachim Raff, César Franck
1824 Carl Reinecke
1829 Louis Moreau Gottschalk, Anton Rubinstein, William Mason
1830 Theodore Leschetizky, Hans von Bülow, Karl Klindworth
1833 Johannes Brahms
1834 Dionys Pruckner
1835 Camille Saint-Saëns, Nikolai Rubinstein
1836 Arabella Goddard
1837 Mily Balakirev
1839 Modest Mussorgsky
1841 Carl Tausig, Giovanni Sgambati
1842 Walter Bache
1844 Amy Fay, Oscar Beringer
1845 Gabriel Fauré
1846 Sophie Menter
1847 Oskar Raif
1849 Count Géza Zichy

Midway through the century there was a brief pause, as if the creative force in nature rested momentarily; then followed a second wave of consummate talent.

1851 Anna Yesipova
1852 Rafael Joseffy, Constantin Sternberg, Max Vogrich, Alfred Grünfeld
1853 Teresa Carreño
1854 Moritz Moszkowski, Paul Pabst
1857 Cecil Chaminade

Positive Piano

1858 Tobias Matthay
1859 Arthur Friedheim
1860 Isaac Albéniz, Edward MacDowell, Ignace Paderewski
1862 Claude Debussy, Moriz Rosenthal, Arthur de Greef
1863 Ernesto Nazareth, Isidore Philipp, Alexander Siloti,
    Felix Blumenfeld, Fannie Bloomfield-Zeisler
1864 Eugen d'Albert
1865 Émile Jaques-Dalcroze
1866 Ferruccio Busoni, Eric Satie
1867 Enrique Granados, Amy Beach, Martinus Sieveking
1868 Scott Joplin
1870 Leopold Godowsky, Sigismond Stojowski
1871 Ernest Hutcheson
1872 Alexander Scriabin, Joaquín Malats
1873 Sergei Rachmaninoff, Harold Bauer, Max Reger, Joseph-Édouard Risler
1874 Josef Lhévinne, Marguerite Long
1875 Maurice Ravel, Albert Schweitzer
1876 Josef Hofmann
1877 Alfred Cortot, Wanda Landowska
1879 Cyril Scott
1880 Nikolai Medtner , Rosina Lhévinne, Olga Samaroff
1881 Egon Petri
1882 Percy Grainger, Igor Stravinsky, Artur Schnabel, Joaquín Turina, Ignaz Friedman
1883 Arnold Bax
1887 Paul Wittgenstein, Artur Rubinstein, Yolanda Mero, Eubie Blake
1888 Heinrich Neuhaus
1890 Dame Myra Hess, Benno Moiseiwitsch

And in the final hours, almost as if was said: "I'm very pleased with my work, but let's throw in just a few more …"

1891 James P. Johnson, Sergei Prokofiev
1892 Mieczyslaw Horszowski
1893 Frederico Mompou, Leo Ornstein
1895 Ernesto Lecuona, Walter Gieseking, Guiomar Novaes, José Iturbi, Clara Haskil
1896 Alexander Brailowsky
1898 George Gershwin, Shin'ichi Suzuki
1899 Duke Ellington

Vladimir Horowitz, the man who was to set the standard for 20th century piano playing, was born in 1903.

It's clear that this stunning illustrative list (not exhaustive) represents a true golden age of intense piano music composition and performance activity yielding extraordinary results, reminiscent of 5th century B.C. Athens or Renaissance Italy for painting, sculpture, poetry, architecture, and philosophy. By the way, that word renaissance is actually French, perhaps indicating that they simply bested the Italians in historical branding. The Italian is *rinascimento* or rebirth. But Paris, along with Vienna and Berlin, was a major focal point for the 19th century musical renaissance.

For whatever political, social, or economic reasons, in the centuries prior to the Renaissance European civilization seems to have experienced a period of relative stagnation. (That's not to say that interesting stuff wasn't happening all over the rest of the planet). Key factors underlying the great flowering of artistic activity were the literary achievements of Petrarch and Dante and a renewed interest in the best of the ancient world. Later on, thanks to Gutenberg's printing press, access to books expanded greatly and top on the best seller lists were those ancient Greek and Roman classics. Artists and architects even journeyed to Rome to measure and study ancient monuments and sculptures.

The men and women of the Renaissance rediscovered the great ideas and techniques of the past and applied them with renewed vigor in their own lives, adding significant new innovations.

It is universally admitted in the present day that the foundation of all true knowledge must be study of the great classics which have been handed down to us by our ancestors. Only thus can we be assured of progress, by gathering new strength for the advancement of knowledge. It also has the negative advantage of convincing empty pretenders of their emptiness. It is a most sorry conceit for any man to neglect the study of the great spirits of former days, and thus say in effect that he's able to produce what they did.
ANTON THIBAUT

Despite the myriad technological advances we now enjoy, compared to the musically vibrant 19th century our contemporary music scene sadly appears to be in a trough resembling that languorous state prior to the Renaissance. Today 'classical' musicians for the most part competently perform a canonical repertoire consisting of a small subset of historical works. A common complaint heard is that though mechanically correct, the playing has to some degree assumed a rather sterile, homogenous and almost museum-like quality.

[**Disclaimer**: Occasionally I'll ascend my virtual soapbox, a 19th century platform, literally, for expressing one's personal opinion. These days it's usually done by way of the Op-ed, blog, YouTube comment, various flavors of social media, just plain texting, and even the once relatively objective 'news'].

Rest assured, ostentatious, stale, boring, and disheartening are not qualities inherent in the music itself but are reflective of our time, our performers, and even our audiences who, after all, must also interpret.

So you really think a poem has only one meaning? Aren't you aware that each poem is transformed by the reader? And it's the same with every musical score.
CLAUDE DEBUSSY

To have great poets, there must be great audiences.
WALT WHITMAN

All too often, critics and audiences alike decry those mechanically proficient yet somehow 'uninspired' performances. To the chagrin of aspiring composers, the words 'new music' often make people literally turn and run.

Dwindling, aging audiences at classical concerts have become the stereotypical norm. Sustainability and economic viability of the arts is in jeopardy. Symphony orchestras are increasingly going bankrupt and music education budgets are routinely reduced. These factors in the acknowledged gradual decline of the musical arts over the past couple of generations are documented in popular books like *Who Killed Classical Music?* by Norman Lebrecht (Carol Publishing Group).

Negativity even surfaces in surveys of professional career satisfaction; many 'classical' musicians are unhappy with their jobs. If they aren't enthusiastic and inspired, heaven help the audience.

A musician cannot move others unless he too is moved. He must feel all the emotions he hopes to arouse in the audience, for the revealing of his own emotion will stimulate a like mood in the listener.
C.P.E. BACH

It's too convenient to simply blame the current state of affairs on the musicians. Over time, audiences have become less discriminating in large part due to that growing neglect of arts education by both government and private sectors.

Why does the public not applaud when a piece finishes softly?
L. M. GOTTSCHALK

The public does not generally care about Adagios; this arises from a sort of shortsightedness of the ear (if such a phrase be permitted), which fails to grasp or embrace the rhythmical scope of the piece.
M. MATHIS LUSSY

Never play slow movements at Court - it bores them.
LISZT

Gone are the days when a majority of concert-goers played a musical instrument, sang, or cultivated knowledge of art and literature. But there is, and always has been, a disproportionate fascination with the spectacle.

People in general like to see exceptional feats, and plume themselves on the ability to distinguish special strokes of skill. They crowd to see acrobats, strong men, jugglers, and singers who can screech a note or two higher than others. Such people will talk of a feat as if it were in itself a concrete universal thing that everyone must see. In reality they are only setting up as admirable the standard of their own meagre understanding.
SIR HUBERT PARRY

The attraction that binds the virtuoso to the public is similar to that which draws crowds to the circus: we always hope that something dangerous will happen. M. Ysaïje will play the violin with M. Colonne on his shoulders, or M. Pugno will finish by seizing the piano with his teeth.
CLAUDE DEBUSSY

Positive Piano

Whenever serpents are strangled the general public wants to know just how big and how dangerous they are, and judge this by the performer's behavior.
WILHELM von LENZ

In large leaps, now and then you must claw a wrong note; otherwise no one will notice that it is difficult.
HANS von BÜLOW

The audience, in fact, responded wildly and recalled the performers four times ... although the Times contended that the reception was perhaps not due to the work or the performance but the audience's desire to see yet again the celebrated trio of performers - exciting as an "enlarged edition" of Siamese twins - for the "agreeable historical remembrance."
THE ARCADIAN (May 1873)

Beethoven once participated in a concert where a man stooped over and played the violin between his legs. In America, L.M. Gottschalk had to compete with blackface minstrel shows. Just like the relationship between customers and business, and citizens and government, performance quality will improve when audiences demand more from artists.

The aphorism "Every country has the government that it deserves" might with equal truth be altered to "Every country has the music it deserves." With music as with everything else, demand and supply go hand-in-hand.
OSCAR BERINGER

A refreshing exception to the above, as in every generation: enthusiastic young music students, sincere and unpretentious in their eagerness to learn and express themselves.

Previous generations have not been immune to occasional lackluster artistic expression, or excessive vanity for that matter – that's been around a long time, dating back to at least the time of Ecclesiastes. But the contemporary 'serious' music scene, excepting a minority of authentic talents working to advance Art, is frankly but a shadow of what it once was. What passes (or fails) as original composition these days doesn't begin to compare with the inspiration, innovation, craftsmanship, and just plain beauty of a previous era.

I recently burned over a ream of my old compositions and am pleased they no longer exist.
C.P.E. BACH

Haydn feared to weary his hearers. Our modern bards have no such vain scruple.
CAMILLE SAINT-SAËNS

If only some of our current 'composers' would similarly raise their standards. The label 'atonal' is nonsensical. Most contemporary offerings have plenty of tones, just very few if any tunes. Music, both pop and 'serious', is largely becoming 'a-tunal'. Of the three main ingredients in music – melody, harmony, and rhythm – melody is perhaps the most powerful for expressing profound human emotion and it's very audibly lacking these days. That's troubling.

You must not promote bad compositions; on the contrary, you should expend every effort to help suppress them. Don't play bad compositions; neither should you listen to them, unless you are forced to.
ROBERT SCHUMANN

They always write too much and think too little.
CLAUDE DEBUSSY

Many modernist composers never even attempt to pronounce a phrase that is musically sensible. … What if the public, one fine day, after being tempted by the struggle with such matter suddenly sensed its superiority and eliminated them and their 'art'?
NICOLAS MEDTNER

I must say that I think the success of those very modern people in painting and music is mainly due to the fact that the audience hasn't the courage to say "No".
ELISABETH SCHWARZKOPF

Something's happened to performance quality as well. Contrast the best of the 19th century. In those good old days, professional pianists were often distinctly recognizable for their unique personality, charisma, interpretative insight, and especially rich and varied tone production - all of which translated directly into exciting performances.

Occasionally, mastery and interpretive application of some specialized area of mechanical technique was so remarkable that a pianist gained notoriety for it. Dreyshock: octaves; Clementi: thirds; Hummel: crystal clarity, elegance; Beethoven: dashingly inventive and profound improvisation; Thalberg: singing quality, arpeggios and 'three-handed effects'; Gottschalk: vibrant ethnic rhythms, scintillating brilliance; Henselt: marvelous tone and sheer virtuosity; Anton Rubinstein: great emotional power and interpretive insight; Chopin, pianissimo filigree, consummate mastery and artistic aesthetic; Liszt: anything and everything, over the top, unbelievable, transcendent, overpowering, sensational, infinitely 'deep.'

Great performing artists often became associated with signature repertoire pieces in which they excelled. Their love for the art was sincerely communicated through their vibrant personalities. Most were also creators of their own original music, from good to masterpiece, constantly premiering innovative new works of great beauty and interest and often pushing the envelope of technique or, as in Liszt's case, shredding it.

In fact their artistic vision drove piano manufacturers to constantly improve the technology of the instrument. When Liszt broke the four-minute mile of piano technique the piano manufacturers rushed to innovate, to satisfy him and incidentally recruit him as a brand ambassador. (His astounding Beatles/Elvis Presley/Michael Jackson viral celebrity status also got their attention)

At the end of the concert Liszt stands as victor on the battlefield. Daunted pianos lie about, smashed strings wave like white flags of surrender, terrified instruments flee into distant corners; the dumbfounded audience recovers as from a natural cataclysm, a dark storm of thunder and lightning, yet mingled with rain and snow of flower petals and a shimmering rainbow.
MORITZ GOTTLIEB SAPHIR

Beethoven was such an influential artist at the beginning of the era that his imagination as a composer virtually demanded more physical capability in the instrument. And amazing as it sounds, the impending deafness of this one man may have also motivated the industry to build a stronger, more powerful piano.

Ask Streicher for me, if he would be kind enough to build a piano especially adapted to my weak hearing; I desire the tone to be as strong as possible. ...I've preferred his instruments ever since 1809. He's the only one who could give me such a piano as I really want.
BEETHOVEN

Piano manufacturing technology eventually peaked towards the end of the 19th century. Those additional bass keys on the Bösendorfer Imperial Grand were recommended by pianist and composer Ferruccio Busoni at the turn of the century. But that extended range is a trifle compared to the more significant earlier innovations along the way that included an iron frame, steel wire for strings, felt-covered hammers, at least two additional octaves, and the double escapement action that enabled quick repeated notes. Another artistic as well as economic boon was vast employment for armies of artisans lovingly crafting their products by hand.

Men, Women, and Pianos by Arthur Loesser (Dover Publications) delightfully chronicles the golden age of the piano. Manufacturers in the 19th century once numbered in the hundreds. We still have some decent pianos today despite the dozen or so remaining brands cutting back on quality and offering more electronic keyboards in order to stay afloat financially.

The new complacency and lowered-bar comfort zone is not inherent in great music of the past but is a symptom of our contemporary mental state. It's been observed that individuality is gradually being supplanted by homogeneity in a global context. The corporate franchise is displacing the 'mom and pops', the endless 24/7 barrage of 'consumer' advertising is persuading us to eat, dress, and buy alike.

We mentioned the book *Who Killed Classical Music*? The author does a good job of recounting the rise of professional artist management and the effect of publicity on the culture. But curiously, he missed the most important one. Now almost totally forgotten, almost as if there's a conspiracy to erase him from memory, Edward Bernays began his career as a booking agent for both the opera singer Enrico Caruso and Sergey Diaghilev's Ballets Russes when in New York City.

Some of the new ideas he implemented?

Positive Piano

All circulars carried a drawing or a photograph which proved that the artists never grew older. The permanent age was about 28. Every artist was 'outstanding'. The word was potent and indefinite enough … and I discovered that words did not always mean what they said. … Caruso saw the powerful influence of publicity and how it developed hero worship.
EDWARD BERNAYS

… a bit of a departure from the 'old school'.

At that time (1860s) the great art of advertising had not as yet been developed and the reputation of an artist was established by the things the audience said about him.
LEOPOLD AUER

If a recommendation for a performer is misleading and untruthful, it is an imposition upon others and a reflection, not only upon the writer of it, but upon all other testimonials that he may have written, and therefore does more harm than good, and should not have been written at all.
E. A. SMITH

In these days of decreased genuine personal interaction we receive most of our information second-hand, often from independent parties hoping to shape our thinking. Apart from the marketed persona, we have little idea of the underlying character of media celebrities and if we were to meet them in person might be disappointed. Glance down at the pedals when some concert pianists play and you may find feet of clay.

One of Bernays' favorite quips was 'gilt by association', where you appeared to be gold-plated by just hanging around celebrities. The idea of money somehow representing a level of quality quickly follows.

America has been brought up on the star system. It overpays top artists and makes gods of its conductors.
JOSÉ ITURBI

Bernays soon realized that he could earn far more from the corporations who began hiring him to persuade people to buy stuff. Paul Mazur, an executive at Lehman Brothers (remember them?)

made a request: "People must be trained to desire new things, even before the old has worn out." Bernays obliged, for a very nice fee; much more than his commissions for booking musicians. Then he graduated to persuading people to 'do' stuff, also making a specialty of fierce mudslinging against his clients' competition in business and politics.

Materialism is a truly ancient concept; there's some serious discussion of it recorded on old clay tablets, papyri, and tanned sheepskins. But it really began picking up steam around the invention of the steam engine and the industrial revolution. Bernard Mandeville published his quirky satire *The Fable of the Bees, or The Grumbling Hive* in 1714. The subtitle is telling: *Private Vices (=) Public Profits.* (The equals sign is mine).

Later on, in 1899 came *The Theory of the Leisure Class* by Thorstein Veblen in which the author coined the familiar term 'conspicuous consumption'. Veblen was a scholar of that 'science' Carlyle deemed 'dismal' (economics). His book, though fascinating, is mainly arm-chair philosophy.

Bernays, however, was the nephew of Sigmund Freud and was the first to exploit psychoanalytic theory in the emerging 'science' of advertising as plied by the 'Mad Men' of Madison Avenue. Later on, I'll tell you something about Edward Bernays that will absolutely shock you.

One generation after Edward Bernays came Jerry Mander, born in 1936. After studying economics (the same dismal science Veblen studied) at Wharton and the Columbia University graduate school of business, Mander eagerly embraced the 1960s – 70s golden age of television advertising now thriving thanks to Bernays' ground breaking contributions.

Bernays coasted into a long gilded retirement, living to the age of 103. He never gave the greater social and moral consequences of his work a second thought. Mander, however, after achieving great success as an executive in the television advertising world, one day had an epiphany, quit, and wrote *Four Arguments For the Elimination of Television* (Quill, 1977).

Mr. Mander - thank you for your magnificent book. If I could copy and paste the whole thing right here I would. Despite the unequal title (and I cannot come up with a substitute, either) this un-name-able ineffable subject matter literally screams truth in a miraculously lucid and gripping manner. Read his book and you will understand why music today is not as vibrant as in the past, and that's the least of the discussion. In the past 'one hundred years of solitude', our world has been transformed from real life - and real art expressing that real life – to virtual unreality, artificial dumbness, and soul-numbing controlled standardization.

The consolation prize? - now you get 31 flavors of it. Our closets and waistlines have expanded relative to the 19th century while original thinking and individuality has shrunk, supplanted by packaged socio-politico-biz propaganda. Today's photo-shopped blemish free images and celebrity hype, along with meticulously edited 'note-perfect' recordings (not to mention *Antares Auto-Tune*) all obscure our humanity. Right up there with celebrity worship, in terms of distortion, are those self-help books that promise a completely effortless, abundant lifestyle if you'll just tune in to the current esoteric fad or buzzword.

It sounds bizarre but actual warming of the globe is one result of the last century's huge snowballing of materialistic consumer mentality and concomitant erosion of individuality and creativity. With one click it has become easy to buy our 'identity' but that is, of course, an illusion.

If we can't even have our own opinion about something, of course this affects our art which, after all, always reflects our thought.

I must protest against the tendency amongst some to imagine that because a great Master lived many years ago and his body has long been dead and buried, his music must also be in a sense dead, unemotional, un-alive and passionless. ... Surely, all these great Masters were pulsating, living beings, at least as alive and fervent as we are, as emotional, as full of passion, as full of strong feeling and thought as the best of us to-day, and probably far more so! Indeed, isn't it evident that it's because of their phenomenal vitality, enthusiasm for their art, and reasoning power, that they were able to give us such masterpieces?
TOBIAS MATTHAY

The player's individuality, influenced by the general cultural and mental tendencies of the times, is the determining element in producing new pianistic tendencies.
JOSEF HOFMANN

We forget that each musical composition by a master was once brand new and cutting edge, emanating from intense artistic and psychological individuality rooted in and reflective of a dynamic cultural milieu. Where are today's uniquely original performers and composers; where are today's great masters? What other factors existed back then that are perhaps different now?

One big difference is that the 19th century artistic outlook was decidedly broad and wholistic. Musical artists were attuned to all the cultural trends in diverse fields. When Beethoven wasn't composing he was often found in the local tavern having a beer or coffee and poring over the political columns of the local newspapers. Liszt was always on top of current events and developments in science and technology; he eagerly read Humboldt and Darwin when first published, and he was a devout Catholic (an open-minded one). In their own field of music they sought to thoroughly master the existing knowledge base, and then pressed forward with innovation.

Liszt insisted that all piano students should learn composition and all students of composition should learn to play the piano; all candidates had to be able to improvise and read from sight, both scores and individual parts.
JAMES HUNEKER

The pianists will have much more to say on the concept of breadth or well-roundedness in subsequent chapters.

Contemporary attitudes in music generally reflect a more narrow compartmented focus and greater conformance to 'tradition' (whatever that is) resulting in markedly less creativity. More than a century ago, for pianists seeking access to Liszt the common advice was 'bring him something new'. The greatest master placed a high value on the individuality and creativity that usually indicated deeper levels of thinking, initiative, love and enthusiasm.

The creation of something new is not accomplished by the intellect but by the play instinct acting from inner necessity. The creative mind plays with the objects it loves.
CARL JUNG

Just as the Florentines looked back at Pericles' Athens for wisdom and inspiration, we can benefit greatly by revisiting and reassessing the accomplishments, attitudes, and methods of the great musical artists of the 19th century. The new assumes mastery of the old, at least the good parts. The intent here is not to simply present a series of short biographies about those prominent pianist/composers - that you can easily obtain from other books or on-line, and it's your first homework assignment.

But I probably should explain my statement that they played the piano better back in the 19th century - a lot better. Let's take a look, for example, at what I'm calling the 3rd-tier of the 19th century - an illustrious group in which only a handful of today's pianists would qualify for membership.

The name Alexander Siloti (b. 1863) is perhaps familiar to piano history buffs, but not too many others. Siloti studied piano at the Moscow Conservatory with Nikolai Rubinstein, graduating with the Gold Medal in 1881. He then worked with Nikolai's more famous brother, the great Anton Rubinstein, and finally was admitted to the inner circle of the greatest pianist of all - Franz Liszt. He satisfied them all with his piano playing. Years later, in 1901 Siloti conducted the world premiere of Rachmaninoff's Piano Concerto No. 2 with the composer at the keyboard. Siloti also edited much music and created dozens of sophisticated arrangements. He's 19th century 3rd tier.

Leopold Godowsky (b. 1870) is arguably the only person to have truly taken piano technique to a level beyond the ground-breaking innovations of Liszt and Chopin – consider those marvelous 53 Studies on Chopin's Études. As any innovator must be, he was largely self-taught. His piano playing, especially of his own intricately complex arrangements and original works, was considered superb, especially in a private setting ... 3rd tier.

How about the women? As a seven-year-old, Teresa Carreño (b. 1853) alternated between playing with her dolls and playing Sigismund Thalberg's virtuoso opera fantasies on the piano. She composed over forty interesting works and had such a spectacular international performance career that critics called her the "Valkyrie of the Piano". She remains one of the most famous women pianists in history ... 3rd tier.

Who are some other great artists comprising the 19th century bronze medal podium? Also distinguished are Josef Hofmann, the above mentioned Sergei Rachmaninoff, the other Sergei - Prokofiev, Paderewski, Blumenfeld, Rosenthal, Busoni, d'Albert, Lhévinne,

Cortot, Schnabel, Gershwin, and J.P. Johnson, the father of 'stride piano' and composer of the 'Charleston'. Artur Rubinstein gets the Mr. Congeniality award for his exuberant love of music, even though he may not have compared technically with some of these others. He once remarked that he'd have to practice 500 years to equal Godowsky.

Remember, this was the era of the likes of Mendelssohn, Robert Schumann, Brahms, Saint-Saëns, Albéniz, and Debussy - all pretty amazing pianists who chose, however, to focus on composing. I would still place them in the silver 2nd tier as pianists, noting that they did not make performance careers a priority.

Who ranks as 2nd tier primarily as a performer? Anton Rubinstein, Sigismund Thalberg, Hans von Bülow, Carl Tausig, Clara Schumann, Johann N. Hummel, and America's greatest pianist Louis Moreau Gottschalk. If some of these names aren't familiar either, you'll presently be hearing more, not necessarily about them, but from them.

So who comprises the coveted gold medal 1st tier of the 19th century, and up till now of all of time? Three men form a trinity of titans. Beethoven rules the pantheon of piano gods as Zeus. Seated on either side of him and slightly below are Liszt as Apollo and Chopin as Orpheus; or if you prefer Christian metaphor: father (Beethoven), son (Liszt), and holy ghost (Chopin). Godowsky was nicknamed 'the Buddha' mainly due to his appearance but it somehow suits his personality too, I think.

How was this pianist's hierarchy determined? It's supported voluminously in the literature, as everyone successively paid some serious homage to those in the tiers above. All pianists publicly worshipped their three superiors upstairs at the top.

Hans von Bülow said that Tausig, Rubinstein and himself, all taken together would not make a Liszt; and what a touching glimpse of Rubinstein's modesty is gleaned from his words "There is only one pianist – Liszt."
CARL LACHMUND

Josef Hofmann (3rd) raved about Anton Rubinstein, with whom he was fortunate to have studied with privately. Anton Rubinstein (2nd), a most remarkably talented musician himself, was in awe of Liszt. Liszt was one of a select few human beings in history ever to have absolutely mastered his craft; and he *absolutely* revered Beethoven.

In the 19th century, as now, Beethoven stood supreme as creator/ pianist, Liszt as prophet/pianist, and Chopin as poet-laureate/pianist. No one living today can compare, either creatively or interpretively, with these three men ... yet!

We still live in a democracy (I think), so if you have your own strong opinion you could write your own book; it's gotten easier with today's publishing technology. In the subsequent pages of this book I'll present some truly weighty opinions - those of the above mentioned famous artists. Incidentally, what they thought of each other will also be revealed; but more importantly, they will teach us invaluable lessons about succeeding in life that are applicable to virtually any field of endeavor.

Some wisdom you must learn from the wise.
EURIPIDES

If you truly want to achieve greatness in this life, it makes sense to learn as much as you can from those who have already done so.

Occasionally I'll have a chunk of prose for you that doesn't really fit in a separate chapter. This will be presented as a short independent compositional work or Intermezzo.

INTERMEZZO

The Origins of Music, In a Nutty Shell

Music was heady stuff from day one. The Greek version has Pan partying with his flute and causing *pan*demonium, usually with nymphs in attendance. Right off the bat music is associated with sex. Hermes was a teenaged trickster who invented the lyre, really to distract from the fact that he had rustled a herd of cattle, for which he is remembered as the patron of thieves. He also assigned each of us our share of intelligence, which is a trifle unsettling. Hermes cut a deal with Apollo over the cattle, giving him the lyre.

Orpheus was the son of a Thracian King and Calliope,

one of the original nine Greek Muses. He inherited the lyre from Apollo, became a virtuoso on it and eventually was labeled the most powerful Jungian archetype in music. He once toured with Jason and the Argonauts and in a 'battle of the bands' scenario outplayed the dreaded Harpies that gave bold Odysseus such a hard time. Orpheus was so talented that his music charmed animals and even rocks. Plenty of today's symphony orchestra development directors would love to have him on staff to bolster their fundraising efforts.

Back in the good old days, the Maenads were groupies of the god Dionysus who, like Mammon, was symbolized by a bull. The Maenads dressed in deer skins and carried around long sticks wrapped in ivy and tipped with pinecones; sometimes they even handled live snakes (is that Freudian, or what?) While partying to music they would dance and drink themselves into a state of ecstatic frenzy. Since there were as yet no Volkswagens to tip over, they instead occasionally uprooted trees or tore a live bull apart with their bare hands, eating its flesh raw.

The life of Orpheus ended tragically when, out on a morning walk to admire the sunrise, he bumped into a group of Maenads who promptly tore him to shreds. As great as the groupie thing may sound theoretically, a lot of rock musicians have similarly deeply regretted getting involved with theirs.

Lutes, flutes, and lyres enervate the mind.
OVID

Greek mythology would seem to indicate that even the 1800's Piano and 1970's Rock scenes were relatively tame in comparison, and our current 'classical' music scene then becomes positively soporific. If Bellini were to today rewrite his opera *La Sonnambula* (The Sleepwalker) it might be about some of our current audiences... or instrumentalists and composers.

It's fun to read about early music history, chock full as it is of psychological meaning and metaphor. The god Hermes was also a mediator of sorts between the underworld and the 'real' world. Carl Jung thought Hermes symbolized the relationship between the conscious and unconscious aspects of the mind, hinting at the possibility that music somehow bridges the divide. Many composers have been inspired to treat the subject of Orpheus musically, including Monteverdi, Gluck, Haydn, Offenbach, Liszt, and Stravinsky.

The importance of music in civilization is underscored by its mention in the Book of Genesis. In verse 4.21 Jubal is credited with originating music by inventing the harp and flute, and maybe also the organ and thus indirectly the keyboards. That Jubal was descended from Cain is not a good sign. The very next verse (Genesis 4.22) explains that a guy named Tubalcain was the first blacksmith and metal forger. Thus we can trace the 1970's metal-music craze back to its ancient sources.

Another example of the power of music from biblical history accentuates its military application: Joshua's trumpets crumbling the walls of Jericho. As soon as it was invented music was used to motivate armies to ferociously duke it out with each other. I absolutely love Sousa marches and although I'm a pacifist at heart, you have to admit that *Semper Fidelis* really makes a person want to kick ass and take names - same with Wagner's *Ride of the Valkyries*, especially after the Hollywood treatment. Thankfully, music can also be used as therapy to repair the harm done when used as a fight song. An early example is David's harp soothing moody Saul.

Music appears virtually everywhere as a powerful spiritual force. In Hinduism, the very supreme deity Lord Krishna enjoys playing the flute, but he probably got that flute from Saraswati because in the Rigveda she's mentioned as the goddess of knowledge, music, the arts, and wisdom. Then there's the Pied Piper ... besides kids, add rats to the list of other animals and rocks.

Women seem to have had minor roles in the history of music. The early Church doesn't come across as particularly inclusive of them, at least not in the executive ranks. Just like today, women eventually bumped up against barriers to promotion, only back then the ceiling was stained glass. However, the patron saint of music is a woman - Saint Cecilia. Now that's powerful.

I hope all this talk of the Bible and Greek gods is not too offensive to agnostics or those who make a cult out of Darwin's 19th century theory of evolution which, after all, is simply scientific research evolving over time and need not be worshipped blindly. Here's a neat musical insight from the world of science: in Europe, they've discovered some pretty old flutes made out of various animal bones (cave bear, mammoth, swan, and vulture) - we're talking real antiques up to 43,000 years old. Several have been found in caves in Germany. What's up with the Germans and classical music? They seem to have been at it forever.

Interestingly, the old bone flutes play the same diatonic scale that we use today. Another *really* interesting thing: the oldest bone flute fragment was discovered in a cave thought to be a Neanderthal site. That's right; it's now looking as if those guys we're used to thinking of as the classic 'cavemen' - brutish, hairy, and dull-witted - might actually have been sensitive artist types. They had larger cranium capacities too, which allowed for larger brains, possibly indicating greater intelligence ... than us. And they may even have had religious ideas because there's evidence that they ceremonially buried their dead.

As we know, or rather as we're taught, the more 'intelligent', handsome and violent Cro-Magnon completely wiped out the Neanderthals, though probably first mating with the better-looking of their females because some of us have remains of Neanderthal DNA mixed in. However, there's another possible explanation for that. Perhaps the Cro-Magnon women, though initially attracted by the chiseled pecs and abs of their handsome guys, eventually tired of their endless narcissism and self-absorption and decided instead to date the artistically sensitive dad-bod Neanderthals, because they actually listened to women once in a while and didn't nag them to lose weight.

It's all highly debatable, being only slightly more provable than the Book of Enoch 'Watchers', a group of angels entrusted with the care of the new human progeny but instead deciding to mate with the human females.

Anyway, it could be that modern Cro-Magnon man appropriated the Neanderthal's musical instruments, which would imply that music actually predates 'modern human' civilization.

Not a sound the silence thrills, of the everlasting hills:
Pan is dead. Great Pan is dead!
ELIZABETH BARRETT BROWNING

Carved in marble, the Seikilos 'epitaph' discovered near Ephesus in modern Turkey is the oldest complete notated musical composition (c. 200 B.C.). It's a song with lyrics along the lines of 'don't worry, be happy'. They've found much older fragments of notated music on cuneiform clay tablets that go back to around 2,000 BC.

But because music is so ethereal, we really don't know very much about how it sounded in the days before recording. The 19th century violinist Leopold Auer makes some interesting comments:

The plastic arts, unlike music, have the advantage of practical immortality. Notre-Dame Cathedral in Paris presents the same appearance today as it did when first completed in 1240. But is the music sung at its solemn dedication to be found even in the manuscript collections of museums or libraries, to say nothing of the interpretation of that music? The Sphinx has survived by many centuries Rameses's triumphal hymns. St. Sophia, at Constantinople, is still outwardly the same as when the Emperor Constantine erected it; but Byzantine music, a rich and elaborate system, is reduced to the paleographic fragments which musical antiquarians exhaust their ingenuity in deciphering and collecting.
LEOPOLD AUER

The intangible 'philosophical meaning' of music and the performer's moral character together somehow have great potential power, for better or worse; and music has always been perceived as a spiritual language that most everyone has experienced. If you haven't, Shakespeare thinks you're not to be trusted. If you're a teenager you'll readily agree; elders, just think back a bit to when you were a teenager.

Other art forms however inspiring don't seem to have the equivalent capability to elicit an intense emotional response. Example: while viewing a painting in a gallery, you probably won't be possessed to guzzle alcohol, get naked, and have sex with the nearest stranger in a mud pit. But with music ... well, think Woodstock. I've experienced similar ecstatic sensations playing Beethoven on the piano, and that's just the slow movements.

Angels may occasionally paint in oils or work in stained glass but they primarily make music with harps, lutes, trumpets, and organs. The devil and his cohorts like music too but they prefer the fiddle. Nero supposedly fiddled away as Rome burned down, at least the wooden parts. It's not that violins are inherently more sinister than pianos, there just weren't any pianos back then.

What a grand composer was Virgil! Such melody and harmony! To him more fitting the dying exclamation: "Qualis artifex pereo!" ('what an artist dies in me') and not to that poser Nero, who had but one inspiration in his life—to set fire one night to the four corners of Rome; a proof that a mediocre man may sometimes have a grand idea.
HECTOR BERLIOZ

Music has always played an audible role in religion and mythology and the big question that these disciplines address is that *meaning* of life. Why are we here? ... how can we be happy? ... what are we supposed to be doing with our lives? ... what's the best way to go about it? The greatest musical artists in history gave it some serious thought.

Chapter 2

......

PURPOSE

I shall be an artist all my life.

—TERESA CARREÑO

How many of us are actively pursuing a truly great and worthy purpose in life, one that embodies and nurtures all our dreams and stimulates and utilizes all our talents? Does what you do reflect who you are and what you want to become? Sadly, the answer usually is: not nearly often enough.

The mass of men lead lives of quiet desperation. ... A stereotyped but unconscious despair is concealed even in the games and amusements of mankind.
HENRY DAVID THOREAU

Thoreau's dreary image is unfortunately still the rule rather than the exception, maybe even more so these days. Way too many of us are frustrated and uninspired, and timidly settling for less. Our huge potential goes undeveloped or under-utilized. What we're actually doing doesn't begin to reflect what we would love to do, and can do.

An inspiring lesson from great artists of the past is the power of vision and self-belief to drive self-actualization and succeed in what you want to do, and should do.

I felt from the very beginning a certain destiny that must be pursued. I had an inner faith, an inner security of feeling about the future that nothing could destroy. ... I was sure I would attain something, with real ambition to become an artist.
PADEREWSKI

There is no greater pleasure for me than to practice and exhibit my art.
BEETHOVEN

A strong nature feels itself brought into the world for its own development, and not for the approbation of the public.
GOETHE

Corporate and non-profit boards often schedule retreats in plush surroundings to compose mission statements. An earth-shattering purpose isn't likely to just magically emerge after a day of 'brainstorming' over coffee, donuts, slide presentations and asking others what they think. That word 'retreat' can also mean to go backwards in the face of defeat. Purpose derives fundamentally from individual imagination and ambition, and is refined and nourished by learning and creative application of reasoning and intelligence.

Right now, as usual, I'm in a strange imaginary state of mind, but that's all right; there's a Polish proverb - 'The crown is only reached by means of the imagination'.
CHOPIN

Brainstorming doesn't amount to much if it's self-centered and short-term. But it can morph into a powerful visionquest when the paradigm broadens to include a life's work that somehow contributes to humanity as a whole. When we think in terms of community, possibilities emerge to accomplish something really special - the brand new, the much better, the previously unattained, the genuinely innovative.

Then it comes down to the difference between talk and action. We need less mission statements and more real missions. A mission statement remains only words, clever and catchy or not so much, until it is lived. A better term might be vocation, and when you discover yours (because we're all born with one inside) it feels like it's branded on your very heart and soul, a spiritual calling that no coach, focus group or self-help book can decide for you.

Who should devote himself to the piano? A delicate question, indeed! I fear a short and sharp reply from the world would say, "No one!" But that would be wrong, if only because of the opulent, glorious literature of the piano, which deserves that an unbroken line of interpreters should arise; interpreters with a mission, of course.And here we have the reply to our question: Those with a mission for it should devote themselves to the piano.
MALWINE BRÉE

Great masters like Beethoven and Liszt possessed a monumental vision of life's potential and committed themselves to fully developing their talents in the service of art. They led amazingly rich lives and in the process evolved into the great human beings who still inspire us centuries later.

What you do with your life is ultimately an expression of everything that went into making the unique human being that is you. Along the way, your actions will create meaning for yourself and others. The work seems endless because it is - it spans your entire lifetime, it is your life. In the process you become yourself.

One note resonating alone does not constitute music. Music only takes on meaning as a contextual relationship of multiple tones in rhythm and harmony with each other.

An abstract sound does not constitute music, just like one single word does not make speech.
CHOPIN

Constantly asking yourself 'what should I be doing with my life?' may not be the right approach. A more purposeful question is: what should we be doing with our lives – together?

Surveys indicate that almost two thirds of American employees are not happy with their jobs, which means they're not happy with their lives. And many aren't sure what kind of job will make them happy. We've seen the advent of a brand new career path; the Life Coach – somebody who helps you figure out what you want to be when, or if, you grow up. They offer to counsel you, for a fee, on how to make it happen. It's a job description not mentioned at all in the

19th century piano literature. Hopefully, two thirds of today's life coaches are not also unhappy with their jobs.

Success in life will always depend partly upon circumstances, including luck, especially where success is shallowly defined in materialistic terms. You might even win the lottery, but if you know anything about probability those odds are dismal. Some people who dream of the jackpot don't even buy a ticket. The probability in that case is zero.

The probability of a truly significant creative event depends on the magnitude and intensity of your dreams and your self-image; in other words, your personal creative vision and your belief in yourself. It starts with who you want to be, and what you want to do, and whether or not you believe it's possible. How clearly and detailed you articulate that vision will eventually determine the subsequent methodology or procedures you devise or adapt, and implement.

It is a practical fact that when the end is foreseen, mental energy will cooperate to carry the fingers through any correlation of motions, but these same fingers will flag and fail in the exact same routine if not braced to reach a definite goal.
WILLIAM MASON

Because we often find the pupil's appetite for some coveted piece bringing him safely through difficulties apparently insurmountable, I put the art of interpretation before technical study. The passion for playing will stimulate technique and create resources.
RICHARD HOFFMAN

Technique should create itself from spirit, not mechanics.
LISZT

The spiritual is the parent of the practical.
THOMAS CARLYLE

But even a combination of brains, talent, skill, ambition, and imagination all together isn't enough. Critically important yes, but they're still individual components of a larger wholistic proposition: the self-actualization of a human life. A paradigm or world view represented by one particularly powerful four letter word just might be the thing that makes everything possible.

Neither a lofty degree of intelligence nor imagination nor both together go to the making of genius. Love, love, love, that is the soul of genius.
MOZART

Amor vincit omnia - Love conquers all

'Passion' seems to be very much in vogue lately; you can even get yourself tested on it, again, for a fee. But passion tends to expend itself fairly quickly. Like sex, it's fun and invigorating but not indefinitely sustainable. But you can love someone or something for a lifetime. Passion is more of a short term tactic than a long term strategy. Love, on the other hand, knows no limits; if cultivated properly it can endure forever. How much you love something will determine how hard you'll work for it, how resilient you'll be, and how you'll adapt and persevere when confronted by change and adversity.

The love of life is necessary to the vigorous prosecution of any undertaking.
DR SAMUEL JOHNSON

Find your pleasure in the endeavor and not the accomplishment.
JOSEF HOFMANN

Ever since human beings began 'thinking' about things, the big question has always been: 'what does it all mean?' ... or more specifically - what's our purpose in life? To be sure, it's not the most straightforward question. People always seem to want answers given to them but with this question, it's up to you to create the meaning for yourself.

There is no outward happiness; you must create it within yourself.
BEETHOVEN

Existential awareness of our mortality brings urgency to the question, usually as a function of age. But here's one way of looking at it: a person's life takes on meaning over time, depending upon that individual's progressive choices and actions. Life is a creative act, or colloquially speaking "it's what you make of it".

Man is not simply a being in the grip of unconscious motives. He is a person in the process of creating himself; one who creates meaning in life; who embodies a dimension of subjective freedom... and is able in his inner life to transcend the material universe.
CARL ROGERS

Some people are just driven to become artists in life. They're gripped by a powerful vocation despite the hardship and financial struggle.

Mournful and yet grand is the destiny of the artist. He does not elect his calling - it elects him, and drives him irresistibly on. However unfavorable may be the conditions, the obstacles that appear insuperable, his will stands firm and he remains focused on Art, the sensuous reproduction of the mysterious and the divine in man and in nature.
LISZT

Artistic success is directly proportional to love and inspiration – the 'why'. The other half of the equation - the how - involves plenty of work, utilizing proper and effective methods. But viewed from a top-down engineering management perspective, the first question remains 'what to be ... or do?'

In life one has to decide whether to conjugate either the verb 'to have' or 'to be'.
LISZT

It was a favorite saying of Liszt, but the sentiment is at least as old as ancient Greece and Rome.

I would rather excel in the knowledge of what is excellent, than in the extent of my power and possessions.
PLUTARCH

Basically, it's that old philosophical difference between materialism and spirituality, the notion that accumulating things can make you happy in life versus a contrasting belief that personal growth, self-actualization, and the resultant inner wisdom are ultimately of greater value.

Materialism has lately adopted a new motto of sorts, attributed to a now deceased publishing tycoon: "He who dies with the most toys wins". It's been an ongoing discussion for some time; although a couple of thousand years ago another well-known figure was saying pretty much the exact opposite:

When I became a man, I gave up childish ways.
SAUL of TARSUS (a.k.a SAINT PAUL)

The golden calf we once worshipped has morphed into a full-grown bull, aptly depicted by artist Arturo Di Modica's *Charging Bull*, a 3 ½ ton shiny bronze sculpture in Bowling Green Park near Wall Street. Ironically, the bull faces up Broadway as if dreaming of a risk-laden career in the performing arts instead of its materially-secure one in finance.

The least of things with a meaning is worth more in life than the greatest of things without it.
CARL JUNG

Eric Fromm's *To Have or To Be* addresses the question from the perspective of modern psychology. To varying degrees all of us accumulate and have material things, many of which are necessary, useful, and pleasurable. It only becomes problematic when our relationship to those things becomes a substitute for our fundamental psychological and spiritual growth. In religious studies parlance it's called idolatry, or attachment.

Fromm says that if our individual identity stems primarily from our things, we'll always crave more, constantly seeking to upgrade or replace them over time. Having 'things' somehow gives the illusion of justifying our existence and we'll become anxious if they're lost or taken away because they ultimately come to represent our soul.

A 'to have' outlook focuses on the material at the expense of the spiritual self, pretty much in direct proportion to the having. The thought of our eventual passing from this life is likely to be extremely traumatic as it dawns upon us that we truly can't take our things with us. But more importantly, day to day existence is unsatisfying because things cannot fulfill us spiritually.

It may well be, I submit, that the more one is inclined or seduced to possess,

conserve, and enjoy material things, the less one may have to give in the personal exchange of souls, minds, and brains.
ARTUR SCHNABEL

We have the potential to be infinitely more than the sum total of those things that we have. A 'to be' perspective reflects a dynamic core identity that throughout life is defined by thought and action, especially in the work we choose to do in life and the moral choices we make.

When willing a thing, God's only command is "Be" – and it is.
THE KORAN

Because it's an organically evolving mental state, our fundamental self-identity is limitless and cannot be externally erased or taken away, like things.

Ask me not what I have, but what I am.
HEINRICH HEINE

There's this idea in our culture that we must 'find ourselves' in life. It sounds like an important existential truth but the language is still materialistic, somehow implying that the self is already fully formed and just exists out there somewhere, maybe hidden under a rock. If we can just locate and acquire it, like any other thing, all our problems in life will be solved.

However, there's a built-in dependency on the element of chance. With all the rocks in this world, we may spend years turning over the wrong ones. What if we don't find ourselves? And is our 'self' really a pre-formed integrated whole just waiting to be discovered? Ambition, initiative, and vision; and personal choice, responsibility, and accountability are not emphasized in such a perspective.

There's an alternative paradigm about life: the metaphor of a journey during which the self evolves, blossoms, and matures over time. Life is not so much about finding yourself as it is about creating yourself as you go along. We may have been born in very different circumstances, with individually unique gifts and talents, but we share the ability to imagine, reason, and guide our personal destiny by the choices we make.

Yes, there are social and economic differences in our respective home environments, and also genetic predispositions to consider; but we all begin the journey as human beings of equal value with a unique birthright of individual talent and potential and the ability to learn, discriminate, and choose.

Almost immediately, every thought, attitude, or experience we have, for better or worse, begins to organically influence our thought and action. Stepwise - daily, weekly, over the years - our personalities evolve, unfold, develop, and strengthen. Ultimately it's the sum total of our actions along the way that defines who we become in life.

A full and faithful account of the efforts and studies of an individual, especially if these efforts and studies be self-chosen, is, in fact, the history of that individual's life.
BETTINA WALKER

We're here to become ourselves and make a positive contribution to this world. Psychologists and neuroscientists study life from the perspective of behavior, reward, pain/pleasure, neurons, and synapses. Philosophers and theologians speculate on more abstract ethical, moral, and existential questions. The mystics, perhaps, have the ultimate insight: a direct channel to a higher intelligence that transcends normal sense experience. And artists use the most powerful means of self-expression – Art. What about us regular people? What should we be doing with our lives?

Especially if relatively young and healthy, most of us don't meditate deeply on our mortality. We're usually booked solid with myriad activities like school, work, entertainment, shopping for both necessities and things of questionable value, playing with our phones, computers, and other gadgets; and having, or thinking about having sex. We don't even give the ultimate end of our brief worldly existence a second thought.

But as our awareness hopefully expands, or we age or become seriously ill, philosophical musing and reflection can be a catalyst for new perspectives.

When a man knows he is to be hanged in a fortnight, it concentrates his

mind wonderfully.
DR. SAMUEL JOHNSON

Unlike cats, humans have just one life, at least on this planet. Metaphysical discussions of the afterlife aside, shouldn't we make the most of this one? Let's get beyond the shopping and instead imagine something magnificent to do and then achieve it, and in the process become supremely happy, fulfilled, fully self-actualized – not to mention make the world a better place as well.

My piano is for me what his ship is to the sailor, or his horse to an Arab – more indeed; it is my very self, my mother tongue, my life, the repository of all that stirred my nature in the passionate days of my youth. I confide to it all my desires, dreams, joys, and sorrows.
LISZT

Hopefully, no obituary lists all the things a man had, like a top-of-the line (insert luxury automobile brand), a teakwood-decked yacht, or an NFL franchise. Or maybe a woman owned a magnificent shoe collection that rivaled those of dictators' wives and more jewelry than most queens. Wait a minute ... I just read an obituary of that publishing tycoon and it mentions his sixty-eight motorcycles, large collection of Fabergé eggs, estimated net worth of a billion dollars, and final birthday party costing millions to fly a name-dropper's dream guest-list to Morocco. Oh well, *de mortuis nihil nisi bonum* - speak no ill of the departed.

Vying for more diverts you – until you go to the grave.
THE KORAN

Remember that when you leave this earth, you can take with you nothing that you have received – only what you have given.
ST. FRANCIS OF ASSISI

Think of your life as a perpetual state of being and giving. More rational obituaries usually describe a person in terms of who he or she was. They ideally list a person's accomplishments in terms of actions, especially their positive influence on others with whom they interacted in the course of their life. A measure of success at this point (the end) is the group of people you inspired, influenced, and served; the number of persons who call themselves your friend.

Don't be too concerned about whether or not the names will be chiseled in marble above you; just make sure you experience the meaningful interactions.

To be nameless in worthy deeds exceeds an infamous history.
Dr. THOMAS BROWNE

If you've selected this book to read, perhaps you'd like to do more with your life, maybe the material side of things alone is not satisfying you 100%.

What are you doing with your life? Who (or what) are you becoming? – that's the question. "To be" is to courageously create your destiny. Merely "to have" equates to the "not-to-be" part in Hamlet's soliloquy and represents a sort of spiritual suicide. After all, we're human-beings, not human-havings.

Many poor souls have tried to symbolically take it with them in the form of ornate mausoleums. As time passes, it's kind of sad to see the hulking slabs of granite or pretentious brass plaques, the lives of the actual individuals being totally forgotten. Take those once-mighty Egyptian pharaohs - at this point tourists are more interested in the architectural photo ops. As the poet Shelly expressed in *Ozymandias*, the 'lesson learned' is the ultimate futility of personal vanity.

After I'm dead I'd rather have people ask why I have no monument rather than why I have one.
CATO THE YOUNGER

Your tombstone won't mean a thing (to you) later on. What matters is the quality of your living, breathing life right now. Get busy with that evolving journey that began when your mom heaved you out and the nurse cut the umbilical cord.

To send light into the darkness of men's hearts - such is the duty of the artist.... how beautiful the period in a young artist's life when, untroubled by thoughts of time or fame, he lives for his ideal only, willing to sacrifice everything to his art, treating the smallest details with the closest industry.
ROBERT SCHUMANN

Though everything else may appear shallow, even the smallest task in music is so absorbing, and carries us so far away from town, country, earth, and all worldly things ...that it's truly a blessed gift of God.
MENDELSSOHN

No art is more noble, nor more surely indicative of general mental cultivation than music. By it we can command, for ourselves and many others, a dignified artistic creative act; and where great progress has been made, we ensure ourselves distinction in the world, which is agreeable to both amateur and professional artist.
CZERNY

In the midst of the greatest difficulties, I have never interrupted my study of music. Dedicated to the profession since my youth, and engrossed in it to the best of my abilities and energies, indeed, whatever interest could I have had?
PALESTRINA

Music is a higher revelation than all wisdom and philosophy, it is the wine of a new procreation, and I am Bacchus who presses out this glorious wine for men and makes them drunk with the spirit. ... Throughout my career I've unselfishly promoted the interests of art, the elevation of popular taste and the flight of my own genius toward loftier ideals. Inevitably, I sacrificed my own advantages and profit to the muse ... never thinking of writing for reputation and honor. What I have in my heart must out; that's why I compose.
BEETHOVEN

Nothing will interfere with my perhaps overbold but at least not ignoble desire to create a new world for myself.
CHOPIN

Claude Debussy, if he's not making music, has no reason for existing.
CLAUDE DEBUSSY

No other life than that of a musician could ever have been possible for me.
AMY BEACH

Man's ultimate direction in life? Love, truth, virtue, and beauty.
SUZUKI

Positive Piano

Music, my only real love, the only bride I'll ever claim.
L. M. GOTTSCHALK

Music is my mistress and she plays second fiddle to none.
DUKE ELLINGTON

I was meant to be a composer and will be I'm sure. Don't ask me to try to forget this 'unpleasant' thing and go play football - please.
SAMUEL BARBER

Now, I may be mistaken but these individuals probably didn't just sit down to take a 'passion quiz', penciling in a list of a dozen possibilities and then whittling it down to the top three or whatever. What do you love? What kind of life are you creating for yourself? Are you still obsessed with making the annual billionaires list so you can buy a lot more stuff?

The worthiest things; art, philosophy, love, nature, good taste and inner satisfaction, are independent from money.
FERUCCIO BUSONI

Or can you envision developing your vast potential talent and becoming part of the solution to this world's frustration and problems? Does your work provide not just financial security but spiritual fulfillment as well? You may still be trying to figure out your true purpose in life; that's okay, keep at it. Questioning leads to dreaming, and then excitement, and the desire to try things, and the effort may just result in a truly magnificent vision.

The greatest artists of the past didn't do it primarily for money, they did it not for a living, but for *living* in the true sense of the word - fully committed, fully engaged, and in love with the process. Often the money did follow and, of course, that's not necessarily a bad thing.

Money puts it in a man's power to do good.
DR. SAMUEL JOHNSON

Get all you can, save all you can, and give all you can.
JOHN WESLEY

It's the greedy, frantic obsession with the stuff that can cause problems. It wasn't solely about those great artists' bank accounts, but their values, and their place and purpose in the greater community of human beings.

Teach your children virtue, for therein alone lies happiness, not in material wealth.
BEETHOVEN

The self can't actualize in a vacuum because most significant personal growth derives from relationships, from relating to people in myriad capacities. We must begin with working on ourselves, and that allows us to influence our environment in the best possible way - by example.

We must be the change we wish to see in the world.
GANDHI

Astute business men and women are critical of the "bottom line = maximize profit" attitude, knowing that entrepreneurial ventures should ideally envision products and services that deliver true value, satisfy legitimate universal needs and desires, and make the world a better place. This, of course, is what great businesses do and a well-managed implementation of a useful, high-quality product or service will always be profitable.

But too many businesses are obviously not paying attention because within several years of startup roughly half of them are history – as in out of business. It's a blunt sort of karmic hint that take, take, take is unsustainable; there needs be more giving.

In the engineering world, clarity in the requirements phase profoundly influences subsequent success in design and implementation. If you're without a strong sense of purpose and real vision in your personal life, then you can't begin to plan, much less execute, and all the resources in the world aren't going to help you – just look at some of those trust-funder types who've had every material advantage in life and still can't get it together.

Money and time are the heaviest burdens of life; the unhappiest of mortals are those who have more of either than they know how to use.
DR. SAMUEL JOHNSON

Positive Piano

How valuable it would be for you to know what it's like to be compelled to financially earn your own way through life. There are many things you would become more interested in. Supposing you had to make the clothes you're wearing – how careful you would be to not waste any material.
LESCHETIZKY

First we must achieve clarity in our personal requirements stage.

I didn't exist to write poems, preach, or paint; neither I nor anyone else. All of that was incidental. … Each man has only one genuine vocation - to find the way to himself.
HERMANN HESSE

Hermann Hesse was born in 1877, a valuable date for Indian Head cents. But for some stimulating philosophical discussion of careers, vocations, and meaning in life try his classic novel *Siddhartha*. Incidentally, it contains one of the best professional resumes I've ever seen, that of the Buddha.

I can think, I can fast, and I can wait.
SIDDHARTHA

I would definitely hire that man, and wouldn't bother to ask him how many golf balls fit in a school bus either. Any fifth grader can answer that interview question. It's the usable volume of the interior of the bus (h x w x l minus the seats, etc.) divided by the volume of a standard golf ball ($4/3 \pi r^3$). (Hint: keep the units of measurement consistent and delegate the computation).

Wouldn't a better interview 'discussion' be about the company mission and how employer and prospective employee might collaborate on that mission?

Let's get beyond the trivia and start thinking big. When J. S. Bach said 'all things must be possible' that's about as big as it gets – all things. We can draw inspiration not only from Bach's glorious music but his professionalism, devotion to art and family, boundless imagination, astounding work ethic, and sense of humor.

The Italian renaissance artists looked back to long lost Greece and Rome for their inspiration. J.S. Bach, too, was temporarily forgotten after his death, his reputation even superseded by his son Carl

Phillip Emanuel (not exactly a slacker either). Mendelssohn, Liszt, and other important 19th century musicians rediscovered father Bach and developed a profound respect for him, building on his legacy and that of others, to create their own musical renaissance.

There's no reason why all things can't be possible for all of us; life fundamentally comes down to choices, no matter what the external environment. Make big choices.

Man is able to confiscate everything but the last of human freedoms: the choice of an attitude under any given set of circumstances to determine his own path.
VIKTOR FRANKL

Psychiatrist and author Viktor Frankl survived the holocaust, managing to retain his optimistic outlook on life – because he chose to. In comparison, let's admit that most of us lead relatively pampered lives with little concept of that kind of suffering. If your desk job, consumer gadgets, and comfort food are ultimately leaving you feeling aimless and bored and you find it difficult to create or even identify something truly important in life ... read Frankl's *Man's Search For Meaning* - it's guaranteed to put life into perspective and get you thinking.

Let's recognize and value our vast potential and remain optimistic about our collective capacity as humans to achieve great things, to create beautiful art, and to sustain a just and equitable society. Find something and somebody to love; perfect your skills and use them to benefit others. Every individual can innovate, because they bring their own unique talents and personality to the table. Make a significant contribution by offering us something brand new, or take an existing something to the next level. Take us to a metaphorical place we haven't been before, or haven't even imagined.

When he reached Weimar, Liszt had to build everything from the ground up, even audiences for concerts. This was to him more an incentive than an obstacle, for his own powers were unlimited and his belief in himself was unbounded.
ARTHUR FRIEDHEIM

After all, does not every efficient worker give his life for his calling?
CLARA SCHUMANN

What you do *is* your life, plain and simple. You don't get a life, you make a life. You owe it to yourself to make it special.

And don't doubt that you can succeed greatly. You can, and you're about to receive invaluable assistance from a very special group of people who succeeded spectacularly.

Chapter 3

......

ROLE MODELS

*First of all, if you can possibly do so, find a
mentor, a pilot who can and will oversee the early
steps in your career; depend upon his advice.*

—*JOSEF HOFMANN*

... or upon *her* advice

Great role models typically have achieved a high level of
mastery and thus possess a wealth of wisdom and experience
to share. But their real power lies in the ability to inspire
through sheer example and by setting the achievement bar at a very
high level. Their accomplishments stoke our imagination, really
make us think about possibilities, and motivate us to set higher
standards for ourselves.

Where does one find a role model? Good question.

*Accomplished performers, whose playing might prove instructive, are not as
common as you might imagine.*
C.P.E. BACH

That statement dates from 1759, and represents an eternal truth:
every generation has a handful of true masters and many more
wannabees. The truly successful people in any 'present' have figured
out that you can also learn a lot from the past.

Persistence, courage, reflection, balance in the total ensemble of your work, and above all, the pursuit of truth will carry you far. Nature's simplicity and strength of sentiment should guide you more than anything else. Whoever strays from these generally falls into absurd incongruities that keep one in a class of mediocrity. ... Plumb the depths of the masters, consult them, interrogate them. They are docile towards those who seek them out. They listen to you. They answer you. They lead you on.

CHRISTOPH W. von GLUCK

For musicians, and pianists in particular, there's no shortage of such role models; the list of great composers and concert performers in history is long and distinguished. But there's one that stands out from the crowd, light-years ahead of the pack, in a class all by himself. And it's not often that everybody unanimously agrees that any one individual is the 'best' in any particular field of endeavor – like never.

Ask painters who was the best and you'll get many different answers: Michelangelo, Leonardo da Vinci, Picasso, van Gogh? ... some billionaires might even lobby for Andy Warhol in wishful defense of their emperor's new (in)vestments. At this writing the most expensive painting is a Gauguin that sold at auction for around $300 million, but what that really says about art is debatable.

How about the most brilliant scientist: was it Einstein, Watson/ Crick, Newton, or Archimedes? Presidents ... poets ... athletes? Insert your own candidates and the inevitable diversity of opinion only serves to emphasize the point. But ask the question: 'who was the greatest pianist of all time?' and the answer is: Franz Liszt (1811- 1886).

Liszt holds a unique place in the history of human achievement in that throughout his life of seventy-five years all of his peers, many of whom themselves were possessed of great genius, unanimously admired his unique talent and accomplishments. The literature abounds with countless testimonials from persons who experienced Liszt as a revelation, not only the greatest pianist of his time but one of the most remarkable human beings of his time.

Chronologically Liszt's life spanned an era from Beethoven to Debussy, both of whom he met. Beethoven was born in 1770, Debussy died in 1918 - that's almost 150 years of music history.

It would be one thing if a matinee idol's many fans and

groupies gushed over him. But even (or especially) the likes of Chopin, Brahms, Berlioz, Wagner, Mendelssohn, Robert and Clara Schumann, Moscheles, Grieg, Anton Rubinstein, Tausig, and Saint-Saëns unanimously acknowledged and praised the unique genius of Liszt.

Liszt played three of my Studies quite admirably. Faultless in the way of execution, by his powers he has completely metamorphosed these pieces; they have become more his than mine. ... I shouldn't like to hear them played in any other way than by him.
IGNAZ MOSCHELES

Not sufficiently remembered today except by connoisseurs, Moscheles pretty much dominated the piano scene in the first two decades of the 19th century. He and Mendelssohn collaborated in composing the *Preciosa* variations in C minor for two pianos. After Moscheles once publicly performed the piece with Liszt he exclaimed: *"It seemed to me that we were sitting together on Pegasus"*. One of the most striking aspects of Liszt's talent was his ability to perceive musical meaning in other composer's works – beyond that of the composer himself (or herself).

A sensitive, insightful person who understands good performance can astonish a composer by revealing more in the music than he was aware of.
C.P.E BACH

This might not be that impressive in the case of works of average composers, but with Liszt, it held true for the great ones as well.

Liszt is at the moment playing my Études. I wish I could steal from him his manner of rendering my own studies.
CHOPIN

In 1853, the twenty-something Brahms travelled to Weimar to meet Liszt for the first time. A group of distinguished musicians had heard good things about Brahms and were eager to hear his compositions. After a friendly chat, Liszt politely asked Brahms to play. A bit nervous, Brahms explained that he was weary from travel, had no chance to practice and so was not up to it at the moment.

Positive Piano

Liszt…picked up the illegible scherzo of Brahms (Opus 4 in E flat minor), said "well, then I shall have to play" and placed the manuscript on the music rack. …He read it off in such a marvelous way – at the same time carrying on a running accompaniment of audible criticism of the music - that Brahms was amazed and delighted.
PETER CORNELIUS

Frankly, anyone that did not hear Liszt has no say in the matter. He comes first, and then, at some considerable distance, no one else at all. His playing was something unique, incomparable, and inimitable.
BRAHMS

Norwegian composer Edward Grieg once asked Liszt for an opinion of his new violin-piano sonata. Liszt had previously never seen the hand-written manuscript.

And what does he do but play the whole thing root and branch, violin and piano, so full and broadly it seemed somehow magnified. The violin got its due in the middle of the piano part. He was literally over the whole piano at once, without missing a note, and how did he play with grandeur, beauty, genius, unique comprehension. I laughed like an idiot… and when I stammered some words of admiration he said: "surely you can expect an old hand like me to manage a bit of sight-reading".
I don't know which to admire most, the composer or the pianist, for his playing was magnificent. He doesn't exactly play – one forgets that he is a musician; he becomes a prophet announcing the day of judgment so that all the spirits of the universe quiver under his fingers. He invades the most secret places of the soul and delves into one's innermost being with a demoniacal power.
EDWARD GREIG

It happened again when Grieg brought Liszt the manuscript of his now famous Piano Concerto in A minor. The story is so good that I reproduce it at length.

I had fortunately just received the manuscript of my pianoforte concerto from Leipzig, and took it with me. Besides myself there were present Winding, Sgambati, and a German Liszt-ite whose name I don't know, but who goes so far in the imitation of his idol that he even wears the gown of an abbé; add to these a Chevalier de Concilium and some young ladies of the kind that would like to eat Liszt, skin, hair, and all, their adulation is simply comical. ... Winding and I were very anxious to see if he would really play my concerto at sight. I considered it impossible; not so Liszt.'Will you play?' he asked, and I made haste to reply: 'No, I cannot' (you know I have never practiced it). Then Liszt took the manuscript, went to the piano, and said to the assembled guests, with his characteristic smile, 'Very well, then, I will show you that I also cannot.' ... he played the cadenza, the most difficult part, best of all. His demeanor is worth any price to see. Not content with playing, he at the same time converses and makes comments, addressing a bright remark now to one, now to another of the assembled guests, nodding significantly to the right or left, particularly when something pleases him. In the adagio, and still more in the finale, he reached a climax both as to his playing and the praise he had to bestow. "A really divine episode I must not forget."

Toward the end of the finale the second theme is repeated in a mighty fortissimo. In the very last measures, when in the first triplets the first tone is changed in the orchestra from G sharp to G, while the pianoforte, in a mighty scale passage, rushes wildly through the whole reach of the keyboard, he suddenly stopped, rose up to his full height, left the piano, and, with big theatric strides and arms uplifted, walked across the large cloister hall, at the same time literally roaring the theme. When he got to the G in question, he stretched out his arms imperiously and exclaimed: 'G, G, not G sharp! Splendid! That is the real Swedish Banko!' to which he added very softly, as in a parenthesis: 'Smetana sent me a sample the other day.' He went back to the piano, repeated the whole strophe, and finished. In conclusion, he handed me the manuscript and said, in a peculiarly cordial tone: "Keep steadily on; I tell you, you've got capability, and— don't let them intimidate you!" This final admonition was of tremendous importance to me; there was something in it that seemed to give it an air of sanctification. At times when disappointment and bitterness are in store for me, I shall recall his words, and the remembrance of that hour will have a wonderful power to uphold me in days of adversity.

EDWARD GRIEG

Most pianists today require many hours, if not days or weeks, to work up that concerto and usually will have heard it before either in performance or on a recording and have an idea (someone else's, that is) of how it 'goes'. It's a considerably different proposition to interpret something brand new and innovative in your own time, something of quality that can endure more than a century and a half into the future.

Few composers and pianists were as sensitive and discriminating as Robert Schumann.

Liszt began to play ... and now the daemon's power began to awake... I have never found any artist, except Paganini, to possess in so high a degree as Liszt the power of subjugating, elevating, and leading the public. We are overwhelmed by a flood of tones and feelings. It is an instantaneous variety of wildness, tenderness, boldness, and airy grace; the instrument glows under the hands of its master ... how extraordinarily he plays, how boldly and breathtakingly, and then again how softly and tenderly – I've now heard it all ... The way he played from my Novelettes, the Fantasy, and the Sonata moved me greatly. The second Novelette, the one in D, gave me especially great pleasure. You will hardly believe what an effect it makes.
ROBERT SCHUMANN

Robert's wife Clara was, of course, an equally sophisticated artist, and an even more advanced pianist than her husband who had to give up performing due to a hand injury.

When I heard Liszt for the first time at Graf's in Vienna, I was overwhelmed and sobbed aloud, it so shook me...it is as though he wanted to be absorbed by the piano...and then again, how heavenly it is when he plays tenderly...how fortunate Liszt is, to be able to play at sight what the likes of us toil over and in the end get nowhere with. I'm now practicing one of his études, beautiful and magnificent, but simply frightfully difficult ...no one can rival him in his mastery of the instrument - but what a pity that so little calm enjoyment can be derived from it. Instead one is swept along as if driven by demons. ... The women were mad about him of course, it was disgusting.
CLARA SCHUMANN

There's a great anecdote about Liszt playing Beethoven at Wagner's villa in Bayreuth. It was late, Wagner had already gone to bed and Liszt and some others were still up drinking coffee and brandy and smoking cigars. The discussion centered on Beethoven's massive piano sonata, the so-called *Hammerklavier* Opus 106, one of the deepest and most technically daunting pieces a pianist will ever attempt to interpret and perform. Liszt praised the wonderful adagio movement, made some specific point, then got up and said *"I'll prove it to you"*. The party reconvened to the adjoining music room.

Liszt sat down, and filled our souls with the mysticism of Beethoven's last works. He seemed once more to have surpassed himself, to have established an inexplicable, direct contact with the dead genius whose interpretation was for him a religious task. When the last bars of that mysterious work had died away, we stood silent and motionless. Suddenly, from the gallery on the upper floor, there came a tremendous uproar and Richard Wagner in his nightshirt came thundering, rather than running, down the stairs. He flung his arms around Liszt's neck and, sobbing with emotion, thanked him in broken phrases for the wonderful gift he had received. Apparently he had crept out of his upstairs bedroom on hearing the first notes and remained there without giving a sign of his presence.
BERTHOLD KELLERMANN

You (Liszt) have the power. I am convinced that you are the greatest musician of all time.
WAGNER

Wagner, as you know, was not prone to complimenting others. Apart from the musicians he amazed, Liszt bowled over virtually every critic of the 19th century, with piano playing that is; many of them were never able to understand Liszt as futuristic composer, but that is another story.

Liszt is the most musical musician of his time, none of his contemporaries could measure up to him, with the possible exception, and only to a degree, of Mendelssohn.
JAMES HUNEKER

If you're wondering what Mendelssohn had to say about Liszt …

Well, isn't it a miracle? I was at Erard's with Liszt, and put the manuscript of my G minor concerto in front of him, and though it's barely legible he played it off at sight with the utmost perfection. It simply cannot be played more beautifully than he played it – absolutely marvelously. Liszt possesses a thoroughly musical feeling that cannot be equaled.
MENDELSSOHN

The list of great musical artists that were astonished and thrilled by Liszt seems endless.

No mortal can compare with Liszt. He dwells alone on a solitary height.
CARL TAUSIG

I already had an impossible preconceived notion of Liszt's immense pianistic genius. Imagine my astonishment when he exceeded all expectations. ... If you never heard him at his peak, it's impossible to describe any idea of it. ... The remembrance of Liszt's playing consoles me for being no longer young.
CAMILLE ST. SAËNS

I have heard only two fine pianists, my old piano teacher Antoinette-Flore Mauté, and Liszt.
CLAUDE DEBUSSY

As recounted by Alan Walker in his incomparable three-volume biography of Liszt (A.A. Knopf 1983-96), in January of 1886 the twenty-three year old Debussy was in Italy after winning the Prix de Rome scholarship with his *Prelude to the Afternoon of a Faun*. He heard Liszt perform several pieces, possibly including *Au Bord d'une Source (Beside A Spring)*, a composition that anticipates by a half century the 'impressionism' associated with Debussy (though he himself disliked that term applied to his music). His 'old piano teacher Antoinette-Flore Mauté' was once a pupil of Chopin and you must appreciate Debussy's wit to realize what that remark said about a lot of other contemporary pianists.

How can you drink my health, or do me honor as a pianist, when Liszt is sitting at the same table? We are all corporals, and he is the one and only Field-Marshal.
ANTON RUBINSTEIN

The great Russian pianist and composer Anton Rubinstein (1829-1894) was one of only two other professional performers in the 19th century ever to be compared, however remotely, with Liszt, the other being Sigismund Thalberg (1812-1874). (Chopin, also compared with Liszt, was, of course, in a class by himself).
A charming anecdote has Anton as a stellar child prodigy once

hearing the more mature Liszt perform and exclaiming in tears *"I can't do that".*

Anton Rubinstein at one of his historical recitals played Liszt's Don Juan Fantasia, and followed it immediately with Thalberg's on the same subject. When asked why, he said "to show the difference between a god and a grocer".
OSCAR BERINGER

It's not like there was less competition in the 19th century. Though we're still inundated with pianists of varying caliber today, back then there were many more fine piano virtuosos, and apparently, just like today, equally many not so fine ones.

There's been no lack of concert-giving pianists this year in Paris. ... Everyone was thumping away and wanting to be heard, if only for appearances' sake, in order to be able to act like a great celebrity.
HEINRICH HEINE

I don't know where there can be so many pianists as in Paris; so many virtuosi, and so many asses.
CHOPIN

My father would not let me take up the piano; otherwise I should no doubt have turned into a formidable pianist in company with 40,000 others.
HECTOR BERLIOZ

Berlioz presciently saw the handwriting on the wall, though his timing was off by more than a century - he took up the guitar. Following his own instincts, Liszt stuck with the keyboard as it rapidly evolved from drawing room puniness to rock venue brawn. He quickly distanced himself from the pack to the point that most professional pianists didn't dare to publicly perform in the same town.

The previously mentioned Thalberg was one of the few who initially did, notably in a much-hyped 'dueling pianos' for an 1837 charity fund-raiser hosted by the Italian Princess Belgiojoso. Who 'won'? Her answer, variously recorded, remains a classic example of tact and diplomacy.

Positive Piano

Thalberg is the best pianist, Liszt is the only pianist.
PRINCESS BELGIOJOSO

There is, though, a letter from Liszt to his romantic flame the Countess Marie d'Agoult where he attributes the remark to her, and also proudly states that Robert Schumann disagreed, saying Liszt was both *'first and only'*.

A great source for information about Liszt is Adrian William's fascinating *Portrait of Liszt – By Himself and His Contemporaries* (1990, Oxford University Press). Reading like a virtual hagiography yet eminently suitable for a beach vacation, it's a vastly entertaining and informative collection of anecdotes about an amazing man.

What would the great Beethoven have said about Liszt had they met? Well, it happened, although the details are a bit hazy. It was either at a public concert in Vienna in 1823 or in Beethoven's apartment (but not the Black Spaniard's House where he died four years later). Czerny and Liszt corroborate the event, and Beethoven's own sketchbooks refer to some kind of meeting.

Beethoven would have been in his early fifties, Liszt a boy of eleven, already a celebrated piano prodigy. Liszt was forever proud of the memory. Beethoven gave him an affectionate kiss on the forehead and said …

"Forge ahead; you're one of the lucky ones! It will be your destiny to bring joy and delight to many people and that's the greatest happiness one can achieve".

No pianist today could so definitively impress such a stellar assembly of music masters. Can you imagine playing to Chopin his études, or a nocturne, or performing a Beethoven sonata with that supreme master sitting next to you, leaning forward intent on every note? The aging, almost totally deaf Beethoven would not necessarily have to hear everything. He would have perceived your body language, demeanor, and physical motion - your inherent rhythm and interpretive skill (or lack thereof) at the keyboard, and could discern your inner character.

In earlier years, often enough when hearing a pianist play his music Beethoven would somewhat disdainfully remark 'that's nothing' and then proceed to overwhelm everyone present with his own interpretation. It wasn't necessarily personal, it's just that his standards were so much higher and the service of Art meant everything.

To the acrobats of the keyboard who abounded in his day Beethoven referred contemptuously as pianists "who prance up and down the key-board with passages in which they have exercised themselves— putsch, putsch, putsch; what does that mean? Nothing. As a rule, in the case of these gentlemen, all reason and feeling are generally lost in the nimbleness of their fingers".
HENRY THEOPHILUS FINCK

Beethoven's improvisation was brilliant and astonishing in the extreme, and no matter who was in attendance, he knew how to make such an impression on the listeners that often there wasn't a single dry eye, and many broke out crying, for aside from the beauty and originality of his ideas, and genial presentation, there was sheer magic in his expression.
CZERNY

Tausig, Debussy, Mendelssohn, St. Saëns, Moscheles, ... and Chopin? For these artists mechanical perfection was simply a starting point for sublime interpretation. Anton Rubinstein was a total monster of a pianist and a significant composer as well. Wagner had a colossal knowledge of music. But let's separate out the musician from the often obnoxious ego. I'm glad the piano wasn't Wagner's main thing; he'd be tough to rationalize later on in my chapter about 'social skills'.

Debussy had seen Wagner but once, but the impression was frightening. "His eyes were terrible" he shrieked. "Ouf, they were scary, But Liszt, ah, that was different. He was goodness itself."
ARTHUR HARTMAN

That fascinating anecdote about Liszt playing Beethoven's Opus 106 at Wahnfried with the teary-eyed Wagner flying down the stairs in his bathrobe just could not be repeated with today's crop of concert pianists.

The longer you live and the more you learn, the more clearly you will feel the difference between the few men who are truly great and the mere virtuosi.
GUSTAV MAHLER

Positive Piano

In the andante of the sonata (Weber No. 2 A-flat Opus 39) I learned in the first four bars more from Liszt than in years from my former good teachers.
WILHELM von LENZ

Wouldn't it be fantastic to reclaim that incredible spirit and creative vitality for our own generation? It's truly exciting to think about once again meeting and exceeding that sky-high standard set by the 19th century and taking piano-playing, composition, and all of society along with it to a new higher level.

As a youth, Liszt was fortunate to have a great teacher in Czerny, possibly the best ever at teaching piano technique and cultivating terrific mental focus and discipline. Czerny was also a celebrated composer and, what speaks loudest, a man who earned Beethoven's respect and friendship.

Be wary of projecting your own mental state onto the notes of those Czerny exercises with words like boring and repetitious; it's entirely possible that you don't appreciate some of the subtle technical aspects or just don't know how to work with them in a wholistic context. It's not just about practicing the notes.

Liszt, who wrote in his own études the most complicated figures of all for the piano, was a pupil of Czerny and used his master's studies to the very last for technical purposes. ...With Czerny one has plenty of chance for endurance and velocity work, and besides, there's always opportunity to study interpretation. He himself laid particular stress on this in the study of his études, requiring them to be played repeatedly in different styles, pianissimo, fortissimo, and, lastly, with 'nuances'.
LESCHETIZKY

Study everything as if there were nothing more difficult; try to interpret studies for the young from the standpoint of the virtuoso. You will be astonished to find how difficult it is to play a Czerny, or Cramer, or even a Clementi study.
FERUCCIO BUSONI

It's one thing to prefer other material, but it's a psychological red flag when a person merely disses a master without specifically articulating why.

And don't dismiss Liszt as some rare genius who didn't have to work at anything, rationalizing that since you're not a genius you couldn't possibly ever achieve such greatness yourself. Liszt undoubtedly spent hundreds of focused hours working on piano 'technique'. (More on the true significance of the term in a moment).

I spend four to five hours on exercises (thirds, sixths, octaves, tremolos, repeated notes, cadenzas, etc.) Provided it doesn't drive me mad – you'll discover an artist in me.
LISZT

Liszt had no 'method' I'm aware of, although he doubtless served his time under Czerny, who must have been one of the best teachers who ever lived… Liszt's finger-technique was something marvelous, and made everybody else's seem coarse and heavy in comparison.
AMY FAY

But 'finger-technique' alone can't explain Liszt's eventual almost supernatural sovereign mastery. How many pianists have slaved away for hours a day, eventually learning to rapidly execute the notes but then what? You must have something important to say with all those notes.

Liszt enchanted and inspired on an unprecedented scale, moving audiences to the point of tears, euphoria and epiphany. His extraordinary personality, intense spirituality, and colossal work ethic propelled him to the forefront of his generation, and so far, all generations.

I know, some people are bound to say "but every conservatory graduate today can play the Liszt Études and Concertos – big deal." That is really missing the point. To be a Liszt today would require you to achieve several not inconsequential things:

Your performance would have to absolutely astound every musical genius on the planet; possibly not too difficult since there are a lot fewer of them around these days. You would have to command the admiration and respect of the Pope and every King, Queen, and President on the planet. There's still only one Pope but there are lots more of the latter today.

You would have to raise the level of what's technically possible in the art of playing the piano with your own amazingly creative and innovative compositions that, at least initially, nobody else would even be able to play at all. And … (and we cannot know this for some time) ... your body of creative work would still be around and admired almost 200 years into the future.

Simple rehashing of somebody else's old stuff does not make you great. Even software programmers know that; they're not going to be impressed with virtuoso handling of FORTRAN or COBOL routines. Again, no offence intended, but comparing any pianist today with Liszt is like comparing a run of the mill preacher with John the Baptist.

But, you say, there are no recordings; nobody knows how Liszt played. Well, we just heard from plenty of people who heard Liszt and wrote about it. And we know what people thought about music back then.

Recording has been great, within limits, for education and entertainment. But there have been some negatives. The advent of mechanical self-playing pianos and early recording technology indirectly encouraged the consumer mentality. Take for example the curious preoccupation with the 'complete works' in vogue today.

We live in an age occupied, preoccupied I would say, with quantities.
ARTUR SCHNABEL

We record a great composer's total output, as if one modern pianist's or conductor's interpretation could be the last word on the life's work of a genius from another generation. Those old masters would probably have been puzzled by our encyclopedic box sets that are purchased and listened to perhaps once or twice, then collect dust on the shelf. Their paradigm was to live a vibrant meaningful life a day at a time, and the artistic masterpieces flowed forth organically, expressive of a dynamically evolving and maturing personality.

Besides the current state of flux in business and distribution models, maybe the recording industry is in decline because people are realizing that collecting commodities is really not that satisfying in itself. The value of an object derives in part from what we can learn from it. In this respect, a study of the great variety in early recordings from the golden age of pianism can be fascinating indeed.

The place to do that is the International Piano Archives at the University of Maryland, College Park (IPAM) - the largest and most comprehensive collection of classical piano recordings since the inception of the technology, starting with Edison's wax cylinders. Unfortunately, by the curator's own admission, this important resource is significantly under-utilized. Almost a half-century ago, a New York Times music critic noted the same thing.

Study of old recordings is one of the most valuable tools in any survey of performance practice, and one largely ignored by students and musicologists.
HAROLD SCHONBERG

Let's briefly explore one example of the 19th century attitude towards studying musical masterworks. The *Mazurka* is a Polish dance form, of which Chopin composed more than fifty for the piano.

Of the Chopin Mazurkas, one must harness a new pianist of the first rank to each of them.
LISZT

Liszt is always right. Do you image that I am satisfied with my own interpretations of the mazurkas? A few times I have been satisfied, in those early concerts, when I could feel the appreciative atmosphere of the audience. Only there must I be heard. The rest of the year is for work.
CHOPIN

Given the above sentiments, how could one of today's pianists be expected to produce a 'definitive' recording of all Chopin's Mazurkas - in a recording studio, no less?

Jan Ignaz Paderewski's 1912 recording of the Mazurka Opus 17.4 often comes up in discussions as a remarkable example of early recording art. How about recruiting fifty-some different pianists to each record a single Chopin mazurka for a CD project? It would be far more interesting than one pianist performing them all, don't you think? And let it be live – in front of an educated and appreciative audience.

Five or ten years later, record the set again twice – first with the original pianists, and then with a whole new crop of younger pianists. We could compare the various versions, and note how life experience (hopefully) matures an artist, and also how each generation brings new insights. It would be quite a challenge to produce but I'd be first in line to subscribe (and I'd like to contribute Opus 67.4 in A minor). It would be enough, and an exercise in humility, to truly 'master' even one of the Mazurkas that you identified with strongly and watch, or hear it evolve over time.

Chopin has written two wonderful mazurkas which are worth more than forty novels and are more elegant than the entire century's literature.
GEORGE SAND

Chopin was the Phoenix of intimacy with the piano. In his Nocturnes and Mazurkas he is unrivalled, unbelievable.... I learnt about many general issues concerning piano playing by working together with Liszt on the Chopin Mazurkas in B-flat major and in A minor from Opus 7. ... He treated them very seriously, especially the at first glance 'easy' bass in the Mazurka in A minor. What a lot of work he took upon himself for my sake. "Only an ass could think that this is easy, but you can tell a virtuoso in those ties. Play it this way to Chopin, and he will certainly notice and be pleased."
WILHELM von LENZ

There are no details in Chopin's playing that are negligible.
EUGÈNE DELACROIX

There are incredible details in Chopin's mazurkas, and he has found how to make them doubly interesting by playing them with the utmost degree of gentleness, with a superlative softness. The hammers just graze the strings so that the hearer is tempted to draw near the instrument and strain his ear, as though he were at a concert of sylphs and will-o'-the-wisps.' ... Unfortunately, scarcely any one besides Chopin himself can play this music and give it the character of something unexpected and unforeseen, one of its chief charms. His performance is veined with a thousand nuances. He holds their secrets, which cannot be pointed out.
HECTOR BERLIOZ.

'One must forget the piano has hammers' was one of Debussy's most frequent sayings. Chopin used to speak in this way to his pupils, one of whom, Mme Mauté d Fleurville, became the first of his teachers.
MARGUERITE LONG.

It was an unforgettable picture to see Chopin sitting at the piano like a clairvoyant, lost in his dreams and how his vision communicated itself

through his playing.
ROBERT SCHUMANN

The masters' attention to detail was infinitely acute and each individual composition could stand alone as a finished artwork. Our modern consumer mentality possibly lies behind the urge to just play and record everything, despite the fact that commoditization often results in decreased quality. We routinely perform our predecessor's music unfazed by the mechanical challenges (more on technique soon to come), but we don't seem to appreciate the composers underlying moral and philosophical outlook and the larger mission of Art that they stood for – and we're therefore missing out.

As this point you may be saying, "okay, you've proved that Liszt was the greatest pianist ever ... but so what?" Actually Liszt considered being the greatest pianist in the world his least accomplishment and in his mid-thirties he completely walked away from his performance career. He realized that there was more to life – much more. He spent the rest of his life helping people realize their dreams, and he can help us too.

What people said about Liszt is indeed fascinating, but what Liszt himself had to say about music, and about life, is even more so. Understanding what Liszt represents as a self-actualization phenomenon can powerfully inspire and motivate us to greater achievement and success by our own efforts.

Let me ask you to think as profoundly as you possibly know how to think, of what you are undertaking if you intend to study to be a real artist. Think of what that means. I take it that you would not be satisfied to be third-rate, or even second-rate; you have something first-rate in your personality.
LESCHETIZKY

Do you really believe that young rivals with as much to stake as I, and joyously eager to stake it, can easily be found? I very much doubt it.
LISZT

Those words speak worlds about a psychological mindset. What's at stake for you? How eager, no, joyously eager are you to stake it all, because it's not just about a resume, a job, or even a career - it's about your life. The great pianists and composers created meaning through both art and their incredibly full and rich relationships with other human beings. Their music and performances expressed this life growth, and to the degree that it embodied elements common to humanity we can relate to it today.

If piano music is to remain the exponent of emotions, it must of necessity turn back to the melodic and therefore personal playing of an earlier time. Combined with the virtuosity of of the present day it would give us the very ideal of piano-playing.
W.F. PECHBE

It's unfair to compare today's pianists with Franz Liszt because he was so much more than a pianist, and that's really the point. It's not that we don't measure up mechanically; these days too few of us are living up to our true potential as fully integrated human beings.

Greatness begins with a great vision. Think how it would alter your approach if you could truly imagine Liszt seated right there in the first row, or right at your side as you practice – the mental exercise alone would enlarge the scope of what's possible for you.

Always play as if a master were present.
ROBERT SCHUMANN

We can, and should, relate to these masters' acquired wisdom, success strategies, and their unwavering belief in themselves.

On the portal of Hell Dante wrote "Abandon all hope, ye who enter here." On the threshold of Art should be written: "Bring with you the undying hope and fervor of your hearts, all you who enter here," for thus only will Art become the dreamed-of heaven to you. The deep, unspeakable joy which a great and beautiful creation gives to an artist's soul will then be yours. ...Learn and work every day - willingly, sincerely, and eagerly - and do so for the very joy of learning and working.
ALBERTO JONÁS

Hope, hard work, and lifelong continuous learning lie behind every successful undertaking in life. The value in emulating a role model is that you work through, in your own way, all the challenges that the mentor or guru has conquered in his or her own life. That's a very different proposition from superficial imitation.

True, I've been successful, but I don't advise you to follow my way, for you lack my personality. ... Learn all you can from my playing, relating to conception, style, and phrasing but don't imitate my touch, which, I'm well aware, isn't a good model to follow.
LISZT

When you're as old as I am, you may do as I do ...if you can.
ANTON RUBINSTEIN

To play exactly as Liszt did would be impossible for anyone unless endowed with an individuality and personality exactly like that of Liszt. Since no two people are exactly alike, it's a futile comparison. To discuss Liszt's playing from the purely technical standpoint is also futile because so much of his technique was self-made, and a mere manual expression of his unique personality, and what his own mind had created.
JOSEF HOFMANN

But that doesn't mean you can't learn a heck of a lot from a mentor.

Liszt became irritated when someone claimed it wasn't possible to do what he suggested. "I've no use for pianists who play only in a manner suitable to family gatherings".
AUGUST GÖLLERICH

If you're fortunate enough to obtain time with a true master who's willing to help you, don't whine that you can't do it. If asked to jump, quickly reply 'how high?' A negative 'I can't' attitude is the underlying reason why you can't do it in the first place. If you're going to be that way you might as well stay home and not waste a professional's time.

It's not just about imitating someone's looks or mannerisms; you become inspired to work out your own unique talent and potential. In *Ends and Means* Aldous Huxley (1894-1963) says that people often see various manifestations of the Divinity as examples to model in attaining transformative personal growth. He notes that this holds as well in our secular world; we can model ourselves after outstanding human figures with amazing results.

Czerny was greatly inspired by Beethoven and shared this enthusiasm with his own students. What might he have told the young Liszt about Beethoven the pianist, composer and man? – probably the same things he tells us in his memoirs.

Beethoven was the greatest prima vista player of his time, even in score-reading; he scanned every new and unfamiliar composition like a divination and his judgment was always correct.
CZERNY

Once Beethoven played 'a vista' a difficult composition by Bach in manuscript, no less than Bach himself would have played it– according to the owner. ... Förster once brought Beethoven a new quartet, and late in the first movement when the cello faltered, Beethoven stood up, still playing his own part (on the viola) and sang the bass accompaniment. "It had to be so", he laughed, "else the composer did not know his craft." ...Once he played a never-before seen presto so rapidly that it must have been impossible to see the notes. "Nor is that necessary," he replied, "if you read a text rapidly there may be a multitude of typographical errors, but you neither see them or heed them, so long as one is familiar with the language."
FRANZ GERHARD WEGELER

It's evident that the young Liszt quickly acquired the most profound respect for Beethoven and a fierce determination to emulate him. Prior to meeting Czerny the boy had even tried to teach himself Beethoven's piano sonata Opus 106, the 'Hammerklavier', despite his father's objections. Beethoven, and everything he stood for, served as a standard in the Czerny/Liszt collaborative 'system' resulting in spectacular virtuosity, including those miraculous sight-reading skills noted earlier, and taking piano artistry to previously unimagined levels.

Beethoven once remarked to Czerny that as a boy he himself had been negligent, that nobody had taken him to task for it, and thus his early general musical training had been mediocre.

'... and yet,' Beethoven continued, 'I had a talent for music'.... It was touching to hear him utter those words with all seriousness, as if nobody suspected it.
CZERNY

Beethoven had a talent for music? ... a major understatement; I also find that very touching. Beethoven also told the ten year-old Czerny's father that his son had talent, and that the father should be more strict! Czerny's father replied *"Ah, Mr. van Beethoven; please remember, he's our only child"* – but he surely took it to heart. Czerny junior became the most disciplined musician of his time.

Years later Czerny probably had the same discussion with Adam Liszt, the father who was also extremely influential in his son's development, and who resembled Leopold Mozart in being a loving parent and role model, greatly sacrificing for his son. When Adam wrote of his boy's success to Czerny, he mentions that he had printed on the concert programs 'Pupil of Carl Czerny", and that many in the audience wanted to meet Czerny, asking if he had any more such astounding students. Adam's reply to them was that any talented pupil willing to work really hard could become a virtuoso under Czerny's astute and empathic guidance.

Vision and proper methodology, inspired and acquired in large part from the role model, are huge factors in the underlying motivation and subsequent application and perseverance of an apprentice. What other Beethoven anecdotes might Czerny have related to his young student?

Beethoven recalled to me – "When I was asked to give lessons to the Duke, he let me wait in the antechamber, and for that I gave his fingers a good twisting. When he asked why I was impatient I explained he had wasted my time. You can hang a medal on someone or knight him, but it won't make him the least bit better. You cannot make a Beethoven, and for that which you cannot make, and are far from being, you must learn to have some respect – it will do you good. After that he never let me wait again."
BETTINA von ARNIM

There's another famous Beethoven anecdote about strolling with Goethe and refusing to stand aside in deference to a passing group of nobles on the principle that they were not inherently superior by birth alone. Some two decades later the thirty-year old Franz Liszt defied Nickolas I, Tsar of Russia by ceasing to play when the Tsar kept talking during the concert. When Nickolas demanded to know why he stopped Liszt simply remarked "When the Tsar speaks, Music herself must remain silent."

Nickolas I is remembered primarily for a corrupt bureaucracy, running the economy into the ground, Russia's disastrous losses in the Crimean War, occupying Hungary (Liszt's homeland), and iron-fisted repression of any dissent. He almost had Fyodor Dostoevsky shot by firing squad, calling it off at the last minute as the prisoner froze in the snow, staring down the barrel of the executioner's rifle. Dostoevsky's crime? - belonging to a book club of sorts, interested primarily in liberal utopian literature, to hopefully help make the world a better place. Today it's difficult to comprehend the power wielded by 19th century despots, greater even than master over slave on the old southern plantations and Caribbean isles because they presided over empires. The Tsar was perhaps the most powerful of all, yet Liszt risked standing up to him in favor of civil (and artistic) rights - shades of Beethoven standing up for respect and equality.

Role models can help us become clear about what we would like to do with our own lives. From a top down perspective, it all begins with a higher purpose. Billionaire status is not enough; the greatest artists didn't do it primarily for the 'pecuniary remuneration'.

Art is not a means of amassing wealth. Become a continually greater artist; the rest will happen of itself.
ROBERT SCHUMANN

I regard artistic duty as higher than material gain.
CLARA SCHUMANN

The virtuoso must have a far greater motivation than that of playing for gain. He has a mission to educate the public.
RACHMANINOFF

If I'm playing only because of the fee I always play badly - worse than the average pianist.
FERUCCIO BUSONI

In late 19th century Germany the rumor was that Liszt had turned down the equivalent of half a million dollars from P.T. Barnum to tour America. Adjusted for inflation, that amount in 1884 would be worth more than $12 million today. Primarily remembered for his circuses and freaky museums, Phineas Taylor Barnum (1810-1891) was also one of the most successful impresarios ever, promoting performing artists like soprano Jenny Lind, the famous *Swedish Nightingale.*

ALOYSIUS: Perhaps the hope of future riches and possessions induces you to choose the life of the musical artists? If this is the case, believe me, you must change your mind; not Plutus but Apollo rules Parnassus. Whoever solely wants riches must take another path.
JOSEPHUS: No, certainly not. Please be sure that I have no other object than to pursue my love of music, without any thought of gain. My teacher often told me one should be content with a simple way of life and strive rather for mastery and a good name rather than wealth, for virtue is its own reward.
JOHAN JOSEPH FUX The Study of Counterpoint 1725

Money, up to a certain point, is very capable of increasing happiness; beyond that point, I don't think so.
BERTRAND RUSSELL

That point, psychologists have demonstrated, is basic self-sufficiency. Once you have the financial security to pay your bills – food, clothing, shelter, insurance, whatever - money ceases to satisfy in a psychic sense and doesn't motivate or empower real psychological or spiritual growth. Liszt's playful response to Barnum's entreaties reflects his amusement at the thought. One intimate reports him exclaiming: *"What? for millions of Deutschmarks, and at age 74, I'm supposed to play my Erlkönig 300 times?"* As far as the millions went, Liszt had already been there and done that in Europe. And apart from the money, he was definitely over the publicity hype thing.

Barnum wasn't all bad. He knew himself and his limitations, and worked hard to achieve success despite many ups, downs, and criticism. His memoirs make fascinating reading; one truth about life he understood very well:

Unless a man enters upon the vocation intended for him by nature, and best suited to his peculiar genius, he cannot succeed.
P. T. BARNUM

Commitment to a truly big vision, one that is *visionary*, may very well result in you eventually becoming *very* much in demand. In the 20th century, a great love of music (and of people and life) resulted in phenomenal success for Liberace. He earned every bit of it through hard work, having also to tolerate petty criticism and personal attacks. Liberace chose to cash in on his unique talent, crying all the way to the bank and then buying the bank. At one time he was the highest paid entertainer in the world.

One moral of the story: simply desiring lots of money won't be enough to bring out your full greatness, but if you focus on bringing out that greatness you'll be compensated handsomely.

To get the process going, first you need a …

Chapter 4

······

GAME PLAN

My work is a game, a very serious game.

—*M.C. ESCHER*

Of course, success requires skill, discipline, talent, and confidence, not to mention externals like tools, (a piano, sheet music, a tuxedo) and all important networking contacts. But if you don't have a target, then good luck hitting anything. And if you don't have a plan to develop your skills, well … don't worry, we'll make a plan.

We'll spend Christmas again in our dear old Weimar. Oh what beautiful apples and trifles we'll hang on the tree! And what talks and compositions, and projects, and plans!
LISZT

I will now tell you briefly my plans for the immediate future, my studies, and the work I'm doing. The principal thing is of course to work as hard as possible at the piano, and to prepare the extensive repertoire that Liszt has suggested for my concert tours.
HANS von BÜLOW

The vision gets things started; you've got to imagine your end result. Then you create a game-plan, a multi-level all-encompassing blueprint from top (big picture) to bottom (individual steps of the finest granularity). Add heaps of confidence, enthusiasm, motivation, focus, and elbow grease and you're on your way.

Assume for the moment you've got the vision. You've been dreaming, thinking, imagining what you'd love to do with your life - it has dawned on you. The dawn has always been a metaphor for possibilities, and for beginnings; how many chapters of Homer's Odyssey begin with that rosy-fingered dawn?

Now it's time to address how to do it. Before you impetuously just leap into manifesting imagination into reality you'll need a comprehensive and effective plan and strategy to work with. First, consider the single most important commodity in life.

It's About Time

Man has no nobler or more valuable possession than time. Every day is lost in which we do not learn something useful; therefore never put off till tomorrow what you can do today.
BEETHOVEN

In the grand existential scheme of things, time is your most valuable resource. People act as if the supply was unlimited but for us mortals, time is most definitely limited and irreplaceable as soon as you use it. You can depend upon it to march on – in one direction. How much time have we got? No one can be absolutely sure but for the sake of discussion let's go with averages.

24 hours x 365 days equals 8,760 hours in a year. How many years? The Biblical three score and ten years, or 70, probably represents a cultural norm for life expectancy once upon a 'time'. Psalm 90 explicitly reminds us that even if we get an extension, say, four or five-score (80, 100 years) life is still eventually going to end. Psalm 90 makes no mention of the inevitable taxes but does suggest you appreciate and value your time.

Teach us to number our days that we may gain a heart of wisdom.
PSALM 90

To determine the hours we've got to work with over the long haul (let's hope it's long) multiply 8,760 x 70 years to get approximately

613,000 hours. I don't know about you, but that doesn't sound like very much for a whole lifetime. Leap days every four years don't help much either. And no guarantees; for any particular individual it could be a bit more, or a lot less.

The common man isn't concerned about the passage of time; the man of talent is driven by it.
SCHOPENHAUER

Here's a sobering thought: according to the *CIA World Factbook* the global individual life expectancy at birth is around 67 years; females (69) tend to outlive males (65). So in the several thousand years since Psalm 90, despite all the advances in science and technology life expectancy hasn't improved as you might expect. We're actually a bit worse off now than we were back then in those 'simpler' times - something to think about.

Ranked number one in life-expectancy are the hoary denizens of Monaco with an average! of 89. Since women outlive men it must be a virtual cougar's den. Americans have an average lifespan of 78, ranking about 50th among all nations. Then there's the very sad situation at the bottom: in most African countries men and women on average only live to about 49 or 50, a statistic we ought to be collectively ashamed of.

But of those total 613,000 hours, how much time do we really have to work with? Subtract one third of our existence right off the top thanks to an average of eight hours of sleep a night. Let's assume we'll 'work' eight hours a day and use the other eight for all other miscellaneous activities. Then the time available for work in life is somewhere around 200,000 hours.

Our very first few years aren't that 'productive', although there have been some over-achieving infant prodigies still in diapers so let's just keep the total intact for now. We should, however, subtract out 6 hours a day for 9 months x 12 years, (about 13,000) for time spent on our basic compulsory education; a great concept but its relative effectiveness is getting a lot of press at the moment.

Education is what remains after one has forgotten what one has learned in school.
(ORIGIN IN DISPUTE)

Positive Piano

That leaves a slimmed down 192,000 hours, call it an even 190,000 in which to do our thing in this life - time that continually ticks away, whether we spend it productively or squander it.

Wolfgang Amadeus Mozart lived for 35 years and 11 months – a fraction more than half the proverbial 70 years allotted. That means he accomplished everything he did in just 95,000 hours. It seems so short ... because it is! Mozart packed it in and left a legacy that most centenarians can't match. Obviously, time (and life) is what you make of it. It's not about occasional quality time but a quality lifetime - every minute of it.

A life of short duration...could be so rich in joy and love that it could contain more meaning than a life lasting eighty years.
VIKTOR FRANKL

The simple message here is that the hours allotted to you in this life are both scarce and sacred. Make them count! Every act you choose is in a sense a withdrawal from your existential bank account. Think about how you spend your precious currency.

The cost of a thing is the amount of what I call life which is required to be exchanged for it immediately or in the long run.
HENRY DAVID THOREAU

One always has enough time if one will apply it well ... nothing is to be rated higher than the value of the day.
GOETHE

How much time should we spend practicing the piano? Some pianists claimed to have hardly practiced at all (yeah, right), and then there's Paderewski. In his memoirs he says early in his career sometimes up to seventeen hours a day! The consensus among great pianists is that, if accomplished with 100% focus and discipline, 3-4 hours a day is a healthy and sufficient amount. They constantly remind us, of course, that with practice time it's not just quantity but quality and consistency.

In piano playing, as in every art, if one wishes to get anywhere, one must do at least something of a technical nature every day. Sickness and other

matters of an unavoidable nature rob us of enough days.
FRIEDRICH WIECK

Seldom practice over four hours a day...if you persist you'll lose your strength with time. The chief aim is to develop the critical sense. Whenever your fingers are at the keyboard, be busy in your brain building up those faculties which discriminate very nicely between what is artistic, effective, or beautiful, and that which is weak, banal, or ugly. It's no exaggeration to say that years are wasted every minute through unintelligent practice.
ALEXANDER LAMBERT

If, with a fixed determination to excel on the piano you dedicate to it three hours daily (about half an hour appropriated to exercises, the same to reviewing established repertoire, and the remaining time to the study of new compositions) this will assuredly enable you, by degrees, to attain a very commanding degree of excellence, without necessarily obliging you to neglect your other pursuits.
CZERNY

If one is to devote his life to the musical art, four hours daily are indispensable.
ERNST PAUER

I practiced two hours in the morning and two in the afternoon, and the rest of the day I played with my dolls.
TERESA CARREÑO

When a pupil said to Lebert "I've practiced six hours today," he replied: "Then you've sat at the piano four hours longer than your mind was capable of acquiring anything." ... Work regularly and conscientiously, but not for too long at a time. Two hours at a stretch of careful practice is quite enough at one sitting, and it's far better to do several periods of work in the day of shorter duration.
MARK HAMBOURG

I practice two hours in the morning and then two hours later in the day. After two hours of hard study I'm exhausted from close concentration ... practicing while tired, either mentally or physically, is a waste ... practice days missed or skipped are gone forever.
EMIL SAUER

A popular motivational book from the mid-19th century was suggesting similar ideas.

Lost wealth may be replaced by industry, lost knowledge by study, lost health by temperance or medicine; but lost time is gone forever.
SAMUEL SMILES

Published in 1859, *Self-Help* by Samuel Smiles (yes, that's his real name) may have coined a whole future publishing genre. Earlier examples are found in the medieval *'Mirrors of Princes'* books and of course the biblical *Proverbs*.

Smiles outlined his motivational approach in the book's introduction.

The object of the book briefly is, to re-inculcate these old-fashioned but wholesome lessons - which perhaps cannot be too often urged,—that youth must work in order to enjoy, that nothing creditable can be accomplished without application and diligence, that the student must not be daunted by difficulties but conquer them by patience and perseverance, and that, above all, he must seek elevation of character, without which capacity is worthless and worldly success is naught.
SAMUEL SMILES

Smiles realized that his book should focus on inspiration and encouragement; the reader him/herself needed to actively do the actual helping otherwise it wouldn't be 'self-help'.

In Smiles' book, and all those letters and diaries of the great pianists of the 19th century I didn't come across a single mention of a so-called 'scientific study' on success. If you live by pop science and psychology without really thinking for yourself, this book may not be for you. However, I'll do my best to entertain you, at least to the equivalent value of three or four sugar-laced frappuccissimos. You won't develop tooth decay or gain weight by reading my book alone (no snacking) and as a side benefit you'll be exposed to some music history.

There's very little in Smiles' *Self-Help* about the author himself. Now, I've done some reading in the genre and things are a bit different today. A sizeable chunk of the more recent books is often self-congratulatory rambling about the author's 'accomplishments', followed by browbeating of the reader over the need to own multiple luxurious mansions around the world and have a 'trophy-wife', or if you're a woman, have a 'perfect' body.

Much of the rest comes across as filler material with occasional suggestions on how to intimidate sharks or play mind games with crystals or burning coals or whatever. Some of today's self-help books are relatively entertaining but to me they don't seem as practical and authentic as the old school.

You know, the trophy wife thing is just another unhealthy attitude born of materialism. A man would do better to concentrate on proving his own worth, perhaps modelling Phocion, statesman of ancient Athens. When a woman once bragged about her jewelry to Phocion's wife she simply replied "Phocion is my ornament". He must have been quite a guy.

Productive use of time demands effective methodology assiduously applied with laser-like focus. When the mind tires and attention wanes it's time to take a break, or you end up wasting time. Worse, continued 'practice' may strain your nerves and the diminishing returns are likely to cause frustration and discouragement.

In *How to Live on 24 Hours a Day* a second 19th century self-help author, Arnold Bennett (1867-1931), advocated time for self-improvement, especially through reading and the arts. When you take a break from the focus on your main activity, relax with an alternate activity that also improves you. Bennett urged full use of time to 'the great end of living', as opposed to 'vegetating'.

He also points out that time is the ultimate playing field leveler.

There exist inequalities today…but no one receives either more or less time than you receive… talk about an ideal democracy! In the realm of time there is no aristocracy of wealth or intellect.
ARNOLD BENNETT

The future is something which everyone reaches at the rate of 60 minutes an hour, whatever he does, whoever he is.
C. S. LEWIS

Nobody gets more time than anyone else at any particular moment; so don't use lack of time as an excuse if comparing yourself with others. You've got the same number of hours per day as did Liszt, Chopin, Brahms, Paderewski … or Beethoven.

Positive Piano

Consider the time, means, and circumstances necessary to your piano studies carefully. Arrange your life in such a manner as to derive from it the greatest physical, intellectual, and mental good.
ALBERTO JONÁS

We're going to devise a success template inspired by, and synthesized from, the collected wisdom and experience of history's greatest pianists. Still, it's easy to fall into the trap of thinking that all we need to do is simply put in the time.

One of pop psychology's latest revelations is that you can master anything in life if you just keep at it for 10,000 hours. Self-help books have jumped on the bandwagon, again presenting 'scientific' studies and speculation about 'geniuses' to try and prove it. I don't think so.

For discussion purposes 10,000 hours is about five years, based on a 40 hour work week with 2 weeks off a year (40 hours x 50 weeks x 5 years = 10,000). It's really not an enormous amount of time to spend on something; anybody who's held a steady job for five years has done it. Most entrepreneurs work more than 40 hours a week and could potentially rack up 10,000 hours in maybe 3 years. At the opposite extreme, despite thousands of hours at their desks some individuals haven't worked a day in their lives.

Which leads to my first question: do meetings count? ... because if they don't the majority of our hypothetical 10,000-hour masters will probably be found in retirement homes. And they say that the average British worker spends 36 days a year answering approximately 9,000 work emails. Is mastery attained in the actual work or in the technique of answering emails?

Americans play too much. How many come to me and say, 'I practice seven hours a day,' in an expectant tone, as though praise were sure to follow such a statement!
LESCHETIZKY

Here's a 19th century pianist's perspective on that flawed 10,000 hours-to-success paradigm:

Oh, the endless leagues that ambitious fingers have traveled over ivory keys. All too often they race like automobiles on a racecourse, in a circle, and after having gone innumerable miles and spent a tremendous amount of energy,

82

they arrive at the same point from which they started, exhausted and worn, with very little to show for their work, and no nearer to their real goal than when they started.
JAMES FRANCIS COOKE

And here's the same author explaining why hours alone is not the answer.

The proportion in which mental and physical activity is compounded determines the distinction between practicing and real study. And the degree in which real study enters into his daily work determines the success of the pianist.
JAMES FRANCIS COOKE

Stop for a second and turn on your rationality switch – of course it's about quality, not quantity! The 'research' claims that nobody seems to have acquired peak excellence in less than 10,000 hours. Well, apparently the 19th century pianist who achieved the absolute highest level of excellence ever somehow improved on that number by 500%.

When Franz Liszt was about nine or ten years old he was presented to Carl Czerny in Vienna as a potential student. The boy had already attracted attention as a prodigy of sorts and was highly praised by both nobles and notables who themselves may or may not have had the expertise to judge excellence.

Here's Czerny's first impression:

He was a pale delicate-looking child, and while playing swayed about on the seat as though drunk, and about to fall on the floor. His playing was quite irregular, careless and confused, and of the principles of fingering he had such scant understanding that he threw his fingers about on the keys quite arbitrarily. Nevertheless, I was amazed at the talent with which nature had endowed him. Some things that I set before him he played at sight, purely by instinct to be sure, but for that very reason in a manner which made it plain that Nature herself had here formed a pianist.
CZERNY

That sounds like a kid with amazing potential but nothing to write home about in terms of acquired skill ... yet. Liszt's father had to go back to Hungary so some time elapsed before they could get started on lessons with Czerny. But upon returning to Vienna a year later, little Franz began studying in earnest.

After only a year I could let him perform publicly, and he aroused a degree of enthusiasm in Vienna that few artists have equaled.
CZERNY

Here's the reaction to the now twelve year old Liszt in public performance in Vienna with, so it is said, Beethoven in attendance – from the Vienna correspondent of the London music journal *The Harmonicon:*

… execution so precise and correct, united with such taste and elegance that the boy already ranks with the greatest pianists of the day. In physical technique, he leaves us nothing to wish for, and indeed seems destined to attain the highest acclaim in the art.
THE HARMONICUM 1823

But no eleven year old boy could have logged 10,000 hours in the one year between these two observations; there just weren't that many hours, even practicing literally 24/7. Some other factor(s) must explain the phenomenal progress.

I gave the boy a lesson almost every evening. Never had I so eager, talented, and diligent a pupil.
CZERNY

Let's analyze Czerny's statement. A lesson almost every evening: that's structure and consistency according to a plan. Talent: that's a birthright we all share to varying degree; the boy Liszt undoubtedly was blessed with an inordinate amount but most of us don't even begin to utilize our gifts effectively or really tap into our own potential. Eager and diligent: these words define an attitude and a character trait, both of which we can all develop if we get excited about something, and work at acquiring discipline.

There's an important lesson here. Countless other pianists of that era slaved away mechanically for the next five or ten years (or twenty or thirty) but are now totally forgotten because they never amounted to anything special. Who knows what they actually did in all those hours or how they went about it; but whatever their method (and attitude) - it didn't work out very well.

Possibly the biggest advantage was having Czerny as a mentor, guide, teacher and friend. Here was a man who set the 19th century bar for discipline and perseverance, a man of good will and character, who had 'studied' with Beethoven, perhaps more closely than any other individual; in fact later he was entrusted with teaching Beethoven's nephew. The closeness to Beethoven was no doubt a wonderful opportunity for learning music, but even more powerful was the direct association, and friendship, with a truly great man of truly great character.

And Czerny really knew how to play the piano. He was an expert; he had a methodology that worked and he knew how to impart that knowledge and to motivate students, which he did predominantly by example.

Pupils that from the outset manifest a desire and love for the thing, and who strongly and rationally apply themselves, will acquire a perfect knowledge of the keys and notes in a relatively short time. Others, frightened at the apparent tediousness of the acquisition, often lose several months in attaining the same object. Which, then, of these two ways is the better? ... I most earnestly recommend you to practice daily, with untiring diligence and the greatest attention.
CZERNY

I don't know if factory workers still punch time clocks but it would simplify tracking their hours to determine when mastery kicks in. After 10,000 hours we should expect a virtuosic level of craftsmanship. But ask quality engineers managing assembly line processes and they'll tell you: it ain't necessarily so.

Constant repetition of a process, in itself, usually results in decreased efficiency as a function of time. Mental and physical strain, boredom and occasional injury, diminishing returns, and the plateau effect all take their toll. Rotating workers through different assignments helps mitigate boredom, but then they aren't working on just one thing for 10,000 hours. According to the 'logic', dividing your time evenly across three distinct tasks would require a total of 30,000 hours or 15 years to master all three.

Study demands that we delve into the minute details of our art, and master them before attempting to advance.
JOSEF HOFMANN

Don't only practice your art, but force your way into its secrets; art deserves that, for it and knowledge can raise man to the Divine.
BEETHOVEN

To claim that attaining mastery in any endeavor is primarily a matter of putting the time in is at best ...

I - R - R - E - S - P - O - N - S - I - B - L - E
(Sorry, had to pause, breathe deeply, and then edit out the F-words).

Yes, most successful people have indeed invested a certain amount of time in mastering their craft but that's not to say that anyone just putting in the same amount of time will be equally successful. Use the rational part of your brain when reading. There's a big difference between truth-sayers and soothsayers; and beware of outliars.

We must always be conscious of what we're doing, and *'what we're doing'* must be truly effective. Simply showing up for some random number of hours doesn't constitute 80% of success, as some might say. Showing up is just the beginning, and the real substantive portion – focused work – is a lot more than 20%. We're not talking about just physically showing up either - your complete attention is required.

Boredom on assembly line type work is often just a symptom of underlying inattention, a lack of focus and concentration mainly due to lack of interest. It's a sure sign that your heart isn't in it. A person will eventually (often quickly) become discouraged by lack of progress. The situation can spiral downwards when few (or no) tangible results are garnered from the procedures implemented. There's no job satisfaction, the negative impact of the frustration makes it all the more difficult to focus, boredom increases ... things get worse ... until you quit.

Genuine inspiration is a must for eventual attainment of mastery. Forget high-brow superficiality; you must have a high-bar vision of what you seek to accomplish and your heart must be in it or you will become disheartened, and may give up prematurely. Are you excited about work? Does it make you feel good about yourself? Is there a sense of pride and ownership in the end product; or total apathy? Do you love your job? (Oh, that very sad statistic – two-thirds of people don't).

Are you part of a collaborative team with a supportive boss assembling the most aesthetically beautiful and reliable product in history; or did you just finish cranking out a couple of thousand cheap ugly plastic widgets that are bound to break as the consumer wrestles with the packaging ... while your jerk of a boss was nagging you the whole time? My heart goes out to you if you've had to put up with that for 10,000 hours because you need to pay the rent and feed your kids.

The popularity of the 10,000 hours idea came out of research published by psychologist K. Anders Ericcson (not to be confused with Eric Erikson) however his paper *The Influence of Experience and Deliberate Practice On the Development of Superior Expert Performance* acknowledged that way back in 1899 Bryan and Harter were claiming that at least ten years were required to become an 'expert'.

Note that Ericcson uses the expression 'deliberate practice', not just any old practice. But that still doesn't adequately address methodology and motivation. A person can practice deliberately for years on a dead-end paradigm; unfortunately it happens all the time. Some other 'seminal' observations in the paper include: a lot of experience is required to become an expert, it takes time, and it helps to be tall in basketball. Okay; got that.

But I disagree with his statement that children require many years to 'master' their first language. Though Mandarin may be daunting to westerners, most Chinese infants pick it up pretty quickly and easily, becoming fairly proficient in a matter of months not years. And let's be honest, who really 'masters' a language anyway, and how would anyone else know? I'm pretty sure both Shakespeare and Samuel Johnson would have said they were continually learning.

Even the experienced artist remains forever a student, and to teach art is a matter of daily learning.
FRIEDRICH WIECK

I would fain grow old learning many things.
PLATO

I am still learning.
MICHELANGELO

A separate paper *'The Making of an Expert'* (Ericcson, Prietula, Cokely) seems to be largely a rewrite of the first, but curiously contains a quote by a famous 19th century violinist that totally contradicts the authors' premise.

It really doesn't matter how many hours a day you practice; if only with the fingers, no amount is enough; if you practice with your head, two hours is plenty.
LEOPOLD AUER

Auer, by the way, was born in 1845. Here's another Auer quote from a hundred year old book comprised of interviews with great violinists. (*Violin Mastery: Talks with Master Violinists and Teachers,* F. H. Martens, 1919). The chapter on Auer, incidentally, is called *"A Method Without Secrets"*.

The right kind of practice is not a matter of hours. Practice should represent the utmost concentration of brain. It is better to play with concentration for two hours than to practice eight without. I should say that four hours would be a good maximum practice time— I never ask more of my pupils— and that during each minute of the time the brain be as active as the fingers.
LEOPOLD AUER

Academic research on 'mastery' usually defines the criteria for expertise in terms of education, experience, and accumulated knowledge. In other words, sounds like it depends on the number of university degrees you rack up, prizes or awards you win, or encyclopedias you memorize.

Never memorize anything you can look up.
EINSTEIN

And, oh yes - also listed as a criterion to indicate mastery was 'social reputation'. I guess things may now depend on the number of Facebook friends you have.

I can have no intercourse, and do not want to have any, with persons who are not willing to believe in me because I have not yet made a wide reputation.
BEETHOVEN

Liszt, the greatest pianist ever, did not attend any college or conservatory. As a teenager he applied to the Paris Conservatory - at that time the best music school in the world. It's still pretty good. He was denied admission simply for being a foreigner – against the 'rules'. Did I mention that Cherubini, an Italian, headed up the conservatory? Go figure.

The American prodigy Louis Moreau Gottschalk met the same fate. In Gottschalk's case, the chair of the piano faculty added an *ad hoc ad hominem* comment:

No; America is a country of steam engines and railroads, not artists.
PIERRE ZIMMERMANN

Gottschalk was soon vindicated when his hugely popular virtuoso piano showpiece *Bamboula* was chosen as a graduation test piece at the conservatory, with Gottschalk occasionally on the examining board. In later years, Liszt reminisced about his experience.

All was lost, my groans and lamentations were unceasing, the wound was deep and bled for a long time. My father tried in vain to comfort me. It was only several years later, thanks to assiduous reading of Kalkbrenner's Piano Method (then in use at the school) and confidential conversations with conservatory students that it healed completely.
LISZT

Kalkbrenner was a popular virtuoso of the day, but also a boorish pedant. He once presumed to give Chopin piano lessons but the proposition was politely declined.

Mendelssohn said afterwards: "Chopin is worth twenty Kalkbrenners!"
LOUIS C. ELSON

The Paris Conservatory faculty no doubt soon felt like those publishers that initially turned down J.K. Rowling's Harry Potter books; Liszt remains the bestselling pianist of all time. He was eventually awarded an honorary doctorate by the University of Konigsberg and his characteristically humble thank you note reveals his definition of education.

Positive Piano

The dignity of Doctor granted by your celebrated faculty makes me happy, and would make me proud were I not so aware of the spirit in which it is granted; I must assume the duty of unceasing learning and untiring labor.
LISZT

The greatest master just kept going, and didn't stop to calculate the hours logged. I've come across a few Ph.D. types that seem instead to know it all after donning that cap and gown.

Liszt had, of course, conquered the piano world years earlier with no degrees. All that Bach, Mozart, Beethoven, and Chopin could muster on their resumes in terms of music education was a few private lessons at one time or another. They didn't win any competitions either because there weren't any back then - another significant comment on our times.

All of these men, however, recognized the value of constant learning, in all fields; and they enthusiastically pursued it through independent reading but even more importantly, through real social networking; that is, conversing with real people about important matters. The stimulation from constant learning and collaboration enabled innovation far beyond the established levels.

Frankly, a lot of similar 'research' by academics reads as if it was conducted in their parents' ivory basement - in dim light. Just the other day, a new study came out stating that roughly two-thirds of this stuff is not reproducible by independent researchers; meaning they're basically junk, a waste of trees, digital storage capacity, and network bandwidth. Maybe that philosophical Roman Emperor was on to something.

Remember that all is opinion.
MARCUS AURELIUS

It depends upon who's doing the opining; I'll go with the 19th century pianists. I feel for the trees but the biggest tragedy is in failing the next generation of young people who are eager to learn.

Apart from that statistic, and assuming he's in the one third of credibility, Ericcson has been partially misinterpreted by the self-help cognoscenti. He specifically states that deliberate practice must be focused and concentrated, and should include continual challenges beyond the established skill levels, i.e. pushing the envelope, or raising the bar.

He also acknowledges the positive influence of parents and role models, and would probably agree that in the case of Mozart and Liszt, the parents' love and guidance was integral to their kids' subsequent achievement. And he discounted as useless the above mentioned popularity, peer-approval, and educational attainment as demonstrable criteria to measure 'mastery'.

I sat next to Paderewski and jokingly offered him a simple means by which to measure the greatness of a success by asking a simple question of his colleagues. One should not ask how he had performed, but rather what appreciation was garnered from the public and the local critics. The level of success could be measured from the answer, just as from a thermometer.
MORIZ ROSENTHAL

But the major benchmark that Ericcson substituted is dismally inappropriate, for music performance at least: exact, unvarying reproduction of nuance in repetition. Maybe for robots building automobiles, but please - not performing artists. In fact, accomplished pianists in the 19th century emphasized the exact opposite.

It's impossible for the performer to give a program repeatedly in identically the same manner. If he did succeed in doing this, his playing would soon become stereotyped.
OSSIP GABRILOWITSCH

How can I play the piece twice exactly alike? I'm a different man today from what I was yesterday, and shall be different tomorrow from what I am today. Each day is a new world, a new life, it's impossible to give two performances of the piece that are identical in every particular. A machine might make a number of identical repetitions, but a human with active thought and emotion, has a broader outlook. ... It's the differences that count in art, not similarities.
HAROLD BAUER

I've learned that I must continually have my mind alert to opportunities for improvement, and be in quest of new beauties. Even while actually playing in public it's possible to conceive of new details that come like revelations. There's always room for improvement; the new gives zest and intellectual interest to the artist's work.
FERRUCCIO BUSONI

Positive Piano

Busoni never played anything twice in the same way. He relied on the inspiration of the moment, and when he was inspired he did amazing things.
ISIDOR PHILIPP

Anton Rubinstein often treated the same program absolutely differently when he played it a second time. But more astounding still, everything came out wonderfully on both occasions.
MATVEY PRESSMAN

Chevillard said "Mon cher ami, yesterday you gave me a different tempo than we just played." Debussy looked at him with intense reflection in his eyes and said "But I don't feel music the same way every day."
FRANÇOIS GILLET

M. Peru, 'the only surviving pupil of Chopin' in an interview reprinted in the Musical Herald says: "Chopin's interpretation of his own music was never twice alike, yet always perfect. He played with very sudden and sharp nuances, and frequent changes of time. As to what we call 'classical' interpretation - that had no meaning for him. Everything was beauty, and even a fugue he made not a dry exercise but a thing of genuine poetic charm."
TOBIAS MATTHAY

When a passage is repeated in a composition, it's a mistake to repeat it in the exact same way.
LILIAS MACKINNON

Systemization is the death of spontaneity, and spontaneity is the very soul of Art.
JOSEF HOFMANN

Shall we repeat it one more time, for emphasis?

Never play anything the same way twice.
LOUIS ARMSTRONG

Nobody really gets excited about a batch of cookies because they're uniformly cut from the same mold; we react to the texture and taste, and praise the individual baker's talent.

Apart from any researcher's ideas about measureable criteria of 'mastery' and how it's achieved, the main factor to consider is whether or not the procedure you execute is properly designed to result in a successful realization of your specific goal.

It's not enough to be busy, so are the ants. The question is, what are we busy about?
HENRY DAVID THOREAU

Put simply, how you go about it is paramount - the means always determine the ends. With any given task, the appropriate means and consistent, focused implementation will effect amazing results. Motivation has got to be part of the formula, and that means love, enthusiasm, significant curiosity or interest, or at minimum, conscientiousness and some sense of responsibility. Hours alone guarantee nothing, except perhaps fatigue, and aging.

Results can be achieved with a great economy of time if the right methods are used.
XAVER SCHARWENKA

By thinking of each note a girl can do more in half an hour than she can do in four with her mind on other things, and if she plays slowly for two hours every day she can gain wonderful facility.
CECIL CHAMINADE

You cannot imagine what may be effected in one single day, if we properly avail ourselves of the time.
CZERNY

It's not the time spent at the keyboard that counts but what your brain brings to the task, and how your time is spent at the keyboard. It wasn't years that gave me my technique, but a well-planned course carefully worked out and filled with that priceless enthusiasm without which musical success is unthinkable.
MARK HAMBOURG

Learning to study well is the main thing; it's half the battle. … If you 'worked' less and thought more, you could play better. What you accomplish by hours of hard work can be done in half the time by relaxation and vision.
LESCHETIZKY

The important thing is not the amount of "hard work," but the way it is

done. It is better to practice an hour daily, with your thoughts concentrated on your work than to practice five hours with your thoughts rambling. Engagement of a cheap, second-rate teacher may prove fatal to the pupil's chances, because a certain attitude of attention, of using the mind, must be taught from the very first lesson.
HENRY THEOPHILUS FINCK

It does not pay to practice the piano in the wrong way! The effect of all practice is to form habits. If the habits are right, progress is sure. If the habits are wrong, the playing is bound to go from bad to worse.
EDWARD M. BOWMAN

I don't know about you, but this musty old 19th century thinking seems reasonable to me.

The problem of inefficient means and motivation isn't just limited to manufacturing; it plagues the service industry as well. A prime example: the U.S. Postal Service. (Note: the following discussion is not 'scientific', being instead largely anecdotal - mostly overheard while waiting in line at the PO).

Quarterly analyses done by the consumer advocate of customer satisfaction data show that improving the reliability of mail delivery offers the greatest opportunity to improve customer satisfaction.
USPS (Chapter Report, 12/20/95, GAO/GGD-96-30).

Is that what they mean by euphemism? ... or just an example of stating the obvious. Well, at least management is tuned in to a cardinal business truth: fulfill your basic mission and you'll keep your customers happy. But in fact, a lot of customers are not happy, and most postal employees are unhappy and immensely relieved if they just make it to retirement without...'going postal'.

Seriously, the intent here is not to pick on the USPS employees *per se*; we're just using the system as an example of government bureaucracy that could use some improvement. (Had to check spelling there and noticed the similarity to 'bureau crazy').

Systemic error and management's lack of leadership and accountability are the main problems - not the employees. The Post Master General is a political appointee; the job is a sinecure, a favor granted to somebody who worked on a campaign or made a hefty donation. Apparently his/her pecuniary remuneration is second only to the President's - that tells you something.

The USPS hasn't worked well because the boss usually was not qualified and didn't work at all. Another scary thought: the job used to be a cabinet level position in line of succession to the Presidency - talk about that old *Peter Principle* where people get promoted to their level of incompetence. Thank God somebody changed that.

We need old Ben Franklin, first Postmaster General of the United States, to come back and set things straight.

Only speak when it benefits others or yourself; avoid trifling conversation ... Resolve to perform what you ought; perform without fail what you resolve. ... Make no expense but to do good to others or yourself; i.e., waste nothing ... Lose no time; be always employed in something useful ... Use no hurtful deceit; think innocently and justly, and, if you speak, speak accordingly ... Imitate Jesus and Socrates.
BENJAMIN FRANKLIN

Wow, that last one really got me, especially in the context of the USPS. We might as well throw in an appeal to the Archangel Gabriel, patron saint of postal workers.

Franklin was actually qualified for his job, having been Postmaster General for the British colonies in America for years and operating it with a budget surplus (those were the days). He was understandably fired when he joined the American Revolution. I guess you know that Franklin played the violin and also composed a string quartet.

But things are looking up. For the first time ever we now have a woman in charge at the USPS and she's made a career of it, having begun as a letter carrier thirty years ago. Ms. Megan Brennan – congratulations and best wishes. I wish you and all your employees (including my younger brother) much success.

People by nature enjoy work but it's difficult to remain motivated and excel in a poorly designed and mismanaged work environment.

All anyone asks for is a chance to work with pride.
W. EDWARDS DEMING

If the process is flawed even apparently simple activities will seem difficult and in the long run you'll get poor results, if any, and waste precious time. The system, for better or worse, will have a profound effect on the people. To solely blame employees is a major copout. Management is responsible for creating a viable system and for leading by example. (Individuals, of course, need to get their act together too).

You know, if I was a post office clerk I'd steer the conversation towards something really dismal, like the relative effectiveness (and moral character) of elected officials, especially the higher-ups. Now there's a real bunch of losers, most of whom will never master their job description. Although furiously busy with their own self-serving shenanigans they rarely, if ever, work at their theoretical real task – serving the interests of the American people. A million hours wouldn't be enough for them to master anything worthwhile.

An honest politician is one who, when he is bought, will stay bought.
SIMON CAMERON (c. 1860's)

When I first heard all the talk in the media about the 1% I thought they were referring to the percentage of politicians that actually care about their constituents. Maybe for the other 99% we ought to revive an old 19th century practice involving tar and feathers.

On the bright side, the USPS recently ranked higher in customer satisfaction than both airlines and cell-phone service providers … maybe not that much of a compliment. Actually, time spent tracking down lost parcels and standing in line at the PO gives you, the customer, an opportunity to practice virtues like forgiveness and meditative deep breathing; things not so easy to attain when on the subject of those politicos.

Well, I'm glad authors can earn a living from writing books; I'm trying to pay some bills with this one myself. But I just wish some of the beautifully crafted self-help (non?)-fiction out there was a bit more responsible in content. Blaming the fact that you're not a billionaire on the year you were born isn't exactly scientific. In science it only takes one exception to throw out the hypothesis and send you back to the drawing board, or coloring book as it may be. The year 1955 may have seen the birth of a few future billionaires but a whole lot of non-billionaire 'exceptions' were also born that year too - like tens of millions.

It's comparable to saying that if you unfortunately live in geographic states beginning with letters in the second half of the alphabet you'll perpetually come in second due to the extra milli-second lost in scrolling down the pop-up window to select your state. I just made that up and I hope that it sounds really silly, because it is.

I'm frankly tired of spending money for books claiming to help me, only to read page after page of how the author made millions flipping real estate or peddling DVDs and seminars to the corporate world and not really accomplishing anything of real substance. I guess the only metaphorical benefit with narrow minded thinking is that it facilitates insertion of the cranium into the rectal canal, but then you're liable to get tunnel vision and start talking out your backside.

The editors did a double take at that one, lecturing me about how a book on classical music should be more 'dignified'. I asked them if they had read any of Mozart's letters.

And now I wish you a very good night,
Just crap in your bed with all your might,
Sleep with peace upon your mind,
And try to kiss your own behind.
MOZART

When it's necessary – speak; and do so in a way that people will remember.
... Whoever is most impertinent has the best chance.
MOZART

You can keep whittling away at that mindless 10,000 hour goal - or you can start thinking about the best way to go about accomplishing something. Then take a hint from those who have truly achieved excellence the old fashioned way, by earning it.

I was obliged to be industrious. Whoever is equally industrious will succeed equally well.
J.S. BACH

Young people can learn from my example that success can be created out of thin air. What I have become is the result of my hard efforts.
JOSEPH HAYDN

And what about those little prodigies who after only a few hundred hours of work do things you couldn't in a million years? (You actually can, in much less time than that). Shouldn't we be analyzing what they are doing, and perhaps try to model their approach?

If your over-all self-development and personal growth is on track, sometimes you don't have to do anything. There's a funny thing about practice and assimilation; just because you're not sitting on your butt strumming the keyboard doesn't mean you're not learning and advancing. Much (most?) analysis, processing, understanding, and absorption (conscious and unconscious) occurs away from the piano, or whatever your main activity is.

When I'm traveling in a carriage, or walking after a good meal, or during the night when I cannot sleep; it is on such occasions that ideas flow best and most abundantly.
MOZART

Many of the most perplexing musical questions and difficulties that ever confronted me have been solved mentally while I was walking in the street or lying in bed at night.
FERRUCCIO BUSONI

Harold Bauer encourages his pupils "to do as much work as possible away from the instrument."
HENRY THEOPHILUS FINCK

One can do much study away from the instrument in thinking about the music; indeed, it is all thinking, in reality. Leschetizky's principle was to do much practice away from the piano.
ALEXANDER BRAILOWSKY

Study should not be timed and regulated by the clock. You are always at it more or less, if you take pleasure in your profession. … I learn useful things at night, like how mistaken we are in our assumed omniscience. You can learn much from peace and quiet – and from music, which begins where thought leaves off.
LESCHETIZKY

But, as previously stated, you need to be 'on track'. Let's examine more closely the issue of systemic or 'built-in' inefficiencies.

William Edwards Deming Ph.D (1900-1993) was born in Sioux

City, Iowa, right at the close of the 19th century. After acing physics and math at MIT he became an expert in engineering quality control utilizing statistical methods. And this guy, not surprisingly (to me, anyway), was also a musician and composer.

As an industry consultant he was instrumental in the rise of a veritable dynasty of Japanese manufacturing efficiency, quality, and profitability. For a whole generation after WWII, Japan dominated the world economy. In a relatively short period of time, its reputation for quality zoomed from rock bottom (remember the pejorative "made in Japan"?) to absolute tops. Everybody loved and bought Japanese cars and electronics. Their stuff is still excellent; my Yamaha piano has served me well over the years.

I just saw a television advertisement where one U.S. automobile company is even calling one of its cars 'America's import'. I wonder how much the ad agency received for that one, and who got promoted? (P.S., that advertisement had a very short lifecycle).

Deming traveled to Japan in 1946 when the country was in ruins. The Japanese people were impressed by his integrity and the fact that he treated them compassionately as equals, not second class citizens. The rest, as noted above, is manufacturing quality history. For some strange reason his work was ignored by American companies. Finally, 35 years later in 1980, NBC television presented a story about him titled 'If Japan Can, Why Can't We?' Hmm… only took 35 years to catch on - now that's an old story.

Deming's approach was basically twofold: 1. ultimate responsibility for success in business and government lies squarely with leadership, and 2. correct system design and implementation is paramount. Conversely, failure can always be traced back to lack of (or dim-witted) leadership and paradigms, or systems that are either not thought out very well, or are downright stupid – or both.

The Eleventh Commandment: "Thou shalt not be stupid!"
LESCHETIZKY

If time and intelligence are properly invested in the system up front, there won't be so many of those frequently asked questions or FAQs later on. The purpose and function of the system will be evident and, most importantly, it will work.

Somebody smart and responsible has to be in charge. In business it's the CEO (forget about those board members); in government the President and Congress are ultimately responsible for the well-being of the nation – pretty grave responsibility I would say … please - get with it ladies and gentlemen.

Weak leadership and poor management unfortunately ripple completely down through any organization. Regarding your progress in playing the piano, or whatever you choose to do, you ultimately must be both CEO and President, and a great one, at that.

To reiterate: process is paramount: how you do something (not just how much) determines your results. To be successful, one must first scientifically analyze for effectiveness each detailed operational procedure and physical component in the total system. If your method, tools, and application aren't sound, thousands of repetitive hours will be to no avail and working yet harder will simply waste additional time and effort.

Hard work and best efforts will not ensure quality, and neither will gadgets, computers or investment in machinery. There is no substitute for knowledge. We have it in abundance…we must learn to use it.
W. EDWARDS DEMING Ph.D.

Deming championed collaboration, as opposed to competition, and he insisted on ethical treatment of people, both customers and employees. (Postmaster, please take note). He actually viewed the monopoly as ideal because 'ideally' it represents the ultimate collaboration – everybody in a whole industry works together, prices are the lowest possible due to economies of scale, needless duplication from competition is avoided, universal standards are easier to establish, getting spare parts is cheaper and easier, the common good is served, etc … in other words, Deming was an intelligent man of character or some kind of innocent, naive saint.

Not surprisingly, Deming was pretty down on that big sacred cow of corporate human resources departments - the performance appraisal and its associated merits (if any) and demerits. He suggested abolishing it completely and just getting down to work, setting up the system correctly, giving employees something useful and interesting to do, training them properly, and treating them with respect. I don't think he mentioned 10,000 hours of anything.

Deming got it right, and he wrote about it. Why aren't his lucid engineering management books flying off the shelves? Or, to update that expression since there aren't many shelves anymore because there aren't many bookstores left – why aren't swarms of drones literally blotting out the light of the sun as they deliver Deming's books to your doorstep? I don't know; but I recommend that you look into this man's work.

If any pianists back in the 19th century music world were advocating thousands of hours of practice alone as the sure way to success ... well, they're long forgotten. I repeat: there's not a single such reference in the surviving literature that I've seen, and that's quite a bit.

Instead, we consistently find great musical artists of the past warning against a mindless 'hours only' approach and advocating quite the opposite: less expenditure of time, but on more focused, tried and true approaches to success – and then spending your new surplus of time on growth experiences in other activities related to your health, social relationships, all-around education, and spirituality. What a concept!

In other words, get good procedural information, use your innate intelligence and common sense to be very focused when working on your main activity, and spend the rest of your time enjoying, and learning from, the great diversity of life.

Common sense is not as common as it should be.
ETUDE MAGAZINE October 1889

The most vital thing in piano playing is to think. Don't repeat a technical illustration hundreds of times with little or no thought directed to the performance. Such work is absolutely useless. Perhaps that's a bit too strong. With countless repetitions there will at least come to be a little improvement, but it will be very small.
SIGISMOND STOWJOWSKI

The mastery of a difficult passage is not at all a question of repetitive mechanical practice; it depends upon the understanding of it, the ability to see it plainly, of making a picture of it in the mind's eye.
LESCHETIZKY

Forming a mental concept is the principal condition to which all ability is subject.
JOSEF HOFMANN

The worst kind of practice is perfunctory practice. The keyboard is a treadmill for thousands of students. They play interminably without considering the musical side of their work – like an actor reciting Hamlet with the same sing-song cadence that a child recites multiplication tables. When you practice, every note, every motif, every phrase, every section, should be filled to the utmost with musical expression.
ALEXANDER LAMBERT

It's not the number of pieces we're intimate with that improves our playing, nor is it the length of time spent at the piano; it is the benefit derived from careful, intelligent practice.
FRANK J. MCDONOUGH

It's not the quantity, but the quality of practice that ensures progress. A merely mechanical or thoughtless exercise of the fingers may strengthen muscles and sinews, but will not produce real progress. Satisfactory progress can only be made when the intellect initiates, assists, and directs the mechanical practice.
ERNST PAUER

Chopin never tired of inculcating that the appropriate exercises are not merely mechanical but claim the intelligence and entire will of the pupil, so that a twentyfold or fortyfold repetition, even nowadays the worshipped arcanum of so many schools, does no good at all; while one hardly dare mention the kind of practice advocated by Kalkbrenner, during which one may occupy oneself reading!
CARL MIKULI

Earlier we mentioned Mozart as an example of a fully self-actualized life. He comes up quite a bit in pop-psychology - Wolfgang that is, not Leopold, the father, mentor, author of an insightful treatise on mastering the art of violin playing, and no doubt a powerful force behind the success of his now more famous son. Leopold deserves some credit too and a good book about him and his ideas would make a great addition to the self-help genre.

One must make a name for himself, attain a certain notoriety, so to speak, before achieving one's fortune in this world....Convince the public of your ability in composition though they've never heard anything of yours yet and

only know of you as a remarkable pianist and childhood prodigy. Make the effort to succeed, and to demonstrate your mastery as a composer in all genres.
LEOPOLD MOZART to his son.

Some people think that simply listening to Wolfgang's music will work wonders for your intelligence quotient, or your child's. Well, I personally agree that exposure to great art is a good thing; but some obvious questions that arise are: might it depend on which piece, who's performing it, and the quality of the recording? Some artists are more insightful than others; a computer MIDI file may not cut it. The much more important question we should be asking is: 'how did Wolfgang Mozart become so successful?' – surely not from just listening to his own yet-to-be composed music while snuggled in the cradle. Maybe his father played Bach to him on the violin or his mother sang folk songs?

I'm inclined to think that a hunt for folk songs is better than a manhunt of those 'heroes' so highly extolled.
BEETHOVEN

Be sure to listen often to all kinds of folksongs; they are a mine of beautiful melodies, and offer you insights into the characters of different nations.
ROBERT SCHUMANN

Ah, … the folk song effect! Perhaps; but hey, what if we actually learned more about music, and even tried to play and compose it? No, our contemporary 'culture' is instead cutting arts education budgets and promoting consumerism … just go buy a CD. The 'secret' of Mozart's greatness is actually quite simple (though much more complex than those CDs) and clues may be found in his character and total life experience. But first, there's a theory making the rounds that I've heard one too many times and now feel obligated to address.

Reincarnation is a sacred concept in some world religions, especially Tibetan Buddhism. The essence or spirit of life is seen as a mysterious whole of which we are fragments. The whole propagates and maintains itself across generations as individuals come and go. Physicists have known about a similar concept for a while, only they call it conservation of energy.

Carl Jung speculated that we are born with the symbolic psychic history of Mankind somehow embedded inside of us. Biologists know that the DNA molecule encodes life - the history of everything it once was and the potential of everything it can be.

That's all really great. Now, I searched through the distant past looking for some Egyptian scribe or Roman senator who had once composed *The Marriage of Figaro* and *Don Giovanni*; I researched the history of noble cities like Ephesus and Constantinople for a long lost composer of *Rondo à la Turk*. ... but drew a huge blank.

The closest I could find was the four Bach brothers, composers who built on the accomplishments of their father. Mozart was definitely influenced by their symphonies and other works, especially those of Johann Christian and Carl Philipp Emanuel – check it out. I also saw some remarkable similarities between the compositions of Wolfgang and his father Leopold.

Well, I thought I was on to something but it turns out that all five of those men were still alive when Wolfgang Amadeus Mozart was born in 1756.

Darwin was a pretty open-minded scientist. It's said that he once attended a séance with Mary Ann Evans (a.k.a authoress George Eliot). Liszt, as we know, eagerly read Darwin (along with tons of religion books) but took a dim view of table-rapping. To claim that Mozart was great because an ancient spirit who happened to be a damned good composer decided to inhabit his body is a bit farfetched, at least for this author.

If only we could just ask Wolfgang Amadeus Mozart how he did it. Actually, we've already heard what he had to say ... and we can't hear it enough.

Neither a lofty degree of intelligence nor imagination nor both together go to the making of genius. Love, love, love, that is the soul of genius.
MOZART

There's much mention in letters of Mozart missing his mom while traveling with his dad, and of missing his pet canary, and later, as a mature man, of loving his wife dearly and missing her too. But there's no mention of a minimum of 10,000 hours in his collected letters, at least not that I've discovered.

Instead of speculating on the 'secrets of success' he was busy working smart; receiving expert guidance, encouragement and support from his father; staying highly motivated to work with amazing discipline at composing masterpieces because he loved music, and also playing a little billiards and cracking jokes every now and then.

Schindler records – and on such points his testimony is reliable – that he heard Beethoven attribute the marvelous developments of Mozart's genius in great measure to the 'consistent instruction of his father.'
A. W. THAYER

There you go Dad. You can't just pop in a CD and wander off to watch the football game or play cards.

Look for opportunities, tirelessly seek out friends, cultivate the relationships relentlessly, revive their interest if it grows dull, and do not believe that 'promised' is as good as 'delivered'!
LEOPOLD MOZART to his son

Show people what you're really made of. Do what you say you're going to do. Create your own opportunities through networking. A truly integrated effective procedural model coupled with your persistent, intelligent application will get results, especially when you absolutely love what you're doing and it becomes a personal mission, a veritable reason for existence.

Living a life of action paradoxically saves time; you'll find yourself less in a 'hurry' with more time to 'spend' on important activities. Ever since we lived in caves there's only been twenty-four hours in a day. But our distant ancestors didn't chop up the day into discrete units; they lived in the moment, closer to nature, perpetually motivated by the task of basic survival. Today we must choose how to spend our minutes and prioritize the important things in life. The trivial, the boring, the time-wasting, and the nonproductive will automatically cease to exist once you discover and commit to your larger purpose in life, your main priority.

Once you've decided to *carpe diem*, you'll need to first apply your second most valuable resource – your mind.

To achieve great things, two things are needed; a plan, and not quite enough time.
LEONARD BERNSTEIN

Procrastinators often harbor the illusion that they have too much time. The worst case would be if we were immortal; we'd never get around to doing anything ever - what would be the point? But we are mortal; our tenure in this world is a proverbial flash of a nanosecond in the greater scheme of things. Plan, yes; then act as if there's not enough time. Planning is just a tool to structure and optimize the part where you actually act. People have known about it for ages.

He that would perfect his work must first sharpen his tools.
CONFUCIUS

Give me six hours to chop down a tree and I'll spend the first four sharpening the axe.
ABRAHAM LINCOLN

By failing to prepare, you're preparing to fail.
BENJAMIN FRANKLIN

And yet, way too few people really take the time to think clearly about important matters and do some simple planning.

We remain barbarously unplanned as individuals.
ALDOUS HUXLEY

The business world has its strategic planning where strengths and weaknesses, opportunities and threats, (or perceived challenges) are all considered. There are even SWOT teams, not to be confused with SWAT teams although there's some overlap.

S   STRENGTHS
W   WEAKNESSES
O   OPPORTUNITIES
T   THREATS

If the profit motive alone becomes the primary why for doing something, the decision of exactly what business to pursue is actually made after planning to do it. In other words, the thinking is: 'we aren't sure exactly what we're going to do but it must be profitable, and hopefully the analysis of the above factors will dictate how to proceed'. The 'planning' becomes more of a survey of what's 'paying'.

A similar situation in your personal life might go like this: you go off to college, you don't know what you really want to do, or you have an idea but lack the courage to try it, so you look at the 'job market', note which professions are hiring and paying well, even if they don't interest you in the least, and then decide to major in one of those fields. It's probably not uncommon; remember that more than two thirds of Americans today are not happy with the jobs they end up in.

As previously noted, income and profit are not necessarily bad things depending upon how you got them and what you do with them. Profit is essential in business or you exit stage 'wrong' and go out of business. Now for individual lives, yes - you need a minimum amount of money to survive - but the real target numbers are happiness, quality of life, and self–fulfillment. The motive of material gain alone is not enough to (get you to) make this happen, and planning a life around money exclusively is a mistake.

To some degree, business strategic planning can be adapted and applied to individuals. If you're not yet sure of your goals in life such an exercise can get you thinking. But the highest purpose of the individual is self-actualization, becoming the person you're destined to be in life and all that entails. Unlike corporate strategic planning and things you can buy with a credit card, mapping out your precious life is a truly priceless proposition.

Consider your individual 'STRENGTHS', they're far greater than you probably imagine. First of all, you share a stunning advantage with every other human being on the planet: you're living in the best possible time - right now. The sum total of all experience, information, and wisdom accrued by civilization since the beginning of time is at your disposal.

Take music as an example: in the last three and a half centuries since the time of Buxtehude (1637) and Bach (1685) onwards, we've amassed an amazing legacy of great music and relevant knowledge. To be sure, previous ages had their own meaningful music and at each particular time in history it was enough. But knowing what I know now of the continuum of music history I can't imagine living prior to the time of Mozart, Beethoven, Chopin, Liszt, Debussy, or Gershwin and many others.

Positive Piano

You and I, as well as a great many other people, ought to be very thankful
that we were not born until after Franz Liszt and William Mason had time
to improve the means of developing piano touch and technique.
EDWARD M. BOWMAN

We possess this truly awesome collective heritage, and yet we have
an obligation to extend it, to build on that past and make our very
own personal contribution today. All high achievers intuit this truth
about their own human net-worth and when coupled with a sense of
community obligation it generates enthusiasm and commitment and
unleashes great personal power.

The expression *Noblesse Oblige* meant that the privileged nobility
of former times were (ideally) obligated to help those whom they
ruled.

Génie Oblige!
LISZT

Liszt adapted/adopted the motto to mean that the same goes for
artists of genius: they are obliged to lead, and contribute to the
common welfare.

True music must repeat the thought and inspirations of the people and the
time. My people are Americans and my time is today.
GEORGE GERSHWIN

Our place and time is here and now. Advances in technology
undreamed of in past centuries provide us with powerful
tools in support of our chosen activities. Computers, network
communications, and transportation have made it much easier to
work on projects and collaborate with others, regardless of geography.

For sure, we still have a lengthy list of challenges, many of which
have gone global. Environmental pollution is greater now than in
the past. The general economy and personal finances always seem
to be an issue. Social injustice is as rampant as ever, maybe more
so. Two things that used to be pretty simple and natural - food and
medicine - are rapidly becoming mankind's worst nightmare ... the
list goes on.

We can become overwhelmed in the face of these and other

perceived problems but anxiety doesn't help matters, in fact it makes things worse by diverting the potential positive force of your mind.

It all comes down to choices. Most of the bad things in life are a result of our own poor ones, and much of the remaining global suffering can be traced back to other choices, often criminal, by a minority of selfish and greedy individuals ... which is all the more reason for the majority of sensible individuals to work together for positive change.

When things get tough, the tough must optimistically envision a better alternative, and then act. The greatest strength of human beings, the very essence of what it means to be human, is our free will and ability to make choices in life.

Free choice is the highest mental process.
MARIA MONTESSORI

You may not be able to control the actions of others but you can control your own. If the environment has become dangerously polluted and depleted of natural resources, choose to be a part of the solution. Live a lifestyle that improves the situation, not one that adds to the problem. Your contribution, however small, will make a difference and the more individual action there is, the greater the difference. You'll be supporting the leaders in alternative causes and the sum total will become powerful indeed.

Our lives today may seem complex in comparison with the past, but it's been relatively so with every generation. Those that follow us will marvel at our simpler life. Complexity is a mindset, a perception; but we can choose to:

Simplify, simplify, simplify.
HENRY DAVID THOREAU

Pure, genuine beauty is always synonymous with simplicity.
FRIEDERICH WIECK

The simplest things are sometimes the grandest ... and the most difficult of attainment.
WILLIAM MASON

More 'things' also make our life seem more complex. Is all that clutter - the material possessions and gadgets - really serving a valuable and nurturing purpose in our lives or does it stem from the short-lived desire for immediate gratification? Aren't the best things in life truly simple? Isn't happiness best found in health, relationships, learning, entertainment, meaningful self-expressive work, and spirituality, all in harmonious balance?

People themselves are always the most important resource. There are more of us alive today than ever before, so there's more opportunity than ever before. If we act intelligently we can efficiently utilize our wealth of natural resources, with plenty for all.

There's strength in numbers. An amazing support team is waiting in the wings ready to serve as cheerleaders, mentors, confidents, and sources of material aid. These are your parents, siblings, friends, peers, fans, fellow-professionals, even your pets. As a group it's probably a lot larger than you think.

A lot of parents are understandably reluctant to encourage their children who show some interest in the arts - because some interest is not enough.

You will see that if you are serious in your music, your parents may become your best friends.
LESCHETIZKY

Ultimately you determine how much help you're going to get by your actions and your belief in yourself. When you demonstrate commitment you'll be perceived as a leader and your team will be inspired to follow.

'WEAKNESSES' are actually a matter of perception and attitude. Instead of viewing things negatively, objectively identify areas for improvement; see them as temporary less productive aspects of yourself to be consciously transformed into strengths. Don't despair thinking that your current situation is all it ever will be. Your own pilgrim's progress is an organic evolution, a constant unfolding of new growth, mindset and strength.

But practically speaking, right now is all you've got to work with. We do learn from the past, we reminisce and cherish fond memories, and we plan for the future – but our actions occur in the present.

What can I think of the future, which does not exist, because it is the future?

And I prefer not to make pronouncements on the past because it no longer exists.
IGOR STRAVINSKY

The moment is supreme.
FRANZ SCHUBERT

We need less talk, especially carping and criticizing, and more action to manifest our inner creative vision. Problems to solve will always exist for you if that's your paradigm - or you can instead focus on creating value, which is what the world really wants and needs.

'OPPORTUNITIES'? - let's just say they're virtually unlimited because you are going to create them at will. Businesses spend countless hours sizing up the competition trying to come up with ways to emulate or undermine them. They second-guess the 'economy' or invent wily new ways to persuade people to buy things - whether or not they are actually useful, desirable, or even safe.

In a way, your personal growth is your very own product or service and it's uniquely valuable because it's the fulfillment of a human life – yours. The scope of your vision, commitment, and level of perseverance will define the end result. Put your energy into developing yourself and you'll create unique value for all your customers.

Helping one's self in the highest sense involves the helping of one's neighbors.
SAMUEL SMILES

Opportunities are often described as something to exploit to advantage. A company analyzes whether or not an objective is attainable (bottom line: financially) and if it's not, they look elsewhere. Now, if you're the decision maker ('decider') and this is about your one precious shot at life – you owe it to yourself to think big!

A great subject generally demands a grand treatment.
LISZT

As far as the 'THREATS' category goes, people can always come up with plenty of reasons for not accomplishing their goals, but these only amount to excuses. The basic threats are the same for everyone and there are only two: you'll lose your health and won't be able to work; or you'll lose your motivation and belief in yourself ... and quit.

If you have a beautiful life dream you must realize it. And how will you know if something is attainable or not if you don't try?

However little talent one has, one should at least try.
SUZUKI

Understand and appreciate your many strengths and count them as blessings. Start thinking about how you can marshal them together and put them to good use. It's the starting point for an action plan with a clearly defined and measurable scheduled sequence of short and long-term goals to be worked on in a context of effective strategic means – until you succeed.

A strategic fit describes how a company's products/services and management structure match up with their external environment. Paradoxically, most companies usually set their objectives after they assess their environment, and often set goals based on what others are already doing. They can obsess about 'the competition' just like many people try to keep up with those Joneses.

But defining what we'll attempt in life by the current environment is simply too timid. Even worse, deciding what's possible in terms of what others have already done means no progress whatsoever – in the whole world. This kind of non-thinking severely blocks creativity and innovation.

It's a mistake to insist that a thing is impossible just because we can't do it.
CICERO (106 - 43 B.C.)

Mediocrities are afraid to be individual and original.
ANNIE W. PATTERSON

Everest can be climbed, you can run a mile in less than four minutes, a man or woman can walk on the moon ... all once considered impossible just because they hadn't been done yet. If you're a piano student, you can flawlessly perform the Chopin Études, the Liszt Études, the Godowsky-Chopin Études, ... or fill in the blank _____. But please don't make a display marathon out of it by trying to play them all in one public concert, just to show off. The three men that composed them were infinitely superior interpretive and executant artists and they programed only a few at a time, knowing inside that they didn't have to prove anything to anybody, focusing instead on simply making music.

Better yet, if you're not already doing it, try creating something new, beautiful and exciting that takes artistic expression and music technique, or business products and services, not just to the next 'level' but into the stratosphere.

To repeat:

The vexation of an obstacle begins when one imagines that it is insurmountable.
MORIZ ROSENTHAL

Each of the above mentioned sets of Études are truly ground breaking musical works; they expanded the vision of what was considered possible and established new standards of beauty and excellence. If that sounds daunting, remember that it took time and resulted from a process of studying diligently what had come before and extending that knowledge through a combination of personal vision, enthusiasm, planning, methodology, and application – a process available to all of us.

As much as creativity and risk-taking are publicly lauded, in practice they are paradoxically feared, shunned, and actually discouraged in favor of the old status-quo-comfort-zone. That mindless mindset always keeps you a step or two (or miles) behind and virtually guarantees perennially playing catch-up and vaguely imitating others who accomplish original things first.

Real leaders and innovators on the cutting-edge aren't intimidated by external environmental factors. The biggest risk in life is to remain self-centered, timid, insecure, cautious, and fearful.

For all the sad words of tongue or pen, the saddest are these: It might have been.
JOHN GREENLEAF WHITTIER

But even if you're totally excited about accomplishing great new things, all the hard work in the world won't help if your methodology, or means, is not realistically grounded in a carefully reasoned approach that is capable of facilitating 'success' when you apply it. Shortly, we'll discuss a fascinating subject of critical importance to the discussion of optimal achievement, and many of you will be hearing of it for the first time.

Businesses that are smart (that is, profitable, or at least still in business) periodically review results and revise strategies to accommodate changing environments. One requisite tool is a series of critical benchmarks by which progress (or not) can be monitored over time. We must do the same over the course of our personal and professional (the same?) development.

Now, about that marketing/demand analysis - don't be afraid that there won't be any takers for your product; the world is always receptive to a sincere artist with a powerful vision who has devoted the time to technically perfect his/her 'Art'. A huge demand exists for talented individuals with something new and exciting to offer. This represents an equally huge opportunity in the world because the supply of these individuals is relatively rare. If you're totally committed to perfecting your art you will have no competition. The fully-actualized self is the real product, and they're in short supply.

Such a thing as a royal road, a secret trick or a patent method to quickly become a great artist does not exist. ....Nothing can take the place of real worth. If you would make a list of the indispensables of pianistic success you must put at its head 'real worth'.
JOSEF HOFMANN

Don't worry about identifying and conforming to trends; set them. By the time you climb aboard the season's genre bandwagon the real trendsetters are off doing something else. Focus on those core strengths you're naturally and temperamentally really suited for, and on what you love – that's what you'll enjoy the most anyway. To paraphrase a now-departed famous tech entrepreneur: "Focus on a core repertoire and make it great".

To be happy, or even successful, you must judge well what is possible for you to achieve, and not spend your lifetime striving to do what others can easily do better.
LESCHETIZKY

Ascertain at the very outset whether nature has adequately supplied you with the necessary tools for what you have in mind.
LEOPOLD AUER

114

Don't strive after a pianistic style that may be unfit for you. ...One hour spent in practicing an aspect of music for which one has a natural physical or imaginational ability will generally prove more fruitful than many hours devoted to problems towards which one is less instinctively impelled.
PERCY GRAINGER

There's as much art in choosing the right compositions as in playing them. There are still some pieces I would not attempt; some that require more power for instance, than I now have.
JOSEF HOFMANN

Under which king will you serve? for you cannot serve two. Better let nature decide for you, and decide she does with marked preferences. I've attended piano recitals and wept silently because the "piano reciter" fondly believed he was versatile and attempted everything from Alkan to Zarembski. What a waste of vital force, what a waste of time.
JAMES HUNEKER

Become expertly accomplished in your inherent strengths. True polished artistry sells; contrived mechanical flash in encyclopedic volumes gets old pretty quickly. There isn't a big market for rapid scale players.

Brilliant passage work fades with time. Mechanical accomplishment is only of value where it serves a higher purpose.
ROBERT SCHUMANN

Acknowledge your own unique personality, identify your niche and then set your sights really high. Raise your personal artistic bar not just a fraction of an inch but at least two hands - that's eight inches in the horse world, a huge increment for humans in the Olympic high jump.

When they set that high jump or pole vault bar at a certain height you have to exceed it to clear it. You will sail over that bar, and greatly exceed your goal with less time and effort via a sound wholistic strategy pursued with enthusiasm and perseverance.

Resolve to create and commit to your very own personal development strategy, one that aims for absolute mastery of your chosen craft or profession and exploits a broad diversity of attributes, strengths, and skills. Your life isn't a short-term product development cycle, it's about the long term (like a lifetime) proposition of creating yourself during your way too short but potentially glorious tenure on this awesome planet.

A side note on the meaning of awesome, a word heard all too often these days. Bringing your own bag to the grocery store or ordering the largest coffee from the barista is not 'awesome'. Awesome means invoking awe. Awe is direct, transformative sensory/emotional experience of reverence, respect, and wonder with a tinge of fear; you know, kind of like what Moses felt when the Hebrew God chatted with him through a burning bush about the future of mankind. Whatever your dream, make it truly awesome.

The greater danger for most of us is not that our aim is too high and we miss it, but that it is too low and we reach it.
MICHELANGELO

In the long run, men hit only what they aim at. Therefore, though they should fail immediately, they had better aim at something high.
HENRY DAVID THOREAU

And make sure it includes lots of good things for everyone else too. Like Beethoven said, you're one of the lucky ones if your destiny includes bringing joy and delight to many people, for that is the true secret of happiness and success.

How we use our time is a major factor in personal success. Time is of the essence in your contract with life. Don't procrastinate, get on with it. Efficient use of time leads to other efficiencies and enhanced productivity. And that increases the chances that you'll be ready to seize opportunities as they arise. Often, it's not just a question of time management but also of timing.

In the matter of concerts you must never put off. Learn to seize the hour when it's favorable to you; if you don't it escapes you for no good reason. ... he who walks in the streets of by and by, ends up in the house of never.
L.M. GOTTSCHALK

So, you have finally decided to appear! You are inclined to come too late. Beware of missing chances; otherwise it may be altogether too late someday.
LISZT

One of Bülow's pupils once requested the opportunity to play in concert. Bülow looked non-committal and made no reply. Six months later the applicant, who had meanwhile given up hope, was given his chance. Appalled at the prospect the pupil stammered 'not ready'. 'Not ready?' exclaimed Bülow, looking through him as if he did not exist, and then turning scornfully on his heel, "An artist is always ready". Stunned by his contempt the youth undertook the concert, slept not during three days and nights of preparation, was successful, and hastening to thank Bülow found him already possessed of the full information, humming snatches of the program in high good humor.
BERNARD BOEKELMAN

Time is very short, especially for an artist who wishes to accomplish anything out of the ordinary.
HANS von BÜLOW

Are you thinking of doing great things someday, then you would better begin today.
ETUDE MAGAZINE October 1889

Remember how you delay, how often you've received an opportunity from the gods, and yet didn't use it. Know that your time is limited, and if you don't use it for clearing away the clouds from your mind, it will go, and you will go, never to return.
MARCUS AURELIUS

Make use of time, let not advantage slip.
SHAKESPEARE

Now is the watchword of the wise.
PROVERB

Each indecision brings its own delays,
And days are lost lamenting lost days
Are you in earnest? Seize this very moment,
Boldness has genius, power and magic in it.
Only engage and then the mind grows heated
Begin it, and then the work will be completed
GOETHE (FAUST)

Ars Longa, Vita Brevis. Art is long, life is short.

This time, like all times, is a very good one, if we but know what to do with it.
RALPH WALDO EMERSON

Time is a great teacher. Unfortunately, it kills all its pupils.
HECTOR BERLIOZ

Pointed classical reminders to get on with it – now!

What to do with your time? Subsequent chapters will offer up powerful advice on creating artistic success from some of the biggest overachievers in history - synthesized into a working template you can apply to your own life. But we must first digress to discuss a 19th century individual whose life's work has the most profound implications for optimal human functioning, health, and achievement. His unique insights provide a powerful context for the subsequent wisdom from history's greatest pianists.

Chapter 5

······

MEANS

Hours of labor are saved by the right mental control.

—ALBERTO JONÁS

Whenever I pick up a book on music, psychology, health, sports, or even business, I turn to the index looking for a particular man's name. It should lie somewhere between *affirmations* and *attraction, law of*; rarely do I find it, in fact almost never. Relatively unknown, he was ahead of his time and to a large degree still is. Initially he pursued a career as a performing artist, not as a pianist but as a professional actor and orator.

Born in Tasmania in 1869, this man discovered a great truth about how the human body and mind naturally function together at optimal levels and how we can be negatively affected by the complex demands of 'civilized' life. He originated a practical so-called 'technique' to educate people in using their bodies more effectively and incidentally avoid health problems stemming from lifestyle stress. He successfully demonstrated his insights to be a powerful approach to enhanced mental and physical well-being and taught his method to many students who also were able to reproduce it.

More than half a century after his death his work is still not properly understood and there are often misconceptions, even among the minority familiar with it. It's not mainstream by any means, despite profound philosophical ramifications for mankind,

119

maybe because it can't be shrink-wrapped and shipped overnight, or sold in vending machines. It requires some serious critical thinking, discipline, and 'work'.

You may have guessed that we're talking about Frederick Matthias Alexander. Known to friends and colleagues as just "FM", that's how I'll refer to him too (it's less typing).

The *Alexander Technique* as it's commonly referred to today presents a unique opportunity to delve into a subject, the awareness and practice of which can literally transform every aspect of your life and greatly facilitate, in fact is absolutely necessary for, the full realization of all your inherent potential.

An impressive list of accomplished individuals, many of them performing artists, have appreciated and benefitted from FM's work.

Aldous Huxley – polymath, novelist (*Brave New World*)
John Dewey - philosopher, psychologist, educator
George Bernard Shaw - playwright, critic
Sir Paul McCartney - that Paul McCartney – *Yesterday*
Sir Yehudi Menuhin - violinist, conductor
James Galway - flutist
Paul Newman - actor, director, race car driver
Sting - aka Gordon Matthew Thomas Sumner
Sir Adrian Boult – conductor, premiered Holst's *The Planets*
Moshé Feldenkreis - created his own bodywork method
Nikolas Tinbergen - scientist, Nobel prize, physiology/medicine

A proposed meeting and demonstration with pioneering 19th century psychologist William James unfortunately did not take place. It would have been a fascinating meeting of minds and had the two men collaborated it may have influenced how FM's work is perceived today.

The greatest weapon against stress is our ability to choose one thought over another.
WILLIAM JAMES

A number of prestigious musical organizations value and teach the subject, including the Juilliard School at Lincoln Center, the Royal Academy of Music in London, the New England Conservatory of Music, and the Los Angeles Philharmonic.

It's not just intellectual liberals and artistic types that vouch for FM - the Israeli Air Force is said to train their pilots in the technique. It's been demonstrated to reduce stress and decrease reaction time, useful when flying jets at supersonic speeds. This group wouldn't invest the time and resources if it didn't work.

I simply offer this as an example of an organization with a critical mission that happens to be extremely efficient at it. (It's the pilots that are efficient, not the politicos that order them around).

The definitive source of information remains the four books FM authored. In order of publication, they are:

Man's Supreme Inheritance 1910
Constructive Conscious Control of the Individual 1923
The Use of the Self 1932
The Universal Constant in Living 1941

You'd think the cool titles alone would spark some interest. I've now read them all, several times over. Considering the challenges of effectively articulating the subject matter intellectually through language the books are at first not easy to read and understand.

It's impossible to put down here more than a bare outline of this technique because the sensory experiences which come to the pupil in the process of acquiring a new direction of his use cannot be conveyed by the written and spoken word.
F.M. ALEXANDER

Why haven't more people been exposed to this? Why isn't it being universally taught in our schools? Well, as we know, new ideas often meet with resistance, especially from those who didn't think of them first. Some people have been known to rise above that, though.

Mozart's defence of Haydn's music was prompt and spirited. When Kozeluch and Mozart were one day listening to a composition of Haydn's, the former called attention to certain strange progressions, asking Mozart if he should have written them so. "I think not," replied the composer, "and for this reason: neither you nor I would have thought of them."
WILLEY FRANCIS GATES

FM observes in his writings that people tend to bend the facts to suit their own ingrained viewpoint, and when emotional attachment is strongly linked to habitual sensory experience, an appeal to reason and science is often difficult, if not impossible. Mental habits are as powerful as physical ones; in fact, both are intimately inter-related.

Old mistakes are often more harmful than new truths.
GOETHE

Tradition too often means a collection of bad habits.
ARTUR SCHNABEL

A great many people think they are thinking when they are merely rearranging their prejudices.
WILLIAM JAMES

Thankfully, there's that optimistic classical notion that truth prevails in the long run, and will set you free if you can grasp it - *Veritas vos Liberat*. Or, if you don't get it, progress marches on and hopefully the next generation will.

A new scientific truth does not triumph by convincing its opponents and making them see the light, but rather because its opponents eventually die, and a new generation grows up that is familiar with it.
MAX PLANCK

FM's work is about getting back in touch with natural processes, becoming happier, healthier and more productive by using our minds and bodies as nature intended, one human being at a time. Perhaps our generation will be the one to finally understand, accept, and implement his work in a big way.

At first, I frankly couldn't understand very much in FM's books, this despite significant exposure to diverse weighty treatises on chemistry, religious studies, philosophy, and psychology. It took time to absorb his ideas intellectually but the turning point was a series of lessons with a teacher. I've experienced the AT hands-on (literally) and if a picture is worth a thousand words, an experience is worth a million. Here's my own brief overview of the basic theoretical premise.

Eons ago our primitive ancestors freely roamed the primeval

forests and savannas. They'd been evolving for many years, perhaps millions, and had acquired three highly effective habits: (1) walking around on two legs searching for something to eat and grabbing it with their opposable thumbs, (2) wooing potential mates to reproduce with, or just practice reproducing with for the fun of it; and (3) looking out for, and escaping from, multifarious nasty predatory beasts.

One of the best methods they devised to handle this last terrifying event was to impulsively run! or conversely to freeze! making themselves as small as possible in order to avoid detection; just like rabbits, for example. (For now, just make a note of that).

The hominids performed their three habits instinctively and well. But along the way something happened that no scientist has ever satisfactorily explained (and need not, incidentally), although religious scriptures and cultural myths offer some profoundly interesting ideas: the dawn of consciousness and reason in Man. At least we think so; watching the nightly news can make you wonder if it really did happen.

Maybe those early humans felt they needed more than just three habits, I don't know. But consciousness, that whopping game-changer of an innovation, has resulted in seven billion of us now dominating every other life form on the planet, as well as each other. So far so good; or is it?

Suddenly we got civilized and swiftly incurred many taxing and stressful new demands on our lifestyle. We had to quickly master a slew of new skills involving tools, fire, clothing, shelter, hunting animals (including the ones that used to hunt us), agriculture, advanced dating psychology, and just plain putting up with many more of ourselves, to name a few.

I realized that in our present state of civilization which calls for continuous and rapid adaptation to a quickly changing environment, the unreasoned, instinctive direction of use such as meets the needs of the cat or dog was no longer sufficient to meet human needs.
F.M. ALEXANDER

Man needed one moral constitution to fit him for his original state; he needs another to fit him for his present state; and he has been, is, and will long continue to be, in process of adaptation.
HERBERT SPENCER

Positive Piano

The passage from the natural to the civilized state produces a very remarkable change in man, by substituting justice for instinct in his conduct.... when the voice of duty replaces physical impulse and appetite, man, previously thinking only of himself, is forced to act on different principles, and to consult his reason before listening to his inclinations.
JEAN-JACQUES ROUSSEAU

It all happened at light-speed relative to the Galapagos tortoise-like pace of evolution, which according to scientists requires millions of years, or at least a few hundred thousand. In the distant past we were content with our three main habits. But then, within 30,000 or so years we went from caves to pyramids to Greek and Roman temples to castles to Gothic cathedrals to steel and glass skyscrapers ... and finally to the moon.

Suddenly we had women (and men) playing hard to get, lots of consumer products to purchase and figure out how to program, warfare, disease, stressful jobs (surveys consistently indicate that 70% of employees aren't happy with theirs) and things called laws.

The more laws and restrictions, the more thieves and robbers
The more ingenious and clever men are, the more strange things happen
The sharper men's weapons, the more trouble in the land.
LAO TZU

The physical and mental demands of a conscious lifestyle totally outstripped our instinctive ability for natural, optimal functioning. Animals were smart enough not to pilfer apples off the Tree of Knowledge or peek into Pandora's Box. They still operate on highly evolved instinct and those in the wild still manage just fine, unless they run into Man.

The evolution of the brain not only overshot the needs of prehistoric man, it's the only example of evolution providing a species with an organ it doesn't know how to use.
ARTHUR KOESTLER

The richest comedy presented by the evolutionary process is that creatures designed by nature to have perfect posture and vision should today represent

124

a picture of bespectacled decrepitude.
RAYMOND DART

Just living in a rapidly changing environment has been a huge challenge; perhaps that's why we generally resist change. We couldn't rapidly evolve new instincts to successfully deal with all the new stimuli. But subconsciously, our instinct remained to drive us to act instinctively in basic tasks. Life suddenly became extremely stressful (threatening?) and rather than first calmly think things through with our new consciousness and reasoning ability, the only thing we could 'remember' to do instinctively in similar situations (like those rabbits) was to freeze!, drawing our head and neck down, forcing our bodies to get as small as possible.

Even today, if you get out of line a policeman will perhaps not so gently bark at you to revert back millions of years. You wishfully hope that the stress and stressors will eventually just go away so you can resume eating and mating but it/they haven't and won't. Life continues to grow seemingly more complex with each generation.

Back in the primeval jungle there were no concert grand pianos and no Bach Fugues, Chopin Études or Beethoven Sonatas. These artistic marvels only became possible with individual human consciousness and creative reasoning ability. YouTube notwithstanding, cats and other animals guided by instinct alone cannot play the piano. Instinctive piano-playing creatures never evolved into their own distinct species, not on this planet anyway, although 'Pianists' do make a brief appearance in Camille Saint-Saëns' *Carnival of the Animals*. Playing the piano successfully, as with any other 'civilized' proposition, depends not upon animal instinct but on our ability to think.

Animal species rely on individual and herd instinct but for humans, although we share the same biological heritage, individual details of implementation are always different because we're all absolutely unique thinking (hopefully) individuals – physically, mentally, and spiritually.

It is not in human nature for all men to tread the same path of development, as animals do of a single species.
MARIA MONTESSORI

Unfortunately the stresses of civilized life have caused us to chronically mis-use our mind/body or 'self'. We no longer function naturally in an optimal manner and this causes us much mental anxiety and physical distress.

That's the basic premise, admittedly a bit of a downer. The good news - and it's very exciting: FM rediscovered and empirically demonstrated how humans can regain true natural function and optimal performance in their daily tasks and achieve unimagined levels of mental and physical productivity and well-being.

First of all, it bears repeating that FM's work transcends the intellect: reading, verbalizing, and even thinking are mere precursors to understanding via wholistic experience. The concept must be grasped and realized experientially over time, a kind of integrated total mind-body makeover that results in paradigm-shifting new insights, transformative higher awareness, and often radically improved health.

Quantum theory provides us with a striking illustration of the fact that we can fully understand a connection though we can only speak of it in images and parables.
WERNER HEISENBERG

Intellect is just one tool in the learning process, but it's still an important one that can prepare you for when an Alexander Technique teacher helps you to experience what in all probability will be next to impossible for you to experience by yourself. (This startling statement will be duly explained).

We probably shouldn't call it the Alexander Technique, which sounds a bit like chiropractic methods or the Heimlich Maneuver or whatever - things which it most assuredly is not. He called it his 'work'; but bowing to convention, I'll occasionally refer to it as the 'AT'. Again, it's less typing.

Alexander's system gives us relief from strain due to maladjustment, and consequent improvement in physical and mental health, increased consciousness of the physical means employed to gain the ends proposed by the will, a general heightening of consciousness on all levels; and also a technique of inhibition, working on the physical level to prevent the body from slipping back, under the influence of greedy 'end-gaining", into its old habits of mal-coordination.
ALDOUS HUXLEY

126

Anyone seeking to master the art of playing the piano (or anything else for that matter), should perk up at the implications of those words by Huxley. FM's paradigm/practice (because it melds thought and action) is very different from mainstream thinking about the mind/body connection that is in all probability informing your current world view.

A number of books about FM's work have been published since he passed in 1955; some are better than others. Reading will hopefully stimulate your interest and inspire you to research and experiment, and to seek out a qualified teacher to assist you. But if you want to see this 'technique' in action immediately, just observe toddlers, kittens, and puppies at play.

To be honest, you learn orchestration far better by listening to the sound of leaves rustling in the wind than by consulting handbooks in which instruments look like anatomical specimens.
CLAUDE DEBUSSY

But like every valuable undertaking this is a life's work. In order to grok it, be prepared to actually do it, and keep doing it. You bring to the table your unique life experience and intellectual capability, but most importantly, your overall open mindedness and mental flexibility. Everyone will understand and appreciate it at a different level. Isn't this true of everything in life, especially interpretation of classical music? Like great music, even if you don't get it right away don't be discouraged; it will eventually come at some point in the future if you stick with it.

Beethoven's works are seldom appreciated and understood at first. Experience has taught us that precisely those works that initially appear to be the most incomprehensible prove themselves over time to be most excellent. However, one also has to play them carefully, which requires study, something missing even with some virtuosos.
CZERNY

Popular notions about FM's work tend to emphasize physical posture. Not simply an over-simplification, this is erroneous, or at best partly true.

There is no such thing as a right position, but there is such thing as a right direction.
F.M. ALEXANDER

Books include illustrations and explanations of various positional learning examples: *lunge, monkey, whispered "Ah", hands-on-the-back-of-the-chair, lengthen neck, widen back*, etc. FM himself talks about these in his writings. It's not just about posture or position alone but a systematic mind/body re-education leading to naturally effective integrated motion, controlled (or not) by the reasoning mind. Your progress and subsequent result is absolutely relative to your unique individual history of physical and mental habits.

When watching a child it's obvious that mind development comes from movement. … Will realizes itself through movement…and this is procured through education of the senses.
MARIA MONTESSORI

Children must learn to do everything easily and gracefully, if it be only standing, walking, or entering a room. For it cannot be expected that a child who is stiff and awkward in everything else can suddenly become easy and graceful at the piano without proper training.
A. KINCAID VIRGIL

So how did FM get into this stuff? In *The Use of Self* he describes in detail how, relatively early in his career, he experienced a significant personal crisis; and it was about the worst thing that could happen to an aspiring actor and orator. He began to lose his voice, and doctors were unable to help. Alexander might have remained just another performance artist who experienced physical problems forcing him to quit his profession, eventually finding some other way to earn a living. Had this been the case we wouldn't be talking about him today.

But that's not the way it happened. He simply refused to accept the grim prospect of chronic suffering and frustration and the inevitable abandonment of his career. He proceeded to carefully investigate the problem, devising an experimental process for detailed self-examination.

Is it not fair to conclude that something I was doing in using my voice was causing the trouble? Very well … I must try and find out for myself.
F.M. ALEXANDER

He cleared the furniture from his living room, placed smoke-free mirrors (that's a joke) along all the walls, and resolutely determined to analyze from all angles every move he made while reciting his lines, noting in particular the effect on his posture but more importantly, the full range of motion and vocal performance. This went on, not just for a few days, but for many months. We now know that FM was an extremely perceptive and persevering individual. The personal voyage of discovery that ensued was both remarkable and unprecedented.

First of all, he reasoned that the hoarseness was merely a symptom of some underlying causative effect(s). Taking a pill, gargling, and even bed rest weren't going to provide a permanent solution because these were therapeutic approaches that, at best, would only temporarily assuage symptoms of the underlying improper use.

There are a thousand hacking at the branches of evil to one who is striking at the root.
HENRY DAVID THOREAU

Over time, FM noticed some things he had been previously unaware of: when reciting his lines he was habitually pulling his head back and down, lifting his chest, and somehow depressing his larynx, causing him to gasp for breath. He noted curiously that in the mirror there was an illusion of appearing 'shorter' in height than normal. (It wasn't an illusion).

He couldn't directly alter the issues with the larynx and breathing but achieved some success in not retracting his head, which actually led to improvement in those other two symptoms. By aligning his head and neck 'forward and up', though it felt unnatural at first, he eventually discovered an inherent control mechanism for optimal use of the body.

FM now realized that a key relationship between head, neck, and spine controls or drives our physical reactions to environmental and psychological stimuli. The most natural and powerful alignment appeared to be that 'forward and up' and 'lengthened' orientation, He termed this the 'primary control'.

This primary control depends upon a certain use of the head and neck in relation to the use of the rest of the body, and once the pupil has inhibited the instinctive misdirection leading to his faulty habitual use, the teacher must begin the process of building up the new use by directing the pupil in the establishment of this primary control. The pupil then mentally projects this direction while the teacher uses his hands to bring about the corresponding activity, the combined procedure securing for the pupil the desired experience of use. This experience, though unfamiliar at first, will become familiar with repetition.
F. M. ALEXANDER

The head, neck, and spine retract backwards and downwards in instinctive response to confusion and stress; the primary control is temporarily lost and mental focus on the task at hand quickly evaporates. Often (almost always) the individual is completely unaware of what's happening. Watch any number of contemporary pianists playing the piano on YouTube and you'll see a variety of truly bizarre, hunched-over postures and motions glaringly indicative of stressful, unnatural use.

The situation is reflected at a subconscious level in many popular expressions. 'Hunker down' means assume a defensive position when challenged. 'Posturing' describes the artificial physical/mental behavior of an individual under stress. 'Don't cramp my style' means don't inhibit my effectiveness. 'Take a stance' is a subtle reminder that mental choices are reflected immediately in body posture. Are you 'on top of the situation' or 'scared stiff'?

If somebody says 'he's out of control' it's not likely to be complimentary. And when they call you 'spineless' or a 'slouch' that's also negative.

Given those examples, now look at this rather amazing old English nursery rhyme that appears to chronicle the mis-use of the self and the resulting degenerative effect on a community.

There was a crooked man, and he walked a crooked mile,
He found a crooked sixpence against a crooked stile;
He bought a crooked cat which caught a crooked mouse,
And they all lived together in a little crooked house.

Back up in time and you'll find some more interesting vernacular. The expression "Thy neck is as a tower of ivory" is found in the Hebrew Masoretic Text (Song of Solomon, King James Bible) and symbolizes elegance, grace, and purity. In Greek mythology, Zeus made Atlas bear the weight of the world on his shoulders. The first cervical vertebra (C1) is called the 'atlas'. It's at the very top of the spine, directly under the skull. There lies the metaphorical power to support the whole world.

He has lost connection and concentration with the head, by which the whole body is supported and held together by its ligaments and sinews, growing as God decrees.
COLLOSIANS 2:19

Run a Bible concordance search on the word 'neck' and you'll find quite a few thought-provoking phrases.

He who is often rebuked and stiffens his neck will be destroyed suddenly, with no remedy.
PROVERBS 29:1

Ancient conquerors had themselves depicted with their feet on the necks of enemies, symbolizing their total subjection. And the words 'a yoke on thy neck' imply mental and physical subjection.

A remarkable development often experienced by those who work with Alexander teachers is a tangible increase in height – because once freed from internal stresses via conscious directives, components of the body release tension and slightly expand. A somewhat mysterious reference to this phenomenon can be detected in the gospel of Luke in the New Testament. 'Taking thought' can also be translated as 'worrying' – either interpretation makes uncanny sense in an Alexandrian context.

And which of you, with taking thought, can add to his stature one cubit?
LUKE 12:25 (KING JAMES)

Effortless ease and confidence are the natural result of efficient thinking, orientation, direction (as in film director) and movement - as expected of an advanced organism that successfully refined itself through millions of years of evolutionary adaptation or, if you like, is the express creation of a perfect being (however, now struggling with the drastic consequences of a fall from grace). Intermediate versions that didn't get things right died out pretty quickly along the way. Stress is a fact of life, but successful species have evolved to deal with it effectively.

When humans become stressed (piano recital?) the head and neck all too often instinctively draws down and back, significantly hampering mental/physical coordination and process. The primary control is thrown out of whack and the organism struggles to function freely and confidently. If the neck and head drawing down and back becomes chronic due to virtually perpetual lifestyle-induced stress, conscious or not, then use becomes habitually flawed. The complex interrelationships between every bone, muscle, tendon, and nerve remain skewed all the time.

The total body adapts to this scenario, gradually adopting a more rigid or fixed 'unnatural' configuration, (even arthritic and 'hunched-back') ... and this becomes the new 'normal' as perceived by the senses. Optimal functioning becomes impossible and because mental and physical are intimately intertwined our mind is negatively affected, resulting in lack of confidence and self-esteem, inability to focus, unhappiness, depression, even despair.

All evil results from the non-adaptation of constitution to conditions. This is true of everything that lives.
HERBERT SPENCER

As you can see, we're beginning to cross over into the area of psychology. Chilean-born pianist Claudio Arrau (1903-1991) was one of the more sophisticated musical artists of the 20th century. He was fortunate to have studied with Martin Krause (1853-1918), a pianist who benefitted from direct association with Franz Liszt. For Arrau, brilliant mechanical piano playing wasn't nearly enough; one should strive for *"complete development of general culture, knowledge, intuition, and human integration in the Jungian sense of the term"*.

I suspect that this enlightened attitude is coming down to us in part from Liszt, through Krause. Arrau once opined that a music conservatory should offer classes in "psychoanalysis and dancing". Please forgive me now for yet another digression nested within the present one, but I believe some further insights from psychoanalysis will add value to this particular discussion.

Wilhelm Reich (1897-1957) is another brilliant original thinker even less generally familiar than F. M. Alexander. After earning a Doctor of Medicine degree at the University of Vienna he became Sigmund Freud's (1856-1939) number one protégé in the emerging discipline of psychoanalysis, though the two eventually parted ways over professional differences.

In general, Freud took a pessimist's view, believing that Man had a basically violent nature buried in his subconscious and that society needed to restrain it. Reich optimistically saw humans as fundamentally noble and good, with great potential for love and creativity through self-actualization.

As a doctor, Reich initially worked with hospital patients, including the mentally-ill. Based on his experience and clinical data he eventually broadened his theories to include everybody. (These days, mental health is all relative.)

It's a concrete jungle out there. Humans are pretty resilient, and most of the time we don't break a sweat over the miniscule stuff but all too often we're forced to come up with myriad ways of physically defending and psychologically shielding ourselves from all the tragic abuse, hostility, and injustice in the world. Individual instances may range from rudeness, insolence, bullying, hazing and racial discrimination, all the way to performance-appraisals and outright physical violence.

Also, 'the system' as a whole isn't necessarily set up to foster and nurture all of our basic natural needs, individually or as a whole. There's no end of prohibitions and rules, some of which are overly and unnaturally restrictive. Example: repressed sexuality comes up often in psychoanalytic discussion.

In the now clichéd Freudian 'office-visit' the patient reclines on a couch and the therapist sits behind him or her, out of the line of sight. There's no touching and little if any eye contact. Reich disagreed. Rather than just watch the clock while a patient rambled, vented, ranted, or melted down, he instead carefully observed their eyes, facial expression, posture, body language, breathing patterns, voice inflection, even how they moved when walking across the room or sitting down.

He took good notes, especially when the conversation hinted at repressed psychological and physical trauma. The patterns that he observed led him to formulate a theory using the analogy of a medieval suit of armor.

Please keep reading. I promise you that this is really important for piano playing, and everything else too. Reich believed that the human body literally 'armors' itself in an attempt to shield or protect from the painful mental/physical trauma and social prohibitions on self-expression, especially regarding healthy sexuality. The mental confusion physically manifests as blockages - literally rigid plates or mesh of muscle, tendon and nerve - something very uncomfortable even to just think about.

The 'armoring' reflects the sum total of a person's emotional life experience; it purports to serve as a defense against future disappointments in life and also internally locks in frustration and anxiety that literally could boil over and explode at inopportune times. In contrast to the hands-off Freudians, Reich considered touching and massage of patients necessary to educate awareness of, and facilitate the loosening of, the body armor. He noticed that when he assisted a physically tense person to let go of the armor, anxiety often erupted as the previously armored 'comfort zone' evaporated.

We experience and react to manifold life stimuli in the form of babysitters, classmates, parents, neighbours, bosses, societal authority figures, comedians, and pretty much everything in the natural environment – and adapt as best we can. As a simple example, a piano teacher might criticize or punish a 'wrong' effort, instead of explaining and demonstrating a more effective approach.

I was never disobedient, but sometimes I received slaps and thrashings due to mere clumsiness. In those days that's how they brought up children; in my opinion, a very unjust one.
LISZT

Nothing is to be gained by noise and scolding, least of all with students to whom nature has been sparing in musical gifts.
LOUIS PLAIDY

Scolding does no good and should be avoided.
SUZUKI

Haydn's piano teacher actually beat him on occasion; the young

Beethoven sometimes got similar treatment from his alcoholic father – not a good thing. Even if it's 'just' a tongue-lashing, a young student (older ones too) may unconsciously attempt to physically inhibit the particular condemned effort by tensing the arm, neck, or back muscles; clenching the jaw, artificially altering their breathing, etc. Usually this is a temporary measure but if repeated over time the inhibitory response may develop into habitual unconscious 'armoring'.

Depending on how resilient we are, or how successfully we adapt, the experience either strengthens or adversely affects our future growth and development. Our 'character armour' can imprison us in rigid and stereotyped reactions to environmental stimuli. The armoring is also a compromise between our impulses and our social obligations--between what we want to do, and what we think we should do to toe the societal line. It's a way of immobilizing the anger and hostility that is often the reaction to trauma. That Reich used the term 'character armor' is significant: physical configuration embodies a human being's total character.

It seems to me that you don't dare to express yourself as you feel. Be bolder, let yourself go more. ... I see that timidity and lack of self-confidence form a kind of armor around you, but through this armor I perceive something else that you don't always dare to express, and so you deprive us all. When you're at the piano, I give you full authority to do whatever you want; follow freely the ideal you've set for yourself and which you must feel within you; be bold and confident in your own powers and strength, and whatever you say will always be good. It would give me so much pleasure to hear you play with complete abandon that I'd find the shameless confidence of the vulgar virtuoso unbearable by comparison.

CHOPIN Emilie von Gretschs, letter of 30 April 1844.

Like Freud and Jung, Reich was a highly intellectual and well-read man. He may have already been familiar with the Hindu concept of chakras when he noted that energy blocks caused by armoring characteristically appeared in seven areas of the body: the forehead, the mouth area, the neck, chest, diaphragm, abdomen, and pelvic region. Blockages in these areas inhibit natural fluidity of function in everything from visual focus, facial expression, and breathing; to athletic motion of all kinds, from simply walking to more complex activities like playing the piano, ballet, or ice skating. It even affects the seemingly relaxing activity of sex.

A suit of armor may defend against a perceived hostile environment but if you're perpetually confined in one, without even knowing it, you cannot be at your best. Men in particular have difficulty shedding armor because they're used to suppressing emotions. Defensive armoring may be a relatively effective short-term avoidance strategy for acute trauma but if retained indefinitely it ultimately robs you of your freedom and potential to fully experience joy and creativity in life.

There's a nice image of this in the film *Robin Hood* (Universal Pictures 2010) starring Russell Crowe and Cate Blanchett. When Robin first meets Lady Marion there's obvious chemistry but they both warily have their defenses up. In a subsequent scene he asks her to help him out of his chain mail tunic, a job normally requiring the assistance of a squire or personal attendant. She helps him 'get the weight off his chest' (his heart) and the heavy metal mesh plummets to the floor with a resounding thud. Crowe's hunkish upper-body (I'm envious) is fully revealed and his human and heroic qualities are symbolically liberated, incidentally empowering the erotic and, of course, man and woman fall romantically in love.

If you haven't actually experienced a medieval suit of armor, in Mark Twain's *A Connecticut Yankee in King Arthur's Court*, the title of Chapter Twelve says it all: *Slow Torture*.

When I trotted, I rattled like a crate of dishes, and that annoyed me; and moreover I couldn't seem to stand that shield slatting and banging, now about my breast, now around my back; and if I dropped into a walk my joints creaked and screeched in that wearisome way that a wheelbarrow does, and as we didn't create any breeze at that gait, I was like to get fried in that stove; and besides, the quieter you went the heavier the iron settled down on you and the more and more tons you seemed to weigh every minute.
MARK TWAIN

Reich saw physical armoring as a direct result of a mental state, similar to the mind/body interactions theorized by FM. Based on his own experiments, FM attributed the manifestation of Reich's character armor to habitual mis-use, physical and mental; the result of end-gaining in a now obsolete instinctual mode as opposed to reasoning out effective new means to accomplish objectives and consciously applying them conscientiously. The two men seem to be describing the same phenomenon from different angles.

You translate everything--whether physical, mental, or spiritual into muscular tension.
F.M. ALEXANDER

Reich believed that therapeutically dismantling the character armor would free underlying emotional blockage, and reassert natural potential for joy and creativity. It might also unleash memories of the childhood repression that had caused the blockage in the first place. FM went beyond Reich in actually figuring out how to achieve this empirically, although his original goal was more pragmatic – the simple re-establishment of optimal function for performance artists. Practitioners of the 'AT' will advise you of the possibility of significant emotional release during the course of lessons.

Researchers theorize that, over time, blocking or locking up emotions by physical armouring along with its consequent unnatural strained body configurations can wind up contributing to serious physical degeneration like rheumatism and arthritis.

Unsurprisingly, F.M. Alexander found that in the course of his work educating individuals in proper 'use of the self', symptoms of these conditions were ameliorated to an amazing degree, as acknowledged by the numerous medical doctors who sent him their 'hopeless' cases.

Health is not merely a condition of matter, but of Mind; nor can the material senses bear reliable testimony on the subject of health.
MARY BAKER EDDY

Reich sensed and appreciated the pulsating rhythms of life and realized that armoring interrupted and restricted the energy flow throughout the body. We may experience this as a stiffness, tension, or lack of 'aliveness'. 'Armoring' can become chronically painful if places in our body permanently retain mental stress and 'lock up', and it reduces our natural capacity for creativity and self-expression. We'll apply this to the all-important concept of rhythm in music in an upcoming chapter.

Wilhelm Reich's story is really quite amazing and far beyond the scope of this book. His work deserves to be carefully studied, expanded and applied. But because he championed individual freedoms in the face of rising world fascism, things unfortunately ended rather badly for him. I'll recap some of the highlights later in this book, but for now we must return to FM and the great pianists.

Descartes' *Cogito ergo sum- I think, therefore I am* - implies that consciousness (thinking) connotes existence (being). Both Reich and Alexander take that statement considerably further in their work. Your emotional and intellectual life experience becomes physically manifest in your body. The postures you adopt, how you move, even how you look - are all accurate reflections of what has happened, and is happening, in your mind.

FM found the correlation between mental attitudes and physical posture/motion to be a two-way street. It seems that Descartes' cogito may be as reversible as a two-tone belt. *'I am, therefore I think'*. The physical configuration assumed by your body can influence, dictate, or limit what's possible for you to think.

We can't truly change our thoughts without changing our bodies. This has profound implications for people concerned with changing 'bad' habits. Mentally willing a change is not enough if the physical body persists in its old habitual orientation, because the physical will persist in dragging the mental back into its previous state.

The influence of the cultivated habitual use acted as an almost irresistible stimulus to me to use myself in my accustomed wrong ways.
F.M. ALEXANDER

Could the young but realize how soon they will become mere walking bundles of habits, they would give more heed to their conduct while in the plastic state.
WILLIAM JAMES

Once familiar with FM's work, you appreciate correlations in the piano literature. I'm convinced that great pianists intuited these concepts, even without intellectual knowledge of the theory later articulated by him. After all, it's simply nature at work in its most unlabored, effective, and natural way.

Gracefulness is necessary; one must begin with posture. ... Beautiful playing depends more on freedom and suppleness than on force.... Stiffened muscles or diverse bad habits may need to be addressed in those who begin late or

have been poorly taught.
FRANÇOIS COUPERIN

I earnestly entreat you to acquire a graceful and appropriate position, when sitting at the pianoforte. Equally important is a graceful position and carriage of the head and upper part of the chest; it must neither be stiff nor bent. Some of my former pupils, whom I used to tease with the reproach of making a cat's back (sitting with their backs bent and oblique) have, in later days, thanked me for the strictness which I showed in this particular. It's not merely that an awkward position is disagreeable and ridiculous, but it also impedes, if not prevents, the development of a free and elegant style of playing.
CZERNY

Regarding one's position at the piano, Liszt was always particular. "Sit upright, look up and away from the ivory, and you will play with greater inspiration." ... (To a young man) "Sit as if you were to be shaved, with the head well up."... (To a young lady) "A pianist should sit like a well-bred society dame, with a quiet air of superiority, then she can phrase better"... (To a young lady who persistently eyed the keys) "Sit as if you were having your photograph taken".
CARL LACHMUND

Like his successor Paderewski, Liszt sat erect, and never bent his proud head over the "stupid keys," as he called them, even deprecating pupils doing so. ....The most divine expression came over his face when he began to play the opening measures of the accompaniment, and I shall never forget the concentration and intensity he put into them if I live to be a hundred!
AMY FAY

I occasionally saw Beethoven momentarily out of sorts or occasionally de-pressed. Very soon he would regain his composure, carry his head erect, stride ahead with his customary purpose and vigor, once more master in the workshop of his genius as though nothing had happened.
ANTON SCHINDLER.

All who saw Anton Rubinstein playing at the piano had to admire his whole bearing, the complete repose of his body and head. He tried to train his pupils to bear themselves in the same reposeful way while playing. Here is an example quoted by Mrs. E. N. Vessel: "How you are sitting at the piano!

Positive Piano

Please get up!" said Rubinstein to a pupil; he himself took the chair and placed it exactly in front of the middle of the keyboard. "Always take care how you sit at the piano. He kept his eye on his pupil during his lessons, for he sat at a piano beside the one on which the pupil played, sometimes himself playing the passages and pieces which he was explaining "You ought to sit at the piano comfortably, your hands and arms must be free, therefore place the chair farther from the keyboard and never lean back in your seat!"
ELLEN von TIDEBOHL

There are certain positions in sitting and standing which strain the nervous system. Ease at the keyboard can never be attained unless one learns to sit easily and comfortably during practice. Another (possible adverse effect) is the position of music on the music rack. In the case of the grand piano the music is somewhat higher than with the upright piano. Consequently the player's head may be held in a strained position. For this reason I discourage sitting too low at the piano. It forces the player to strain his neck while reading music. The great network of nerve ganglia located at the back of the neck is then strained.
ALBERTO JONÁS

As FM continued to experiment in front of mirrors an unexpected and very frustrating fact emerged: he found he couldn't always consciously do what he willed to do. He was astonished to discover that his actual motions were often the exact opposite of what he had mentally set out to do and thought he was doing. Apparently his habitual wrong ways of doing things had become so comfortably ingrained that they affected his sensory experience, which was now working against him.

Here was startling proof that I was doing the opposite of what I believed, and of what I had decided I ought to do. ... The belief is very generally held, that if only we are told what to do in order to correct a wrong way of doing something, we can do it, and that if we feel we are doing it, all is well. All my experience, however, goes to show that this belief is a delusion. ... There was nothing for it but to persevere, and I practiced patiently month after month, as I had been doing hitherto, with varying experiences of success and failure.
F.M. ALEXANDER

Over time, as we perform diverse activities we develop a habitual sensory calibration level or comfort zone that 'feels' right. Even if our self-use is all wrong our habitual actions feel okay simply because we've gotten used to them. When a golfer slices the ball he's not conscious of the underlying sensation of improper use of the body …. he just blurts out 'f#@k'. In fact, his unsuccessful action probably 'felt' just fine, otherwise why would he do it that way? It's usually not his method and execution that frustrates him but the end result: the ball in the woods, or a sand trap, or through a neighbor's windshield. If he'd been more aware of, and had consciously implemented, a truly effective procedural usage of the 'self' - the ball would likely have sailed straight and far.

When people are wrong, the thing which is right is bound to feel wrong to them.
F.M. ALEXANDER

FM noted that the basic desire to swing at the ball dominates. If a coach explains a better overall technical approach, the external words alone will not wield the same power as the old ingrained habit within. Also, if the coaching calls for corrective inhibition, it conflicts with the lower-level impulsive desire to act immediately.

The generalization "keep your eyes on the ball" doesn't consider that wrong use of eyes is inextricably linked to wrong use of the whole body, including the whole mind; otherwise we'd all be golf champions. An FM teacher can help you to properly align everything – head, neck, spine, pelvis, etc., and maintain that optimal alignment while envisioning your goal, internalizing the correct procedural methodology step-wise, almost as if chanting a mantra while your eyes focus on their target and you swing through cleanly. As you can imagine, an intense process of near total sensory re-education is involved.

If feeling can become untrustworthy as a means of direction, it should also be possible to make it trustworthy again.
F.M. ALEXANDER

With the AT, the first steps toward relearning naturally efficient body/mind functioning often feel weird and unnatural. If we're given new directions on how to consider and accomplish a movement, initially we don't implement them correctly even if we think we are, because the old habits are too strongly ingrained and still 'feel' right.

It's surprising how many people miscomprehend where they stand in their musical studies. Where they think they are, and where they really stand may be far apart.
ERNEST HUTCHESON

FM discovered something infinitely more profound than 'fix your posture, stand up straight, and you'll function better'. He wasn't just interested in the proper way to sit in a chair, although that served as a good demonstration for starters. FM figured out how to regain an immense mental and physical clarity and how to effectively apply our 'selves' to anything we seek to accomplish in life.

Nature, to be commanded, must be obeyed.
FRANCIS BACON

Given the full scope and significance of his discovery it's truly amazing that he was able to do what he did, all by himself, especially knowing now that sensory perception has become 'tainted' and misleading. Even when wrong, we often feel perfectly fine as our sense perceptions mistakenly register everything as 'business as usual'.

Imagine a laboratory scientist (or a chef) using a thermometer that was perpetually off by twenty percent, or a carpenter using a skewed level or a tape measure with several inches cut off. The end result will be frustrating and confusing, and never get better until the sensory device is recalibrated true.

This subject is difficult to write about and I keep looking for ways to explain it by comparison with subjects I'm somewhat familiar with. Some worldviews, take Buddhism for example, are fond of saying that we're living an illusion of sorts. FM's paradigm reminds me of Buddhism's Four Noble Truths - 1) Life is suffering, 2) the origin of suffering is desire, 3) this situation can be overcome, and 4) the answer lies in the eightfold path consisting of right view, intention, speech, action, livelihood, effort, mindfulness, and concentration.

Consider the book of Genesis: the first Man and Woman live in god-like perfection until they eat of the tree of knowledge, after which all of Mankind flounders in a fallen state, endlessly desiring everything they can now possibly imagine but weren't necessarily equipped to handle and mostly screwing things up.

End-gaining, without due consideration to means-whereby has got to go. Rational thought and planned action continuously monitored by properly calibrated senses is the only way to get back to any semblance of Eden.

This end-gaining business has got to such a point - it's worse than a drug.
F.M. ALEXANDER

As William Blake noticed several hundred years ago, people seem to want everything, even the moon. Well, we've proven that we can have it if we're willing to think, plan, and execute properly. The accomplishment of the men and women of the 1960's NASA program remains a magnificent example. Bravo!

We're often frustrated in our desires because they are primarily short-term instinctually-driven emotional urges to satisfy our own perceived selfish needs. We try too hard and too fast without sufficient awareness of, and attention to, the proper means required to achieve a desired goal … or understanding of the consequences of poor choices.

We sell the thrones of angels for a short and turbulent pleasure.
RALPH WALDO EMERSON

Our higher potential is sacrificed to immediate gratification. To complicate matters, when impulsively striving for something, what we perceive with our senses … is often not what we're actually doing at all. Yet the now habitual faulty sense perceptions feel totally comfortable – and 'right'. FM used the catchy Victorian expression 'debauched kinesthesia'. (If you don't believe your sensory mechanisms can let you down, start by wiki-ing 'optical illusion'.)

Consider the following series of events: we desire a goal, e.g, virtuosic performance of a piano étude to express our inner artist or maybe just to impress someone. We approach it instinctively, without any rational planning of how this goal might reasonably be attained, or any monitoring or feedback of actual progress. We're driven by an almost hypnotic fascination with the music. Even if (when) the first results are not satisfactory and we experience frustration because the impulse to immediate gratification is thwarted, our habitual use feels perfectly natural because it's what we're used to.

If our fundamental wholistic use of the self (integrated mind/ body) is unfortunately out of whack due to years of bad mental/ physical habits (and in all probability this is the case) then chances are we cannot live up to our potential, despite all good intentions and 'trying'.

You can't do something you don't know, if you keep on doing what you do know.
F.M. ALEXANDER

It's frustrating to fail, as we often must under those circumstances. We become discouraged and lose confidence, which again negatively affects our overall health in subtle ways, further weakening us. Eventually we may begin to believe that the goal or task is actually impossible, because no matter how hard we try, success remains elusive. To remain blissfully (or miserably) unaware of your faulty method and just keep at it for another 9,999 hours in order to somehow attain mastery is completely nonsensical.

Insanity: doing the same thing over and over again and expecting different results.
EINSTEIN

When a person has reached a given stage of unsatisfactory use and functioning, his habit of "end-gaining" will prove to be the impeding factor in all of his attempts to profit by any teaching method whatsoever. Ordinary teaching methods, in whatever sphere, cannot deal with this phenomenon, indeed, they tend actually to encourage end-gaining.
F.M. ALEXANDER

Always try to avoid making the pupils 'do'; always try to make them think.
TOBIAS MATTHAY

If you're still not sure what end-gaining means, try making a recording of your piano practice session, or video yourself attempting pretty much anything new. Chances are you'll be shocked at all the starts and stops, the repeated errors, and the tension and the frustration evident, most of which you weren't

144

even aware of when you were carrying out the activity.

That's end-gaining or 'trying' impulsively as opposed to working methodically within a cycle of feedback and correction. It's virtual seduction by desire and precludes awareness of a reasoned 'means-whereby' that could actually achieve the desire, in other words, one that works.

Artur Rubinstein said that major advances in his piano playing only came after he began recording because, of course, he critically analyzed the takes and started paying more attention to what he was doing. Glen Gould, the 20th century's master recording artist, called the now technologically dated tape recorder the 'best teacher' because of the critical feedback it provided.

Incidentally, Gould's recordings, though marvelous works of art, cannot be compared to live performances because they contain hundreds of meticulous splices, similar to film editing, in a personal quest to realize 'perfection' of artistic vision.

A pattern of error due to underlying incorrect methodology and faulty application can quickly spiral down, becoming a vicious cycle where each subsequent iteration results in further frustration, discouragement and even physical degeneration. If that sounds like a scary proposition, well - it is.

But there's hope, says FM. We can inhibit our negative knee-jerk reactions and substitute a reasoned, effective sequence of planned actions, effective because they will be in harmony with natural processes. Thus we can reverse that downwards spiral, transforming the vicious cycle into a victorious one, forward and up, so to speak. Through the higher plane of conscious control we can rise above our habitual dependence on inapplicable and misguided instincts, flawed sensory perception, and the tyranny of immediate gratification.

Conscious control means primarily a plane to be reached, rather than a method of reaching it.
F.M. ALEXANDER

The above sentence puzzled me at first, but I think it's sort of like saying 'success' is not something you do, but rather the end result of a process encompassing successful actions. Alexander's work is not an immediate quick-fix but a long-term proposition and requires discipline and perseverance. We can morally reeducate 'debauched kinesthesia' and our sense mechanisms can be recalibrated to their original natural state. A healthy primary control can be reestablished empowering our total potential as human beings for disciplined reasoning, vibrant health, and the relatively effortless manifestation of our creative potential.

Just 'buying in' to a new approach intellectually isn't enough. All those bad habits that felt right will relentlessly kick in once again if you revert to end-gaining, and your sensory apparatus will again resort to transmitting erroneous feedback data.

Working on the new principle means working against a habit of life, and difficult as that is (as anyone who tries it will find out) the difficulty is enormously increased when one is working contrary to the habit of "end-gaining", for this habit is so closely bound up with faulty habits of use that feel right, that to give it up means giving up the lifelong familiar habits of use that go with it, and employing instead a new use which feels wrong.
F.M. ALEXANDER

Unless you're still in diapers, mastering the art of piano-playing, or anything else, unfortunately means having to first unlearn lots of bad habits, and then implement new and more effective ones. This requires elevating your awareness, a good thing in itself.

The greatest possible relaxation plays a very significant role in piano technique. ...The difficulty is that the sensation of passivity or relaxation in piano playing is unfamiliar and unaccustomed for most people and must be reacquired and practiced. The tendency towards active intervention persists and is difficult to unlearn.
FRIEDRICH A. STEINHAUSEN

FM realized that the habit of end-gaining was so powerfully ingrained that even in the simplest of activities, like sitting in a chair, you had to initially inhibit those ineffectual thoughts and procedures you always thought were so right for achieving the goal. Only then could you mentally project to yourself (without yet acting out) the new, proper sequence of steps to optimally effect the action - step one, two, three..."all-together, one after the other" - while a teacher uses his/her hands to simultaneously coax your body into a new alignment giving you the new sensory experience associated with truly natural use, which will at first feel 'wrong'.

Even the simplest procedure involving motion presumes a many-sided adaptation in advance. Much of this is obviously inborn or inherited; the rest is acquired by development. Practice and adaptation comprise our whole life and being.
FRIEDRICH A. STEINHAUSEN

At your first lesson you might spend the whole hour just relearning how to properly sit down in a chair and then stand back up again, as an example of the over-all re-education process. That 'simple' act becomes a totally different experience when you don't unknowingly retract your head and neck backwards and down, and instead the orientation is forward and up, leading the whole body in a coordinated motion.

Even admitting the necessity of muscular automaticity, reflection is imperative in acquiring it; walking, running, and breathing, purely automatic as they must be in the end, are all the better for a little reflection on the right ways of doing them.
TOBIAS MATTHAY

And for pianists, simply getting on and off a piano bench is just the first step of what can be an amazing complex proposition – playing the piano.

Wholistic reeducation, which is what the AT really is, means heightened awareness of what you are in fact thinking and doing, including weighing the consequences of your choices and actions along with gradual familiarization and habituation to the initially brand-new sensations of executing correct procedures. With practice, a re-calibrated, more accurate sensory feedback capability supplants the previous skewed and deceptive one that facilitated self-defeating mis-use. In effect, a new standard of normality is created and implemented with which to perceive and react to life's never-ending stimuli.

The first step is to reign in that instinctive desire to do something as quickly as possible without logical reasoning as to how it can be accomplished most effectively. Be skeptical of shoe salesmen urging you to "just do it", folksy sayings like "if at first you don't succeed, try, try again" or self-help book authors adding: "just keep at it for

10,000 hours and you'll become a master!" There's even one author egging people on to 20,000 hours.

Just as you have the impulse to do something, stop.
ZEN SAYING

We must inhibit immediate gratification and first think things through. Consider a simple piano-playing example. Paradoxically, our intense desire for self-expression works against us. Fascinated by its artistic beauty, (or mediocrity often enough) we're 'driven' to play a piece of music primarily through instinct and trial and error; our mind takes a back seat.

The very essence of success is of course, practice. But students who are gifted are very likely to be so enchanted with a composition that they dream away the priceless practice minutes without any more definite purpose than that of amusing themselves. It is human to crave pleasure and the more musical the student, the more that student is inclined to revel in the musical beauties of a new work rather than devote the practice time to the more laborious but vastly more productive process of real hard music study.
PADEREWSKI

Athletes know that mere mechanical bending and stretching of the limbs is not enough; there must be an intense wish to attain such a result behind each movement. How much more, then, is an alert, attentive mind needed in piano playing, where the muscular movements are so much more complicated and subtle!
HENRY THEOPHILUS FINCK

The storehouse of experience and drill rests in the region of the subconscious, not the unconscious, because at any time we can bring any detail about walking or grasping, formerly relegated to the mechanical, back into full consciousness, to be thoroughly analyzed. Indeed, we do this all the time, whenever a long-automatic procedure gets interrupted, as in a 'mistake'.... The attention is directed to the fault. The whole procedure is brought out of the subconscious into clear consciousness. It is revised and not permitted to sink down again until the whole detailed procedure has once again been adapted to the purpose, the 'ideal'.
FRIEDRICH A. STEINHAUSEN

A note's most striking and definite fact is its transition from non-existence to existence, from silence to sound; for this is an absolutely definite point of demarcation at the piano. When playing, we cannot definitely think a note unless we think the time-place of the beginning of the sound. This has a far deeper significance. We cannot experience any act of consciousness, cannot direct our minds and think about or realize anything definitely, without just such an act of timing - a timing of our consciousness. The act of directing our thought or attention upon anything is therefore a rhythmical process; thought and rhythm are inseparable.

TOBIAS MATTHAY

Many of us will invariably struggle in frustration, and yet true masters always make it look so effortless and graceful - because they invested the time in right thinking, and effective methodology and application.

Liszt's hand is constantly in graceful motion on the keys; free, without contortion. … He intuits all possible nuances, seemingly without the need to study. … His ability to stamp his passionate vision on the keys, as on a canvas or in philosophical discourse, constitutes a psychological process to actualize talent.

Mme. AUGUSTE BOISSIER

Does the eagle practice flying? He looks upwards, gazes towards the sun, unfolds his pinions, and soars towards its burning light. Don't imagine that Liszt does anything – he 'does' nothing at all; he thinks, and what he thinks takes on form. Can it really be called piano-playing? Liszt then, cannot be expected to practice scales and finger exercises, as is the custom among schools and professors.

WILHEM von LENZ

FM often commented on the ubiquity of mis-use. Someone asked him once if he had ever encountered anybody who could 'properly' use their mind and body as nature intended, and wasn't a total mess like the majority of the population. In *The Use of The Self* FM does make tantalizing mention of one such natural, untainted individual who apparently was an astounding virtuoso at billiards.

The lives of Liszt and Alexander overlapped by seventeen years. It's interesting to speculate what FM would have thought of the ultimate self-actualized pianist but they unfortunately never met.

Tasmania is quite a ways from Weimar, Rome, or Budapest, the three cities Liszt called home in his final years.

Wilfred Barlow M.D. was one of the most prominent first-generation Alexander pupils and founded the Society of Teachers of the Alexander Technique. Barlow once performed a simple study on 108 students, aged 17 to 22, to see if in fact the head and neck were unknowingly retracted and stiffened as a person went from standing to sitting position, as FM noticed in virtually everyone. The result: 107 of 108 did indeed behave exactly as FM had observed - that's just a tad over 99%. Younger students did it a bit less.

More interesting, when it was pointed out to the students, and they were asked to refrain from it, only 11 could do so. That means 90% couldn't immediately change, even if aware of the problem.

We cannot alter our habitual way of doing things simply by deciding to do them some other way. Our will is potentially free, but to free it for effective action we need certain principles of use on which to base our actions.
WILFRED BARLOW M.D. (The Alexander Technique, Healing Arts Press)

Intrigued by the concept of end-gaining, Barlow also decided to measure electrical activity in a person's forearm when actual movement of the fingers was initiated, and then compare the results with when the person only mentally considered moving his fingers. The test data clearly showed that a small fluctuation in the level of muscular electrical activity was evident when the person simply thought about taking action. The body is always chomping at the bit to attempt to 'do' what we're craving or imagining.

Dr. Barlow's book presents a medical doctor's scientific approach to the subject, perhaps emphasizing the physical aspects. A complementary book is *The Expanding Self* by Goddard Binkley (STAT Books, 1993). Binkley is another man who learned from Alexander himself, and he kept a diary of his lessons in the 1950s. It's a profoundly spiritual and philosophical document.

Alexander distrusted the traditional paradigm of mind/body dichotomy or duality, instead substituting the term 'Self' to better convey the inseparable and integrated nature of the mental/physical. These two books approach the subject from opposite ends and meet in the middle. Please make an attempt to obtain and read them; you will learn much if you keep an open mind.

When I returned from my lesson with Alexander I had a good session at the piano. Never have I felt such power and certainty in my playing.
GODDARD BINKLEY

Humans are now faced with infinitely complex tasks that we couldn't possibly have evolved to handle by instinct alone. The great differentiating factor between humans and animals is, believe it or not, our minds. If we can imagine something it's probably doable – if we first use our brains to carefully reason out the proper means.

Our only idea is to go from wrong to right in a moment; in spite of the fact that it has taken us years to get to wrong. ... Everyone wants to be right, but no one stops to consider if their idea of right is right.
F.M. ALEXANDER

Playing the piano is an activity that conscious, imaginative humans literally dreamed up; it requires an exceedingly complex skill-set. In real time, the eyes scan a score and the brain decodes relative pitch and rhythmic duration data in a framework of musical notation while instantaneously directing nerves, tendons, and muscles in the back, arms, wrists, hands, and fingers to execute scales and chords, while the feet are mobilized to gauge and manipulate coloring and sustaining effects through pedaling, with the ears, of course, directing sound waves back to the brain's analytical feedback mechanisms.

That brief description was necessarily minimalist and barely begins to describe the details; I'm sure an anatomy or neurology professor could say it more eloquently. And yet children can do all this quite easily; some prodigies even find a way to tackle the most complex creations of the masters.

A mechanical instrument not found in nature had to be invented to make a piano recital possible. It's actually a pretty simple device. Unlike many instruments where the pitch must be sought out and actually created, note and pitch on the keyboard are identical - you just depress a key (the right key).

There's nothing remarkable about it. All one has to do is hit the right keys at the right time and the instrument plays itself.
J.S. BACH

Perhaps Bach understated the problem and no doubt he smiled when he said that, but he probably was sincere. As a musician, he obviously developed and applied a personal strategy or means-whereby that for him proved to be highly effective.

Control of the muscles by the mind is vital to piano technique. It's the principle that allows imparting of light and shade, and gradations of expression and tempo - the life which changes the sounds of the mechanical instrument into music.
MARK HAMBOURG

But performance requires a continuous stream of varied notes (and rests) in a rhythmic and dynamic context, mentally/physically directed via the brain, head and neck. And we haven't even mentioned musical interpretation, a kind of mental selection and fine tuning of 'the varieties of musical experience' - the accumulated life wisdom of the musician.

The apparent complexity amazes, and yet the whole process can and should be absolutely simple, natural, and effortless, based on correct principles.

In every activity the use of required mechanisms will be satisfactory or unsatisfactory according to whether our direction of that use is satisfactory or otherwise.
F.M. ALEXANDER

Concentrate the whole attention on the movement to be performed, making as it were, a mental map of the entire route from brain to finger tips.
LUDWIG DEPPE

There are three 'tracks' in the human body used in piano playing: from ear to brain, from eye to brain, and from brain to keyboard.
W. MACDONALD SMITH

The impulse of the will travels so quickly to the muscle that the desire to move and the movement appear as one. This may account for the notion that the will appears to reside in the finger itself.
FRIEDRICH A. STEINHAUSEN

Thought is most essential in the study of pieces; for the way by which they are learned, or rather memorized, goes from brain to fingers, and never in the other direction.
MALWINE BRÉE

We know what doesn't work: blind faith in unexamined bad habits and unreasoned trial and error approaches without due consideration of whether or not the methods used are truly effective in a wholistic context. That is why failures outweigh successes and frustration is rampant. Emotional disturbance resulting from 'failure' simultaneously manifests itself in the physical body, which again exacerbates the mis-use, making it all the more likely that the person will fail again with repeated attempts.

(Even if this is sounding too theoretical, please keep reading; we'll get more specific shortly.)

Not to say that trial and error experimentation is necessarily a bad thing, as long as it isn't haphazard, and devoid of the all-important feedback and refinement cycle.

Liszt reduces everything to the fundamentals; explores all variants, executing every conceivable combination of tone and shading. ... logical and open-minded, he works in a disciplined manner one step at a time. His amazingly organized mind, coupled with a detailed knowledge of harmony and habitual frequent sight-reading, allows him to decipher and conquer passages in all keys.
Mme. AUGUSTE BOISSIER

It's necessary to look deeper than so-called piano methods in order to find the underlying principles. Perhaps the most important of all is relaxation.
LEOPOLD GODOWSKY

While performing music, all concentration should begin above the eyes; it should not involve the shoulders because any tension there will make it impossible to relax arms and hands completely.
ARTUR SCHNABEL

When someone says relax, we might imagine a sandy beach, palm trees, and sipping coconut water through a straw while reclining in a bamboo chaise. (Be sure to take Adrian William's *Portrait of Liszt* with you). Relaxation means a composite of a quiescent state (repose) plus the relative degree of natural tension, both physiological and mental, of a healthy organism subtly aware of its environment and always prepared to react.

Without energy input, muscles become tense and rigid, not relaxed; that's the meaning of "rigor mortis." Paradoxically, in order to relax our muscles we must use vital energy. When our vitality is at low ebb, all the muscles of our body tend to approximate to the state of death; resulting in more stiffness, less ease and relaxation. Any gymnastic exertion (piano playing, singing, etc.) we undertake under such unfavorable conditions of mind and body, will be impeded while the muscles remain tense and restrictive.
TOBIAS MATTHAY

Has anyone ever characterized your playing as 'lifeless' or 'death warmed over'? Relaxation in a living organism requires an electric tension. That means we also need our rest to maintain our vitality. Relaxation brings to mind muscles, and energy, but there's an equally important mental component: the letting go of that ubiquitous desire for immediate gratification, or end-gaining.

It's challenging to fully and flawlessly render your personal interpretation of a great master's composition at the piano. Relax and be patient, the process takes time.

One does not become an artist in a day.
LESCHETIZKY

Don't rush headlong into the process trusting that subconscious instincts will get it right, even though mind/body orientation/ function is probably confused and out of sync. Let's back up to the 19th century music scene for a moment. Besides piano exercises and concert music, Czerny also wrote quite a bit about music and playing the piano. His first impressions of the young Liszt bear repeating.

Knowing from long experience that such geniuses, whose spiritual and intellectual attainments outstrip their physical resources, usually neglect to attain a solid technical foundation, I deemed it essential to use the first few months to regulate and strengthen the boy's mechanical dexterity in such a

154

way that it would not deteriorate in later years.
CZERNY

The words *"such geniuses, whose spiritual and intellectual attainments outstrip their physical resources"* recall FM's description of our collective situation. After acquiring consciousness and reason, the accelerated pace and increased demands of 'civilized' life outstrips Man's instinctive ability to effectively deal with previously non-existent environmental stimuli.

In my early years I wasn't patient enough to 'make haste slowly' and thoroughly develop myself in an orderly, logical, and progressive way. I desired immediate results, and took short cuts, so to speak, accomplishing my ambitious goals through sheer willpower. I wish now that I'd progressed by logical steps instead of by leaps.
LISZT

Nature does not proceed by leaps. Natura non facit saltus.
LINNAEUS

The interpretation of virtuoso piano masterpieces is a perfect example of a complex human activity - like one of the most. To succeed, we need an eminently practical and workable strategy, a way to study and practice that virtually guarantees ultimate technical mastery and boundless artistic freedom to express ourselves fully and spontaneously. It's not the end that justifies the means, but exactly the reverse. The means used will always determine the end result.

Some pianists try to conquer everything by force; and imagine that they shall succeed in this by practicing for hours, laboriously indeed, but in an inattentive and thoughtless manner, and by hastily playing over all kinds of difficulties innumerable times. These persons play till their fingers are lamed; but confusedly, too hastily, and without expression, or what's worse, with a false expression.
CZERNY

Assuming you can get yourself onto the piano bench properly and attain a physical (and mental) 'posture' that fully marshals all your physical/mental energy for the task at hand, the first thing to do when learning a new piece of music is … nothing.

Liszt said to Valérie: "Don't play quite so much." That says a lot if you know his method.
Mme. AUGUSTE BOISSIER

Resist the urge to launch into it instinctively, like you've always done. The most basic advice from great pianists on learning music is to slow down. Take your time, tune in to the various requirements of the task; start gradually, one step at a time.

I fear the artist too often likes to feel and enjoy, but loathes the troublesome process of learning to understand the working of his own machinery. Equally important as actually giving our mind to our work is that we apply ourselves in the right way.
TOBIAS MATTHAY

Your fingers are like capering horses, spirited and willing, but ignorant of where to go without a guide. Put on your bridle and reign them in till they learn to obey you, or they will not serve you well.
LESCHETIZKY

'Hold your horses' is a metaphor for mental discipline as old as Plato's charioteer. First, get familiar with the overall structure of your piano piece (or task). What's the key, time signature, and general form? (Most pianists can't answer this question for all the pieces in their repertoire). Read though each hand separately; note harmonies, chords, progressions, and modulations. Interpret the melodic lines vocally; the melody is probably the main thing that caught your interest in the first place. Resist the urge to impulsively jump in and recreate the music for yourself despite dozens of wrong notes, inconsistent tempo, and erratic rhythm. You may instantly gratify your desire for expression, but you'll also be setting the stage for bad habits, making real mastery much more difficult in the future.

'Success' is a controlled continuous, lifelong process of forming and reinforcing good habits on a daily basis. It takes time.

Every pianist advances at a rate commensurate with his ability. Some develop slowly, others with wonderful natural gifts advance very quickly. No matter the rate, the time and effort required to gain mastery is far greater than the ordinary non-professional music lover can imagine.
VLADIMIR de PACHMANN

Speed - the royal road to man's physical and mental derangement.
F.M. ALEXANDER

Say we agree on this sound advice, that we should initially adopt methods of slow, focused practice. Now comes that interesting phenomenon observed by FM: a person reasons out a logical approach and sincerely thinks he's applying it but in fact he's not! Lack of awareness leading to chronic clueless misuse of the self over time results in corrupted sensory and feedback mechanism. Often when piano students are asked to "try it again more slowly and deliberately" they nod, and then promptly repeat the passage at the exact same tempo – a sure sign that awareness is lacking.

The first step is inhibition. This means consciously exercising a choice to not do, thus effectively blocking the habitual misuse. Not doing habitual flawed actions makes possible the substitution of a new way of doing, one that is consciously thought out and applied in a controlled manner. It would be a positive step in the right direction if, when asked to repeat a phrase more slowly, the piano student just sat there pondering…..what is slow? … what does ½ speed sound like … where is my metronome?

Practice non-doing, and everything falls into place.
LAO TZU

Prevent the things you've been doing and you're half-way home. You're doing what's called leaving yourself alone…. Everyone is always teaching us what to do, leaving us still doing the things we shouldn't do.
F.M. ALEXANDER

Often the way we 'deal' with the ups and downs of life doesn't work because the underlying paradigm is ineffective. A paradigm is a philosophical mindset, a way of thinking, a theoretical idea of how a process works. The expression 'dealing with life' is a paradigm of sorts; a reactive, defensive, and non-creative one at that. An alternate paradigm, for example, might be 'I choose to manifest my creative vision'. The planning and execution of these two mindsets will be considerably different and yield different results.

The 'therapy' paradigm is particularly widespread. Focusing on trying to fix or change a perceived problem by ameliorating its symptoms is not the same as investing time and resources in creating a favorable situation in the first place. Therapeutic intervention often involves purchasing products and services. If the root causes are not addressed, the need for therapy becomes chronic and the consumption continues, sometimes without end. Companies selling products love this.

FM cautions that most so-called therapeutic processes by design affect the subconscious level, bypassing your assertion of your own conscious control. Manipulative physical methods, hypnotism, drugs, even repetitive affirmations if they are mindless and self-hypnotic, can't effect success in the sense of restoring a fully conscious state of enlightened analysis and choice.

Exercise and sports, even so-called relaxing ones like golf, if not done properly don't address underlying defective use of the mind/body that has evolved over time. They can actually exacerbate the situation, even things like yoga and breathing 'exercises'. A faulty kinesthetic system (unreliable feedback from the senses) cannot be remedied by physical exercise alone.

Another common paradigm is 'prevention', but again, the focus is still on the 'negative' and how to prevent it. Prevention, of course, implies the existence of a satisfactory state to be preserved from degradation. But FM says few individuals are free from manifestations of deficient use and functioning. We must first regain a pristine state through a process of reeducation before we can maintain it, or prevent relapse.

Whether the goal is health, artistic/business success or fulfilling relationships, the most powerful of life's paradigms is 'creation' – the visualization of a desired state, followed by wholistic planning, strategy, tactics, and persistent action to make it manifest.

Our biggest challenge in life may be to relinquish defeatist paradigms and open ourselves up to new possibilities.

It's not the degree of 'willing' or 'trying', but the manner in which the energy is directed, that's going to be effective.... Trying is only emphasizing the

thing we already know. … If people will go on believing that they 'know', it's impossible to teach them anything.
F.M. ALEXANDER.

It is not enough to be thoroughly anxious to help our pupil; our hard trying will end in sore disappointment unless we know what help to give and how to give it.
TOBIAS MATTHAY

When you think, and say, '*I can't*' it becomes a self-fulfilling prophecy. If the body is not optimally aligned (and used) then neither is the mind; it can't adopt a confident attitude. This leads to a certain reticence, and the adoption of risk-aversion strategies rooted in fear and lack of self-confidence.

A person comes to me with a crippling defect due to the improper use of some organ or set of muscles. After analysis, when I show that person how to use that organ or muscles in the proper way, I'm often met with the reply "But I can't". … The negative reply confirms that the control of the part affected is entirely subconscious – if it weren't we could substitute the hopeful "I can" for that despondent "I can't".
F.M. ALEXANDER

New experiences, with their potential for learning and innovation are avoided; personal growth and enhanced awareness are restricted. The corrupt usage continually undermines your confidence, and fetters your imaginative vision of what's possible in life. Body/mind is a unity, not two distinct entities. Unsound body, unsound mind.

Mens sana in corpore sano. A sound mind in a sound body.

How many millions of people have wanted to play the piano, have tried and gone about it in all the wrong ways unaware of what their minds and bodies are actually doing, and have all too quickly given up saying I can't, it's too hard, it's impossible? Certainly not Bach and Busoni - look at what they accomplished with their faith in possibilities, their mindset and method.

Often, despite all our trying, a successful solution can't and won't present itself until a paradigm shift empowers an enlightened perspective, one that is grounded in a natural, optimal human body/ mind function, and mentally says 'I can'. When a gifted AT teacher assists you to attain that natural harmony and balance, you'll be astonished by the instantaneous rush of confidence and optimism. Mental states can be altered by rehabilitating or re-educating the physical.

Theories are … exactly that: theories. None can ever be completely certain since future experimentation may shed further, possibly conflicting light. Newton's Law of Universal Gravitation has been partially superseded by Einstein's Theory of Relativity, but that doesn't mean that Newton's ideas aren't still extremely useful in practice; they are, in a relativistic framework. Isn't everything relative to something? Isn't that the elegance of Einstein's work?

You're on the right track when your hypothesis is empirically demonstrable. FM repeatedly demonstrated his work with interested scientists and medical doctors in attendance. And he maintained that his research was a process, an evolving life's work, always remaining open to significant fresh data and new insights.

I do not profess to offer a final perfected theory…we are only at the beginnings of understanding, and I wish to keep my theory simple and avoid dogma. … I should not be true to my principles if I weren't willing to accept amendments should new facts so indicate.
F.M. ALEXANDER

Here are a few more thoughts for consideration.

First, say to yourself what you would be, and then do what you have to do.
EPICTETUS

You can have neither a greater nor lesser dominion than that over yourself.
LEONARDO DA VINCI

Habit is overcome by habit.
THOMAS à KEMPIS The Imitation of Christ

We cannot solve our problems with the same thinking we used when we created them.
ALBERT EINSTEIN

Alexander stumbled on to something major, then set out to devise a rigorous methodology to establish conscious control of behavior over the instinctive plane. He realized we can't directly apply a quick fix to a rigid, habitual situation. We must methodically work though a set of new and indirect procedures that will achieve the desired result.

For example: if for optimal function the spine needed to be in a lengthened state with the head freely balanced forward and upwards, initial conscious direction had to focus on achieving exactly that; and not prematurely jump forward to 'achieving' some larger desired goal, like 'whip off this complete étude at presto tempo *now*!"

FM's experience taught him that first he had to get his whole body into that stress-less natural state, a tricky undertaking since at first it felt 'wrong'. Then, to achieve his ultimate action goal he had to successively execute a number of steps in sequence while maintaining that original pristine configuration throughout - which required immense focus. At first, he would lose his composure as soon as he proceeded to the second step. But then he devised a way to mentally give orders in sequence, and ultimately execute them all together in a fluid integrated process. In initial attempts to train at it, the 'direction' was cumulative: 1, 1+2, 1+2+3, 1+2+3+4 etc. At the same time, bad habits had to be inhibited.

Like a type of mental yoga, the process rejuvenates the mind and the subsequent clarity of focus empowers startling results. (I know that was redundant; yoga *is* mental). You will find yourself much more conscious of your surroundings. Think of what that focus will enable you to do in learning to play the piano, or any other complex task.

Human activity is primarily a process of reacting unceasingly through the sensory mechanisms, to stimuli from within and without the self... One must substitute conscious for instinctive direction to change use
F.M. ALEXANDER

FM's work is about living in harmony with nature, through awareness, individual choice, and reasoning - meaning self-empowerment in the fullest sense. Therapies, whether psychoanalytic, medical, nutritional, recreational, massage (even those lovable therapy dogs) may provide some benefit in the short term. But if root causes are not addressed, it simply means inevitable dependency on externals. Individual freedom and self-reliance through natural health creation and maintenance is the real goal.

The AT is deep stuff. It's not simply repetitive exercise, as in 'three sets of ten reps'. It's not about trying and practicing but about analysis, heightened awareness of how you use yourself, and enlightened choice to change for the better, through consciously controlled action,

Everybody wants to change the world, but nobody wants to change themselves.
TOLSTOY

In any task, cycles of repetitive practice must governed by consciousness and control. Good habits are formed over time and the grand result is superior performance with less wasted effort.

The thousand mile journey does indeed begin with a single step – but that first step, and each and every one that follows, must be characterized by wholistic effective use of the self. It begins with recognizing and inhibiting previously established bad habits, then re-education via a new, more effective, natural paradigm so that we may effortlessly express what we imagine, (like 'in this lifetime') without wasting precious time floundering about in developmental dead-ends.

We can throw away the habit of a lifetime in a few minutes if we use our brains.
F.M. ALEXANDER

Change your use = change your habits.

Business leaders who don't stop, think, create, and efficiently execute a reasonable business plan usually fail; and that's at least half of all new ones within the first five years. But that 'plan' doesn't do anything by itself except collect dust or occupy storage bytes.

The best laid plans of mice and men often go astray.
ROBERT BURNS

You must proactively plan *and implement* your plan. When engineering projects go awry, the fault lies in either of two key places: the requirements phase, where the desired end result must be clearly articulated; and the actual design or means of satisfying the requirements which must be implemented through conscientious analysis and work.

If you aren't able to "hit a right note" while playing, remember the trouble is not in your hands and arms but in your head, your mental poise. The nerves control the muscles of fingers, hands, and arms. But the nucleus of all these nerves is situated in the cortex, in the head, whence are issued the orders that set these nerves in motion. Quiet your mental self, gain command over it, and watch the immediate change in the greater quiet and certainty of your motions.
ALBERTO JONÁS

FM rediscovered the essence of natural integration of body and mind (the self) guided by conscious thought. When the body is whole, so is the mind, and therein lies peak potential. FM said that anybody could figure out how to readjust themselves, if they had the discipline. For most of us the training will initially be a deeply collaborative effort with an experienced teacher.

Inappropriate (wrong) self-use of the organism has far-reaching physical and psychological ramifications, from basic individual issues of mental and physical health, happiness, and efficiency, to global issues born of poor choices, like environmental degradation, inefficient and inequitable use of natural resources, crime, violence and warfare.

I cannot insist too strongly – the conscious mind must be quickened.
F.M. ALEXANDER

Reading the works of F.M. Alexander and creating a one chapter summary has been by far the most challenging aspect of writing this book. I hope my presentation has been thought-provoking and that you're motivated to further research this important subject. If you're reading about it for the first time, without direct experience, it's normal to perhaps be a bit skeptical. But many very intelligent people and some pretty prestigious organizations are absolutely convinced. If you're thinking it's just for long-hairs, high-brows and egg-heads let me mention once more … supersonic jet pilots with the right stuff.

Be docile and divest yourself of any prejudices you may have; it's absolutely necessary to successfully play my compositions.
FRANÇOIS COUPERIN

Teaching does not consist in merely pointing out the existence of faults but in making clear the cause of each fault and the direct means of its correction. People must be taught to attend, to analyze, to notice on their own account - to observe, tone and duration, and time; how they should be, and also, how they really appear. Once you get a pupil to attend mentally and physically his playing becomes infinitely more musical. Much that at first seemed hopelessly wrong, at once becomes better, and often to a quite surprising extent. A pupil who perhaps seemed 'hopelessly unmusical' gradually seems to become endowed with quite musical instincts!
TOBIAS MATTHAY

The work of F. M Alexander is deeply connected with what is perhaps the most important thing in life ...

Chapter 6

······

HEALTH

May God give you good humor, health, and strength; those are such necessary things.

— CHOPIN

Awholistic perspective by definition takes everything into consideration. But if you had to pick just one critical factor, optimal physical and mental health is the single most important requisite to any great undertaking, and small ones too.

Once you've determined to become a concert performer, let nothing stand in the way of study except the consideration of your health. Success with a broken-down body and a shattered mind is a worthless conquest.
FANNY BLOOMFIELD-ZEISLER

Without vibrant health you can't succeed in a big way and even if you do it's not worth it. Put health at the top of your list.

But if this had been Chapter One you might have thought this was just another diet and fitness book. It's not, but health is so fundamental to life that it virtually defines the quality of it. It's almost synonymous with happiness and productivity - many of the pianists absolutely agree.

Few people realize what a vital factor health is to the concert pianist. I have a certain diet and a certain amount of exercise and sleep, without which I

cannot play successfully.
EMIL SAUER

It cannot be too much insisted on, that no matter how talented, it will be impossible for a professional pianist to attain the highest eminence unless he enjoys at the same time excellent general health and strength.
W. MACDONALD SMITH

But what does health or 'healthy' really mean these days? We talk about vitamins or certain vegetables being healthy - broccoli, for example. Okay, but that's a fragmented way of thinking about it. Health has recently been defined by the World Health Organization as the condition of being sound in body, mind, and spirit; not simply freedom from physical disease or pain.

The energy, strength, and mental well-being that health provides are precious assets that enable us to live, work, and realize our dreams. Much failure is not due just to lack of smarts or work ethic but also underlying poor health.

There's no doubt that the unaccountable failure of some people with really great talent has been due to their neglect of health and their consequent inability through sheer physical weakness to face the tests put upon them.
MARK HAMBOURG

If you lose your health, for whatever reason, it won't matter who you are or how skilled you are at anything.

Owing to my unfortunate illness I am unable to work or earn anything.
MOZART

If I could give as definite expression to my thoughts about my illness as to my thoughts in music, I would soon help myself.
BEETHOVEN

I was at the point of death and during the whole summer dangerously ill. … My health since then has become very fragile and I cannot yet get rid of a teasing cough.
CARL MARIA von WEBER

For nearly a week I was confined to bed with a very severe fever, which might easily have become more serious still. My second concert was obliged to be put off on account of it. Today my doctor has given me permission to play on Wednesday. I don't really know whether I shall be able to do it, for my hand trembles fearfully.
LISZT

There are dozens of such instances in letters of the great composers. Today most artists with any degree of humility don't see themselves even coming close to equaling the accomplishments of history's artistic superstars. I feel the same way about that but it's somewhat beside the point. Our job is to become the best that we possibly can as individuals and thus make our own unique contribution in life.

Personal health is actually one area in which we can potentially surpass history's great artists. Timeless wisdom (and some real scientific knowledge) of what truly constitutes vibrant natural health has greater dissemination and exposure today than it did in the past. Sadly, for many of those great composers it wasn't always a given, and for lack of accurate information and/or motivation many of them suffered terribly. Unfortunately, the sickly composer dying young is a valid stereotype.

Everyone can potentially excel at health because it's quite simply our birthright as a species. It's the normal state of affairs in nature only we humans have gotten off track, like way off. We've literally lost it, and the new 'normal' is becoming pathetic. It's not that we must get healthy, we must regain health. Medicine and so-called 'health care' are not health but 'fixes' we inevitably resort to when we lose our health.

Helping people deal with the symptoms of disease can be an amazingly complex proposition requiring many years of study in anatomy, physiology, biochemistry, pharmacology, immunology, surgery ... and lots more. Medical school attracts and challenges some of our most brilliant minds. On the other hand, you could explain the basic fundamentals of health to anyone in a day, if not an hour or so.

Knowing how to regain (and retain) health requires a relatively small up-front investment in learning, but here's the catch-88: conscientiously applying the fundamentals requires that you exert yourself, with great vigilance and discipline, every single day of your life - especially at mealtimes.

A wholistic view of health must address a number of important factors. Jotted down by a pianist in the 19th century, the following list holds true today, as it will forever.

We live in an age where there's a colossal appeal for more efficiency. Standards of musicianship constantly ascend. Here are a few essentials: Good healthy simple food, cooked without unnecessary strong spices, eaten at leisure amid congenial surroundings, not swallowed down in haste with the mind worried, for the right mental condition during meals is important. Exercise, and deep breathing, in the open air, not occasionally, but every day. Plenty of physical and mental work done with joy, and sensible regulation of the day's work; and see that intervals of repose come between your intervals of energy.
Good moral habits - immorality of any sort eventually undermines the strongest nervous system, and is the surest, quickest, deadliest enemy of good nerves. Consider: is this a wise or foolish thing you're attempting at any point? Method and calm deliberation as to the distribution of your work and executing daily tasks. When confronted with a number of things to do, don't fret, but dispose of them one at a time, calmly and with care. Maintain consistent early hours of retirement as far as possible.
ALBERTO JONÁS

A search for 'health and fitness' books on *Amazon.com* often results in over 100,000 listings, depending on the day of the week, it seems. That's a lot of books, far more than a person could read in a lifetime. Since there are often duplicates in large databases let's really reduce the number, like by 90%. Still, that would be 10,000 unique books. Authors aren't writing them solely for charity; the economics of the situation are fairly transparent. The huge supply at robust prices indicates an equally huge demand for health information. And that means that way too many of us suffer from poor health and are searching for answers.

When feeling fine we tend to take health for granted but anyone who gets seriously ill knows that nothing in life is of value without it. Even that old 'common cold' feeling is a real drag. And if we're immobile in a hospital bed, suffering excruciating pain or tragically facing impending premature death, we suddenly don't care anymore about all the activities we once cherished or the material things we own or once desired. We just want to feel better and regain our health.

When one is no longer master of one's own freedom of movement, life has no further value, no matter whether it's the result of sickness, old age, imprisonment or the glorious distractions of the current times.
FERUCCIO BUSONI

Why has regaining health become so challenging? A couple of things come to mind: information and motivation. Let's start with the information.

You'd think that learning about something as natural as health would be simple and straightforward but there's a veritable deluge of information out there and it's often complicated, contradictory, and confusing. It's not that we're obtuse, most of the information is abstruse.

Besides all the books in print, lots of often deceptive and propagandistic 'health' advertising and so-called 'news' inundates our media. Subtle and not-so-subtle product placement abounds in film and television. There's nothing wrong with advertising and selling a good product but it's becoming painfully clear that some of these products aren't actually 'good' for us, and might eventually cause us some real pain, both in body and wallet. If you literally buy-into the label of 'consumer', better adopt that motto *caveat emptor* – buyer beware. It's up to us to shift gears into self-reliance mode.

It's time to educate ourselves instead of taking dictation from special interests. A nation expects every citizen to know and understand the laws of the land; quite a remarkable responsibility given the sheer volume of statutes and regulations. The nation doesn't expect us to know a thing about health, except that now we must know all about the new laws increasing mandatory medical practices and insurance obligations or we'll end up paying stiff fines or even going to jail.

It would be difficult for any one individual to master all the intricacies of medicine (or insurance). I wonder if a single senator or congressperson actually read that so-called 'Affordable Care Act' legislation. We the people must educate ourselves on the basics of health. Establishing a truly healthy lifestyle goes a long way towards preventing future problems and is a lot less expensive in the long run.

When it comes to health it's healthy to cultivate flexible open-minded thinking that also includes a large dose of that plain old-fashioned common sense. The discussion should be grounded in the scientific method, and I'm not talking about the current plague of academic resume-padding 'studies', or 'research' funded by corporations with (in)vested interests in the results.

A healthy lifestyle is characterized by a combination of proper nutrition, exercise, rest, mental poise, and purpose reflected in meaningful work. Let's take them one at a time.

Get the best book you can on diet and eating, the right selection of foods, etc., and then use all of your willpower to create habits of correct eating. This may show in your playing and study. Who knows, it may be just what you need most to get rid of nervousness.
ALBERTO JONÁS

Will power is needed not only for the purpose of concentrating the attention on one thing at a time, but for refusing tempting offers at a time when it would be suicidal to accept them.
HENRY THEOPHILUS FINCK

Allow me to repeat, for emphasis: get the best book you can find, then…

Use all of your willpower to create habits of correct eating

USE ALL OF YOUR WILLPOWER
TO CREATE HABITS OF
CORRECT EATING

A well governed appetite is the greater part of liberty.
SENECA

Once upon a time eating food was about nutrition. Now it has become synonymous with entertainment and self-therapy. I was just reading the book *Mere Christianity* by C.S. Lewis and came across an interesting remark:

You can get a large audience together to watch a woman undress on stage, but you can't fill a theater by simply displaying a covered plate on that stage and slowly lifting the cover to let people see if it contained a lamb chop or a bit of bacon.
C.S. LEWIS

Ah, Mr. Lewis; times have changed, and relatively quickly too. Today we have 'food-porn' in countless magazines and television shows, a clear indication of skewed or screwed-up thought paradigms. What your body needs for health is not food but nutrition.

Truth be told, our poor eating habits have been a problem for a long time. For centuries, gluttony (*gastimargia* or 'gut-madness' in Greek, *gula* in Latin) has been considered one of the seven deadly sins.

The Viennese repasts are famous all over Europe, and the one ordered for us was so luxurious that Beethoven could not help making remarks on the profusion which it displayed. "Why such a variety of dishes?" he exclaimed, "Man is but little above other animals if his chief pleasure is confined to the dinner table."
EDWARD SCHULTZ

The eminent 19th century pianist Alberto Jonás recognized that what we choose to eat and drink and thus put in our bodies is paramount. It's simple common sense to maximize our intake of fresh, natural and nutritious foods and minimize or eliminate unnatural toxic processed 'stuff' and chemical stimulants that undermine health.

Tell me what you eat and I'll tell you what you are.
J.A. BRILLAT-SAVARIN (1755-1826)

The Physiology of Taste or Meditations on Transcendental Gastronomy by Jeane Anthelme Brillat-Savarin is a fascinating food classic from the early 19th century. With its emphasis on quality fresh food it's helpful, but perhaps isn't the right one for focusing on total health.

Find the best book you can ... hmmm ... tens of thousands out there.

Look for a book that is not only well written and entertaining but is also based in science and that good ole' common sense. My opinion? I liked *Fit for Life* by Harvey and Marilyn Diamond (1985 Warner Books). It's very straightforward and readable. The authors advocate a diet rich in whole, natural foods like fruits, nuts, vegetables; the more raw the better. (Remember: ketchup is not a vegetable).

The authors also suggested minimizing processed foods and avoiding some completely, like refined white sugar. The book is almost forty years old now and these simple observations are not exactly earth-shattering anymore, at least not to reasonably intelligent people.

If implemented conscientiously, such an approach will get positive results. Apparently plenty of people saw value in the book because it was a New York Times Bestseller with millions of copies sold worldwide. Hard to believe that after decades the book is still attacked by some in the establishment who characterize it as a 'fad diet' even though the title of the first chapter is *'Diets Don't Work'*. Did they even read the book? Fruit and salads - really? Come on guys, the authors even included a recipe for grilled chicken.

For a concert pianist on tour the most important thing is sound sleep and a good digestion.
ALFRED CORTOT

Where else to get recommendations and ideas? Seek out genuinely healthy and fit people and ask them what they did, and do; consider their logic when deciding what to do for yourself. When you find something that works to create improved health – act on it. For cutting edge comprehensive health and science information, sign up for Dr. Mercola's free email newsletter at www.mercola.com - *"the world's #1 one natural health website"* by the numbers.

Going organic is a great way to avoid harmful pesticides. If you can't think or act without a 'study', there are dozens of them providing evidence that most industrial crop pesticides are highly toxic when they find their way into your bloodstream, so don't eat pesticide sprayed food items. A monster of a company is genetically engineering crops to withstand increased pesticide spraying. Did I miss the logic in some executive's brainchild?

But just because something is labeled 'organic' doesn't mean it's healthy; I mean you can buy organic white refined cane sugar, something best avoided, kind of like the plague. Another book recommendation: *Sugar Blues* by William Dufty (1975 Grand Central Life & Style).

We don't need a study to tell us there's a direct correlation between levels of health, energy and achievement. Common sense dictates that processed foods, devoid of any life energy, are probably not as healthy as natural whole foods like fruits and vegetables.

INTERMEZZO

News Flash!

Some half-century ago the refined-sugar industry apparently was aware that its product was unhealthy for humans and was connected to tooth decay and obesity, among other things. The CEOs, Boards, and share-holders didn't really see any advantage in publicizing that fact back then. I used to go to a dentist who told me that diet was irrelevant and that I just needed to brush and floss a lot. The receptionist kept a bowl of hard candy on the counter, I guess to make you feel better after that filling or root canal - plus I got a 'free' toothbrush after paying my hefty bill.

Weston Price D.D.S. (b. 1870) traveled the world studying the dental health of indigenous populations. Those that still dined on whole, natural local foodstuffs had beautiful cavity-free teeth; most had never even heard of a toothbrush. As the company store and refined 'civilized' diets (processed) took over, things turned rotten; especially people's teeth. A fascinating book is Price's *Nutrition and Physical Degeneration* (1939). One of the original founders of the research arm of the American Dental Association, he was metaphorically drawn and quartered by his colleagues for hinting at how we might get by with fewer dentists.

A similar case is that of William Bates M.D. (b 1860). An ophthalmologist by training, Bates theorized that stressful lifestyle was adversely affecting eyesight. He developed natural methods for dealing with the problem; large scale adoption and implementation might result in better vision and general health – and less eye doctors. His metaphorical fate: burning at the stake. Additional fascinating reading is Bates' *Perfect Sight Without Glasses* (1920). As with F.M. Alexander, Aldous Huxley saw value in Bates' work and wrote about it in T*he Art of Seeing* (1942).

Within a couple of months I was reading without spectacles and, what was better still, without strain and fatigue.
ALDOUS HUXLEY

Incidentally airplane pilots were among the first to use the Bates method to improve their vision. It seems like when you have a kick-ass job that puts your life on the line daily, you go with results.

And pianists - the Bates 'long-swing' works relaxation wonders prior to going out on stage to perform.

Processed food is a billion dollar industry, snack foods alone account for much of the total. The obesity epidemic is so well documented that the American Medical Association recently labelled it a disease. I guess that now means you'll be able to get health insurance to protect yourself from it. Tip: forgo that insurance and try eating better and more moderately.

The European Union just designated obesity a bona-fide disability. Of course truly disabled individuals should be helped, but this perspective doesn't encourage health and healthy living.

Here's an interesting twist on corporate diversification: some processed food companies are expanding (no pun) into … the weight loss and 'fitness' industries. At this writing, Jenny Craig is owned by Nestlé, the largest food company in the world based on revenues. Mostly associated with chocolate, they make lots of other processed food products including breakfast cereals, ice cream, and plenty of those 'snacks'. Even doctors know that devouring boatloads of processed foods may be (is?) linked to obesity; if that's the case, the more a company sells, the more weight-loss customers they'll potentially have … a sweet (pun intended) synergistic supply and demand relationship. Weight Watchers has been around for half a century now, a good indication that its services are much in demand. According to their website the new President and CEO's brilliant resume lists high-level executive experience … at Kraft, Cadbury, and Nabisco.

No children can be brought up to healthy manhood on sweetmeats and pastry.
ROBERT SCHUMANN

Mastering the art of playing the piano will place immense demands on mental and physical energies. You won't become great at anything if you're weak and sick all the time.

To be successful you must endure the strain of long hours in travel, night after night appearing in big important engagements, with all the responsibility they entail; much nervous excitement, and great bodily fatigue. In spite of that, on arrival you must always be ready to play with energy, spirit and unflagging interest, otherwise you'll not inspire or convince your audience. Your nerves must be well under control and healthy, or you'll never survive the tension of public life. Health and strength are absolutely indispensable to the modern professional pianist. Build up strength by constant exercise and fresh air. The audience does not excuse one because of ill health or because one looks tired; nothing short of perfection satisfies.
MARK HAMBOURG

One should eat lightly before a performance. The body uses a lot of energy to digest food; that's why you often get sleepy after a big meal.

I make it a practice not to eat for a few hours before the concert … my mind will be in better shape.
PEPITO ARRIOLA

We cannot employ the mind to advantage when we are filled with excessive food and drink.
CICERO

The opera singer Enrico Caruso habitually did not eat for six hours prior to a performance. Note: the Kama Sutra recommends sex on an empty stomach. All that bodily energy directed towards digestion will detract from more pressing concerns.

Most doctors, of course, agree that nutritious diet and moderate exercise are beneficial for health. But those very coy and supremely expensive Super Bowl drug company advertisements are fond of reciting themes like "when diet and exercise aren't enough... take drugs". A diet and exercise approach really can go a long ways towards getting and keeping you healthy - if you give it a chance by actually doing it.

Besides eating, we must drink. Plain old H_2O is more than sufficient for survival providing it's really plain, or pure.

Beethoven's favorite beverage was fresh spring water which, in summer, he drank in well-nigh inordinate quantities.
ANTON SCHINDLER

Unfortunately, Beethoven's usual fare included plenty of coffee and mac' n' cheese.

Among Beethoven's favorite dishes was macaroni and Parmesan cheese. ... Coffee seems to have been the nourishment with which he could least dispense.
ANTON SCHINDLER

After water, every other liquid you put into your body is primarily entertainment, and there's usually a distinct pleasure versus payback ratio.

Learning and performing musical masterpieces demands prodigious memory. Liquid substances that negatively affect this function should be minimized or avoided all together. I was taught that the kind of alcohol we drink is tough on brain cells (ethanol, C_2H_5OH). To memorize music pianists need their brain cells to be fully functioning or at minimum just be there. Ethanol denatures proteins and dissolves lipids - things your brain requires to work well. In excess, cirrhosis of the over-taxed liver and mental illness may result over time.

Recovery from my illness is not complete. For about a year now, when I get up in the morning I suffer from nausea, but not the rest of the day. I know the cause is bad diet, too many strong cigars, and too much brandy, but not

as much as people say.
LISZT

Almost half of all automobile crash fatalities are alcohol-related and the risk of a fatal car accident increases exponentially with the level of alcohol in the driver's blood. Please don't drink and drive. And do yourself another favor: don't drink and play the piano at the same time either; it won't be pretty.

People have said to me after some particularly brilliant number "Ah, you must have taken a bottle of champagne to play like that." Nothing could be further from the truth. A half a bottle of beer would ruin a recital for me. The habit of taking alcohol with the idea that it promotes a fiery performance is a dangerous custom that has been the ruin of more than one pianist. The performer who would be at his best must live a very careful, almost abstemious life. Any unnatural excess is sure to mar his playing and lead to his downfall with the public. I've seen alcohol tear down in a few years what has taken decades of hard practice and earnest study to build up.
EMIL SAUER

Before the concert I drank half a bottle of red wine. This caused me to wake up in the middle of the opening number, the Bach Fugue in E minor. ... the next day the Munich critics said that I played that first number with astonishing coldness and lack of feeling but that the rest of the program was okay.
GEORGE ANTHEIL

The music was worthy of the occasion, but the endless toasts spoiled everything. We drank to the memory of the immortal Haydn, and toasted all musical celebrities, living and dead, absent and present; the consequence was that some of the executants' fingers were rather heavy when it came to the second part of the music.
IGNAZ MOSCHELES

The evidence is uncompromisingly against the abuse of alcohol or any drug destined to affect the nerves. An exception might in some cases be made for an occasional high-quality glass of beer or wine, partaken of in moderation. Abstain from strong stimulants.
ALBERTO JONÁS

At the highest level, mechanical technique thrives on economy of means. During all those practice hours, pianists are (or should be) primarily exercising their mental powers. Moving the fingers, wrists, and arms around while sitting on your butt doesn't burn up a lot of calories, even in up-tempo études. Plus, it's just not a good thing to sit in an office chair or on a piano bench for long periods of time.

Go out regularly and get some genuine exercise. Not only are sports healthy and fun, they help build coordination and an all-around confidence that will support your piano playing.

He worked through ninety-six Cramer études one after another without complaint. It rather knocked him out. But then his father bought him a riding horse and now he rides for an hour every day, and refreshes himself in the open air. It has restored his strength and now he barely breaks a sweat at both Clementi and Cramer.
FRIEDRICH WIECK

Learn to swim, fence, ride – do things, become accomplished until you gain confidence. That is one way of overcoming nervousness.
LESCHETIZKY

Everything is possible if one has developed the nervous power of one's own body. I've found rowing at the sea-side and the handling of a heavy boat in getting it into and out of the water excellent for developing the muscles. The same may be said of almost any hard work requiring half an hour.
JOSEF HOFMANN

Rowing a boat is good to develop wrists for octave playing.
WILHELM BACHAUS

Mr. Joseffy believes in the use of light dumb-bells to prepare and strengthen the wrist for octaves.
Mrs. HENRY THEOPHILUS FINCK

I asked the concierge where was Joseffy ..."Oh, that one's right close; he has his billiards match at the café".
MORIZ ROSENTHAL

Rhythmic pulse is best explained by recalling one's stride in walking or

running - one had to learn to feel pulse before he could encompass either of those accomplishments! Just as we imagine the swing of walking or running; we establish a gait for every piece we play. How vivid do the Beethoven themes become if we hum them in our rambles through the woods - conceived as so many of them doubtless were under a similar impression of fresh air and the accompaniment of a healthy walking stride.
TOBIAS MATTHAY

Beethoven is a famous pedestrian and delights in walks of many hours, particularly through wild and romantic scenery. Nay, I was told that he sometimes passes whole nights on such excursions and is frequently missed at home for several days.
EDWARD SCHULZ

I spend all my mornings with the muses; and they bless me also in my walks.
BEETHOVEN

Oscar Raif is an enthusiastic member and officer of the Swiss Alpine Club. He vacations in Switzerland, making frequent tours often alone without even a guide into the regions of eternal snow, with which he is as familiar as the streets of a city.
JAMES HUNEKER

Henselt still follows his course of physical exercises every evening, forcing, in spite of sweat and fatigue, his hands and feet to perform all sorts of complicated evolutions on the horizontal bar. He once got a notion that Swedish gymnastics was beneficial.
WILHELM von LENZ

I've always been fond of swimming and I spent many hours during the summer at my favorite sport. One time I swam from Bensonhurst to Coney Island and back in a matter of three hours.
ARTHUR FRIEDHEIM

If the arms are weak, they can be strengthened by proper physical exercises ... to develop muscles and render them firm and vigorous. The pianist can invent special ones of his own. Care should of course be taken not to overdo it.
HARRIETTE BROWER

Positive Piano

I like best to work in the country. Often in the summer, when tired of practicing, I go out in the fields and labor for an hour or two – with bare hands. I wish I could have such opportunity for manual labor when on a concert tour. Its effect upon nerves and muscles is more restorative than anything else.
PADEREWSKI

The pianist must learn to work mentally. But if he wishes to avoid fatigue, he cannot dispense with bodily exercise in the form of all kinds of sport. Where the limit is, just what may be pursued without danger to his fine manual technique, each individual must find out for himself. No general rule may be stated.
FRIEDRICH A. STEINHAUSEN

Rock climbing is just too tough on my fingers and wrists.

Here's a mental benefit derived from the challenge of sports. After deciding to attempt a 100-mile (Century) bike ride, I trained for several months, averaging three 25-30 mile rides a week. I visualized myself cycling the whole 100 miles while there was still daylight. On the big day it took me over eight hours, but I did it. Apart from the satisfaction of attaining a very fun personal athletic goal (with the only downside being a temporarily sore butt) I very shortly marveled at one amazing development.

The next week, the large scale piano solos I was working on seemed less daunting. Before, with the Beethoven Sonatas and the Liszt Opera fantasies, it was plenty to work on just one movement or section at a time. Now I played through complete sonatas easily, not once but multiple times in a row. The Liszt pieces that previously seemed so long and complicated now seemed more compact, and I rehearsed not just one but five different ones sequentially in one sitting. The cycling milestone had somehow upped the mental scope of my beliefs, rippling through to any task I now attempted.

One 19th century concert pianist and composer was into bodybuilding. At his peak, music critics favorably compared Martinus Sieveking to Paderewski, Rosenthal and Joseffy. Google the images of this guy on the Internet and you'll see that he was definitely ripped.

Sieveking spent time in Leschetizky's class in Vienna, and was considered one of the favorites. Mark Hambourg described his physique as "more of a house than a man." His large hands could span the interval of a 12th. He once sketched out his reach on music manuscript paper; it ranged from middle C on the treble clef to high G. I'm speculating, but I bet you anything he handed it to his date.

Size may or may not matter for some things in life; in piano playing you're alright if you can grab an octave. In fact an unusually long span can actually be a problem for pianists; large hands are not a prerequisite for great performance. Attitude and attentiveness will carry the day, same as that other very popular human activity!

The flip side of exercise and practice is rest and sleep. The body must constantly recuperate, repair, and recharge. This is always good for your Art too.

That old notion of a composer suddenly having a terrific idea and sitting up all night to write it out is nonsense. Nighttime is for sleeping.
BENJAMIN BRITTEN

It is quite certain that at no time did Beethoven employ the evening hours for composition. At ten o'clock at the latest he went to bed.
ANTON SCHINDLER

If progress is not rapid at the beginning, don't fancy that you can improve matters by sitting at the piano from morning till evening; that's harmful to health, and besides, it is impossible to pay close and careful attention for so long.
MALWINE BRÉE

Every effort requires nervous expenditure. It then becomes necessary for new nerve force to form. Just as a storage battery which has been used up needs to be charged again, the nerves must be recharged with force for future endeavors.
ALBERTO JONÁS

We spent the summer on Squirrel Island, coast of Maine, one of the best places I know of in which to rest and have a good time, the kind of a "good time" which makes one feel, after it is over, like going earnestly to work again at the piano.
EDWARD M. BOWMAN

Too many of us are tired, run down, and sleep-deprived. This adversely affects physical health, mental concentration and confidence. The 19th century by day was lit by sunlight and after perhaps an hour or two of candles and firelight in the evening it went pitch black, and people slept. Things still followed a fairly natural rhythm in that respect.

Our dependence on artificial light has drastically changed all that. Working a full night shift, or even just late hours in an environment of artificial lighting and electronics can result in reduced reaction time and confusion. Learning ability and memory degenerate with sleep deprivation; you may even become more accident prone. Those études and fugues are going to seem even more complicated. Get your rest. Sweet dreams.

Now I see the secret of making the best person: it is to grow in the open air and to eat and sleep with the earth.
WALT WHITMAN

There's really nothing magical about fresh air, we simply must breathe to live. You can go without food for weeks and without water for a few days, but you'll last a couple of minutes at most without air. Outside is where we human beings lived exclusively for tens of thousands of years and that's the environment in which we thrive. Inside, on the other hand, tends to be fairly toxic these days and can adversely affect health.

Take the building materials themselves: the lumber may have been 'treated' (think arsenic), the sheetrock may contain similar nasty chemicals, the roofing material, the insulation, paints, varnishes – all that stuff can be unhealthy. This may be one area where they had an advantage back in the 19th century. A hundred and fifty years ago a lot of these chemical substances didn't exist yet; homes and public buildings were probably less toxic.

Inside, synthetic fabrics (or natural ones treated with 'flame proofing' chemicals), plastics, aerosols, and detergents can all result in off-gassing of noxious elements into the air you breathe. Cooking with gas or propane and wood burning fireplaces can also degrade air quality.

Closer to your body, even some cosmetics and shampoos (actually plenty of them) can be toxic. While you're thinking about what you put in your body also consider what you put on it, especially those hands of yours. Go for the skin care products with organic and natural ingredients. I like the British company Neal's Yard Remedies and also Weleda out of Germany.

Other stuff to be aware of and try to avoid or minimize: air-borne dust particles from laser printer toner, and electromagnetic pollution from computers, televisions and other gadgets. Even the electrical currents swirling around in the wiring of every wall of your house may have subtle negative influences on your health.

Those were man-made issues. Mother Nature is finally getting so pissed off at our atonal unharmonious ways that many of our buildings are now riddled with toxic mold. This can make you really sick, and may result in severe neurological symptoms. You may not even know where it's all coming from. Learning and memorizing Bach fugues will unfortunately become 'im-possible' if you become severely weakened from unknowingly ingesting mold and can't even think straight.

Home Sweet Home unfortunately is not always so sweet, especially on the inside, which may actually be quite insidious. The song has an interesting history. The lyrics come from John Payne's 1823 opera *Clari, Maid of Milan;* Sir Henry Bishop added the melody to create the popular song. Donizetti used the theme in his *Ana Bolena,* and both Sigismund Thalberg and Louis Moreau Gottschalk (and probably others) created virtuoso concert versions for piano. It was popular during the American Civil War to the point of inciting desertions among soldiers and Adelina Patti sang it for Lincoln at the White House.

Get outside as often as you can. You don't want to get sunburned, but natural light is healthy and health professionals tout the vitamin D angle. If you live in a major urban city, outside may not be any better than inside due to all the traffic or industrial pollution. Environmental toxins including (especially) noise pollution are a much bigger problem today than in the 19th century. Visit the country as often as you can, enjoy your vacations in a natural setting.

In summer I exchange the rush of travel, the catching of trains, for the repose and quiet of a vacation by the sea.
JOSEF HOFMANN

Positive Piano

Do you move about often enough in the open air? Much outdoor exercise in every kind of weather makes for strong, durable fingers. Musty air in a room makes for sickly, nervous, tense, and fallible playing.
FRIEDRICH WIECK

The pianist will unwisely waste his time with long continued periods of practice without relaxation, general bodily exercise, and plenty of deep breathing. A quick walk around the block, interspersed with good full breaths, often restores the nerve force and ensures progress.
ALBERTO JONÁS

It would be difficult to tell you how I work, but I can tell you where; always in the open, if possible. I like to sit out of doors; I want to be in the midst of nature.
AMY BEACH

Deppe told his pupils to "live a child's life", and keep much in the open air, to wear no gloves.
BETTINA WALKER

It's really important to cultivate a relaxed and positive attitude towards your work and the people around you. Mental poise means calm, peace of mind, and personal satisfaction. Poise allows for conservation of energy and enhanced focus.

Very little artistic pleasure is derived when there is no repose, no poise.
JOSEF LHÉVINNE

Should I be offered a salary of 2000 florins by the Archbishop of Salzburg, or 1000 florins from someone else, I would take the second offer; for in place of the difference I would have health and peace of mind.
MOZART

Loss of mental poise usually means worry, anxiety, and even depression and the concomitant loss of productivity. Perhaps the most insidious aspect of all disease is that accompanying depression that saps our motivation and our will. Nobody ever accomplished great things when they despaired of life itself.

Keep your melancholy within bounds and see that it does not last. Life is

precious and negative moods can consume us body and soul, we must at all costs overcome it, or not let it come into being. Don't imagine that life has little more in store for you. It's not true. Suffer sorrow calmly, happier times are sure to follow. Why do you suppose man was given the divine gift of hope?
BRAHMS

I forbid you to be depressed.
GABRIEL FAURÉ

The number one medical condition in America is not heart disease or cancer but depression. September is suicide prevention month; I hope it's not connected with going back to school. But it's very sad that the condition is so widespread that we have to have a month to advocate awareness of it. Incidentally, that business of naming a month for some cause goes back to Edward Bernays, publicity guru. The publicity act in itself does little or nothing to address causes.

But symptoms of depression no doubt result from myriad complex factors in life, least of which, (if at all) is an inherent natural deficiency of psychiatric drugs.

The whole organism is responsible for specific trouble. Proof of this is that we eradicate specific defects in process.
F.M. ALEXANDER

Negativity, moodiness, ill-humor and depression all extract a heavy toll on everyone else in the community as well. It's tough to remain positive around negative people.

Those who habitually wallow in their own emotionally bad health and fill their own minds with the rank poisons of suspicion, jealousy and hatred, as a rule take umbrage if you refuse to do likewise, and they find a perverted relief in trying to denigrate you.
BRAHMS

Wilhelm Reich thought mental illness resembled a biological plague that could go viral and rapidly spread through society (look around); all the more reason for each one of us to work harder on ourselves, and thus be kind to our neighbors.

Constant worrying about things is a choice, and a poor one at that.

It not only makes you miserable, it makes you less effective.

I don't go around regretting things that don't happen. Let your mind alone, and see what happens.
VIRGIL THOMPSON

The things that don't exist are the most difficult to get rid of.
F.M. ALEXANDER

Worry is just the sign of an uncontrolled mind. The person who worries allows his mind to wander to things that do not concern the present, to things that have happened in the past, or to things that very probably may never happen at all.
LILIAS MACKINNON

I've been through some terrible things in my life, some of which actually happened.
MARK TWAIN

Mark Twain's daughter Clara wrote about her husband Ossip in *My Husband Gabrilowitsch.* (1938 Harper Bros.) In his native Russia he studied with Anton Rubinstein and Leschetizky and became a talented concert pianist, conductor, and a founding director of the Detroit Symphony Orchestra. What a great experience to have had Mark Twain for a father-in-law!

Get rid of the idea or habit of worrying ... jot down that you and all your petty worries will be out of the way only a few years hence. This is a world of trouble or joy pretty much as you choose to look at it. ... The normal cure for nervous conditions is not to be found so much in medicine bottles as in work accomplished without hurry and flurry, with care and a happy mind, plenty of rest, the right food and the right mental attitude.
ALBERTO JONÁS

An absolute balance between the physical and mental powers with regard to health and vigor is necessary for satisfactory practice. Mind and body must both be vigorous when you practice. If you feel unwell, better leave off for a while until you have recovered.
ERNST PAUER

There was but one piano in the house and three of us to practice on it. Naturally sometimes practicing was inconvenient. I fumed and worried because my endeavors were checked...I finally lost both sleep and appetite, and the doctor was called. Finding no definable ailment, he prescribed 'change of air and scene'. ...I said, 'There's something that will cure me without sending me away, but I'm afraid you will not care to do it ... give me a piano all to myself and let me play on it as much as I like!'
BETTINA WALKER

Exasperatingly, we remain very much at the mercy of our bodily moods wrought by our current state of health! It's all about vitality. It's possible to be inspired or 'in the mood' when our vitality is high, but not when it is low. When our vitality is high we feel mentally keen and alert, open to new impressions, and alive to the promptings of an active healthy imagination. But when the tide of vitality is at its lower ebb, we can't assimilate new impressions, nor will our brain provide any.
TOBIAS MATTHAY

Wholesome nutrition, invigorating exercise, fresh air, cultivation of mental poise, avoidance of environmental toxins - certainly nothing new there and most would wholeheartedly agree on the benefits of a proactive wholistic approach for building and maintaining health.

But the mind is funny; sometimes you can intellectually agree with something and yet continue to do the exact opposite simply because of awareness-blocking habit. The light bulb hasn't gone on yet, the *aha*! or eureka moment hasn't arrived, the something new has not truly dawned on you.

A paradigm shift is that moment when a new perspective instantaneously elevates your consciousness and empowers you to think and act differently. You discard previous ineffectual thought patterns almost magically, no matter how ingrained they've become, and exchange them for better ones.

Parents, teachers, sales persons ... virtually anyone seeking to persuade often wonders how to convince somebody of something, especially if they're trying to help them. It's more powerful when we convince ourselves. Sometimes what's required is a ...

WAKE UP CALL ... HELLO ...

Currently, the United States spends a larger percentage of its gross domestic product on 'health care' than any other country in the world – over 15%, or more than 2 trillion dollars. A trillion is a number that gets tossed around plenty these days, usually in reference to the national debt, but it's basically incomprehensible to humans who aren't professional mathematicians. It's one followed by twelve zeros:

$$1,000,000,000,000$$

One trillion single dollar bills is a mind-bogglingly huge pile of paper. Do you think you might practice the piano for a trillion seconds in your lifetime? A second goes by pretty quickly doesn't it? Practicing the piano (non-stop) for a trillion seconds would take 31,688 years. Imagine yourself practicing in a cave, your partner painting pictures on the rock walls and your pet woolly mammoth outside, hopefully plowing that ice off your driveway. Maybe you'd get pretty good at playing the piano (pop-psychology's magical 10,000 hours!) but there's no guarantee unless you had a clear vision of what you wanted to accomplish and also were practicing effectively.

In comparison, a billion seconds is 31.7 years, and a million seconds is only 13 days. Scientists estimate that your brain contains 100 billion brain cells, give or take a few. That number now looks like a pittance in comparison to our national 'health care' budget, a good chunk of which is tragically wasted. Let's not waste our brain cells, we don't really have that many, perhaps 5 percent of the annual 'health' budget in dollars, but check my math please.

Even with all the mega-spending, the World Health Organization recently ranked the United States at only 37th in terms of health care. Remember, they usually only give medals to the top three in anything. We just narrowly beat out Slovenia, but trail behind both Costa Rica and Dominica. (But Slovenia bested the United States with a lower infant mortality rate). Now, no disrespect to these countries is intended; considering their much smaller GNP's, the fact that they can be ranked anywhere near the U.S. is a testament to their efficiency.

The sandy beaches and palm trees of Costa Rica and Dominica bring to mind an interesting trend: people now use their vacation time to travel to countries where health care is not only cheaper, but better. Something's seriously wrong; it doesn't take a rocket scientist or a concert pianist to realize that. Maybe our paradigm, or how we conceive of the health issue in the first place, is largely to blame for why we've gotten so off track.

Where all is but dream, reasoning and arguments are of no use, truth and knowledge nothing.
JOHN LOCKE

In the vernacular, the above sentiment is expressed as: 'you're dreamin'. The 'health care' cartel of hospitals, pharmaceutical and insurance companies focuses on treating the symptoms of illness and is predominantly a profit-driven industry larger even than 'big oil' or the military-industrial-complex (also pretty big). Automobiles aren't even listed in the top three anymore, at least in the United States.

'Health care' corporations are mandated by law to turn a profit and in order to do that they need a growing revenue stream of sick people. A two year old could spot the conflict of interest in that scenario, and she wouldn't have to be a prodigy banging out a Prokofiev concerto either. Whatever the 'health care' system is doing to/for people, it's not calculated to be wildly successful or one sixth of our economy is going down the tubes when everybody gets better. Incidentally, the quotes around 'health care' are intended to imply 'so-called'; a more accurate term for the discussion might be *disease management.*

And 'philanthropic health nonprofits' (those pesky quotes again) also must consider their budgets and growth targets, or at least survival. If they really help people get healthy they just might put themselves out of business.

Repeat business is a simple prerequisite for economic sustainability. Manufacturers of consumer products have a neat thing called planned obsolescence; your gadget du jour rather quickly becomes obsolete or falls apart on its own so you have to buy another one.

But there's a perplexing difference between the 'health' industry and just about every other; unlike when the plumber comes over to fix a leaky faucet there are simply no guarantees. Unless it's really gross malpractice, most of the time, whatever happens, you still have to pay up. If you end up dead, your estate will be billed.

An ounce of prevention is worth a ton of the cures that are being peddled these days. It's best to get and stay healthy.

An artist owes it to himself and the public to remain in perfect condition – for he must never offer the public anything but the best.
WILHELM BACHAUS

Of course, if you become seriously ill you'll need to become part of the system as a patient. It's extremely costly, very uncomfortable - a definite hassle. And often it's not a long term fix you get for your money but simply short-term amelioration of your symptoms. If you don't make some meaningful lifestyle changes you may soon find yourself right back in the waiting room, or worse, the emergency room.

Another nagging phenomenon is iatrogenic or medical-system induced disease (we'll give the practitioner's a break here by laying it on the system). Studies indicate the incidence of iatrogenic disease to be as high as twenty-five percent. That says you might visit a doctor and come away with something you didn't have before, just like you might flip a coin twice and have it come up heads both times.

Invasive testing methods - lots of prodding, poking, cutting, slicing, and irradiating - may be one factor. When you think about it though, wouldn't it be better to learn how, then assiduously act to prevent dis-ease by living in a way that promotes ease and health rather than wake up one day to find that you've seriously flunked your diagnostic test, as in 'F', and now that you're 'F'd' you're faced with some super expensive gnarly operation or toxic drug therapy.

I am interested in medicine, especially surgery – on somebody else.
JOSÉ ITURBI

Side effects from drugs alone are responsible for tens of thousands of deaths every year.

Adverse drug events (ADEs) result in more than 770,000 injuries and deaths each year and cost up to $5.6 million per hospital, depending on size.
US DEPARTMENT OF HEALTH AND HUMAN SERVICES AGENCY FOR HEALTHCARE
RESEARCH AND QUALITY

Even the government agrees that much of this is largely preventable so let's do our part as individuals to help out. Regaining health and remaining healthy in the first place is still primarily our responsibility. In fact, unless you're a child dependent upon parental guidance it's totally your responsibility, not that of your doctor, the government, your piano teacher, or anyone else.

Doctors and nurses can be highly effective in assisting with serious acute trauma from accidents like burns and broken bones. Biomedical engineers have contributed amazing technology that really helps people too. But as individuals we're each responsible for prevention of the much greater incidence of health problems arising primarily from lifestyle - like what and how much we eat, whether we exercise or not, where and how we choose to live, and how tuned in we are to our actions.

The government, of course, ought to lead in the larger issues of environmental pollution, industrial safety, and banning seriously harmful products foisted on an unsuspecting public. Yes, I did say 'ought to'.

If more than half of us are obese and the other half is depressed, then we are sick, sick, sick. Isn't there a similar line somewhere in Bernstein's *West Side Story*? The International Classification of Diseases is a medical classification system. Its new ICD-10 codes now describe almost 70,000 "diseases, signs, symptoms, abnormal findings, complaints, social circumstances and external causes of injury or disease".

Future generations, if they aren't living in caves, will surely thumb through historical archives and assume that in our age we were all mad. If we don't wake up to reveille, pretty soon we're going to be hearing taps.

Faulty paradigms and misinformation can be propagated through our educational systems and the 'popular' media (that's not unanimous, by the way). With so many health and fitness books out there, not to mention government publications and the daily onslaught of charming television advertisements from the pharmaceutical and comfort food companies, how do you know what's 'true', or at least accurate and effective? You have homework to do, for the rest of your life.

A healthy, beautiful and optimally functional body and mind result from a lifestyle in harmony with nature. Many frustrated and unhappy people resort to artificial means to circumvent their inability to maintain their health, and there's always someone willing to oblige and profit from their despair. Surgical procedures for weight loss have their dangers and with few exceptions constitute an ill-advised quick-fix substitute for a genuinely healthy lifestyle. If the underlying habits aren't addressed, it's just a matter of time before the situation repeats itself.

The prevalence of vanity cosmetic surgery (as opposed to genuine treatment for accident victims or congenital defects) is another sad commentary on our society. We're all so beautiful as children yet too often something happens to our self-image; our self-esteem becomes degraded and we lose faith in ourselves. We resort to artificial means that cannot possibly succeed because the whole of our being is ignored for just one or two details of the physical.

Back in the 1960's, the plastic surgeon Maxwell Maltz puzzled over why many of his patients were not mentally 'convinced' that they looked better after successful surgery, as corroborated by everybody else. They still retained their former low self-esteem, and could not 'see' the physical difference. If ever there was a clear demonstration of the indivisible mind-body connection, that's one.

In *Psycho-Cybernetics* (Prentice-Hall, 1960) Maltz explains how he devised a way to address the underlying mental issues with a program of visualizing and setting and attaining goals. He realized that a person's external thought and action reflect what's on the inside, the belief system within the mind. Unless the interior self-image is healthy and confident, no amount of external tweaking (or tampering) will make a difference. In addition, cosmetic surgery procedures have their own physical risks, as is known by the many unfortunate souls who have later regretted it.

The 19th century music world had a curious parallel; a type of self-mutilation was once in vogue to supposedly improve piano playing. The web of flesh and muscle between the fingers was surgically cut to increase the hand's reach or span across the keyboard and provide a larger range of motion of so-called weaker fingers.

One of Leschetizky's pupils found great difficulty in training two fingers, and the father, who was a doctor, wanted to cut the muscle between them. Leschetizky forbade it but the father insisted. Leschetizky then refused to teach the girl any longer. The family said he was obstinate and only

wanted his way.
ETHEL NEWCOMB

I earnestly beg you to think no more of having the barbarous operation. Better to play every octave and chord wrong throughout your life than to commit such a mad attack upon your hands.
LISZT

The practice was rooted in complete ignorance of what playing the piano is really all about. Once, a woman approached Josef Hofmann and Leopold Godowsky after a concert, and noting their relatively small hands asked "How can you great artists play the piano so magnificently with such small hands?"

Where in the world did you get the idea that we play the piano with our hands?
GODOWSKY

Playing the piano is primarily a mental process. There's really no shortcut around a basic fact of life - the need to think.

To try and serve music successfully with fingers is quite hopeless.
ARTUR SCHNABEL

The temptation is great to give an unfavorably-built hand a greater expansive breadth by stretching and over-expansion. All such efforts should be discarded, however, for they only lead to injury and stiffening of the joints. With normal hands, the fundamental rule of technique (physiological and psychological) is that it can be improved only through natural practice on the instrument itself.
FRIEDERICH A. STEINHAUSEN

The average student has a fixed idea that piano practice is purely gymnastic exercise and lives in the hope that with enough repetition the piece may at last 'do itself' without his thinking about it at all, a mere exercising of the muscles concerned.
TOBIAS MATTHAY

Logier's Chiroplast, Herz's Dactylion and Kalkbrenner's Hand Guide were weird gadgets whose advertisements promised a virtuoso technique. The trite cliché no pain, no gain definitely does not apply to piano practice. The history of pianism has its share of horror stories about career-ending injuries that could have been avoided. Robert Schumann experimented with one of those trendy mechanical devices claiming to miraculously strengthen a pianist's hands and fingers.

I reached the point when, whenever I had to double under my fourth finger, my whole body would twist convulsively and after six minutes of finger exercises I felt the most interminable pain in my arm, as if it were broken.
ROBERT SCHUMANN

It ended disastrously. Schumann permanently injured one of his fingers and was forced to abandon his performance career. It's not clear whether experimenting with the device alone was responsible. Schumann was becoming a very sick man, his condition exacerbated, or probably caused, by the then cutting-edge medical technology of ingesting mercury for various ailments. Of course he was seriously poisoned by it. The symptoms include fatigue, headache, memory loss, trouble performing complex tasks, depressed mood, joint or muscle pain, and insomnia, among others. Schumann eventually became suicidal and died in an insane asylum.

You can develop strain and carpal tunnel syndrome from practicing even without gadgets. It's not from practicing too much but from not practicing correctly – incorrect 'use of the self'.

Leschetizky constantly cautioned against any stretching or pulling of the hand, and it was never his idea to practice with paper wads or a house key pulled up between the fingers.
ETHEL NEWCOMB

So-called dumb keyboards (a double entendre) are less physically dangerous, but ultimately have little value either. Unless you're listening to the sound you produce you're not making music and, therefore not 'practicing' either.

'Dumb keyboards' have been invented; practice on them for a while, in order to see that they lead to nothing.
ROBERT SCHUMANN

In Dante's Hell there's a dumb piano, and Lucifer sees to it that they practice without ceasing.
LISZT

Another controversial health issue that's been around since the time even of Mozart and Liszt is medical vaccination and immunization.

After vaccination there began a period of sickness in which the boy struggled alternately with nervous disorders and fevers, several times bringing him close to death. Once during his second or third year, we thought we had lost him and had a coffin prepared. This alarming condition lasted until his sixth year.
ADAM LISZT

They are trying to persuade me to let my boy be inoculated with smallpox, but as I have expressed sufficiently clearly my aversion to this impertinence they are leaving me in peace. Here inoculation is the general fashion.
LEOPOLD MOZART

The immunization paradigm believes that health can be acquired externally, by purchase. That's 180 degrees diametrically opposed to the paradigm that health is a natural birthright that must be individually cultivated through proper nutrition and lifestyle. It wouldn't be such a big deal if it was just about money well spent – or not. But a significant number of people (like one or more, especially if you happen to be that one) have been seriously harmed and have possibly even died from adverse effects of immunizations.

Although the 'technology' has advanced in two hundred years, unfortunately the mistaken paradigm remains the same. Why are we as taxpayers funding a special government program to compensate individuals deemed to be injured by vaccines? The following statement appears on the website of the U.S Department of Health and Human Services.

On October 1, 1988, the National Childhood Vaccine Injury Act of 1986 (Public Law 99-660) created the National Vaccine Injury Compensation Program (VICP). The VICP was established to ensure an adequate supply of vaccines, stabilize vaccine costs, and establish and maintain an accessible and efficient forum for individuals found to be injured by certain vaccines. The VICP is a no-fault alternative to the traditional tort system for resolving vaccine injury

claims that provides compensation to people found to be injured by certain vaccines. The U. S. Court of Federal Claims decides who will be paid.
U.S. DEPARTMENT OF HEALTH AND HUMAN SERVICES

I'm not a lawyer but I think the 'no-fault alternative' part means that the manufacturers are off the hook and that we the people will cover the costs of damages for them. And there's now a strong push to legally mandate this questionable 'health' practice for all, and take away a parents right to choose when it comes to their child's health despite the existence of this damage claims program ... and little or no discussion of some pretty nice financial donations to politicians by the drug companies.

Are we to be inoculated against every known disease till our bodies become depressed and enervated sterilities, incapable of action on their own account? I pray not, for such a physical condition would imply a mental condition even more pitiable.
F.M. ALEXANDER

It's thought by some that the rise in autism rates is related to vaccinating. You as a taxpayer are paying for litigious claims settlements because the drug companies have been exempted by law. The safety incentive in the vaccine industry is thus seriously compromised. This important discussion is beyond the scope of a book on mere piano playing, but a good source is the National Vaccine Information Center (NVIC), at www.NVIC.org.

There are cures that are worse than disease.
ALDOUS HUXLEY

Wholistic health works in the context of a system of inter-related parts. In the previous chapter we discussed the body work of F. M. Alexander. Basically everything we do with our bodies affects our overall health, for better or worse.

We can picture the effect on the vital organs, their general disorganization, the harmful irritation caused by undue compression, the interference with the natural flow of blood, lymph, and digestive fluids. In fact we find a condition of stagnation and fermentation, causing the manufacture

196

*of poisons which more or less clog the mental and physical organism. ...
Look to that wonderful instrument, the human body, for the true solution
of our difficulty, an instrument so inimitably adapted, so full of marvelous
potentialities of resistance and recuperation that it is able, when properly
used, to overcome the force of disease which may be arrayed against it.*
F.M. ALEXANDER

Without health, energy and optimism, even simple tasks like tying
your shoe laces can become desperately difficult, if not impossible
- not to mention that major long term goal of a spectacular concert
performance before an enthusiastic and expectant full house at
Carnegie Hall.

A healthy lifestyle will go a long ways towards regaining and
maintaining vibrant health. We can educate ourselves and find the
discipline to make significant lifestyle changes. Eventually it won't
require so much discipline because the perceived sacrifice will evolve
into a great joy in and of itself.

*To me art is joy. The more intensely studious the artist, the more joyous he
will be in his art. Everything connected with art and the study of art should
be easy, natural, individualistic, untrammeled, and instinctive.*
PERCY GRAINGER

Combine your instinctual common sense with logic and education
and create your own personal health program that includes a nutritious
and nurturing tasty diet along with energizing, invigorating exercise
that is both fun and gives a sense of achievement.

Cultivate an optimistic attitude, healthy social interactions, and
meaningful, productive work and you will evolve mental poise.
Getting and staying healthy is a lifelong process, with ups and
downs, successes and setbacks. But your inner physical system, your
outward appearance, your mind, level of happiness, and of course
your piano playing and every other activity you engage in will all
beautifully blossom when you make health a priority in your life. We
need more patience and less patients; more ease and less dis-ease.

*It's a strange characteristic of our age that, as regards pleasure of both mind
and table, we cannot adequately digest our food, speedily become sated with
each dish, and yet never tire of sweetmeats. You may call this the spirit of*

progress; yet why be ashamed of retracing our steps to our great ancestors? Borrow some of their calmness, stability, and strength, and so gain the beautiful and loving spirit that has given us so many peaceful, refreshing, and lively melodies.
ANTON THIBAUT On The Purity of Tone Art

Thibaut's work 'On the Purity of Tone-art" is a fine book about music. Read it frequently when you are older.
ROBERT SCHUMANN

An honest discussion of health doesn't have to be an emotional rant on the sad state of affairs, the corrupt corporations, and lack of real leadership by our elected officials, although the outrage is becoming justifiable. Live your life with quiet integrity and vote fortissimo with your wallet. They will get that message.

The Wall Street Journal recently reported that for the past 40 years real per-capita 'health-care' spending has been growing at twice the rate of real per-capita income, not only in the United States but in the whole developed world as well. You don't have to be a mathematician to realize that's impossible to sustain in the long run.

Beware the medical-industrial complex - it's careening out of control. The 37th-ranked Goliath is lumbering across the countryside; first doing considerable harm, but nevertheless doing considerable right by Wall Street.

Goliath looked at David and saw that he was little more than a boy, glowing with health, and handsome … and he despised him.
THE BIBLE I SAMUEL 17:42

The system is majorly flawed. People are clamoring in droves for alternatives. Unfortunately, open-minded persons proposing those alternatives are subject to witch-hunts; persecuted, and tossed to wild beasts in corporate legal amphitheaters.

If anything's sacred, the human body is sacred … and your very flesh shall be a great poem.
WALT WHITMAN

Regain and maintain vibrant health. True health care must be self-care. Please take care of yourself.

When you exchange an ineffective paradigm for one that really works, and when you do your utmost to regain health through intelligent life-style choices and self-discipline, you accomplish a very great thing. But in the wholistic toolkit of extraordinary life success there's yet another critical factor to consider ...

Chapter 7

......

SOCIAL SKILLS

The very way one greets people and expresses oneself is art. If a musician wants to become a fine artist, he must first become a finer person.

— *SUZUKI*

The piano is a wonderful musical instrument but it remains just an inanimate object until a real human being expresses emotion by playing it.

We often say the piano as an instrument expresses every emotion, when we really know it can say nothing at all without the pianist. If he has many emotions and the ability to express them, the piano will do his bidding.
JOSEF HOFMANN

If the ultimate source of music is human emotion, then the way to become a better pianist, meaning a better musical artist, is always to become a better person.

I wish you to esteem me greater as a man, not an artist.
BEETHOVEN

In 1870 I had the good fortune to attend the Weimar Beethoven Festival with Tausig and there I met Liszt for the first time, getting the opportunity to know him from every point of view, as pianist, conductor, composer, and

in his private capacity as a man – every aspect seemed to me magnificent.
OSCAR BERINGER

Contrary to what you might surmise while perusing the Internet, there's no shortage of talent, brains, or beauty on this planet. Nor is there a scarcity of hard-working individuals who when faced with a challenge are willing to work and persevere. So with all that potential out there, why are so few people truly successful at what they do? Why don't more of us realize our dreams and ambitions?

The kind of tact that many musicians need is 'contact'. They haughtily hold themselves aloof from pupils, parents, and public until they freeze them out. Then they wonder why they do not succeed as well as a less competent musician who is more genial and social.
ERNST PAUER

I firmly believe that the most important thing in life is health; but many great composers in history managed to create beautiful masterpieces despite struggling with severe illness. In every generation there are always plenty of musicians with colossal talent, drive, and even great health who never advance beyond the lower tiers of the profession simply because they lack the absolute minimal qualifications of friendliness, courtesy, punctuality, reliability, and 'likeability'. The simple truth is that a major factor holding us back in our careers is often plain old lack of basic social skills.

That's unfortunate because life is infinitely more pleasant and productive when we all get along, and unnecessary because just like scales and études, social skills can be learned and perfected with practice. A skill is gradually assimilated over time and eventually absorbed into your total personality; it becomes a part of you.

Until we die we should spare no time or effort in changing our weaknesses into merits. It is pleasant and interesting work.
SUZUKI

Your social development is stimulated when you consciously and deliberately tune into others and respect and appreciate them.

Applying 'people skills' by default results in the added benefit of acquiring many more friends and professional contacts. But best of all, when exercising these skills you're in the modes of doing and being, where you set examples and inspire others. Back in the 19th century, anyone who attained prominence in any field made a point of cultivating social skills to a virtuoso level.

Anton Rubinstein is behaving very nicely to me and I like him more and more. He must be a most good-natured creature, free from any trace of jealousy, and he is the only person here who is perfectly sincere; but everybody is very hostile to him and endless difficulties are put in the way of his concerts. All the other artists are more or less two-faced.
CLARA SCHUMANN

In the salons, Liszt spellbound lords and ladies with his irresistible personality, brilliant conversation, and knightly bearing and manners.
ARTHUR FRIEDHEIM

Liszt's conversation is charming. I never met a person whose manner of telling a story was so piquant. Liszt's replies were always felicitous and characteristic. Talking of Madame d'Agoult he told us that when her novel Nélida appeared, in which Liszt himself is pilloried as a delinquent, he asked her, 'But why have you so mistreated that poor Lehmann?'
GEORGE ELIOT

Liszt's conversation is always brilliant. It is occasionally dashed with satire or spiced with humor.
CHARLOTTE MOSCHELES

Chopin had an indefinable power of attraction inherent in his nature. George Sand attempted to define it as "a mixture of tenderness and sincerity, of passion and chastity." La Fontaine described it as "a personality infused with the gift of charm." When Chopin was alive, no one could resist it.
ALFRED CORTOT

In those days letters of recommendation had real value, and this partly explains the social as well as artistic success that almost invariably attended Moscheles. Recommendations inspired confidence in him, and there followed pleasure in his artistic performances. To this must be added the charm of

modest, unassuming manners, which made the stranger a welcome guest, then a friend—not for months, or even years, but for life itself.
CHARLOTTE MOSCHELES

Moscheles' greatest charm lay in his soft, benign manner and gentle voice.
W. F. PECHBE

Moritz Moszkowski is one of the most brilliant conversationalists of our time, adding to his gifts as a musician the attractiveness of a man of keen wit. The Parisians find it hard to believe that he is not French. His wit, caustic as it may sometimes be, always harms nobody, and his barbs are free of venom.
CECIL CHAMINADE

Debussy received us in his hotel room in shirt sleeves, apologizing with an adorable sans-gêne, with such lovable simplicity that when I recall that scene now and then look around and contrast it with the swollen-headedness displayed by non-entities puffed up with their own imaginary importance, I am profoundly moved.
VITTORIO GUI

So how do we learn and practice social skills? The important lessons in life are learned through experience and by example. Our parents and teachers serve as powerful role models early in the development process and hopefully we've been lucky in these.

Compendio 'El Carreño' (1853) - Manual of Civility and Good Manners - for the use of both sexes; in which is encountered the principal rules of politeness and etiquette to be observed in manifold social situations, preceded by a short treatise on the moral obligations of Man.
MANUEL ANTONIO CARREÑO

The father of pianist/composer Teresa, Manuel Antonio Carreño authored a best-selling self-help book that achieved wide circulation in Spanish speaking countries - the *Compendio Del Manual De Urbanidad Y Buenas Manera* (1853). His little seven-year-old daughter promptly imitated her father by jotting down her own list of eleven maxims of 'success'. Number eight is *"children should always imitate a good example"*. Then there are friends, associates, colleagues, and neighbors – virtually anyone we cross paths with. There really is something to that old adage about the company you keep ...

Together with your old sofas kick out the tedious hangers-on, whom for years on one pretext or another, you've tolerated far too indulgently. Too many experiences have taught me to be inexorable.
LISZT

Look well to the company you keep, and let your chief ambition be to excel in all that is noble and worthy.
ÉTUDE MAGAZINE October 1889

I recognize no other accomplishments or advantages than those which place one amongst the better class of men; where I find them, there is my home.
BEETHOVEN

Don't associate with people who are either not worth being listened to themselves, or do not possess the faculty of listening with attention to others. Chatty people get often into the habit of not listening and this habit carries itself into all they do. A person who gives way to this habit will lose by degrees the power of concentrating his attention.
LUDWIG DEPPE

Don't amuse yourself by listening to the foolish advice of some people and the tittle-tattle of others. As behooves sensible and serious-minded people, let us simply do what we know to be right.
LISZT

I know your aversion to useless conversations - something which I share with you.
HANS von BÜLOW (To Liszt)

We are like chameleons, we take the hue and color of our moral character from those around us.
JOHN LOCKE

Often we look back at how we were brought up, dwell on the negatives, and adopt the attitude of a victim. Enough of that. Just like a placebo, the real antidote lies in your mind: awareness, followed by choice - both of which can occur pretty quickly if we want them to. Even if we weren't fortunate in our upbringing and didn't have a 'perfect' nurturing environment growing up (there isn't one) we can commit to improving ourselves and our situation, right now.

A disagreeable adult, or one unable to do good work is brought up that way. Good or bad however, we must live with ourselves until the day we die, facing the inevitable question of how to live. Our ability wasn't developed for us; we have to develop it ourselves. Instead of being defeated by misfortune, make something good of your life.
SUZUKI

The first step is that awareness – start thinking about it! Reading a book can stimulate the process intellectually but for genuine transformation you must regularly and attentively practice life skills amongst other human beings.

Recognize and avoid behavior that alienates. In order to succeed, you must also please, and often it's just a simple matter of you behaving yourself.

Nothing can afford a more glaring contrast than John Field's beautiful Nocturnes and his often cynical manners. There was quite a commotion yesterday amongst the ladies when at a party he drew from his pocket a miniature portrait of his wife and loudly proclaimed the fact that she had been his pupil, and that he had only married her because she never paid for her lessons, and he knew she never would. He also bragged of going to sleep whilst giving lessons to the ladies of St. Petersburg, adding that they would often rouse him with the question, 'Why does one pay twenty roubles an hour, if you go to sleep?
IGNAZ MOSCHELES

Bamboozler, our keyboard player, has fine hands, but is unable to put them to good use except when the governess momentarily excuses herself, leaving him alone with his female students.
DER CRITISCHE MUSICUS AN DER SPREE, 1749

The classic book on social skills is *How to Win Friends and Influence People* by Dale Carnegie (1888-1955). His treatment is both entertaining and enlightening; a few of the specific examples may now be a bit dated but the underlying principles are timeless. The book has been so 'influential' that you hear offshoots of the catchy title in other genres – e.g. *Win Audiences and Influence Impresarios*.

First published in 1936 it has sold over 15 million copies worldwide to date. That's a huge number of sales for a book in any category. Just for fun, let's do some more math. There are currently over 7 billion people on the planet; 15 million (book sales) as a percentage of that is only 0.002 percent. That means two one thousandth's of one percent of all people may have bought the book. Even if we generously multiply this number by 100 to account for library borrowings and shared/second hand copies, at 0.2 we're still under 1 percent for people who may have read it. And those sales numbers now span two generations.

The math underscores the fact that most people are under-educated on the topic (okay, a large number are totally clueless) and woefully unaware of how they interact with others, and the consequences. Imagine yourself in a big auditorium along with 1,000 people. By the percentages, maybe one person will have read *Win Friends...*, possibly more if it's a business/sales convention. Also, how many of the people who have read it actually took it to heart and are practicing it? (which recalls other best-selling books in the religion genre ...)

Perhaps that's an indication of why life can be, shall we say, a bit uncomfortable at times. Of course a person's level of social skills is not solely dependent on the reading of one book; but ... you get the point. Just observing everyday life, it seems that most of us could at best benefit from a bit of training; at worst we're talking about tons of immaturity, self-absorption, selfishness, narcissism, and egoism out there, whether in ignorance or not. These behaviors don't facilitate 'success', to say the least.

If you find yourself constantly complaining of your lack of success, then maybe it's time to grow/wake up and get working on social skills. All those great 19th century musical artists successfully went through a similar positive process (with the possible exception of Richard Wagner, and most of us are not as talented or hard-working as he was).

Many a vigorous and unconsidered word drops from my mouth for which reason I am considered mad.
BEETHOVEN

Many people mistakenly thought that Beethoven was by nature a morose and ill-tempered man. He was sometimes irritable, passionate, and melancholy due to the deafness which, in his later days, increased to an alarming extent. But opposed to these peculiarities in his temperament, he possessed a kind heart, and most acute feelings. Any disagreeable occurrence, arising from his betrayal of irritability, he manifested the utmost anxiety to remove, by every possible acknowledgement of his indiscretion.
CIPRIANI POTTER

You can't imagine how being a child prodigy spoils you ... think, to what point ill-considered outbursts can have troublesome and unforeseen consequences for the unreflective minds which surrender themselves to them.
LISZT

Felix Weingartner, the only conductor who understood the genius of Liszt the composer once said to me: "Liszt was the most decent of them all." The word 'decent' in German seems a strange one to apply to this extraordinary personality, but the more I think of it, the more I realize it's the right one. Indeed I go further than that. Liszt was the Good Samaritan of his day and generation.
FREDERIC LAMOND

It's the musician's behavior to the outside world that gives him personal respect. A singer in a New York music hall can make headlines by bathing in milk, but a genuine respect comes through a strong character, a lovely disposition, and a dignified demeanor. This last instance is, to my mind, an ideal example of good social advertising.
JAMES FRANCIS COOKE

Woe to the artist if ever in public he violates the forms of etiquette and politeness. The singer Bordogni was hissed, because, from forgetfulness or intention, he did not offer to conduct Mademoiselle Cinti back to her seat after finishing their duet.
IGNAZ MOSCHELES

Avoid envy; never get angry, although you may have cause to be so. Be not haughty, that you may be loved by others.
TERESA CARREÑO

Dear Henselt, my whole career has been based upon the worthiness of artists. Lately I have become confused, and have almost come to the conclusion that artists are not nobler than the public; then came your letter. I see, I hear, I believe.
ANTON RUBINSTEIN

Although he was occasionally disappointed where he had hoped to find a nature nobler than his own, Gottschalk maintained a certain loving trust in humanity, and a kind and generous heart.
OCTAVIA HENSEL

Dale Carnegie started out teaching public speaking skills to businessmen but soon realized that the 'fine art of getting along with people in everyday social contacts' was the real key to success. Finding no 'practical textbooks' on the subject, he promptly sat down and wrote one. He interviewed many prominent successful people like President Franklin Roosevelt, Thomas Edison, and Clark Gable - creating a curriculum of sorts that he tested and refined for years.

It's amazing that a simple demonstration of kindness, tact, and sincerity will have an almost profound effect on a person – because it's so rare. The silver lining in this thundercloud is actually a bit of a health hazard – you're liable to stub your toe on that social skills bar when you stumble over it, because it's now lying on the ground.

Shouldn't great social behavior be the norm rather than the exception, especially since it's easy and costs nothing? The wisdom in *How to Win Friends and Influence People* often seems obvious because it's just common sense. When Carnegie counsels to not be so critical and complaining, to avoid arguments, and let the other person save face … it's all been said before.

Formerly, I was too forward in expressing my opinions and made enemies for myself – now I judge no one because I do not wish to injure anyone. And besides, I think to myself: if it be something real, then it will maintain itself in spite of all enmity and envy, but if it be not solid, it will tumble down of its own accord, no matter how they try to prop it up.
BEETHOVEN

Silence at the proper season is wisdom, and better than any speech. Know

how to listen, and you'll profit even from those who talk badly.
PLUTARCH

A gentle word, a kind look, a good-natured smile can work wonders and accomplish miracles.
WILLIAM HAZLITT

In order to achieve harmony, one person must gracefully give in to the other, and it is nobler to be the one who gives in than the one who forces the other to give in.
SUZUKI

Leschetizky talked a lot about the efforts one should make to be fair in one's lifetime, and he used the English word "fair" – he thought the word was very beautiful.
ETHEL NEWCOMB

I like the noble simplicity of English manners.
BEETHOVEN

Take delight in the contacts you make on journeys; the people you meet have been placed there by destiny. Therefore, greet them. It may lead to a conversation... Rather than talking about yourself, learn to draw the other person out, and above all, listen ... it's the basis of pleasant human relations, love, harmony, improvement of one's fate, and grasping opportunity. The other person lives a quite different life from you, and knows something you don't, and you are bound to learn something.
SUZUKI

If you've lately experienced public transportation in a major urban area you know how far we've come, or regressed, since the above suggestion was offered some seventy years ago. Desperate for a gig and unable to comprehend why you aren't being offered one, you might find yourself on the subway sitting right next to a booking agent intent on discovering the world's next great concert pianist.

Sometimes our light goes out, but is blown again into instant flame by an encounter with another human being.
ALBERT SCHWEITZER

... but you're still crushing digital candy or humoring your irritable feathered friends on your 'smart' phone; or simply just staring at your tennis shoes with a glum expression on your face.

Booking agent? ... highly unlikely? ... maybe in the small town I live in, where we don't even have a subway. Teresa Carreño once boarded a train departing Paris for England. Already an international superstar pianist, she still had not 'conquered' the most demanding audience of all - the Germans - and she dreamed of performing with the great conductor Hans Richter. Now let me just say, it's possible that Teresa was at the time mentally distracted by one of her several divorces ...

Opposite her compartment sat a German man reading his newspaper. Ignoring him, she and her companion carried on a boisterous conversation. Then, curious about the scenery opposite, she crossed over and stared out the man's window without even greeting him and then actually bumped into him without apologizing. She returned to her seat and then made some facetious remark, luckily in Spanish, along the lines of "our portly friend may think I want to make love to him but I just wanted to look out the window".

Well, you can guess what's coming ... when the train stopped a mass of musicians were there to greet, much to her chagrin ... uberconductor Hans Richter. (She later did perform with him several times; the incident was never mentioned by either of them).

All the great and famous pianists of a generation seem to have been acquainted with each other, and they spent a lot of time just hanging out. We might think that because the population was relatively smaller 150 years ago (as were towns and cities) it was easier to meet and know people. But travel by horse and carriage (and later railroad and steamship) was actually more tedious back then. Still, people that were 'going places' knew and associated with each other because that's what great people do. They see the value in others committed to the 'ideal', they gravitate towards each other, and they invest time in networking.

It was in the summer of that same year that, I first met that wonderfully fascinating man Franz Liszt, in some of whose works I was to sing the bass soli. Liszt was beyond expectation kind to me, and only too readily I accepted his most cordial invitation to visit him in Weimar. I settled for some weeks in that famous little capital and daily went to the "Gartnerei," a charming little garden residence placed at Liszt's disposal by its owner, the reigning Grand-Duke. There Liszt, who, by the way, invariably greeted me by kissing me on both cheeks, held a sort of court, the picturesque old town fairly swarming with past, present and would-be pupils and disciples of the master, male and female, in velvet coats and huge neckties, and with long flowing hair.

It was, however, by no means pupils only that flocked to those world-famed Sunday morning "At Homes". On one of those occasions, for instance, it was my good luck not only to see but also to hear in that historical music-room, besides the illustrious host himself, no fewer and no lesser stars than Anton Rubinstein, Carl Tausig, and Hans von Bülow.

Here there were the four greatest pianists of the time together, not in a vast concert hall, but in a small private room, in their shirtsleeves, so to say, enabling us privileged fellow-guests to compare, not from memory or distance, but by immediate impression, within the compass of an hour or so, the stupendous power of a Rubinstein with the polished infallibility of a Tausig, the irreproachable classicism of a Bülow with the enchanting grace and romanticism of a Liszt. They are gone, all those four great ones, but the memory of that Sunday morning is more real, more living to me to-day than any reproduction of their playing could be by the wonderfully ingenious musical inventions of this electric age.

SIR GEORGE HENSCHEL

Networking is as imperative as ever, perhaps even more so. But today we have networking meet-ups where you can (again) pay a fee to be in a room full of people who don't know how to accomplish it naturally; most of the time they talk to you nonstop about themselves without asking you anything about yourself. A more productive formula might be 60 seconds about you, then 60 seconds about me, then an hour about how you and I can collaborate to make the whole greater than the sum of the parts, as Aristotle might say. More recently, the 19th century-born Buckminster Fuller (1895-1983) once offered three questions to ponder regarding networking and collaboration.

1. Where is nothing being done? 2. Where are unrecognized resources for potential collaboration passing each other, unaware of each other's existence? 3. Where are known resources simply 'slipping through the cracks' because no one ever thought to put them together?

BUCKMINSTER FULLER

211

Collaboration with the right people is critical for mutual self-development. Mediocre musicians all too often avoid it out of pettiness and insecurity, opting mistakenly to remain small fry in puddles. Most of those from the 19th century are all but forgotten, just like similar personalities are seldom known today beyond their home towns, if there. Seek out leaders in your field and get to know them but be sure to make it worth their while too. Don't just text, tweet, Facebook or Instagram it. Get in front of people in the flesh and genuinely interact with a positive mindset.

MOTHER: My son will go to cafés if I leave him with you in Vienna.
LESCHETIZKY: Most certainly.
MOTHER: But professor; he will become fond of the ladies.
LESCHETIZKY: I only hope so.

Technological progress has reduced physical contact, and thus impoverished the spiritual relations between the members of a community.
ALDOUS HUXLEY

That quote by Huxley , by the way, is over half a century old now. The true test of your people skills comes when you're affronted or ill-treated. It's not always easy to keep your cool and not stoop to someone else's low level, however, it's much to be admired. Grace under pressure empowers superior performance in everything you attempt in life.

It is incumbent upon you to maintain self-respect when faced with occasional adversity from the musical fraternity.
BRAHMS

To conquer and win the unfriendly souls is part of every artist's task.
PADEREWSKI

One cannot play one's best in the presence of these nobles, fawning upon an Italian prima donna ; it doesn't matter whether I or any other artist plays the piano, they don't care about it, their applause on these occasions, I regard as an expression of delight that they have got rid of me. My wife and I sacrifice as short a time as possible to such soirees, and hurry home again, as soon as good manners will allow us.
IGNAZ MOSCHELES

212

No pioneer, no advocate of the new, ever operates without being misunderstood and suffering from envy and the evil effects of cabals.
ARTHUR FRIEDHEIM

On no account let yourself be discouraged or put out of countenance by the envious. The intrigues are the same everywhere, but one must make a way through it all for oneself by force!
LEOPOLD MOZART to his son

Leschetizky was a wonderfully true friend. What he did not do for young artists who came to him to learn. Even in cases where he incurred only ingratitude and animosity, he kept his poise and good temper.
EDOUARD SCHÜTT

You will find gentle people full of faith and goodness who will receive you and your words with joy; but you will also find others, and in greater numbers, the faithless, proud blasphemers who will speak evil of you, resisting you. Resolutely endure everything with patience and humility.
ST. FRANCIS (Paul Sabatier (1858-1928) 'The Road to Assisi')

I know that a great many of the people who approach me with a smile on their lips, and protestations of friendship on their tongues, want nothing better than to pull me to pieces as best they can as soon as they are outside my door. It is, moreover, the fate of the entire world. I resign myself to it willingly, as I do to all the absurd and odious necessities of this lower world. The good lesson is that one learns to better appreciate, and relish the devotion of the few friends whom chance has thrown in your path.
LISZT

Sgambati presented the appearance of one in complete harmony with all around him. His manners were most easy and engaging.
BETTINA WALKER

Rubinstein, Sander and I went to lunch at the finest restaurant in town, 'The Golden Goose', of which, needless to say, I had up to then only seen the outside. We seated ourselves at the large table in the center of the room, at the other end of which—it was already past the usual lunch hour—the only other person in the room, a well-known musical amateur by profession an Army surgeon, had nearly finished his mid-day meal.

213

Rubinstein, Sander, and I were just on the point of commencing ours, when from across the table the penetrating military voice of the surgeon called out to Sander: "I say, Sander, how did you like Tausig the other day?" (Tausig had given a piano recital in Breslau the week before.) Sander, by nature a very shy and retiring little man, got quite red in the face with embarrassment, and was still composing an appropriate answer to the perplexing question, when the irrepressible surgeon trumpeted to us: "Well, I can only tell you, compared to Tausig, Rubinstein is nothing but a thrashing flail!"

Now in German a flail does not merely mean the agricultural implement, but is figuratively used to indicate a particularly rude, uncouth, ill-mannered person. An awful silence followed. Our spoons just raised to our lips nearly dropped into the soup, and for a moment we did not quite know what would happen next. The unfortunate Army surgeon, evidently becoming aware of something being wrong, clapped his monocle in his eye and, surveying our party, recognized the lion-head of the smiling Rubinstein, who, shaking his mighty mane, bade us pay no attention to the incident. "A public man," he said, "must not mind such things. To tell you the truth, they rather amuse me." The surgeon, however, looking anything but amused; got up hurriedly paid his bill, and left by the back door so as not to pass us.

The concert in the evening was a tremendous success. Rubinstein received a perfect ovation at the end of his D Minor Concerto, and when, that night, I was lying awake in bed and dreaming for a long time before finding sleep, I came to the conclusion that there was not a bad name in the world I should mind being called as long as I could play as well and be as famous as Rubinstein.

SIR GEORGE HENSCHEL

If you absolutely must put someone in their place, try to be as diplomatic as you can.

Be convinced that mankind, even in your case, will always be sacred to me.
BEETHOVEN

If I decide to be an idiot, then I'll be an idiot on my own accord.
J.S. BACH

Something quite obnoxious found way too often in the performing arts world is the big ego – with the result that musicians have coined a couple of pejorative labels now used in all walks of life. Think of what the words *diva* and *prima donna* have come to represent.

... a young girl who had spent several years abroad studying the piano begged permission to play something for me, then, without explanation or apology, sat down and—would you believe it ?—played through the complete solo part of a lengthy concerto! Her one idea was to impress me with her "accomplishment," but the only thing she impressed on me was her vanity. She played later in public and was, of course, a dismal failure.
HENRY THEOPHILUS FINCK

What Weingartner says of the tempo rubato conductor is also true of the performing artist - they suffer from virtuoso or importance mania.
EDWARD GRIEG

Excessive vanity can be a real social turn-off, not to mention thoroughly spoil a performance. It's the exact opposite with humility, which is refreshingly pleasant for everyone involved, and opens the door to greater depths of interpretation.

When anything about himself or his achievements came up in the course of a talk, Joseffy always gave the conversation a sudden shove in the opposite direction. He was in fact the most modest of men, having none of the bravado and braggadocio which one is so accustomed to associate with the virtuoso who has conquered the concert audiences of two continents.
EDWIN HUGHES

Sterndale Bennett's words were few, and ever well-chosen and to the point; and there was a ring of truth in all that he uttered that carried conviction to the hearer, that here was one that could not and would not lie – no, nor dilute the truth by telling it by halves.
BETTINA WALKER

Your field of action is this whole great world, and the more your good deeds are known, the more good you will be able to do. If you are a teacher in a little country town, and the musical world knows that you have done something to your credit, that "something" is not to be forgotten.
J. FRANCIS COOKE

Chopin acquired that scrupulous politeness essential to the social relationships of Polish high society. Liszt, who knew all about it, described Chopin's bearing as being "princely".
ALFRED CORTOT

If you're struggling with jealousy - get over it. This powerful negative emotion will hamper your efforts to improve yourself. Simply acknowledge the merits of others; after all, they've worked hard for them. Now get to work on yourself.

A genuine virtuoso of proved worth knows no jealousy.
CHOPIN

Liszt was a noble and good man, one of the best I've ever known. Jealousy and ill-will were unknown to him.... I stress this absence of jealousy in his character because I've never seen it to such a degree in an important man having rivals in his own profession.
COUNT ALBERT APPONYI

Jealousy is absurd because if we wish to be more loved, we have only to make ourselves more lovable. The more we value someone's affection, the greater the pains we must take to deserve it. Noble hearts, oblivious to the vile torments of jealousy, transform objects of jealousy into ones of emulation.
LISZT

When Liszt and Rubinstein both sat down to play a new concerto by the latter (which Liszt with incredible intuition read at sight) it was really as good as a play to watch the gray-haired master following his younger artist, and allowing himself, as if on purpose, to be surpassed in fervor and enthusiastic powers.
SALOMON MOSENTHAL

The person who is jealous acknowledges his or her own inferiority, and our pride must teach us not to be jealous.
TERESA CARREÑO

Beethoven and Wölffl respected each other because they appreciated each other. They followed the principle that the road to Art is broad enough for many, and that it is not necessary to lose oneself in envy pushing forward

for the goal of fame.
IGNAZ von SEYFRIED

*Had I the privilege of composing an opera for your theater I would run a
great risk, for scarcely any man can stand beside the great Mozart. I wish
I could impress on every friend of music, and on great men in particular,
my own depth of musical sympathy and profound appreciation of his
inimitable music; then nations would vie with each other to possess such
a jewel in their land. It's outrageous that the unparalleled Mozart is not
yet engaged by some imperial or royal court! Forgive my excitement, but
I love the man so dearly.*
JOSEPH HAYDN

*If only I could absorb your pure and clean mind, dear Haydn; nobody has a
greater reverence for you than I do.*
FRANZ SCHUBERT

*Trustworthy contemporaries are of opinion that Moscheles could not
compete with Hummel's legato playing; Hummel's touch was soft as velvet,
his running passages perfect as a string of pearls; whereas Moscheles, with
his dashing bravura and youthful enthusiasm, carried away his hearers with
irresistible force. There was no sort of personal rivalry between the two
artists. We have seen how Moscheles preferred Hummel's Septet to his own
composition of the same kind. In return Hummel gave Moscheles tokens of
the most sincere acknowledgment.*
CHARLOTTE MOSCHELES

*Maurice Moszkowski is a man who listens attentively to a performer, no
matter who it is, and is never stingy of recognition when the performance
merits it.*
HENRY T. FINCK

*When he heard an effect that pleased him Leschetizky would often say "How
do you do that?" - an indication of the simplicity of the man. How many
masters would ask that of a pupil?*
IGNAZ FRIEDMAN

*Sgambati was Liszt's outstanding Italian pupil, the most notable musician
of his country except Verdi who, of course, stood alone. He was one of those*

rare individuals who know of professional jealousy only by hearsay and this was a quality which made him universally respected and liked.
ARTHUR FRIEDHEIM

Some of Sgambati's well-developed character must have rubbed off on Friedheim because he evolved into the kind of man and musician who puts Art first, accepts the truth about matters, and eschews shallow (un)professional rivalry. That demonstrates a lot of self-confidence.

I recall remarking at one of Paderewski's many recitals during the first winter that, quite apart from the great magnetism of his personality, he was the foremost all-around player of his time. A woman of marked musical ability who was sitting near me seemed astonished. "How can you, a pianist, be so unstinted in your praise of another pianist?" she asked. It is because I am a pianist, I explained, that I know what I'm talking about.
ARTHUR FRIEDHEIM

To recognize and acknowledge true greatness in others is a stepping-stone to greatness in ourselves.
ETUDE MAGAZINE October 1889

Pretentiousness and superior airs stem from a psychological sense of inferiority. Such behavior just reinforces the fact that maybe you ought to work on yourself a bit.

Henselt hated all shows and shams, and roundabout speeches which not only involve loss of time, but cloud our perceptions of the truth.... And was a foe to all compromises and half-measures, of all veneer and pretension.
BETTINA WALKER

A pretentious manner was disturbing to Leschetizky.
ETHEL NEWCOMB

His earlier friends all bear testimony to the simplicity and modesty with which Gottschalk received congratulations showered upon him after his first brilliant concert at Niblo's in New York.
OCTAVIA HENSEL

A true artist is a person with beautiful and fine feelings, thoughts, and actions. … To attain high art and musical sense, a pure mind is absolutely indispensable.
SUZUKI

I cannot tell you how gracious Liszt was to me. … he was like a humble child showing you his homework. (On Liszt's St Elisabeth oratorio) ….magnificent!
FAURÉ

Negative emotional states like jealousy and envy are primarily reactive. You can break their strangle hold by choosing to take positive action. Resolve to be kind.

How much more beautiful life would be if the dissensions and misunderstandings did not arise. Seen through the perspective of the years, bitterness and resentment appear very wasteful.
ARTHUR FRIEDHEIM

Love as long as you can
Whoever touches your heart, do for them all the loving things you can,
 make every hour happy for them, no hour dreary,
The hour will come when you stand by graves and lament,
Take care that your heart glows, and harbors love,
And watch your tongue; a harsh word escapes all too quickly,
It wasn't meant to be cruel, but the other walks away weeping.
'Oh Love' by
FERDINAND FREILIGRATH

How many pianists play that third *Liebesträum* of Liszt and heed the words of the poem the original song was based on?

You cannot do a kindness too soon, for you never know how soon it will be too late.
RALPH WALDO EMERSON

A musician's personality is one of the first things that will bring him business. And surely as you make yourself objectionable personally, you will lose the interest of the public. This pertains to your appearance as well as to your manners.
JAMES FRANCIS COOKE

There, that wasn't too painful, was it? – a fairly diplomatic discussion of the musician's need for social skills. Well, it's been mild because the editors had a field day toning it down, but I decided to sneak in a few parting words.

Looking for that one good man, Diogenes probably maintained the patience of Job; but if he were alive today he might just toss that lamp in the trash and give up in despair.

The aim of a college education is to teach you to know a good man when you see one.
WILLIAM JAMES

Too many of today's performing musicians are just too obnoxiously vain and self-centered, which really means immature and undeveloped.

What times! What manners!
CICERO

The feeling of inferiority rules the mental life and is clearly recognized in the sense of incompleteness and lack of fulfillment.
ALFRED ADLER

The reason why 'classical' musicians aren't listed up there with those cell-phone providers, used car salesman and politicians is that the general public is just losing interest. Diogenes would have stopped before dozens of 19th century pianists because they were men and women of noble character. We're not going to have another Golden Age until a whole lot of our pianists resume the role of cultivated, cultured, elegant and refined leaders … same in any other field. (I've given up on politicians).

Let's consider the related topic of your physical appearance; it's more important than you might think, especially when in the public eye as a performer. Like people skills, your appearance, dress, and grooming ideally should be a 24/7 consideration, or at least 16/7 (we won't worry about your pajamas).

John T. Molly's *Dress for Success* coined a new expression in the 1970's, but the general concept has also been around for a while.

Chopin's polished shoes? The most glittering I have ever seen. And he always wore a double-breasted frock-coat, buttoned high and cut in the latest style. He was invariably most fashionable and distinguished. One always heard of him as being "dressed to the nines."
GEORGES MATHIAS

Leschetizky was the keenest of observers and had an aesthetic sense, noticing every detail of one's dress, appearance, and conduct. If one dressed elaborately he expected the playing to have some resemblance to the dress. If one was shabby in appearance he generally found some shabbiness in the playing, and of such appearance he was particularly critical. Colors that did not harmonize were an annoyance to him. But more annoying still was an ungraceful and awkward bearing. This he noticed instantly and put down to lack of rhythm, which he compared to balance.
ETHEL NEWCOMB

You are not artistic-looking in the least. It isn't easy to distinguish oneself in this world, there are many good ones. Be thankful these days if you can look like anything.
LESCHETIZKY

Though many sensible people profess themselves 'above' the superficialities of appearance and dress, yet these matters must be considered by the public artist. … The great point is to dress as well as possible, and with suitability to all occasions. Costliness is not so much to be aimed at as becomingness. Indeed, in no way is one's own sense of refinement and culture more certainly shown than in mode of dress.
LOUIS C. ELSON

Klindworth, Pruckner, and I were asked to perform the Bach triple concerto at the ducal palace. An hour before the carriage arrived to take me to the concert, a servant came from the Altenburg with a package that Liszt had requested him to be sure to deliver to me. On opening it, I found two or three white ties. It was a hint from Liszt that I must dress suitably to play at court. This incident shows the care that Liszt bestowed on little things relating to the customs and amenities of social life. He evidently sent the ties as a precautionary measure. Possibly he was not sure whether Americans were civilized enough to wear white ties with evening dress, and was afraid I might appear in a red-white-and-blue one. Seriously, however, it was very

kind of him to think of a little thing like this.
WILLIAM MASON

In those days, you just couldn't get on here in London unless you appeared to be the right sort.
F.M. ALEXANDER

People appreciate neatness in a musician just as much as they do in a physician or a minister. Bohemianism is a complete failure in music, especially teaching.
JAMES FRANCIS COOKE

Mikuli gave instructions to his tailor to fashion me a suit of the best material and sent me to a famous dance instructor to teach me a perfect elegant bow to perform on the evening of the concert.
MORIZ ROSENTHAL

"Here's a girl who plays beautifully. … She requires some good clothes which she now has not, so we must do something for her. I'm going to buy her a dress." Leschetizky took out his shabby old pocket book and paid several large bills for a certain pretty grey evening dress he had seen. "She should have some silk stockings, shouldn't she? …then of course, there must be shoes." We found some quite beautiful grey satin shoes. Still Leschetizky thought the outfit incomplete without some ornament for the hair.
That night a very smartly gowned girl appeared on the stage, her hair dressed beautifully with an ornament placed very becomingly at the side of her head. She glanced over the audience, smiling in rather amazed but grateful and dignified fashion in acknowledgement of the warm reception …. from first to last her playing was of a style remarkably beautiful. …. Leschetizky congratulated her on her splendid playing, and remarked that she looked very charming. "Yes", she replied, "there has been a fairy godmother to me in Vienna, if only I could find her."
ETHEL NEWCOMB

I once attended a 'classical' concert where the pianist walked on stage without a jacket and his shirttails out. My first impression was of lack of respect for the other musicians who were in traditional concert attire, not to mention the audience, most of whom looked a lot better than the soloist. He botched his Mendelssohn concerto significantly, in several places, just what you would expect according to Lechetizky's observations.

If you're serious about your performance, show up looking the part. Your outward appearance really is a reflection of what's going on inside your mind and also signals a mark of respect (or indifference) for others. Do dress for success, especially for a paying audience. That's part of the presentation; they expect it, and they'll appreciate it. You'll look good in their eyes and it'll add to your confidence.

Dress doesn't necessarily have to be formal all the time. Learn to recognize what's appropriate in different social settings and venues. If you don't have the fashion design talent yourself, then get help from a friend who knows how. Emily Post's *Etiquette* is valuable; I also like the Debrett's *Guide to Etiquette and Modern Manners.*

I'm not sure how helpful the following anecdotes are but they're kind of fun.

One morning Liszt said: "The weather's fine, let's go for a walk, but what kind of greatcoat are you wearing?" "A sort of brown velvet tiger skin", I replied. "I bought it in Hamburg and it fits beautifully". He said, "in Paris it will only make you conspicuous. I'm the only man in Paris who would dare give you his arm whilst you wear that Hansealtic pelt! Come, we will have some macaroni at Broschi's, opposite the Grand Opera. Rossini goes there, we'll sit at his table". As we walked along the boulevards, and people looked at us curiously, I understood Liszt's remark that he alone would dare show himself with someone wearing such a coat.
WILHELM von LENZ

Vladimir de Pachmann was in his apartment playing the Chopin D-flat Nocturne wearing a coat that had once belonged to Chopin. It was of mohair of a chocolate brown color, with large collar and long length.
HARRIETTE BROWER

As Paderewski and I stepped outside the wind was blowing a gale. His great mass of golden hair was tossing like an agitated sea of flame, and my own more somber mane was equally disturbed. Two newsboys were passing at the moment; "Just look at those two damn fools!" they shouted. "Get a haircut! Get a haircut!"
ARTHUR FRIEDHEIM

Positive Piano

Cut it short please; I don't want to look like a musician.
JOSÉ ITURBI

Know first who you are, and then adorn yourself accordingly.
EPICTETUS

It may seem paradoxical, but one of the best ways to get better at something is to do lots of other things. Apart from the physical and mental rest from mindful practice on your main activity, you gain additional skills, knowledge, and experiential wisdom; all of which newly inform your practice when you go back at it.

The call for breath in musical art has been insistent since the earliest days of its history. Keep in touch with the great movements of your time and of the past in art, science, history, and philosophy. The student who sacrifices these things can never hope to climb to fame on a ladder of technique.
PADEREWSKI

The human body is so complex that no one sport or exercise fully utilizes every one of its many muscles. Like moves in a game of chess, there are a potentially infinite number of possible muscular combinations to stimulate the body.

Athletes practice cross-training, resting some muscles while using others, building stamina and all-around body strength. Runners can alternate their runs with swimming laps in the pool. A mountaineer will do pushups and situps, or resort to cycling between expeditions. Yoga is a great activity to add to any fitness (or musical) routine.

A neuroscientist might say that diversity in tasks requiring mental direction results in a greater compass of neural networks established. But there's more to it than just muscle, bone, and nerves. Mind and body are an integral whole with spirit and soul, none of which can be separated out.

Consciousness and/or awareness (or lack thereof) is behind every physical action. Whenever you deliberately interact with your environment in a positive, productive way, especially when other human beings are involved, your life experience is enriched, personal growth is the inevitable result, and your 'main' activity greatly benefits.

224

There's no treatise likely to be too learned for me. Without laying claim to real learning, still, since childhood I've acquainted myself with the minds of the best and wisest of every period of time. It's a disgrace for every artist who does not try to do as much.
BEETHOVEN

Liszt is the most universally educated musician who has ever lived.
AUGUST GÖLLERICH

It's been said often, but it doesn't hurt to say it again: there's a great need for more breadth in music study. The more a man knows, the more he has experienced, the wider his mental vision in all branches of human information, the more he will have to say. We need men in music with big minds, wide grasp and definite aims. Musicians are far too prone to become overspecialized.
HAROLD BAUER

In vain do I look for musicians; that is, musicians who can play passably well on one or two instruments, and who are cultivated men.
ROBERT SCHUMANN

To be an interesting interpreter one must be an interesting person; and the intelligent musician must study subjects other than music.
LILIAS MACKINNON

Bülow loved culture passionately. There's an authentic story of his making a day's journey to Stockholm with a well-known savant and discussing with him every current topic of politics, literature, science, and art, except music. In the evening the gentleman was astonished and delighted to find his companion on the platform giving a piano recital.
BERNARD BOEKELMAN

"When I'm on a tour I employ my leisure moments in reading great literature," said Anton Rubinstein, after welcoming us with the genial cordiality which was one of his marked characteristics. "It is surprising how much that is calculated to broaden the mind may be gained in moments that might otherwise be wasted."
AUBERTINE WOODWARD MOORE

Today's musician must have general knowledge, or the individuality is small. Hearing good orchestral music, the theater, ballet, painting, literature, poetry, and travel; all tend to a general development, without which one is like a mechanical engineer who only knows how to put a few screws together. Don't neglect your general education and risk becoming what used to be called 'music simple'. It's an inestimable advantage to the virtuoso to have his brain alive to every branch of intellectual endeavor. The broader and more enlightened his vision of life, so much the finer and profounder his own art will become.
MARK HAMBOURG

Do you never observe how much higher and stronger the musicians stand who enjoy things outside their art?
HUBERT C. PARRY

Everything you study helps everything else, especially when you study great things.
RAFAEL JOSEFFY

Much is learned through many things, and in the course of study different and similar passages perfect each other.
LOUIS PLAIDY

Due to his extensive traveling, Alexander Brailowsky became an expert on railroad timetables, collecting them as others collect coins or stamps and he could work out a better itinerary than anyone in his manager's office.
CAMILLE SAINT-SAËNS

Life is a meal, and music is the roast beef. But who can survive on just roast beef? One must have one's brandy and dessert and cigar. And so I must have my boxing, and my airplane, and my motorcycle.
JOSÉ ITURBI

'Breadth', or well-roundedness, results from a kind of social and intellectual cross-training and a love of many things in life, as exemplified by the concept of Renaissance Man (or Woman)! Whatever happened to them, by the way? Once upon a time people seemed to be able to do many things well, whether creative artistic types or self-reliant farmers, artisans, and homemakers. Leonardo da Vinci (an exceptional being, of course) was not just one of the greatest painters, but also an accomplished sculptor, scientist, inventor/engineer, architect, musician, mathematician, and author.

Today, too many people perfunctorily spend most of their hours at a job they don't like, or sleeping too much (on the job sometimes) or pseudo-socializing with their electronic gadgets inadvertently absorbing a plethora of consumer advertising and/or political propaganda.

Contrast that passive scenario with a person on a genuinely enthusiastic moral and aesthetic mission and with a deep love of all learning for its own sake. That's when we'll see more real da Vinci types and fewer armchair cult-cryptographers.

Bach, Haydn, Mozart and Beethoven were not only proficient at the keyboard, they played string instruments, could sing and improvise, could lead an ensemble, were highly knowledgeable of the music that came before them, kept informed of the latest developments in music (and other subjects) and of course, composed their own beautiful music. Today's concert pianist, for the most part, is content to perform that subset of 'established' repertoire and it's rare indeed to see any original composing activity, and even rarer for it to have substantial merit.

Besides his amazingly insightful and virtuosic piano playing, Liszt composed innovative piano pieces, concertos, songs, transcriptions and arrangements of popular music (especially opera) and original orchestral works. He also conducted orchestras, including premier productions of some now famous operas, especially those by Wagner. Plus he was capable of astonishing management and administrative activity in support of musical culture (The Bonn Beethoven Monument, charity concerts for victims of the Danube floods – this list is lengthy) as well as teaching and writing.

Liszt would be immensely gratified to find musicians, on the whole, giving a great deal more attention to general culture. Liszt was a broad-gauged man ...he was cultured; and by culture he did not mean a few accomplishments, but, rather the serious study of the important problems of life and art.
MORIZ ROSENTHAL

Why are there precious few such individuals anymore? The standard excuse is that narrow specialization is a response to the

227

increasing complexity of life. Right; they'll be saying the same thing in another twenty years when things get even more 'narrow'. Paleontologists blame evolutionary specialization for the extinction of a bunch of powerful creatures – the dinosaurs. Artists: please, let's not go the way of the dodo.

Soulfully expressive musically fine style cannot be merely taught, it is rather the result of many causes. Intellectual power of comprehension, receptivity, depth of character, and general aesthetic culture in the player are needed for it.
LOUIS PLAIDY

Diverse, multi-faceted engagement in life builds confidence. Back in high school football there were days when I just hated those grueling two-a-day summer practices, and didn't at all get it when our coach laughingly called it 'character-building'. But boy were those Friday night games fun, and looking back, I'm glad I persevered and didn't quit.

The more comprehensive and inclusive our individual experience of life, the more we appreciate our universal human condition and the challenges facing our global community. Our modern over-specialized society is losing the ability to grasp the big picture and think beyond individual concerns. Maybe that's one reason why a pianist today can perform works of past great masters, and yet bore his audience to tears.

Art is all-embracing and all aspects of life are intimately bound up in it.
FRIEDRICH WIECK

You cannot set art off in a corner and hope for it to have vitality, reality, and substance.
CHARLES IVES

The sum of your life experience, education, and spiritual and philosophical values and outlook will shape your belief paradigms and not only determine how you act, but what you can imagine. And what you can imagine determines what you can ultimately accomplish in life.

Great composers and pianists were fully engaged in life. Over time they amassed an amazingly comprehensive self-directed education and were rich in significant personal relationships, with profound interest and involvement in the deeper issues of life; liberal in the sense of being open-minded and questioning; and conservative in the sense of respecting and valuing great ideas and accomplishments of the past (something quite different from two current groups of clowns parading as politicians).

Diverse growth experiences are a big part of the formula for taking your art to a higher level. Sports, (quality) reading, the Arts, games, entertainment, socializing, travel, pets, volunteering, mentoring, you name it - these things will unquestionably make you a deeper artist, a more successful businessman or woman, a better parent, or just a better human being.

Intellectually, pianists of the first class represent a very remarkable kind of mentality. Speaking in foreign languages, they find little difficulty in expressing themselves with rapidity and fluency. These pianists are wonderfully well-read, many being acquainted with the literature of three or more languages in the original. They are familiar with art, science, politics, and manufacturing, even in its most recent developments.
JAMES FRANCIS COOKE

You don't have to become an expert in everything, but some sincere interest in, and general understanding of, a variety of subjects will help make you an expert in one main thing – yourself.

Being well-rounded also makes you more flexible, adaptable, and more interesting to greater numbers of persons, and affords greater opportunities to be friends with and also help those people.

I love the study of nature as well as art. No one can study too much, but let us have the heart of everything, not only the formal side.
PERCY GRAINGER

Without travel, at least for those who cultivate learning and the arts, man is but a poor creature. A man of mediocre talent remains a mediocrity whether he travels or not, but one of superior talents will do no good if he is forever tied to one place.
MOZART

Acquaint yourself with the lives and portraits of the great composers. Your

interest will intensify as you seem to meet them in their works.
ERNST PAUER

It is well to make ourselves familiar with the best that has preceded us, both in performance and composition. The master pianists Anton Rubinstein and Liszt were both marvelously broad in the scope of their knowledge. They knew the literature of the piano in all its branches. They made themselves familiar with every possible phase of musical advancement. This is the reason for their gigantic prominence. Their greatness was not the hollow shell of acquired technique. Oh, for more students in these days with the genuine thirst for real musical knowledge, and not just a desire to make a superficial exhibition at the keyboard.
RACHMANINOFF

I've read a good deal, but even better is observation and experience. I've lived in different countries and studied the people, and that is the best education, after all.
EDOUARD ZELDEN

One should have a good all-round education. When young people come to me for instruction, I ask what they are doing in school. If they have left school in order to devote their whole time to the piano, I say, 'Go back to school, and come to me later, when you have finished your school course.'
BERTHA FIERING TAPPER

See to it that you don't starve your mind and your heart in the effort to acquire fleet, strong fingers and light, powerful wrists.
ALBERTO JONÁS

Those aspiring to become concert pianists should have the broadest possible culture, must live in the world of arts and letters. The wider their range of information, experience, and sympathies, the larger will be the audience they will reach from the concert platform. He who has seen and known the world and has become acquainted with the great masterpieces of art and the wonderful achievements of science has little difficulty in securing an audience providing he has mastered the means of expressing his ideas.
EMIL SAUER

Leo Ornstein is an omnivorous reader, declaring that he is "thoroughly unhappy" unless he gets a certain amount of real reading done in the course of every twenty-four hours—modern literature, modern history, political economy in its latest phases—for Ornstein is not only a modernist in music!
FREDERICK MARTENS

With an excellent technique, fine touch, an artistic temperament, and a broad musical and general education, the aspirant may be said to be equipped to enter the virtuoso field.
OSSIP GABRILOWITSCH

Study the public. Find what pleases it, but never lower the standards of your art. Read the best literature, study pictures, travel, broaden your mind and acquire general culture.
FANNY BLOOMFIELD-ZEISLER

Artists should also know how to cook, and if they are women should know how to make a dress; seasoning of food is an art, and in dress making there is form, composition, embellishment, and color to be studied.
LESCHETIZKY

Here's a fun anecdote about Beethoven throwing a dinner party: the guests find Beethoven busy at the hearth, wearing a short evening jacket, a 'stately nightcap on his bristly shock of hair', and a blue kitchen apron.

After waiting patiently for an hour and a half, dinner was served. The soup recalled those charitable leavings distributed to beggars in taverns, the beef was but half done, and calculated to gratify only an ostrich; the vegetables floated in a mixture of water and grease; and the roast seemed to have been smoked in the chimney.
Nevertheless, our host did full justice to every dish, and, anticipating applause, humorously compared himself to the chef in a then popular play, and tried to animate the guests by extravagant praise of the remaining dainties. They, however, found it barely possible to choke down a few morsels, and stuck to the bread, fruit, and wine. Soon after this memorable banquet, Beethoven fortunately grew weary of ruling the kitchen and returned to his writing desk, which he now thankfully would rarely leave in order to procure

indigestion from his own cuisine.
IGNAZ von SEYFRIED

It's remarkable that so few people are able to play waltz time, they swallow the third quarter note as unimportant, whereas the three quarter notes have equal value. Also few are able to dance a waltz well. I've danced few waltzes in my life but I'm able to do it. Yes, to hear a Strauss waltz, for example, played well is among the greatest rarities.
LISZT

Concentration should not be on music alone; to better understand music the artist must embrace the total universe.
CLAUDIO ARRAU

To play the piano one must understand composition, be a singer, and an accompanist all together.
LESCHETIZKY

As far as possible, we should become acquainted with the works of all the great composers and not by any means tie ourselves down to any favorite author.
CZERNY

In certain professions it is well to be a specialist, but not in music, for music is not so vast a science as some others. The pianist who is a specialist gets less out of music than the one who's interested in all good composers. A player may play one composer best, but that's no reason to specialize. The man whose mind is big enough to understand one composer can understand others.
JOSEF HOFMANN

We play as we think. The mind must be continually improved or the fingers will grow dull. In order to see the beauties in music, we must see the beauties in other studies. Music students ought to read a great deal. It makes them think and gives them poetical thoughts. I like Shakespeare, Goethe, Schiller, Cervantes and others…my favorite book is The Three Musketeers. Music is, after all, only another kind of poetry, and if we get poetical ideas from books, we become more poetical, and our music becomes more beautiful. Piano playing is much more than hammering down keys, one has to tell people

things with music that cannot be told with words.
PEPITO ARRIOLA (age 12)

There are a few among us who may be considered the last radiations, faint memories of the grand old school. A fresh sprout of the former many-sidedness is quite conceivable.
ARTUR SCHNABEL

Diverse life experience always broadens and enriches musical interpretation, and even mechanical ability - even when not physically practicing the piano!

Now, let's outline an integrated mental/physical paradigm for achieving your dream using piano playing as an example. If you don't play the piano, you may soon want to take it up. In any case, use your imagination to see the relevance to your own activities. Coming up is a tried and true approach to getting results; tried because a bunch of highly successful people habitually implemented it, and true because it works.

Some will say that revealing these secrets of my studies goes against my own best interests, but I unreservedly renounce them forever if they are useful to others.
FRANÇOIS COUPERIN L'art de Toucher Le Clavecin

Chapter 8

......

BEST PRACTICE

*One cannot improve technique until he is
clear about its essence.*
—FRIEDRICH A. STEINHAUSEN

*A few good principles are sufficient to solve
all problems.*
—C.P.E. BACH

Best practice is a procedural approach demonstrated to achieve results. Sounds reasonable enough, but procedures in a manual don't get results - you do. And these days the world is so dynamic that repeatedly applying one fixed methodology inevitably results in you and what you're doing becoming obsolete, often rather quickly. Is anyone still around faithfully implementing a 'best practice' for manufacturing those buggy-whips?

Let's take a closer look at this business buzzword that a number of organizations apparently aren't even using very much, if at all. For a business, the goal is usually to design, create, and successfully market superior products and services, and hopefully not just spend a lot of time in meetings talking about it. At least I think that's the basic goal, although in reality it seems to be more like: 'always make the numbers'. Important, yes; but infatuation with those 'numbers' alone undoubtedly plays a role in a very depressing business statistic: about 50% of all new business ventures disappear within the first five years - as in out-of-business. Your chances are much better with a truly worthy vision that ethically fulfills legitimate needs, paired with sound engineering and management principles. If you've got that the numbers will take care of themselves.

A few obvious points to keep in mind about a best practice: (1) it needs to be based in reality, not wishful thinking; (2) it must actually be read, understood, and followed by everybody at all levels, and here's the tough part – especially management; and (3) there must be measurable objectives and periodic auditing; in other words, regularly asking and following up on the question: *is this working*? If your best-practice is to consistently result in superior performance it must include benchmarks for self-assessment because you've simply got to pay attention to what you're doing to check if it works or not.

Unnecessary complexity should be avoided. Things should always go smoothly.

It should flow like oil.
MOZART

Take Josef Hofmann as a model - you can. It should flow like oil.
LESCHETIZKY

Ideally, a best practice could be conceptualized in an algorithm, programmed in software, and implemented by a robot that would mechanically execute with precision, *ad infinitum*. That's fine for machines and discrete tasks that don't evolve significantly over time; but with human beings you can't expect one comprehensive blueprint for every detail of everybody's life. You are responsible for creating and dynamically modifying and fine-tuning your very own unique best practice, one day at a time.

That's why best practice must be a wholistic strategy. It doesn't get any more all-inclusive than self-actualization over the course of a lifetime. Start with a clear vision and purpose and get on a mission to manifest it. You'll need optimal physical and mental health to provide energy, strength, and confidence to realize your intentions through persistent application. No corporate best practice is going to work if the employees are perpetually calling in sick. And you've got to be able to work with people, even if your ambition is to be a hermit. Plenty of people still sought advice from St. Simeon the

Stylite, even though he lived on top of a marble column in the Syrian wilderness.

The best practice must be framed in a context of a logical strategy with planned, practical, executable and effective tactics; plus tangible metrics and cycles of analysis and refinement.

System in daily work is perhaps the most essential thing I practice. You must have some comprehensive design, chart, or plan for your development. It should embrace as many things as you can do superlatively well, and no more.
PADEREWSKI

Earlier we heard Josef Hofmann say *'systemization is the death of spontaneity'*. That was in the context of musical interpretation and live performance. As far as work and practice methods go, systemization is essential.

Regularity, system, and precision are excellent general qualities reckoned among the principle conditions that ensure a useful practice, and guarantee a successful performance.
ERNST PAUER

Some of my father's old-fashioned maxims bear helpfully on piano study, as well as on many other things in life. Here is one: "Whatever you do - if it's nothing but throwing straws against the wind - have a system." Another: "Let your head save your heels!" Another: "Let your last effort be better than the one that preceded it."
EDWARD MORRIS BOWMAN

Your best practice must be intelligently implemented with discipline and enthusiasm.

We must be prompted by enthusiasm ('with the gods'). Imagination, hard work, yes, they are the fuel, but enthusiasm is the spark which makes the whole leap into flame.
TOBIAS MATTHAY

Nothing can be accomplished in art without enthusiasm.
ROBERT SCHUMANN

Personal growth always ensues with any progress and the scope of individual imagination or vision also broadens. You previously 'just' saw yourself hiking up a Colorado 14'er but having accomplished that you now find yourself eyeing Everest or its artistic counterpart Parnassus.

Go as far as you can and when you arrive you'll be able to see farther.
THOMAS CARLYLE

Your original goal and strategic plan, along with all its implementation details will have to be periodically revisited and revised, subject to the continuous feedback loop with which you monitor your progress and self-development.

Advice from mentors, friends, and critics may have value; but if you're going to 'succeed' you'll need to be self-reliant, discriminating, discerning, flexible and open-minded, and have the highest possible standards for yourself. And before you can innovate you must master the basics. Yes, it would have been better to plant that tree years ago but if you haven't done it yet, the best time is right now.

Many futile methods have been tried to teach playing the piano. They are analogous to teaching someone to walk on their hands in order that they may go for a stroll. As a result, people have forgotten how to walk properly and are unable to play music in the real sense. The difficulties (theoretical and 'acrobatic') they practice have nothing to do with the works of the great masters. I go straight to the root of the matter.
CHOPIN

First of all, what's lacking is the right foundation on which something secure can be constructed... How can one begin without a foundation stone upon which to lay something better? How build a roof when the pillars do not rest on solid ground? ... Without step by step development and continuity; without plan, reflection, thought, and speculation; without method, nothing works.
FRIEDRICH WIECK

One must first acquire a firm background of technical principles by which difficulties can be solved in the most logical and profitable manner.
MARK HAMBOURG

To master the technical side of the art of piano playing, cultivate a positive technique grounded in proven principles, and begin your study with the exactness and seriousness one would adopt in taking up any other art or science.
HARRIETTE BROWER

If you absorb just one thing from the brief discussion of F.M. Alexander, let it be this: the means always determine the end. How you go about something absolutely determines your end result, desired or not.

We'll now outline a practice paradigm that permits optimal results. Note the word permits - in order to actually get optimal results, you must do the getting. We'll use the art of playing the piano as an example.

No two students are exactly alike, nor do any two see things in precisely the same light. This is really a psychological matter...I recommend William James' Talks on Psychology – a very helpful book.
SIGISMOND STOWJOWSKI

From day one, you're personally invested in the outcome because you are the sole proprietor and CEO of the business that is your life. That requires significant input (from you) including real work and personal accountability, but also plenty of mature reflection and analysis ... soul-searching, if you will. Your motivation, method, self-confidence, health, and natural talent affect the results. But ultimately your vision, love, enthusiasm, tenacity and perseverance effect the final outcome. Start believing in something that you previously thought impossible for yourself. Once you've done it, the only thing you won't believe is that you didn't just simply do it years ago.

For the longest time, the four-minute mile symbolized the impossible. Maintaining an average speed of about 15 miles per hour for 1,760 yards was deemed total nonsense. Well, in 1954, the Englishman Roger Bannister ran a mile in 3:59.4 minutes. Then, of course, within weeks it seemed like everyone was doing it; eventually several high school students accomplished the feat.

But do we remember the names of those hundred or so men who have done it since? Bannister is remembered not so much for running a mile under four minutes but for a major paradigm shift. The current world record of 3:43.13 minutes was set by Hicham El Guerrouj; hey man, you rock! No woman has yet run a four minute mile and I guess some people (mostly men) will maintain it's impossible. Ladies, I say: go for it.

Major accomplishments require belief, motivation, focus, and work. Vladimir de Pachmann relates how his teacher assigned him the first prelude and fugue from J. S. Bach's Well-Tempered Clavier …

He didn't know that I had mastered the art of concentration so that I could obliterate every suggestion of any other thought from my mind except that upon which I was working. He underestimated my youthful zeal and intensity. I couldn't be satisfied unless I spent the entire day working with all my artistic might and main. I couldn't stop when I had memorized the first fugue, so I went to the next … and the next … and next.

At the next lesson, de Pachmann placed the book unopened on top of the piano and with all the cockiness of youth asked his teacher to name a prelude and fugue to be played.

After I had finished playing he was dumbfounded. An actor learns page after page in a few days, why should the musician go stumbling along for months endeavoring to learn something which he could master in a few hours with the proper interest and the burning concentration without which all music study is a farce?
VLADIMIR de PACHMANN

One way of defining 'focus' is the removal of distractions, so you can attend to the most important detail. Meditation and yoga are ancient 'technologies' to help you do exactly that. When you practice meditation, you are in essence removing tedious and worrisome mental distractions and instead cultivating a tranquil state of mind empowering the positive. Focusing on a single *asana* or pose can literally make it happen, no matter how challenging it may at first 'seem'.

Pruckner asserted that to play a scale wrong once through absent-mindedness was to undo all the previous good of playing of it correctly.
MARK HAMBOURG

Positive Piano

What is talent without serious, earnest study leading to artistic and technical perfection?
PADEREWSKI

We take things apart to find out how they are made. We put them back together to indicate our mastery of knowledge. The measure of musicianship is the ability to do (not just analyze).
KATHARINE GOODSON

It's no secret; the ability 'to do' requires working at it. Even that white-haired old man in the Bible had to work at things – apparently it took him a whole week to create the universe, and then Man.

What a piece of work is a man!
SHAKESPEARE

Remember, all the talk in that whole big universe isn't going to add up to much without work. And …

Nobody else can do your work for you.
ALBERTO JONÁS

So far I've accumulated some eighty printed sheets of my thoughts, not including all my other editorial work, and also poured my heart's blood into completing ten major compositions in two years. I spend several hours a day studying Bach and Beethoven and much of my own music, and have dealt promptly with an extensive correspondence that was often difficult and detailed. I'm a young man of twenty-eight, a quick blooded artist who in spite of this has not set foot outside Saxony for the last eight years, sitting here quietly, careful with my money and spending nothing on drink or horses, quietly minding my own business.
ROBERT SCHUMANN

Under the inspiration of Liszt's playing everybody worked "tooth and nail" to achieve the impossible. A smile of approbation from him was all we cared for. That's how he turned out such a grand school of piano-playing.
AMY FAY

The child becomes a person through work.
MARIA MONTESSORI

If one would learn a thing, it has to be thoroughly mastered by repeating it again and again.
SUZUKI

Discipline, work. Work, discipline.
GUSTAV MAHLER

The master pianist has often climbed to his place over Matterhorns and Mont Blancs of industry. Years of study and practice are part of the biography of almost everyone who has attained real greatness. What a pity to destroy old-time illusions of artist heroes dreaming their lives away in the hectic cafés of Pesth or buried in the melancholy, absinthe, and paresis of a morbid cabaret in Paris. In some quiet country villa, miles away from the unlicensed Bacchanalian revels, the virtuoso may be found working hard upon next season's repertoire. After all, the greatest thing in the artist's life is work.
JAMES FRANCIS COOKE

Inspiration does not come without hard work… There's no short cut to glory. No great work of art has ever come into the world save as the fruit of years of earnest, unremitting endeavor on the part of its creator; and no great artist ever blasphemed his ancestors.
FREDERICK DELIUS

The fault with many students is the very erroneous idea that genius or talent will take the place of study and work.
LEOPOLD GODOWSKY

Technique rightly studied and applied is the basis for achievement by geniuses as well as those of ordinary ability. And without work, it is needless to say, nothing is done.
WILLIAM MASON

Masters can put you on the road, but they can't make you go. You must do that for yourself. … If you want to do a thing, you've got to keep doing it. You mustn't stop - certainly not! Eventually one must succeed.
AMY FAY

Positive Piano

No-one could possibly believe more in self-help than I. One who imagines that a teacher will cast some magic spell to make him a musician without working has an unpleasant surprise in store for him.
VLADIMIR de PACHMANN

"Idleness is the mother of all vices" is the simple proverb to serve you. It leads straight to the corollary maxim, which I recommend you ponder and practice: "Work is the father of all virtues". By virtues we mean strength, superiority, nobility, greatness.
LISZT

"I have no ability" – what sadness and despair are occasioned by this nonsensical belief which is really only an excuse for avoiding work.
SUZUKI

If God can work through me, he can work through anyone.
ST FRANCIS of ASSISI

Liszt was devoted to St. Francis and everything he represents. Remember those epigraphs about belief in the front matter of this book? Bach, Busoni, and Rosenthal are basically advocating a major shakeup of your personal possibility paradigm, stimulating you to think outside the coffin and set your sights much higher (not six feet under). St. Francis lived and breathed the belief paradigm about five hundred years earlier and Liszt was very much aware of his teachings.

Start by doing what's necessary, then what's possible, and suddenly you're doing the impossible.
ST. FRANCIS of ASSISI

The concept of work-ethic is ancient, a perpetual theme among wise men and women.

Pray as though everything depended on God. Work as though everything depended on you.
ST AUGUSTINE

Pleasure in the job puts perfection in the work.
ARISTOTLE

242

Life grants nothing to us mortals without hard work.
HORACE

When nature has work to be done, she creates a genius to do it.
RALPH WALDO EMERSON

If you have built castles in the air, your work need not be lost; that is where they should be. Now put the foundations under them.
HENRY DAVID THOREAU

The best preparation for tomorrow is to do today's work superbly well.
WILLIAM OSLER

A person who has not done half his day's work by ten o'clock runs a chance of leaving the other half undone.
EMILY BRONTË

Work is not man's punishment; it is his reward, strength and pleasure.
GEORGE SAND

Our work is the presentation of our capabilities.
EDWARD GIBBON

Every man's work, whether it be literature, music, painting, architecture, or anything else, is always a portrait of himself.
SAMUEL BUTLER

The artist is nothing without the gift, but the gift is nothing without work.
EMILE ZOLA

The average American worker has fifty interruptions a day, of which seventy percent have nothing to do with work.
W. EDWARDS DEMING

Keep up the good work!

But we must work smart and go about things the 'right' way. And it's critical to first step back and seriously think about what we're trying to accomplish, and how.

Positive Piano

Eliminate all that is not essential, and find what is best and most needed for your advancement.
CECIL CHAMINADE

Best practice should be simple, straightforward, and smart. Everyone knows that animals are smarter than most people, so I thought of them first. I love dogs, I mean I really love dogs; and when thinking of 'best-practice' I'm reminded of some basic similarities to their world.
Come - Sit - Stay - Good - Down - Treat
The action-word *come* is a way of saying 'show up', get started, and actually perform a constructive act rather than just talking about it.

I dread beginning works of such magnitude, but once I have begun, then all goes well.
BEETHOVEN

After you've identified something you'd like to do in life, the first step is obviously ... to take that first step.
Sit is my metaphor for naturally effective use of a healthy mind/body, along with all the relevant lifestyle attributes it implies. Here's a thought by way of example: if, due to a lifetime of mental and physical un-natural 'misuse' of your body; and, if you harbor psychologically repressed trauma in the form of physically manifested blockages - your mind/body will not even be able to 'sit' down on the piano bench 'naturally', and that legacy of misuse and subconscious internalized trauma will hold you back. It may even make it impossible for you to ever achieve your dream in life, or even have a dream in the first place.
But knowledge is power; you can do this if you are determined. *Stay* requires discipline and perseverance; you're going to have to hang in there for the duration.
Good is a kind of reward, but also represents positive feedback. *Good* is achieved by monitoring progress, by checking if things are going according to plan, that is, if the 'practice' methodology is being implemented correctly and the results are satisfactory. For pianists, listening is essential to know when adjustments and refinements are required to make it good. Everybody else: just 'pay attention' to what

244

you're doing; it's really what listening is all about.

Down symbolizes full involvement, at the deepest levels, both physically and mentally. For pianists it includes the concept of weight playing; natural, relaxed, full use of the body's mass of muscle, bone, and tendon in a state of mental/physical relaxation, yet energized and ready for action. Details to follow.

Come - Sit - Stay and *Down* are commands. We may give orders to the dog but when it comes to playing the piano you're responsible for choosing to make each individual step happen, from imagined goal and selection of appropriate means to planning, focusing and executing; often repeatedly, to obtain the desired results. That requires discipline, or rather, self-discipline.

Speaking of commands, *mits'vah*, the Hebrew word for 'commandment' (as in the Big Ten) is more subtly translated as a type of signpost or way, pointing in a direction … you must choose whether or not to go.

Treat is the real reward for achievement. Aside from any material reward that comes your way, you'll find that a job well done is one of the most satisfying things in life.

Music is its own reward.
CLAUDE DEBUSSY

So come; let's explore the process in more detail. We shall begin at the beginning, and we will do it well from the start.

Never begin a new thing badly.
LESCHETIZKY

With piano playing, the first step is easy.

Before you touch the piano, let me suggest one prosaic little hint: wash the keyboard as clean as you did your hands.
JOSEF HOFMANN

Clean hands and tools are both practical and symbolic. 'Clean' becomes symbolic of your performance in general. Unfocused practice can easily become 'littered' with mistakes – bad notes, inconsistent rhythms, and weak (or neglected) dynamics.

Positive Piano

The average student pays no attention to the difference between a piano and a pianissimo, to making sharp distinctions between fortes, fortissimos and mezzo-fortes, and above all he ignores the value of the crescendo and diminuendo.

LEOPOLD AUER

Keep it literally clean, and it will enhance your awareness and power of concentration. Liszt often used similar terminology:

Don't wash your dirty linen in public.

LISZT

Make a habit of maintaining a clean, orderly, and aesthetically appealing work environment. Clear the clutter and dust from the piano. How well-organized you are physically (and mentally) is going to significantly influence how efficiently you practice.

Debussy's studio struck me by its remarkable neatness ... not a piece of paper or music to be seen anywhere, a piano covered by a silk cloth, a large and elegant desk, bookshelves containing, among other things, several volumes of Kipling.

CYRIL SCOTT

Debussy's study, the 'sacred room of the house' was typical of its master. It was not large and cluttered, as associated with busy composers, but everything was carefully selected and refined. There was a small upright piano, in between the high well-lit windows was a desk on which were several carved wooden animals and a bowl of beautiful goldfish. The colors of the room were subdued, the furnishings practical. Only a few precious prints and watercolors adorned the walls.

E. ROBERT SCHMITZ

Pianist and author Harriette Brower (1869-1928) interviewed dozens of famous 19th century concert pianists, usually in their private homes.

As a man's surroundings and environment are often reflections of his character, it's always a matter of deep interest to get in touch with the surroundings of the creative or executive musician.

HARRIETTE BROWER

246

Successful concert pianists back then were invariably neat and well-organized. Their homes and studios were described as artistic, elegant, and charming; characterized by tasteful design, antiques, paintings, tapestries, and beautiful views.

I am now in a beautiful room appointed in quiet elegance, costly but in exquisite taste, and where absolute peace and quiet reign. The wide windows open upon a lovely green garden, which adds the final touch of restful repose to the whole picture. (Home of Harold Bauer, Paris)

The music room is lighted at one end by a great arched window so placed that the trees in the garden are seen through its panes. All the appointments of this room, and indeed the whole house, every article of furniture and each touch of color betoken the artistic sense of what is appropriate. Miss Goodson has a keen and exquisite sense for harmony in colors as well as for color in the harmonies she brings from her instrument. (Home of Katharine Goodson, London)

Liszt had some pretty amazing digs, from the Altenberg Villa he shared with Princess Carolyne zu Sayn-Wittgenstein in Weimar to his flat in the Villa d'Este in Tivoli overlooking the cypresses and water fountains, or his monastic cell in Rome with a view of the Forum.

What does your home environment say about you? Is it aesthetically pleasing, stimulating, functional, efficient, neat, and conducive to work? Feng-shui works both ways. Your personal, individual environment reflects your inner psychological state of mind and it also affects that state. You can actually clean up your act by cleaning and clearing your space. Getting organized, clearing clutter, and tastefully decorating can help improve your productivity. Where's the scientific proof, you ask? … start experimenting.

Many respected 19th century artists and educators maintained that environmental quality is critical to learning and creativity.

The environment must be rich in motives which lend interest to activity and invite the child to conduct his own experiences.
MARIA MONTESSORI

Nurturing environmental conditions produce superior abilities. What does

not exist in the environment will not develop in the child.
SUZUKI

A well-ordered and peaceful house is essential for a profitable and successful day – the contrary, most infuriating.
LESCHETIZKY

In Leschetizky's music room were two large pianos side by side. They were covered with piles of music kept in perfect order according to a system of his own, whereby he could instantly find any composition he wanted.
ETHEL NEWCOMB

Besides organization and relative tidiness, additional factors to consider are privacy (or peace and quiet), lighting, and various other ergonomic issues like chairs (but more importantly how you sit in them). Hopefully in the earlier discussion of the work of F.M. Alexander you gained a heightened awareness that natural use of the self (body and mind) is more important than chic office furniture.

Practice in itself may become a source of nervousness if proper conditions are not met. Practice in privacy; avoid petty disturbances such as people passing in and out of the room. Have a comfortable chair while practicing. See to it that the distribution of light in the practice room is right. The windows (and likewise the artificial light) should be behind or at the side of the performer, never in front of him. Eye strain may tire and lead to nervousness almost as quickly as in any other way.
ALBERTO JONÁS

Someone's bound to bring up a notable exception to this discussion, our loveable Beethoven, who happened to be a chronic 'messy'.

Picture to yourself the dirtiest, most disorderly place imaginable, blotches of moisture covered the ceiling, an oldish grand piano on which dust vied for space with various engraved music and manuscripts … a quantity of pens encrusted with ink, compared with the proverbial tavern pens would shine … cane-seated chairs covered with clothes and plates bearing the remains of last night's supper.
J.G. PROD'HOMME

A truly admirable confusion ruled Beethoven's household. Books and music were strewn about in every corner; here the fragments of a cold snack, there bottles still sealed, or half-emptied. On his desk was a hurried sketch of a new quartet; elsewhere were the débris of his breakfast. ... The floor was covered with letters, business and personal; between the windows stood a respectable loaf of Strachino; beside it the notable ruins of a Verona salami.
IGNAZ von SEYFRIED

That clutter and lack of organization often thwarted Beethoven in his daily tasks.

When something he wanted had to be hunted for hours, days, even weeks; and all endeavors to find it remained fruitless, he looked about for a victim to blame, wailing pitifully: "yes, yes, it's my misfortune, nothing is left where I put it, everything moved about, done to play me a trick." The servants understood the good-natured growler and let him growl to his heart's content; after a few minutes all was forgotten ... until the next, similar scene.
IGNAZ von SEYFRIED

You and I are not Beethoven; he's in a class by himself. If we don't have his talent, all the more reason to be as effective as possible in every other way. Get, and stay, as well-organized, clutter-free, and aesthetically aware as you can. I'd like to personally recommend to you a wonderful little book on the subject: *The Life-Changing Magic of Tidying Up* by Marie Kondo. I loved it; and since it's selling briskly, a number of others obviously did too.

What follows is a best practice outline for practicing the piano (from the perspective of a five-year old female black Labrador Retriever). I invite you to use your imagination to apply it to what you do as well. The real wisdom is in the quotes and I hope you enjoy them.

COME!

Carpe diem, but start fresh.

The value of the morning hour above any other time is not generally appreciated. The mental freshness gained from sleep is a tremendous help. Play away for an hour, or a half hour even, before breakfast.
JOSEF HOFMANN

Positive Piano

Piano should be studied when one is fresh, attentive, and eager; otherwise, success is unthinkable.
FRIEDRICH WIECK

Divide your hours for practicing: one and a half in the morning, the same in the afternoon, one hour in the evening.
ALEXANDER LAMBERT

It is well to begin the study period in the morning with a few technical exercises - enough to get the hands into good playing condition. Afterward, alternate technique and pieces, so that the mind remains fresh, which is not the case when one works constantly at one or the other.
LESCHETIZKY

Beethoven rose at daybreak, no matter what the season, and went at once to his table.
ANTON SCHINDLER

Take advantage of the morning, when you're rested. As you tire and lose focus, stop and take a break. Hold it - here's an even better idea.

A good rule is to stop practicing, not when tired, but before you get tired.
LILIAS MACKINNON

It's kind of like eating. Better to stop before you're completely 'full', to avoid overdoing it and becoming 'stuffed'. Meditation, reading, walking, or more vigorous exercise are all great ways to relax in between practice sessions.

One who works in short spells and who works well can do more than another who is 'always at it', and who does not give his mind the rest it requires.
LILIAS MACKINNON

Morning is definitely best, but it also helps greatly to mix it up once in a while.

One shouldn't become accustomed to practicing at a fixed time every day. Practicing at a certain hour becomes a fixed habit, and as a result hampers the performer, who should be able to play at any time. Practice at different

times in the day instead of at fixed ones, and then the muscles will always
be ready to act.
JOSEF HOFMANN

SIT!

After reading F.M. Alexander's books or taking some lessons in
his 'technique' you'll probably never again view the 'simple' act
of sitting in the same way. But beyond the practical experience of
proper mind/body use (which you unfortunately can't get from a
book alone) there are some simple practical considerations.

To be seated at the proper height, the underside of the elbows, the wrists, and
the fingers should be kept on one level.
FRANÇOIS COUPERIN

The seat should be just so high that the elbows, when hanging down freely,
are slightly less elevated than the upper surface of the keys. Always sit
exactly facing the middle of the keyboard, and at such a distance from it that
the tips of the elbows may be a little nearer to the keys than the shoulders.
The forearm (elbow to the fingers) should form a perfectly straight horizontal
line, for the hand must neither rise upwards, nor be bent so as to slope
downwards. The fingers are to be so bent that the tips of them, together
with that of the thumb, when extended outwards, may form one right line;
and so that the keys may always be struck with the soft and fleshy tips of
the fingers, and that neither the nails nor the flat surface of the fingers shall
touch the keys.
CZERNY

Sit easy and erect at the piano, like a good rider on his horse, and yield to
the arm movements, as far as needed, just as the horseman yields to the
movements of his steed.
LESCHETIZKY

Many eminent artists place too little stress on a graceful position at the
keyboard. ... Owing to the weaker leverage too low a seat will cause increased
exertion in performance, so that the player is forced to raise his shoulders in
an ungraceful fashion when trying to use any power.
MALWINE BRÉE

Positive Piano

For long practice periods, a cane-seat (or perforated wood) chair is best.
EDWARD M. BOWMAN

Air circulation? - I don't know, but I included that one out of curiosity.

Now, you probably think you're ready to just start blazing away with your pyrotechnics.

STAY!

Hold on; take it easy. Think things through, don't impetuously dive into that pool of immediate gratification head first; it may not hold water. *Stay!* by default inhibits action that may unknowingly be ineffective or even harmful. Conquering the masterpieces of piano literature will require time and technique, the right kind, and lots of it.

When you begin to learn a new and somewhat difficult piece, devote the first hours to slowly deciphering the notes strictly and correctly, fix upon the fingering to be employed, and gain a general insight over the whole. ... Then play the whole piece over quietly and composedly, attentively and without distraction, till able to execute it without trouble, and in the exact time indicated by the author. Single passages of great difficulty may be practiced apart. Still, they ought to be often repeated in connection with the rest of the piece.
CZERNY

Let's take a moment to explore the meaning of this word *technique*, so often used in reference to ability and excellence. Like any other word, it means different things to different people. Generally it's associated with mechanical ability, for example, playing rapid, accurate scales or arpeggios. But in a wholistic context, technique means much more.

People think technique is just the ability to play very rapidly, and perform very difficult passages upon the keyboard, moving the fingers and hands with special 'digital dexterity'. That's important and necessary, but only one small part of the whole immense subject; and the pianist who has given all his attention to that branch alone can certainly not be called in the

*best sense of the word a great technician, nor can he arrive at the highest
artistic results with only that.*
MARK HAMBOURG

In its broadest sense, technique encompasses all possible means at
your disposal to manifest the desired result imagined by the mind.
Heinrich Neuhaus (1888-1964) points out that the Greek root of the
word τεχυε means universal Art with a capital A, and implies a
complete integration of mechanics and aesthetics, intellect and spirit.
His book *The Art of Piano Playing* is a must read.

No-one should dare to be a poor musician in order to become a fine virtuoso.
ROBERT SCHUMANN

*I doubt if the truism 'technique is only a means to an end' should be accepted
without question, suggesting as it does the advisability of studying something
that is not music, and believed to at some future time to be capable of being
marvelously transformed into artistic expression. Properly understood,
technique is art, and must be studied as such. There should be no technique
in music which is not musical. ...The only technical study of any kind I've
ever done has been that technique with an immediate relation to the musical
message of the piece studied.*
HAROLD BAUER

*Never touch the piano without trying to make music. ... Play through a
passage for the express purpose of really knowing it better both physically
and mentally, from each bar to the piece as a whole. First, to grasp its
musical content and shape; and second, technically; meaning that each
rendition helps us to better realize what to do and avoid doing at the
keyboard. All this implies a constant process of minute analysis of what
should be, and actually is being done.
This requires a high degree of mental concentration. 'Genius' implies natural
capacity for concentration, and by learning concentration in our work we
can all approximate to the genius level. ...To concentration, add vividness of
imagination. Here indeed we have the most salient feature of genius and of
real talent – imagination, the ability keenly to visualize, or imagine things
in our mind's eye.*
TOBIAS MATTHAY

Liszt, speaking of one of his pupils, said: "What I like about him is that he's not a mere 'finger virtuoso': he doesn't worship the keyboard; it's not his patron saint, but simply the altar before which he pays homage to composer." A perfect technique is more than a wonderful power of prestidigitation or facility in the manipulation of an instrument. It implies qualities of mind and heart which are essential to an all-round musical development and the ability to give them adequate expression.
WILLIAM MASON

Technique is of little value in itself and is useful only as a means of expressing beauty.
LESCHETIZKY

The technical ability of the performer should be such that it can be applied immediately to all the artistic demands of the composition to be interpreted. ... the hands, and the mind, of the player must be trained to encompass the difficulties found in modern compositions.
RACHMANINOFF

I differentiate between the mechanics of piano study and the art of piano technique. To the former belong all forms of hand culture, finger training, and gymnastic exercises. To the latter all the finer qualities of touch, tone, fingering, phrasing, pedaling, agogics, and nuance - each an art in itself.
LEOPOLD GODOWSKY

What is technique but the means by which you can express yourself – the outward and material sign through which you're able to say what's in your heart: therefore it is subordinate, but it must be individual. Not to be belittled, one must have technique, it's a necessity; but it sinks into insignificance before the meaning of the message one has to deliver.
LEO ORNSTEIN

Attend to your technical apparatus so that you are prepared and armed for every possible event; then, when you study a new piece you can turn all your power to the intellectual content; you won't be held up by the technical problems.
FERRUCCIO BUSONI

Technical ability, after all is said and done, depends upon nothing more

than physiologically correct motion applied to the artistic needs of the
masterpiece to be performed.
MAX PAUER

How to acquire it? Technique, by definition, is highly personal
because it's intimately intertwined with your artistic conception.
For pianists it's literally hand-crafted and mind-crafted over time.
What's required for one person to express their vision may not
work for another, precisely because our minds and spirits are all
totally unique.

Technical systems are best when they are individual. Every hand, every arm,
every set of ten fingers, everybody, and what is of the greatest importance,
every intellect is different from every other. I consequently endeavored to
get down to the basic laws underlying the subject of technique and make a
system of my own.
FERRUCCIO BUSONI

Technique depends upon so many individual, personal things: the physique,
the mentality, the amount of nervous energy one has, the hand and wrist.
ERNEST SCHELLING

That's why best practice must come from within, tailored to your
individual nature and tweaked by your experience - not devised by
and recommended, much less imposed, by an external authority. We
educate ourselves, appropriate the best of others' experience, and
create our own highly individual methodology.

If you'd really like to do something in life but find you lack
some particular skill - that's telling you something. You may
have to spend extra time (and focus) on things that don't come
naturally to you.

The special study of areas of technique not natural to one must be insisted upon.
LESCHETIZKY

Recall that *Stay!* represents discipline in general. Especially in the
early stages, working up specialized technique to eventually serve
you at the highest levels of mastery may not seem easy. Look at it as
transforming your weaknesses into strengths. Hang in there.

I don't like technique, but it is like money. You may despise it, but you must have it.
MORIZ ROSENTHAL

The need for technique must not be underestimated; it demands patient, painstaking, persistent study. Art without technique is invertebrate, shapeless, characterless.
PADEREWSKI

I find piano practicing a great effort, yet dare not ignore it. It's like an animal whose heads are continually growing again, however many one cuts off.
FERRUCCIO BUSONI

Everyone knows that technique is only a means to an end; but without this means, one does not reach the end.
JOSEF LHÉVINNE

Understanding that mechanical technique is incidental to interpretation does not mean that you can skip it.

"He makes up in expression what he lacks in execution" is sheer nonsense; an excuse; a hackneyed plea for indulgence. Insufficient command of execution means halting, stilted, and ineffective expression. The perfect rendering of all the emotions inspired by the music can only be obtained through unlimited control of technique implying absolute mastery of manual dexterity. The more physical capacity the artist possesses for clothing his thoughts, the less hampered will he be in giving expression to the best that is in him. ...This can only be gained in years of hard work, which should precede any serious attempt at performance.
MARK HAMBOURG

Without technical control gained through thorough study and training, emotion is apt to be only a hindrance, a distortion of good taste and good sense. But added to the proper training, it is the fine flower of an artistic performance. It wins the heart, it subdues and softens, it conquers the world.
HARRIETTE BROWER

It's a mistake to suppose that the knowledge that Schubert was inspired by a certain poem, or Chopin was inspired by a certain legend, could ever make

256

up for a lack of the real essentials leading to good piano playing. Composer inspiration is interesting to a point, but one must understand the main points of musical relationship in a composition; what gives the work unity, cohesion, force, or grace, and how to bring out these elements.
RACHMANINOFF

Of course, it's frustrating to have a great musical concept in your head and not be able to reproduce it at the piano. But hang on to that concept; it's like gold for goldbugs because it's the underlying driving force for your eventual action. The greater the artistic concept, the more it will want 'out'. With patient work, we can develop the means to express it. Since creating Art is identical to expressing your evolving self, development of technique only ends when you end.

Some years ago I felt that technical development must cease at a certain age. This is all idiocy. I feel that I now have many times the technique I ever had before and I've acquired it all in recent years.
VLADIMIR de PACHMANN

The piano has evolved over the course of 300 years into an amazingly expressive instrument. But teaching piano-playing to beginners still revolves around a lecture about fingers and finger exercises. That lecture should instead be about the Mind; about imagination and the brain and how to use it.

Teachers lay great stress upon formation of good hand position, why not develop early on the habit of noting the phrases. Why not a little mind formation? It's a great deal nearer the real musical aim than the mere digital work. ... What a splendid thing it would be if little children at their first lessons were taught the desirability of observing melodic phrases.
KATHARINE GOODSON

All unmusical playing is insufferable. No amount of technical study will make a musician, and all technical study which only aims to make the fingers go faster or play complicated rhythms is wasted unless there is the foundation and culture of the real musician behind it. ... The technique which takes time is the technique of the brain, which directs the fingers to the right place at the right time.
FRANZ XAVER SCHWARENKA

257

Positive Piano

All the muscle will not do what nervous force will, and that comes from the mind. Muscle may be a help, and I dare say it is; but it will never equal the force of the mind that gives impulse in playing.
EDOUARD ZELDEN

When you want to strike a key on the piano, your mind telegraphs along a nerve to the muscle; the muscle pulls on the right tendon, and the finger that is under the control of that tendon strikes the key as directed. This, my boy, is a very simple description of a very wonderful act.
EDWARD M. BOWMAN

The best way to avoid mistakes is to think. While at the piano, think of nothing but what you are playing, however sure you may be of it. Thought is like reins for the fingers, to keep them on the right road.
MALWINE BRÉE

Much industry, patience and energy are necessary to attain results worthy of the beautiful art of music. Nor is it less essential that the student endeavor to cultivate in himself the utmost purity of taste, and a fine musical ear, and strive, by every possible means, to fan the flame of artistic enthusiasm in his soul. Meanwhile the mutual "discipline of brain and hands" must go steadily on, till the whole playing apparatus, from shoulder to finger tips, is used harmoniously and with reflection.
ELISABETH CALAND

The sum learned in the first year of life is enormous. The contrast between the beginning and end of this first learning period lies in the development of the brain and not the muscles. The infant already had fingers at birth and would have been able to grasp with them had the brain only known what grasping was. In the final analysis, the seat of motion is the brain.

Practice is predominantly intellectual labor, a process of the mind. Memory is stored experience obtained through the body itself. It can be so faithful that it appears mechanical, and to the casual observer lacking in spiritual content. A fatal mistake – for growth derives from planned and purposeful procedure.
FRIEDRICH A. STEINHAUSEN

The mere mechanical practice of instrumentalists is worse than a waste of

258

time because it prevents concentration.
LILIAS MACKINNON

Ear training and tone study are combined with mental training - in fact, it is all mental training.
HARRIETTE BROWER

A curiously false view of the nature of piano practice as gymnastics has developed over the course of time...What the main misconceptions have in common is that they are limited to the mere mechanical apparatus and ignore the higher psychic elements. i.e. they emphasize the muscular, try to make it flexible, isolate individual parts and make them independent, and equalize the differences in the five fingers ....The object of this mistaken practice has less do with cognition, refinement, gradation, and coordination than with so-called brute-strength. The poor misguided beginner proceeds to work at the expense of health.
FRIEDRICH A. STEINHAUSEN

Earlier we discussed the importance of doing some planning. Well, now's the time to plan at finer levels of granularity. In the ideal practice session, every single repetition at the keyboard should be planned, and have its own miniature goal.

For every repetition give yourself a reason. A reason will arouse your interest and interest is the secret of concentration. Don't allow yourself to repeat a passage even once without deciding beforehand the end in view. Say to yourself, 'what do I want to do with this passage? What does it mean musically? What shall I do with it technically?' If you cannot get the effect you wish, seek the cause for the failure before you try again.... Form the habit of taking one thing at a time, and doing it thoroughly, whatever it might be. Pianists may play a passage once to improve phrasing; again, trying to improve the quality of the bass; yet again, perfecting the pedaling.
LILIAS MACKINNON

Each practice session should be a highly structured event, with time resources carefully mapped out and allocated to discrete goal-oriented tasks. It doesn't mean anything to just say "I practiced for an hour."

Positive Piano

I hate being told 'I worked eight hours today' when half that time would suffice. Nor do I care to have much ground covered. I prefer two pages played with finish to the longest piece.
LESCHETIZKY

Better a little which is well done, than a great deal imperfectly.
PLATO

Everything does credit to the player which is well played.
CZERNY

Much more useful and productive is something like this, for example: "I will practice measures 18 to 22, first slowly, hands separately for precision and clarity; then hands together, adjusting dynamics (the indications for which I carefully checked in the score) then, I gradually increase tempo by one metronome setting for ten repetitions, each time listening to my tone quality, etc."

Similar goals should be set before starting to practice.

Equally important, having gained success at your short-term goal, make sure that you understand how and why you accomplished it.

The pianist should strive for musical effects in each practice session. If he feels his music, he may subconsciously make some particularly beautiful effect in his playing. It is his duty to notice how he made it. He must seize that effect, crystallize it, and only by realizing how he made it, can he be sure how he can reproduce it in performance.
LILIAS MACKINNON

And ... only one thing at a time - it's all you can do anyway. Multi-tasking is no myth; it's a falsehood. Myth at least incorporates valuable psychology that can operate on your subconscious. Multi-tasking is a 'figment of your imagination' – it doesn't exist. Parallel processing is useful, though. Put the coffee on, go get dressed. Then the coffee will be done percolating by the time you've laced up your shoes. Get all the independent processes going in parallel; but by yourself, you can only do one thing at a time.

As it is impossible to concentrate one's attention on more than one point at a time, the best course obviously is to master each difficulty separately

– one at a time.
TOBIAS MATTHAY

We have a mental concept of what we want to create, the big picture seen from the 'top down'. Now - what about tools to manifest it? Pianists, for example, obviously do use their hands and fingers a lot. The real learning and understanding of the issue 'at hand' is best approached slowly and deliberately from the 'bottom up'.

At first, Beethoven kept me on scales in all the keys and showed me the correct positions of the hands and fingers, in particular, how to use the thumb, the usefulness of which I didn't fully appreciate until a much later date. He especially called my attention to the legato, which he himself controlled to an incomparable degree.
CZERNY

Note that Czerny first mentions position of hands and not which specific fingers. Basic fingering may be somewhat important in the initial stages of playing the piano, but it's the overall hand position driven by a clear mental picture of the goal that's going to empower real results. Then you can almost use any finger you want.

Hand and fingers should be arched, muscles relaxed. … Stiffness hampers all movement; keyboard stretches demand elasticity.
C.P.E BACH

Muscular flexibility contributes more to good playing than strength.
FRANÇOIS COUPERIN

One needs only to study a certain positioning of the hand in relation to the keys to easily obtain the most beautiful sounds, to know how to play long notes and short notes and to achieve certain unlimited dexterity. A well-formed technique, it seems to me, can control and vary a beautiful sound quality.
CHOPIN

Take great care that you do not strike any key sideways or obliquely; as a contiguous key may chance to be mistakenly touched; and in music, nothing is worse than playing wrong notes. While one finger strikes, the other fingers must be kept close to the keys, but always curved, and poised quite freely in

the air. The most important of the fingers is the thumb. It must never be allowed to hang down below the keyboard, but should be held over the keys in such a way that its tip may be elevated a little higher than the upper surface of the black keys; and it must strike from this position. The elbows should never be too distant from the body; and that the arms, from the shoulder downwards, should hang freely, without being pressed against the body.
CZERNY

In a well-trained hand, the fingers are adjusted to each new position that they are to take on the keys, before the keys are touched. Ask any trained pianist to shape his hands to play any required chord or passage and he will take the proper position instantly without the necessity of placing his hands near the keyboard.
EDWARD MORIS BOWMAN

It's helpful to imagine a sequence of individual notes played as a chord (multiple tones played together at once). The hand position for the chord hints at the position for taking the notes individually. Those seemingly impossible Chopin Études become much easier as the hand finds the optimal position and then uses weight to pivot between succeeding positions.

Experiment with different fingerings of your own devising, or those prescribed by the composer or editors.

Debussy believed in the omission of fingering, and this is remarked on in the preface to his Études. The player may make his own decisions. 'One is never so well served as by himself.'
MARGUERITE LONG

The essence of independence is to be able to do something for one's self. ... He who is served is limited in his independence.
MARIA MONTESSORI

Simultaneously experiment with effective hand/wrist positions as you slowly practice the notes, paying special attention to places where the wrist must pivot to a new leverage base, usually involving turning of the thumb.

Sometimes the 'best' (best for you; that is) or most advantageous fingering cannot be discovered until the passage is attempted at performance tempo. One approach is to simply simulate the vector in space, moving your hand and arm slowly across the keyboard in an arc without actually playing (just gently wiggle your fingers above the keys, if you like) but focusing on the position that the hand and arm will assume during actual execution. Be conscious of wrist, arm, back, and neck, as well. Try to find the most comfortable overall body position.

Then go back and actually depress the keys with your fingers. Gradually work it up to performance speed. Listen to your results. Look at your results. Make adjustments. Keep at it, always striving to make music, not just play notes.

Anyone can acquire the ability to play rapidly with confidence and accuracy, if they can first imagine the end result.

If I can think the pieces right, my fingers will always play the notes.
PEPITO ARRIOLA

The energy of movement is determined by the intensity of the conception that unleashes it. The imagined concept is revealed, as far as possible, in this movement.
FRIEDRICH A. STEINHAUSEN

The most perfectly formed hand in the world would be worthless for the musician unless the mind that operates that hand has had a real musical training.
KATHARINE GOODSON

Successful fast playing is built on a foundation of imagination and slow practice. Don't be tugging on the leash.

Make haste slowly. Festina lente.
EMPEROR AUGUSTUS

It is much easier to play a thing quickly than to play it slowly.
MOZART

A firm and rock-like foundation for piano playing can only be laid by patient and persevering slow practice… one difficulty at a time, one hand at a time. Practice slowly and in sections. Not only must all the notes be there, they must be dwelt on. Without the control to play a piece slowly, one certainly

cannot play it fast. … practice a few measures slowly, till you know them, then play faster; take the next few measures in the same way, but at first don't practice the whole piece through at once.
WILLIAM MASON

Practice slowly. As a rule, students work too quickly. The only way to acquire grace and lightness of touch is to practice without ever hurrying. Count two upon each note when playing scales and exercises.
CECIL CHAMINADE

My mother insisted upon slow systematic regular practice.
EMIL SAUER

I couldn't believe my ears. Rachmaninoff was practicing Chopin's Étude in Thirds, but at such a snail's pace that it took a while to recognize it because so much time elapsed between each note. Fascinated, I clocked this remarkable exhibition; twenty seconds per bar was his pace for almost an hour while I waited riveted to the spot, quite unable to ring the doorbell.
ABRAM CHASINS

Always begin your practice slowly and gradually advance the tempo. The worst possible thing is to start practicing too fast. It invariably leads to bad results and to lengthy delays.
ERNEST SCHELLING

It's never right to play ragtime fast.
SCOTT JOPLIN

Practice at first very slowly, gradually increasing the speed until the proper tempo is attained. … The pianist who can practice intricate and rapid successions of passages in slow tempo, and pianissimo, with rhythm, is often doing thereby something that is actually harder to achieve than the showy splash-dash which amazes the uninitiated.
MARK HAMBOURG

Liszt says always listen; then carefully correct through slow, regular practice.
Mme. AUGUSTE BOISSIER

In *Nurtured by Love* Suzuki relates how a young pupil was

convinced that her fingers were too slow and clumsy to play a violin piece at the required tempo. He gently disagrees, suggesting that she simply misjudged herself and explains that her fingers are just not working together with her head, that's all.

He tells her that when he was her age he also practiced the wrong way, because no one corrected him. He suggests placing the fingers slowly and carefully in the positions required for the desired tempo. This is to be repeated slowly for three days; then, on the fourth day, a little faster for two more days. On the sixth day, he predicts, success will come. The little girl did exactly as told, succeeded, and regained her confidence.

When faced with a similar situation, how many of us just give up; unwilling or unable to work at it slowly for one whole week, or even one hour? A fresh perspective and a few kind words from a mentor can work wonders. The magic in slow practice is that it gives you time to think clearly, and to listen.

Thinking is rendered easier by practicing at first very slowly, and not playing faster until you are sure of your ground.
MALWINE BRÉE

Paderewski lays great stress on legato playing, and desires everything to be studied slowly, with deep touch, and with full clear tone.
ANTOINETTE SZUMOWSKA

A woman should never fight the keys, especially if she is good-looking. Effortlessness and ease is always more attractive than a perceived technical struggle.
LESCHETIZKY

(The same goes for men, incidentally)

One character trait is so powerful that it's traditionally been considered a virtue.

Be patient with yourself. You ruin everything if you wish to hasten; calmly take each step in turn to be certain of reaching the top; be patient; nature itself works slowly, follow her example. Your efforts, led wisely, will be honored with success, but if you want to acquire everything too quickly, you would lose time and fail ... place your foot securely on every step in order to

reach the heights on a secure footing.
LISZT

All impatience, the urge to force things along, leads only to unseemliness.
FRIEDRICH WIECK

I must content myself with everlasting patience which, someone once said, can sometimes be a substitute for genius.
CLAUDE DEBUSSY

How to study? Even if you sight read to acquaint yourself with piano literature, a good bit of time is required; but, if you wish to study a thing as a work of art, that is different, and each piece requires weeks of practice.
MARK HAMBOURG

To concentrate you must learn to direct your thoughts, and to prevent them from wandering away from a thing you must train them instead to wander around it.
LILIAS MACKINNON

Concentration and focus are essential. I've left a couple of typos in this manuscript just to test you. (If you find one, please let me know).
Besides being patient, we must also be consistent ...

If possible, let no day pass without touching your piano ... and never play carelessly, even when nobody's listening, or the occasion seems unimportant.
FERRUCCIO BUSONI

If I don't practice for a day, I know it; if I don't practice for two days, the critics know it; after three days ... the audience knows it.
PADEREWSKI

(The above also variously attributed to Anton Rubinstein and Hans von Bülow)

Besides being consistent, we must be thorough.

Every difficulty slurred over will be a ghost to disturb your repose later on.
CHOPIN

Practice as long at one time as you can practice well, and do not try to crowd several months work into one hour. Do everything you do as finely as you can, even though you succeed in learning no more than a few measures.
ALEXANDER LAMBERT

STAY!

... equals wait, think, plan, practice slowly, have patience, be consistent, and persevere.

Circulating in any given generation is a mixture of truths and untruths, reasonable and wishful thinking, and common sense and ignorance. Take piano playing in the 19th century - some people were approaching it correctly and it still shows, and plenty of others were probably doing it wrong, and we've forgotten them. In the following century a more narrow, compartmentalized and pedantic approach gained favor.

Here's an early 20th century recommendation for practicing Chopin's Étude in G flat major Opus 10.5, which uses mostly the black keys of the piano:

In slow practice play the first note from one-half supination, (as preparation) with pronation compounded with articulation: play the second note with metacarpo-phalangeal articulation; play the third note by shift of weight and pivot on it while abducting upper arm; adduct upper arm on fourth note, while articulating; play the fifth note by metacarpo-phalangeal articulation; shift weight on the sixth note and pivot on it while supinating the forearm and the hand. Continue reproducing this cycle of actions every six notes.
E. ROBERT SCHMITZ

I promise you, I didn't make that up. Robert Schmitz was a decent concert pianist, and an engineer with an obvious penchant for mechanical detail. But intriguing as it is in theory, this recommendation is pretty much impossible to implement; nature doesn't work that way. More importantly there's no mention of any creative vision to guide an interpretation; and no emphasis on feedback, on listening to the results of your effort to guide fine-tuning of progress. It's just about depressing keys on a piano keyboard ... and that's depressing.

Positive Piano

We expend useless effort if we try to make what is naturally an unconscious procedure into a conscious one.
FRIEDRICH A. STEINHAUSEN

Attempted realization of the precise locality of the muscles concerned in piano playing is not only futile, but is bound to impede the learner's progress, since it must take his attention away from the points where it is most directly needed.
TOBIAS MATTHAY

The points where attention is most directly needed are precisely the creative vision, and the feedback process to 'manage' refinement and improvement. Now back up again to the 19th century artist's perspective.

Play it with your nose but make it sound well.
ANTON RUBINSTEIN

Implied in that pithy one-liner (recorded by Josef Hofmann) is that you must pay attention to what you're doing to register whether or not it works, that is: if it sounds well.
How will you know if it's ...

GOOD!

... if you don't listen?
Science originates in curiosity, a wondering about a how or a why. You think about it, and then devise a hypothesis. The next step can be very creative - designing an experiment to test that hypothesis. Careful observation and monitoring of the test results provides feedback for subsequent tweaking of both experimental procedures and the original hypothesis. Further iterations of testing and refinement result in additional information.
If some company funds you to do 'science' about their product, forget it; that's not science. That's called either a conflict of interest, pseudoscience, or just plain old bovine fecal matter. The first two really stink; if you've been on a small farm, you know that the latter really isn't that bad.
Effective music practice also requires a reliable feedback mechanism, a way to verify progress (or not) in order to make

adjustments for improvement. That feedback mechanism is critical listening; not just hearing, but focused and mindful listening. The main organ involved is your brain. Ears help by collecting and funneling sound wave impressions but it takes the brain to process and make sense of them.

If you think some of the following quotes are redundant, be advised that you're being deliberately beat over the head with them to reinforce the concept.

Successful musical progress depends upon learning to listen. Every sound produced during the practice period should be heard. At my own recitals, no one in the audience listens more attentively than I do. I strive to hear every note and while I'm playing my attention is so concentrated on delivering the work in the most artistic manner dictated by the composer's demands and my conception of the piece, that I am little conscious of anything else. ... If you don't listen to your playing, it's very probable that other people will not care to listen to it either.
FERRUCCIO BUSONI

I listened more than I studied... therefore little by little my knowledge and ability were developed.
JOSEPH HAYDN

Listen, open your ears, always listen ... Listening to the inward singing of a phrase is of far more value than playing it a dozen times... If you listen well, that in itself is a means of attracting many emotional qualities. ... Piano study is very similar to cooking. A good cook tastes the cooking every few minutes to see whether it's progressing properly. Just so, a piano student who knows how to study makes pauses constantly in his playing, to hear if the passage just played corresponded to the effect desired, for it is only during these pauses that one can listen properly.
LESCHETIZKY

You are always your first hearer; to be one's own critic is the most difficult of all.
HANS von BÜLOW

Pedaling cannot be written down; it varies with the instrument, the room or the hall. Entrust it to your ear.
CLAUDE DEBUSSY

Positive Piano

To hear is not to listen. Listen more attentively to your own playing and I promise you three very desirable results: (1) a great many points which have hitherto never occurred to you will present themselves for consideration; (2) you will instinctively reach an easy conclusion in these considerations and acquire a correct and natural manner of rendering a melody, and (3) all those who have previously listened to you playing out of mere politeness will henceforth enjoy your playing, and that is relatively rare among students.
CONSTANTIN VON STERNBERG

I am obliged to say a hundred times a week 'Listen to what you are playing'. ... Stop and Listen. Do you express the composers thought and mood? Do you express what you feel and wish? Whatever it is, by all means express something!
JOSEF LHÉVINNE

Listen to your own playing.
LUDWIG DEPPE

Listen to the music as you play; work with the mind more than the fingers. Generally one works too much with the fingers and too little with the intelligence.
THALBERG

Most importantly, listen properly to yourself to judge of your own performance with accuracy. He who does not possess this gift, is apt, in practicing alone, to spoil all that he has acquired correctly in the presence of his teacher.
CZERNY

Listen to yourself as if a stranger were playing – one might almost say as if a rival were playing. This makes for concentration and is always profitable.
ALEXANDER LAMBERT

You did (such and such). Did you perceive it?
STERNDALE BENNETT

Franz Liszt – I bow as I mention that name – listened to his inner voice. They said he was inspired; he was simply listening to himself.
VLADIMIR de PACHMANN

270

Self-hearing is by far the most important factor in all music study.
KARL LEIMER

The majority play without thinking or listening. The first point is to listen to what one is playing; it's not a mere matter of proper tempo, but also tone-production and variety of touch. The way that one listens to things brings the finish and develops the artistic side of the performance. After playing a certain passage through once, listen intently until the buzz is out of the ear.
MARK HAMBOURG

Once, when I was playing a Nocturne, Paderewski called to me from the other end of the room: "Why do you always play that note with the fourth finger? I can hear you do it; the effect is bad."
SIGISMOND STOJOWSKI

One of Mr. Joseffy's pupils was playing. He had his back to her and certainly could not see, but he corrected her and told her to use the third, not the fourth finger in a certain rapid run.
Mrs. HENRY T. FINCK

When once you listen to your own playing as if you were listening to someone else, and find yourself unhappy and dissatisfied, then it is that your real study begins.
LESCHETIZKY

He that has ears, let him hear.
The BIBLE

And those with a brain, let them pay attention.

Listen Listen Listen Listen Listen Listen Listen
LISTEN!

Whenever, and whatever you are practicing, always remember to make music.

People talk about using the music of Bach to accomplish some technical purpose in a perfectly heart-breaking manner. They don't seem to think of interpreting Bach, but, rather make of him a kind of technical elevator by

means of which they hope to reach some marvelous musical heights. We even hear of the studies of Chopin being perverted in a similar vicious manner, but Bach, the master of masters, suffers most.
HAROLD BAUER

The polyphonic character of Bach's works trains the mind ingeniously, and at the same time the fingers receive a discipline which hardly any other study can secure.
FANNY BLOOMFIELD-ZEISLER

When great artists recommend Bach for building technique, they mean at the absolute highest level, where musical art and mechanical technique are fused into an indivisible whole. Practicing the music of Bach mindlessly, as if mere finger exercises (but even those should always be practiced mindfully and artistically) is not the answer.

Besides listening to yourself, listen to other (good) artists as well.

A highly developed sense of hearing is of immense value to the student who attends concerts for the purpose of promoting his musical knowledge.
KATHARINE GOODSON

I'm convinced that many who think they have no taste for music would learn to appreciate it and partake of its blessings, if they often listened to good instrumental music with earnestness and attention.
FERDINAND HILLER

I've learned as much from hearing the concerts of great performers as from any other source of educational inspiration. One should listen intelligently and earnestly. When he hears what appeals to him as a particularly fine tonal effect, he should endeavor to note the means the pianist employs to produce this effect, and learn to discriminate between affection or needless movement and the legitimate means to an end.
OSSIP GABRILOWITSCH

Notice the words "a particularly fine tonal effect" – he didn't say to parrot how someone else played the notes. The interpretation must be uniquely your own.

'GOOD' is made possible by listening. Listening is 'GOOD'. And guys, really listening carefully to your wife or girlfriend can make a huge difference in her quality of life (and yours).

To achieve our desired goals in the shortest possible time, we must practice intelligently. We must develop some good study habits.

Practice is a means of cultivating habits. Play correctly (phrasing, fingering, tone, touch, pedaling, dynamic effects) from the start to form good habits.
FANNY BLOOMFIELD-ZEISLER

The technique of an art is to a certain extent, mainly habit. We get used to measuring skips for instance, with eye and hand, until we can locate them automatically, from habit. It's the same with all sorts of technical figures; we acquire the habit of doing them through constant repetition.
PERCY GRAINGER

Right playing, like good manners in a well-trained child, becomes habitual from always doing right. As we are influenced for good or bad by those we associate with, so are we influenced by the character and quality of the tones we make and hear. Be earnest; put your heart, your whole soul, your whole self into your playing.
WILLIAM MASON

This continual playing of a piece over and over again is not what I call study. ... Until you learn to think an hour for every hour you play, you have not learned to study. ... Learn a passage just once; afterwards, only repeat it. That's what I call intelligent piano study.
LESCHETIZKY

Don't try to "correct" a fault, whether slip of the finger, wrong note, wrong time, tone or duration, by playing the right effect after the wrong one - such proceeding is indeed "un-practice". By playing the right note in succession after the wrong one we impress a totally wrong succession upon our minds, and therefore risk repeating the blunder and its supposed correction the very next time we play the passage. The only true correction is to substitute the correct succession of sounds - to go back and move across the damaged place while carefully omitting the hiatus.
TOBIAS MATTHAY

Now begins the time when we must also learn to play our piece with beauty and elegance. All the marks of expression must be observed with redoubled

attention; and we must seize correctly on the character of the composition, and enforce it in our performance according to its total effect.
CZERNY

Imagine what an exhilarating advantage it must have been for the ten-year-old boy Liszt to spend a year with Czerny, who had learned from Beethoven himself, as great music history was being forged in the fire. But even more importantly, Czerny burned with an enthusiasm and respect for Art inspired by direct association with its greatest exponent. That's what inspiration, motivation and education should be all about.

To play a concert piece through as mere physical exercise is not only useless, but positively harmful musically, and this applies equally to the study of études, even scales; for in all repetitions we always form and fix musical and technical habits, and it behooves us to insist upon good habits, and not bad ones, habits of keen attention, and not laxity of attention.
TOBIAS MATTHAY

Just as a prayer uttered glibly by the lips, but which does not come from the heart is worthless, so an exercise played as a matter of form, as a self-imposed duty, is without value.
ALBERTO JONÁS

When practicing, mentally direct your mind as if taking it into another room, a kind of chamber of practice. While the mind is in the imaginary room there should be no intrusions from the outside, no looking out of mental windows.

Don't do things in the hardest possible way; take the natural simple way – be yourself. Wrinkled foreheads and nervous anxiety will not lead to results in practicing. ... All work at the keyboard is for control. It does not come by forgiving slips, blunders, or getting stupidly excited. Every pupil can get a hold of himself and retain that hold so that mistakes become the exception and not the rule.
ALEXANDER LAMBERT

Remain resolutely in control of yourself, however trying the task. Like in Shakespeare's Hamlet, "Do not saw the air too much with your hand

thus, but use all gently, for in the very torrent, tempest, and whirlwind of your passion, you must acquire and beget a temperance that may give it smoothness".
IGNAZ MOSCHELES

If you want to save time in your music study, see that you comprehend your musical problems thoroughly. You must see it right in your mind, you must hear it right, you must feel it right. Before you place your fingers on the keyboard, you should have formed your ideal mental conception of the proper rhythm, the proper tonal quality, the aesthetic values, and the harmonic content.
FRANZ XAVER SCHWARENKA

That you should 'practice' only what you need to should be obvious (but obviously is some kind of 'secret'). A sure sign of Alexandrian end-gaining is when pianists play, over and over again, the things they already know (and are thus 'easier') to avoid really working on the details of thorny issues. These people can't leave off the visceral entertainment, and lack the discipline to tackle the challenging portions. You're not 'practicing' or improving yourself by repeating what you already know.

Few pupils realize that hours and hours are wasted at the piano keyboard doing those things which we are already able to do, and in this quest of something which we already possess.
FRANZ XAVER SCHWARENKA

Your own difficulty is the one which you should practice the most. Why waste time practicing passages you can already play perfectly well?
FERRUCCIO BUSONI

Once a field is conquered, a difficulty overcome, seek other fields. Personal experience will soon teach you that some exercises have ceased to give you any trouble, even when taken at reasonably fast tempo. Never practice them again. ... When should exercises with direct bearing on difficult passages of your piece be taken up? - at once, as soon as the basics of piano technique have been mastered. This is the secret of the virtuoso who says he never practices technical exercises.
ALBERTO JONÁS

Positive Piano

Develop your weak points, the strong points will take care of themselves.
JOSEF LHÉVINNE

To play a piece, one must be able to do even the hardest measure in it.
LESCHETIZKY

*One must know which exercises to choose, and how to practice them. ...
Students spend too much time in playing, and too little in work.*
PADEREWSKI

*A person who learns to work to a principle in doing one exercise will
have learned to do all exercises, but the person who learns just to "do an
exercise" will most assuredly have to go on learning to "do exercises"
ad infinitum.*
F.M. ALEXANDER

Go to the spot you perceive to be the most difficult in your piece
and proceed to transform it into the easiest. It's entirely possible to
do this in a short period of time if you think and focus.

*I must practice diligently. With every piece approached, I'm conscious as if
only just beginning to practice it properly.*
CLARA SCHUMANN

*Geometrically speaking, the shortest distance between two points is a straight
line. Find the straight line of technique which will carry you from first steps
to technical proficiency without wandering about endless lanes and avenues
which lead to no particular end.*
FRANZ XAVER SCHWARENKA

*Avoid worry and distractions of any kind. Your mind must be always
focused on what you're doing or the value of your practicing will be lessened
enormously. By intense concentration, love of your work, and the spirit in
which you approach it, you can do more in half an hour than in several
hours spent without purpose. Don't think you've been practicing if you have
played a single note with your mind on anything else.*
JOSEF LHÉVINNE

Don't stammer through your practice; if you stumble in a passage, leave off

at once; then attack the obstacle again till you manage to overcome it.
ERNST PAUER

Concentration is the vertebrae of musical success. The student who cannot concentrate had better abandon musical study. In fact the person that cannot concentrate is not likely to be a conspicuous success in any line of activity.
EMIL SAUER

This matter of concentration is far more important than most teachers imagine, and the perusal of some standard work on psychology will reveal things which should help the student greatly. ... Many make the mistake of thinking that only a certain kind of music demands concentration, whereas it is quite as necessary to concentrate the mind upon the playing of a simple scale as for the study of a Beethoven sonata.
HAROLD BAUER

Concentration is a matter of such great importance that few artists would hesitate to place it at the very foundation of all serious work. It is a mental process attained only after much intellectual effort. Direct your thinking powers towards one thing, and keep them on it until your definite purpose is accomplished.
OLGA SAMAROFF

Leo Ornstein was an indefatigable worker. He rose at five in the morning, and the old cobbler living beneath him once told him he was the only one in the house to get to work before he did. He toiled at his piano and at composition, and amid the constrained and depressing conditions of his external existence, the misery, gloom and unhappiness which he saw about him on every side, he found his consolation in work.
FREDERICK MARTENS

After being for years before the public, Busoni realized that his trill was not what he wished it to be and he set about perfecting it, we know with what splendid results.
HARRIETTE BROWER

I concentrated upon my work with iron perseverance, and found redemption in it.
EUGEN d'ALBERT

Positive Piano

Every repetition for Henselt was an intense upward struggle out of the 'fleshly' into the 'spiritual'. … one may seem to have achieved much and yet still be on a low plane, one may be gasping because the plane we have struggled up to is high, and one cannot remain on it without growing giddy.
BETTINA WALKER

One of my students was bright and intelligent but extremely averse to application in study, and the challenge was to invent some way to compel mental concentration, for she was constantly looking at the clock to see if her practice-hour was up. In playing a scale up one octave and back in 9/8 time, there are nine complete repetitions of the scale until the beginning C falls again upon the initial note of a measure. Such an exercise is called a rhythmus, and the repetitions compel mental concentration just as surely as the addition of a column of figures does. If played four octaves at a moderate rate of speed, the nine repetitions of the scale would require three to four minutes. A state of mental concentration could not be avoided by the pupil, and in this lay a basic principle. I gave it to her, and when the next lesson-hour came around and I asked her how she fared, she exclaimed: "Why, you've played a pretty trick on me! It took me nearly an hour to accomplish it; but I like it. Why did you not give it to me before!" I said, "I invented it simply to force you to focus."
WILIAM MASON

Paderewski advises studying scales and arpeggios with accents, for instance, accenting every third note, thus enabling each finger in turn to make the accent impulse: this will secure evenness of touch.
ANTOINETTE SZUMOWSKA

Better inaction than half-effort – for in the former you rest; and if you have a conscience, you will tire of inaction, rouse yourself up, and push vigorously on; whereas in the latter case you may indeed be moving, but you are not advancing, and every one of those half-efforts tends to weary the mental system and deprive it of the energy to focus in a given direction.
BETTINA WALKER

Misdirected energy is worse than indolence, and there is much of it. It's said that Leschetizky pronounces the words 'hard work' with scorn, and gets annoyed with those energetic Americans who seem to think that the one requisite in music is the same as a lumberjack's conquest of a forest: work,

work, work. Talent, judgment, and brains are also required in music.
HENRY THEOPHILUS FINCK

After a productive practice session, take a break and rest up a bit. When you're committed to a mission, progress occurs whether you're sitting on the bench practicing or off doing something totally different. The subconscious is perpetually working away at things, even during sleep. A piece you've been diligently working on sometimes mysteriously gets easier after you've given it a break for a while.

One's best study can be done away from the piano. I carry a phrase in my mind and go on long walks to study how best to play the piece. One can more easily imagine the beauties of music than one can reveal them in actual playing. Tempos and shadings can especially be learned away from the piano, much time can be saved. ... Believe me, the time you learn the most is when you go to the window to think it over, not when you are plodding at the piano.
LESCHETIZKY

The phenomenon that one can accomplish something that he couldn't do earlier without practicing in the meantime is especially evident in the inner maturing process of mastering technical difficulties on a musical instrument.
FRIEDRICH A. STEINHAUSEN

When you pick up a score again after a respite, you find things that you have never seen before, no matter how much you may know.
MARK HAMBOURG

This isn't a new idea, exclusive to pianists.

Occasionally desist and relax. When you return to your work your judgment will be surer; to remain constantly at work will cause you to lose power of judgment.
LEONARDO da VINCI

Then ... continue integrating larger sections. Charles Cooke has a very helpful description of this process in *Playing the Piano For Pleasure* (Simon and Schuster, 1941). The general principle is known as 'divide and conquer'. Start with manageable chunks and persevere until the whole is mastered. But make sure the fragments are truly seamlessly integrated.

With your overall artistic concept guiding from the top down, you work from the bottom up (individual notes and the mechanics of execution); and back to the top, which will now probably have matured and expanded, and the cycle repeats.

The most difficult problem for the pupil is to keep the big picture in mind as a continuous progression, and not to allow the necessary attention to each detail, as it comes along, to distract him from a persistent purpose to keep shape and outline perfectly clear.
TOBIAS MATTHAY

A vital point is the bridging over of one passage to another, the securing of continuity in the performance of a work. Without this bridging over we have neither breadth nor cohesiveness... there is neither the mastery of intellectuality nor the value of artistic finish.
MARK HAMBOURG

Remember, it's not just how and how much you practice; when and even where you practice are equally important.

Practice always when fresh. Progress will be ten-fold.
FRIEDRICH WIECK

No technical exercises the last thing at night before bed; far better to play pieces with a variety of technique and touch.
LESCHETIZKY

Sometimes it helps to mix it up and deliberately change your approach by trying something totally different. Let's revisit that Chopin 'black-key' étude for a moment. Hans von Bülow recommended transposing it to the key of G major; that is, mostly on the white keys. It mentally challenges you to think, forcing you to analyse hand positions and harmonic structure and chord changes, ultimately making the original easier to understand and execute.

It's a far more productive exercise than virtual dissection of the infinitely complex anatomy of your hand coupled with the hopelessly impossible task of artificially commanding your neural networks.

That's not the way your mind and body work together when playing the piano. And it's not what F. M. Alexander meant by conscious control.

By the way, a note on the piece: it's intended to be light music, salon entertainment in the best sense of the word, and a valuable study piece. Don't make yourself look silly by putting on airs in a supposedly 'profound' performance.

Did Wieck (Clara Schumann) play my étude well? Why could she not choose something more substantial than the least interesting of the études – at least for those that don't know it uses mostly the black keys. Better had she just sat quietly.
CHOPIN

If the end goal requires playing quickly, at some point you have to experiment with that too.

Many players make the mistake of at once playing quickly, after the slow practice; I find it better to acquire speed gradually. ... When I thoroughly know the piece, I gradually go faster, until I've worked up the required tempo. It comes without much trouble when one thoroughly knows the notes.
LEO ORNSTEIN

There are different opinions on the subject. It can be beneficial once in a while to just let go and push the envelope to see what happens.

Joseffy counseled practicing for perfection and endurance. For the former, slow practice was necessary, with well-raised fingers and minute attention to every detail. For endurance, the opposite course was observed. 'Play for speed, and keep it up, no matter if some of the notes are dropped,' he would say. 'Go through the piece several times without stopping and do not yield to fatigue; overcome fatigue!'
ROSE WOLF

Technique is the correlation of nervous action, rather than mere flexibility. Since correct timeliness of movement presupposes a thought and a 'willingness', successful study of it depends also on exercises in up-tempo motion, not just slow tempo to control finger accuracy.
AUGUST OETIKER

Effective practicing means work that counts. Develop a laser-like focus on trouble spots and absolutely master them, transforming them into the strongest portions of your piece. Then they won't come back to haunt you in performance and instead will bring you extra pleasure and confidence in execution. The quality of practice, or work, is always determined by thinking and musicality.

If we practice a piece of real music with no other idea than that of developing some technical point, it often ceases to become a piece of music and results in being a kind of technical machinery. Once a piece is mechanical it is difficult to make it otherwise.
HAROLD BAUER

Out of four hours' study, one who goes about his work properly will play perhaps only one-half of that time. The rest goes for pauses to think about what has gone before, and to construct mentally the following passage.
LESCHETIZKY

Good practice is intelligent repetition, but there is little intelligence in repeating anything without concentration of mind. Concentrate upon the difficult passages and work on them until they sound as fluent and simple as the ones that are now easy to you.
ALEXANDER LAMBERT

Henselt would go listen to a pupil practicing if he got the chance, and if he considered that the work was being done without conscience, the next time the pupil was playing to him would observe 'No wonder you haven't conquered the difficulty; you've been working with so little method'.
BETTINA WALKER

"Moving the fingers," says Fannie Bloomfield Zeisler, "is not practicing, for in piano work the fingers accomplish one-fourth and the brain three-fourths of the result."
HENRY THEOPHILUS FINCK

Practice regularly or not at all. Pupils think they can skip a day without affecting their work if they practice twice as much the next. Absurd! This is like going without food for a week and making up for it by eating ten dinners in one sitting to catch up. The main advantage in regular practice is that the

mind goes at it after regular periods of rest. The mind must be fresh and clear every moment. Constant watch must be kept for unnecessary movements. Always practice systematically. Do as much as you can learn perfectly.
ALBERTO JONÁS

But don't practice and reinforce mistakes. Resist the "end-gaining" of constantly repeating errors. If you make a mistake, stop and analyze the situation. Almost always it stems from lack of mental clarity and focus and understanding of what is to be executed in the first place. Overlap the beginning and ending of the phrase with the prior and succeeding material.

Conscious control is the result of the thought, discipline, focus, and slow practice required to initially 'cement' the music accurately in place.

As a rule, students work too quickly. The only way to acquire grace and lightness of touch is to practice without ever hurrying. Above all, keep their mind and attention fixed upon what you're doing. It requires an abundance of patience and determination.
CECIL CHAMINADE

Through practice one can develop habits of nerve control that are themselves remedial. Unless one cultivates the habit of repose, he may continue to be nervous the rest of his life. ... don't develop an artificial eagerness to get things done before they may possibly be done. If you're in a train, remember, you will not get to your destination until the train gets there. ... Impatience is the juggernaut that grinds down more nervous systems than anything else except drugs.
ALBERTO JONÁS

If a passage offers some particular technical difficulty, go through all similar passages you can remember in other places; in this way you will bring system into the kind of playing in question. ... Never leave a passage that has been unsuccessful without repeating it; if you can't do it immediately because in the presence of others, then do it subsequently.
FERRUCCIO BUSONI

About that 'being in the presence of others': Busoni was occasionally known to silently re-work phrases during the course of

283

publicly performing a concerto, when the orchestra played without the piano.

The great pianists first practiced 'pure' technique, like the various scales in all the major and minor keys.

Technique is firstly scales, secondly scales, and thirdly ... scales.
J. N. HUMMEL

Then they applied it to a specific piece, an étude, for example. In addition to the mechanical aspects of execution (like hand positon and fingering), phrasing and relative dynamics would then need to be taken into account, all in the context of a vibrant rhythm. And with the compositions of masters, it's wonderful to experience how they somehow stamp their ineffable spirit onto the notes.

Always join technical practice with the study of the interpretation; the difficulty often does not lie in the notes, but in the dynamic shading prescribed.
FERRUCCIO BUSONI

As you progress, your mental image of what's possible for you will naturally expand. You'll want to achieve more, because now you know that you can. You can help this process along at the front end with visualization and constant learning. Always set your sights continually higher, keep telling yourself you can accomplish more; much more.

You cannot actually do what I am assigning you at present, but in the effort to do it, you are roused and stimulated, and this is what you need.
STERNDALE BENNETT

A wise teacher will start with a few simple pieces and then gradually introduce more challenging works so that the student won't even notice increased difficulty. My illustrious father actually started his pupils with pieces of moderate difficulty.
C.P.E. BACH

I've offended God and Mankind because my work didn't reach the quality it should have.
LEONARDO da VINCI

Now it's time to get …

DOWN!

… to some weighty details.

As far as playing the modern piano goes, if there really are any magical 'secrets' the first is truly believing in your ultimate ability to do it, and the second is playing with 'weight'. Like F.M. Alexander's 'Self', playing with full body participation is not just either a purely intellectual concept or a physical one - it's both. It must be understood conceptually and then practically implemented over time through experimentation and experience.

First you need awareness. Weight in piano playing is an analogy for literally digging deeply into any task you can think of in life.

In rapid passages, every tone must be produced with a fitting pressure or the effect will be turgid and chaotic.
C.P.E. BACH

On three occasions I played to Liszt compositions with prominent legato chords and octaves. I had learned how to cling to the keys tolerably well (you always want to cling whenever there is a chance for it in piano playing) and to use flexibility of the forearm at the wrist in many such cases, instead of tossing the hand up and down, as generally done, according to ordinary methods. In each one of these pieces Liszt came over to the piano while I was playing and bore down heavily upon my hands. He held them down steadily in such a manner that I could neither raise knuckles nor wrist and then he told me to go on playing.
W.H. SHERWOOD

More frequent employment of arm weight in the production of singing tone I attribute to the influence of Anton Rubinstein, who developed it more and more in his playing as he advanced in age. … The beauty of the result is indisputable, but has not been adopted universally.
MORIZ ROSENTHAL

Play with weight. …don't strike, but let the fingers fall.
LUDWIG DEPPE

Positive Piano

The constant alternation between de-vitalization and reconstruction keeps the muscles always fresh for their work and enables the player to rest while playing. The force is so distributed that each and every muscle has ample opportunity to rest while yet in a state of activity. ... (One could) practically play all day without fatigue. Furthermore the tones resulting from this touch are sonorous and full of energy and life. To eventually acquire a state of habitual muscular elasticity and flexibility...allow the arms to hang limp by your side, either in a sitting or standing posture, and then shake them rigorously with the utmost possible looseness.
WILLIAM MASON

I was anxious to enlarge my repertoire as much as possible and was practicing a great deal, sometimes twelve and fourteen hours – practically all day. At the end of the day, after a couple of hours rest, I would sit down to the piano in the evening and play awhile and often noticed that despite being weak, I played effortlessly, with pleasure. Why should playing after a hard day's work seem easy, when the next morning, at a time when I should be feeling fresh, the same things did not seem easy; on the contrary, were more fatiguing?

I concluded that, owing to weariness, my arms hung down with their own weight, and I made no effort to hold them up. I was playing with relaxed arm weight, and this did not tire me in the least. I developed this principle for myself in many ways, and found it of the greatest benefit. Many other pianists do this of course; Anton Rubinstein certainly exemplified relaxed weight. He had such heavy hands and arms he didn't try to hold them up any more than absolutely necessary. Yet he was unable to explain the principle. Weight, relaxation, and economy of motion are the foundation stones of technique of interpretation and mechanism in piano playing.

... In weight playing the fingers seem to mold the piano keys under them, the hand and the arm are relaxed, but never heavy ... the fingers are virtually "glued to the keys" in that they leave them the least possible distance in order to accomplish their essential aims. This results in no wasted motion of any kind, no loss of power, and consequently the greatest possible conservation of energy. ... The maximum of relaxation results in the minimum of fatigue.
LEOPOLD GODOWSKY

The hands are not meant to hover in the air over the piano, but to enter into it.
CLAUDE DEBUSSY

286

Weight playing saves fatigue. It develops the whole arm instead of merely the finger and hand. Just as clock-hands are moved by a spring, so the finger action depends on the arm action. The shoulder, arm and elbow and all joints are kept flexible instead of stiff. The fingers are thrown down loosely instead of forced down. The keys are pressed by a fall of weight instead of beaten down. Weight is used in place of muscular tension; the training begins with the shoulder instead of the fingers.
ARTHUR ELSON

But the weight is only useful up until the moment of tone production. Owing to the mechanical engineering of the instrument, after that it's irrelevant until the next tone is produced. On the piano, there's no equivalent to the vibrato technique of the string instrument. Once created, piano tone cannot be physically altered and immediately begins to decay.

Sequential piano tones can, however, be imaginatively crafted in a relativistic sense to create beautiful effects.

In melodious playing Plaidy held that the fingers should be kept on the surface of the keys, and pressed firmly down upon them, this pressure being maintained until the next key was depressed. Curiously, he did not realize that this unnecessary continuance of pressure, after the production of the tone required, was a total waste of force.
OSCAR BERINGER

My black Lab remembers her tricks day after day, especially if they are reinforced with treats. Memory is not just an accumulation of static, isolated, impressions. First of all, it's rooted in awareness.

The true art of memory is the art of attention.
DR. SAMUEL JOHNSON

It's also a dynamic process of association, and relativity. It's strengthened over time by repeated exposure and repetition. If you want to keep things memorized, keep reinforcing your repertoire by revisiting it regularly.

The mental effort necessary to fix notes, phrasing and expression marks in mind is indispensable to a complete mastery of the piece, and its performance

with abandon. Memory is required for expressive playing; for the thought cannot be wholly given up to interpreting soulfully if the eyes have to be fastened on the printed page. One cannot think of the angelic host as singing from music paper! Much bad playing, stumbling and stuttering, often arises from not realizing that all memorizing, whatever its nature, can only be achieved by impressing upon our mind the requisite and correct progressions, sequences, continuities, or chains of succession of the music in all its details.
TOBIAS MATTHAY

When I want to learn a new piece I don't keep the notes in front of me on the music-rack; I throw them on top of the piano, so that I have to get up every time to look at them. After the image of the passage to be memorized is well in mind, I sit down at the instrument and try to reproduce it—notes, touch, pedaling and all. Perhaps it doesn't go the first time. Then I get up and take another look. This time I make a more strenuous effort—to avoid the trouble of having to stand up once more!
LESCHETIZKY

It's good practice to rehearse memorized pieces in the dark.
C.P.E. BACH

Learning Braille helped me to work up a damn good memory.
RAY CHARLES

Best practice must be founded on a fundamentally sound paradigm, one demonstrated to get results. It should be wholistic, and consider every possible factor that comes into play in the successful achievement of a goal. If we're talking about human best practice - it cannot execute by itself. We must choose to do our own work, mindfully, efficiently, and enthusiastically.

The process of individuation consists of three parts: insight, endurance, and action. Psychology is needed only in the first part. But in the second and third parts moral strength plays the predominant role.
CARL JUNG

It's not surprising that a psychologist of Jung's stature would say that reflection and thinking things through, along with persevering in productive action to accomplish a goal are all part of the deep process of psychological maturation. Interestingly, Jung says that sustained action depends mainly on moral strength.

If best practice methodology is to be a Royal Road to success it must facilitate human spiritual growth and development. You just read this whole chapter, but now I'm rather reluctant to inform you that, in fact, there is no 'best practice', only best people. That's right, best practices are just logical and straight-forward things that best people do constantly, consistently, and enthusiastically until they achieve their desired results.

Work intelligently and persistently with the preceding recommendations in mind and you'll be well on your way to becoming the *best of breed*. Next we'll discuss the transformative growth process that pulls it all together - becoming *Man's best friend*.

Chapter 9

......

CHARACTER

Produce great men, the rest follows.

—WALT WHITMAN

E thos (ἔθος) refers to moral character not as a static philosophical concept but as real-time dynamic action. Aristotle says that for character to be credible, individuals must literally live it and exude it. As far as your influence on ancient audiences was concerned, your character preceded you just like your reputation.

Character reveals moral purpose as evidenced by man's choices. It carries with it a credibility that is perhaps the most effective means of persuasion.
ARISTOTLE

'Character' includes the wisdom to make good choices - the right choices. And traits like honesty, integrity and authenticity influence others through example.

Morality is the strength of men who distinguish themselves over others, and it is mine. ... Socrates and Jesus were my exemplars.
BEETHOVEN

Good character is not formed in a week or a month. It is created little by little,

day by day. Protracted and patient effort is needed to develop it.
HERACLITUS

Live simply; carry out your duties with humble gratitude for the Providence which has permitted them to be well-taught to you; be of serene and equable humor, reflect seriously but without becoming sullen.
LISZT

Music study based upon true educational principles is most assuredly character building.
A. KINCAID VIRGIL

It's puzzling how popular notions of the lives and character of great artists degenerate into caricature over time. Plain old ignorance is one reason; human vanity is another - that thing about us being so much smarter than people in the past. Vanity and arrogance have their psychological origins in insecurity, so if we feel we must disparage our predecessors … just saying.

Today Beethoven is often presented as a cantankerous misanthrope with bad hair, Liszt a seductive circus showman with great hair, and Mozart some sort of goofy idiot-savant in a powdered wig. These simplistic notions are inaccurate and misleading and say more about the persons projecting them than they do about the artists.

Let's discuss Beethoven for a minute. Yes he could be cranky, but who wouldn't be under the circumstances.

One cause for mistaking Beethoven's overall disposition was the traveler's ambition of contemplating the greatest genius in Vienna and hearing him play. But when, from their unmusical questions and heterodox remarks he discovered that a tourist's curiosity and not musical feeling had motivated them, he was not at all disposed to accede to their selfish importunities, interpreting their visit as impertinent and intrusive, and consequently feeling highly offended, was not scrupulous in exhibiting his displeasure in the most pointed and abrupt manner.
CIPRIANI POTTER

If you'd like to learn about Beethoven and don't have time for Thayer's massive volume, a wonderful little book now re-published by Dover Publications is *Beethoven, Impressions By His Contemporaries*.

And if you've no time for that at least read the several pages of Beethoven's *Das Heiligenstädter Testament.*

O ye men who think or say that I am malevolent, stubborn, or misanthropic, how greatly do you wrong me, you do not know the secret causes ... from childhood my heart and mind were disposed to the gentle feelings of good will, I was ever eager to accomplish great deeds ....
BEETHOVEN

The impending deafness of history's greatest musical artist forced him into the life of a recluse and depressed him to the brink of suicide, but his character and faith ultimately pulled him through, for which we are eternally grateful.

The great pianists and composers were human and had failings. They faced challenges and adversities in their lives similar to ours, maybe more so. The difference is in how they dealt with things. Their prodigious and sublime creative output resulted from a very special quality: great moral character and the resultant personal power to persevere and succeed in a worthy cause.

Character is not measured by awards, diplomas, and election to public office; especially that last one, with the exception of Paderewski who nobly served as the prime minister of Poland and represented that country at the Paris Peace Conference of 1919.

My great motivation was to become somebody and so to help Poland.
PADEREWSKI

Character cannot be acquired in a material sense, nor is it derived intellectually from books alone, helpful though they may be. Character formation cannot be taught. It comes from experience and not from explanation.
MARIA MONTESSORI

It evolves out of the experience of interacting with other human beings and ultimately defines who you are as a person. Character is developed as a result of conscious choices at every step. Like music, it may be discussed in the abstract but for it to take on any real meaning it must express itself dynamically. Just as music must be realized in sound, character must be realized in action.

Many qualities are mentioned in describing character, but it's always greater than the sum of the individual parts.

AUTHENTICITY

Authenticity simply means real, not phony. It's a mindset, the natural result of self-acceptance and self-esteem, of knowing and accepting what you're all about. Authenticity is synonymous with uniqueness and originality ... and with being.

It was a serious moment for me when Beethoven appeared. Was I to try to follow in the footsteps of such a genius? For a while I did not know what I stood on, but finally I realized that it was best to remain true to myself and my own nature.
J. N. HUMMEL

From my piano quartet and caprice you seem to find a resemblance to Beethoven, and flattering as this may appear to many, it's far from agreeable to me. I abhor everything that bears the stamp of imitation, and my views differ far too much from Beethoven's. ... Though I certainly can't boast of his great genius, I can vindicate the logic and phrasing of my own music. ... To be a true artist, you must be a true man.
CARL MARIA von WEBER

Even should the world take less interest in my performances, my desire will be the more ardent to cultivate music in accordance with my own taste and convictions.
IGNAZ MOSCHELES

A person of any mental quality has ideas of his own. If he wants to make use of his abilities, he must be allowed to work in accordance with his ideas. This is common sense.
LISZT

The virtuoso's most indispensable attribute is sincerity, else he's nothing more than a showman. The greater the individuality: the greater the artist. Someone said that we continually think the thoughts of other people because we're too lazy to think our own. The artist should unceasingly strive to get down to his ideas, find out what he himself really thinks.
MARK HAMBOURG

Whenever the performance of any artist was mentioned, it was characteristic of Debussy to ask "Is he or she sincere?" I think sincerity was a religion with him.
LOUISA LIEBICH

Why was Liszt greater than any pianist in his time? - because he discovered things independently, by himself, that Czerny and his contemporaries had failed to. Why has Godowsky attained his wonderful rank? ... because he has worked out certain contrapuntal and technical challenges which place him in a category all by himself. Why does Busoni produce inimitable results at the keyboard? Because he was not satisfied or content with the knowledge he had obtained from others. Originality in piano playing is nothing more than the interpretation of one's real self, the true voice of the heart, instead of the artificial self which traditions, mistaken advisors, and our own natural sense of mimicry impose upon us.
VLADIMIR de PACHMANN

Gottschalk was not afraid to show his humanity and establish a music of his own. He stands at the head of an army of artists who dare to be themselves.
OCTAVIA HENSEL

He who has been cast in an original mold cannot abdicate his individuality.
L. M. GOTTSCHALK

Individualism is one of the first virtues required of an artist.
MANUEL de FALLA

All that I'm attempting to do is to express myself as honestly and convincingly as I can in the present.
LEO ORNSTEIN

Leo Ornstein is that rare thing—an individual pianist.
JAMES HUNEKER

One cannot talk with Leo Ornstein for five minutes without realizing he is absolutely sincere in his work. His fixed purpose is to express himself and his times with fidelity and honesty, according to his lights, no matter what critics or others should say to the contrary.
HARRIETTE BROWER

Although the pupil must take the playing of his teacher, or other masters, as a model, let him avoid becoming a copy. Mimicking the striking peculiarities of masters will generally lead to a mere outside caricature. Let the teacher lead the pupil to a manner of performance drawn from his own individuality and in harmony with his own convictions.
LOUIS PLAIDY

Great pianists chose to be authentic; then the authenticity radiated all by itself. A person must take a stand and have an opinion of sorts, and nowhere is this more evident than in the interpretation of 'rules'.

We cannot be content any longer with pedantic musicians who memorize rules and follow them mechanically; something more is required.
C.P.E. BACH

Once, while out walking with Beethoven I mentioned two perfect fifths, of outstanding beauty, in one of his earlier violin quartets in C minor. He didn't recall them and insisted it was wrong to call them fifths. Since he habitually carried manuscript paper with him, I asked for some and set down the passage in all four parts. When he saw I was right he said "well, and who has forbidden them?" and when I couldn't answer he repeated it several times. I finally replied "it's a fundamental rule; Marburg, Kirnberger, Fuchs, etc; all the theorists" ... "And so I allow them!" was his answer.
FERDINAND RIES

'Wholistic' ought to be spelled with a 'w' ... and so I allow it.
AUTHOR, POSITIVE PIANO

Beethoven will never do anything according to rule.
JOHANN ALBRECHTSBERGER

Beethoven's real lesson for us was not that we should just preserve age-old forms, and neither that we should plant our footsteps where he first dared to tread. We should look out through open windows into clear skies.
CLAUDE DEBUSSY

If a man doesn't keep pace with his companions, perhaps it's because he hears a different drummer. Let him step to the music which he hears, however

measured and far away.
HENRY DAVID THOREAU

Whoso would be a man must be a nonconformist. ... use what language you will, you can never say anything but what you are.
RALPH WALDO EMERSON

When you've made the psychological leap to independent reasoning, people around you sense it. Your newly gained personal power has tangible effects on your environment. That's the power of conviction.

People in those old times had convictions; we moderns have only opinions. And it needs more than a mere opinion to erect a Gothic cathedral.
HEINRICH HEINE

Just get down to it and, regardless of anything else, apply yourself to your work, like the building of the Seville cathedral, where future generations may have remarked "they were mad to undertake something so extraordinary". And yet the cathedral stands there still!
LISZT

The kind of technical study that passes the student through a certain process, apparently destined to make him as much like his predecessors as possible, is hardly that needed to make a great artist. The preservation of one's individuality is most difficult and yet most essential in studying the piano.
MAX PAUER

In art there is no escaping from one's true inner nature, neither for a beginner nor for the finished artist.
PERCY GRAINGER

At all times, the semblance of the machine in playing should be resisted through the culture of individuality and personality.
RUDOLPH GANZ

Teresa Carreño's fire and passion are the very traits that differentiate her from the numberless hordes of pianists of both sexes who are technically

296

capable but don't stand out with any particular artistic individuality. She should not repress these qualities, or else she will be robbed of her most beautiful jewel, her own personality.
NEUE ZEITSCHRIFT FÜR MUSIK 1896

Every concert is a test of the artist's sincerity, not merely an exhibition of his prowess, or acrobatic accomplishments on the keyboard. .... Indeed, individuality, character, and temperament have become most significant in the highly organized art of piano playing. Remove these and the artist becomes little better than a piano-playing machine that can never achieve the distinguishing charm this trinity brings.
LEOPOLD GODOWSKY

What every artist can and must aim at is a perfectly sincere point of view... the work of a sincere artist is almost certain to have some value; the work of an insincere artist is of its very nature worthless.
JAMES FRANCIS COOKE

Sincerity, individuality, and temperament in a performer's personality are inestimable in winning the approval of the audience. Technical mastery being presupposed, the artist can lose himself in re-creating the composer's mood and thus sway his audience. A pleasing appearance is undoubtedly helpful, but the sheer intensity of personality in the performing artist can result in a magnetism that is almost hypnotic. The artist who cannot thus sway audiences must remain a mediocrity.
FANNY BLOOMFIELD-ZEISLER

Anton Rubinstein was conspicuously different from the opaque mass of self-styled composer-pianists who don't even know what it is to play the piano, still less understand what fuel is necessary to heat one's self in order to compose. With what they lack in talent for composition they fancy themselves pianists, and vice versa.
LISZT

Imitation of other performer's mannerisms disgraces an artist. It may be a good thing for financial success, but it is degradation.
EDOUARD ZELDEN

A fool imitates. It is better to do inferior work of one's own than to copy

someone else's.
GEORGE BIZET

A genius is the one most like himself... Play what you want and let the public pick up on what you're doing, even if it takes them fifteen, twenty years.
THELONIUS MONK

Be yourself; either you make it as yourself or you don't make it.
RAY CHARLES

After having attained, or so my biographer avers, a primary objective of my youth – that of being called the "Paganini of the Piano" – it seems to me, naturally, that I should seriously aspire to being called by my own name, and that I rely enough on the results of persevering determination and work to hope that in future editions of the Lexikon a place will be made for me that is more in accordance with my aims.
LISZT

Boy, you can sense the irritation between the lines. Liszt was in his early twenties when he first heard the great violinist Paganini, possibly the only other instrumentalist Liszt felt exceeded his own level of mechanical execution. The experience motivated him to explore higher levels of piano technique, which he did with brilliant success. In doing so he became not another Paganini, but himself. Later Liszt realized that Paganini had been too self-absorbed, and that musical genius should serve a higher purpose. This is one source of Liszt's famous line: *Génie oblige.*

May the artist of the future gladly and readily decline to play the conceited and egotistical role which we hope has had in Paganini its last brilliant representative... though the saying is Noblesse oblige, much more than nobility, it is Génie oblige!
LISZT

COURAGE

Born in the same year that Liszt passed (1886), theologian Paul Tillich explored man's moral challenges and existential anxiety in *The Courage To Be*. The title pretty much says it all.

Courage consists not in hazarding without fear; but being resolutely minded in a just cause.
PLUTARCH

Liszt listened to the tale of my adventures in Paris and shook his head. "You must never lose courage," he admonished.
ARTHUR FRIEDHEIM

Liszt was not afraid, and like him, his pupils are not afraid, either. It is they who have revealed Liszt's beautiful compositions and brilliant concert-style to the world.
AMY FAY

Nec Aspera Terrent - They don't fear difficulties.
Never shrink from any difficulty.
IGNAZ MOSCHELES

Exercise yourself cheerfully and courageously in this very honorable art. If the labor is great, the pleasure and reward which you may gain thereby are still greater.
CZERNY

The English make it a point of honor not to be nervous. What a splendid trait.
LESCHETIZKY

To surrender to the thought of having no talent and give up the effort is cowardly.
SUZUKI

Don't minimize the matter of courage. ... Of every conceivable requisite of good nerve control – intellectual, physical, and moral – I would choose that word courage as embodying them all. It takes courage at all times to make the nerves subservient to the will; courage to regulate one's life habits, courage to be oneself when in the presence of others, courage to entertain one's own artistic convictions.
ALBERTO JONÁS

Aside from young d'Albert's ease and readiness in the most stunning technical difficulties, his playing bristled with fire, energy, spirit, self-

conviction and, above all, courage - qualifications that recalled to Liszt his own youth, and were after his own heart. No wonder he exclaimed: "Little lion, just like Tausig!"

CARL LACHMUND

The most trying part of the pianist's profession is the self-struggle between sensational effect and true artistic values, the former being the lever by which success is sometimes measured, the latter being the musician's religion. Added to this is the sight of others gaining ground through the false methods - something that must always be painful to the human side of the artist. It requires great moral courage to be a noble pianist.

FANNIE EDGAR THOMAS

Leschetizky dislikes nothing more than dejection on the part of the pupil.

ETHEL NEWCOMB

I have been told, by several who knew Liszt well, that there was nothing he disliked more than timidity and shyness, that pluck and even a little boldness were passports to his favor.

BETTINA WALKER

Courage - above all, courage.

LISZT

DISCIPLINE

The evolution of character is inseparable from the process of individuation (Jung) or self-actualization (Maslow). By definition, choice involves at least two paths and there are always inherent moral/ethical considerations. Discipline is essential for technical development and mastery; self-discipline is essential for developing and maintaining 'character'.

The successful piano student must have purpose, perseverance, and will power – but these qualities are often lacking in the beginning. It is quite wonderful, however, what persistent effort on the part of a teacher will do to arouse the power of thought and determination in students.

A. KINCAID VIRGIL

*I shall always be eager to perform in accordance with the Spanish motto
of mine that you have been pleased to notice: Pundonoroso! (honorable,
scrupulous, punctilious).*
LISZT

*Emil Sauer would have studied a whole hour on these two or three bars to
bring out clearly the meaning of the notes if he were not satisfied with them.
Concentration and right habits of study count more than time spent. Still,
you should enjoy time spent on music.*
LESCHETIZKY

It takes a lot of discipline to continually work at difficult tasks.
Most pianists would agree that Sviatoslav Richter was a supremely
gifted master pianist. Prokofiev's 9th Piano Sonata is dedicated to
Richter, and in *The Art of Piano Playing* Heinrich Neuhaus relates
how he was especially impressed with Richter's rendering of several
complicated measures in the third movement. Richter admitted that
he had once practiced that spot exclusively with absolute focus for
two hours.

Somebody else once overheard Vladimir Horowitz practicing just
a miniscule fragment of a Chopin Mazurka for over an hour.

*Concerning a certain arpeggio passage in the G major Concerto of Beethoven,
Joseffy once said to me with a smile: "That you must repeat 5,000 times
until it's absolutely perfect".*
EDWIN HUGHES

*Thalberg declared that he never ventured to perform one of his pieces in
public till he had practiced it at least 1,500 times.*
HENRY THEOPHILUS FINCK

Having just waded through the last chapter, we know how these
gentlemen clearly envisioned a desired end result, established a
short term practice goal, went about it in a calculated way, listened to
what they were doing, made adjustments, experimented, noted what
worked and didn't – in every repetition. They worked at it.

*Often the case among executive artists, they have rich imaginations and
great temporary zeal, but lack the inclination or ability to regard music as a*

serious art worthy of a great life struggle.
PADEREWSKI

Instead of carrying around letters of recommendation from Queens, it would be better if you did some serious practicing.
LISZT

One of my favorite Liszt quotes! Throughout his life, legions of aspiring pianists approached Liszt with letters of recommendation, hoping for an audience with the great master. He never read a single one, merely gesturing to the piano and saying: 'recommend yourself'.

Art is not obtained by birth or heredity, but must be acquired by the individual. Were it otherwise, the artist's crown would be easily won, but of slight value. When any one says he learns everything without effort, he either tells an untruth, or what he learns is valueless. Thought alone springs effortless from the brain; the technics of every art must be acquired step by step. Practice makes perfect.
MALWINE BRÉE

This then, is my life's secret, I have no other – work, unending work. Today I'm just as keenly interested in my progress as I was many years ago in my youth. Work is the greatest intoxication, the greatest blessing, the greatest solace we can know. Therefore work, work, work.
VLADIMIR de PACHMANN

Nobody else can do your work for you.
ALBERTO JONÁS

Yes, there's that Alberto Jonás quote once again; a 19th century revelation; who knew?

Nobody else can do your work for you.

Nobody else can do your work for you.

Nobody else can do your work for you!

The human life force adapts itself to its environment, trains itself, and develops ability. This cannot be accomplished by mere thinking and theorizing, but only through action and practice. ... An idle person will not develop ability.
SUZUKI

Study the piano seriously. Take the trouble to acquire some talents and you will soon see that work and study don't go with idle musings.
LISZT

A lack of vital interest in study and improvement was incomprehensible to Leschetizky, and he was patient with, and admired, only those whose energies were equal to their desires in fulfilling their duty to their talent.
ETHEL NEWCOMB

I often go straight home from a concert and practice on pieces I just played, because during the concert, new ideas came to me. These ideas are very precious and must not be postponed for future development.
FERRUCCIO BUSONI

Making progress on the piano is not like walking along a road, where you can see what you have just left behind, and what you are just about to walk over... you advance by leaps and pauses. You seem to have a barrier before you and you can't climb over it, and you keep struggling and striving either to get over it or push it aside, and some happy day you find yourself over it; and for a short space you feel you have made a stride. But there before you lies another barrier, and you are restless again, and the struggle and the effort must begin again.
STERNDALE BENNETT

I think heaven will always help those who are truly talented.
ROBERT SCHUMANN

Man, help yourself!
BEETHOVEN

Quite confident in the ability of Ignaz Moscheles, Beethoven assigned him the job of creating a piano score of his opera *Fidelio*. Moscheles, of course, was thrilled, and later often proudly told his friends about how the great Beethoven had entrusted him with the

job. When finished, he wrote at the end of the score *"completed with the assistance of God"*. Beethoven picked up the score, glanced at the comment and gleefully scribbled below it: *"Man, help yourself"*.
Beethoven was a man of deep religious faith, but he possessed the equally strong conviction that it's up to us to develop our God-given talent.

Divine One, you see my inmost soul, you know that therein dwells the love of Mankind and the desire to do good. ... despite all the limitations of Nature nevertheless did I do everything within my powers to become accepted among worthy artists and men.
BEETHOVEN

Nobody else can do your work for you.

There is no reputation gained in anything that is not deserved.
LESCHETIZKY

HONOR

Honor is another of those character traits that naturally become yours as a consequence of your actions. An honorable person is honest, trustworthy, upright, chivalrous, and ethical. I'd add 'law-abiding' but there are plenty of perfectly legal ways to screw people, as many discover when they review their investment fund statements.

Being honorable in all things is the way to go in life. Everything you can possibly achieve, attain, or obtain in life won't be of much value if others can't truly say that you're honorable.

From childhood I learned to love virtue and everything good and beautiful. ... but especially the truth; for that I hold you to a strict accountability. To me the highest thing, after God, is my honor.
BEETHOVEN

From seeing diverse men in all latitudes resemble each other, though changed in name, I have eventually recognized that there is really but one nation – humanity; but one country – the globe; but one code – that of justice and morality.
L. M. GOTTSCHALK

It's easy enough to think you are a great man when you are not obliged to prove it. ... What I want to be in this world is an honest man.
LESCHETIZKY

That Franz Liszt possessed the cardinal virtues of justice and neighborly love, friend and foe have always agreed.
ARTHUR FRIEDHEIM

However things may be, never capitulate to what is idle, cowardly, or false – however high your position may become. ... It doesn't require too much philosophical resignation to remain indifferent to all the petty barking, dull-witted recriminations, and shrill jealousies. The most important thing is simply to be honest, and to form an inner core and essence of one's work and achievements.
LISZT

It is the heart which ennobles the man, and though I am not a count, my honor is as valuable, perhaps more valuable than many a count.
MOZART

Prince, you are you by accident of birth; I am I through my own efforts. There have been thousands of princes and will be thousands more; but there is only one Beethoven. I too, am a king! My nobility is here, and here (pointing to his heart and head).
BEETHOVEN

No virtue, in my opinion, is as exhilarating as goodness.
PADEREWSKI

Music forces mankind to confront its nobility.
ALFRED CORTOT

A good indication of character is if you always do what you say you're going to do, even (or especially) the little things. Your word and your promise represent your honor, which becomes your 'reputation'.

Anyone who doesn't take truth seriously in small matters cannot be trusted in large ones either.
ALBERT EINSTEIN

Justice, personal decency, the moral code, a devout mind and religious purity meant more to Beethoven than all else; these virtues were enthroned in him and he demanded that others cultivate them. "A man is as good as his word" was his motto, and nothing angered him more than an un-kept promise.
IGNAZ von SEYFRIED

Character is formed primarily through interactions with people, through example and experience. Still, books can be powerful when they communicate similar experiences through language. I've always been intrigued with the reading lists of the great pianists and composers; the books that influenced both their technique, and their 'take' on life.

Beethoven's amusement when he is alone consists in reading the old Greek classics, and several of Sir Walter Scott's novels, which delight him.
IGNAZ MOSCHELES

Beethoven liked to read Plutarch and when listening to his music one often imagines that one can see the outline of one of Plutarch's heroes.
BRAHMS

I have often cursed my creator and my existence. Plutarch has taught me resignation.
BEETHOVEN

Plutarch discoursed on life's moral challenges in his *Lives of the Noble Greeks and Romans,* one of whom was the Roman general and would-be politician Caius Martius Coriolanus. Beethoven clearly had an interest in this particular story; his Opus 62 is the overture written for Heinrich Joseph von Collin's tragedy *Coriolan.*

Had I a dozen sons, each in my love alike and none less dear than thine… I had rather eleven die nobly for their country than one voluptuously surfeit out of action.
VOLUMNIA, ACT 1 SCENE 3 CORIOLANUS SHAKESPEARE

The history of Mankind is a romance, a mask, a tragedy, constructed upon the principles of poetical justice… We may depend upon it that what men delight to read in books, they will put in practice in reality.
WILLIAM HAZLITT

William Hazlitt (1778-1830) published his comprehensive literary critique *Characters of Shakespeare's Plays* in 1817. The books that great composers and pianists read offer clues about the process of character formation.

I shall work. I must go forward and not look back. The Imitation of Christ teaches: "what is undertaken must be brought to a conclusion".
LISZT

Imitation is the first instinct of the awakening mind.
MARIA MONTESSORI

The Imitation of Christ is a 15th century spiritual guidebook written in Latin that first circulated in the Netherlands. Although there have been several theories about possible authors, modern scholarship pretty much agrees that it was Thomas à Kempis.

After *The Bible*, *The Imitation of Christ* is said to be the second most widely read book ever and it's also number two after *The Bible* in terms of translations in various languages. These statistics may be a bit dated. It looks like the *Harry Potter* books and the *Da Vinci Code* are giving them a run for their money; fun books, but kind of a statement about how things change.

When interpreting great music, we owe it to ourselves to understand, as best we can, the cultural milieu that helped shape the composer's personalities. And if a particular source of inspiration was a major influence on their character and ultimately their art, might we not benefit from similar exposure?

Liszt found powerful inspiration in *The Imitation of Christ* and pianists might want to explore this influence on the greatest pianist the world has ever known.

I understand only two things: work, and Chapter V of 'The Imitation of Christ'.
LISZT

Examining this tantalizing reference more closely, we find first of all that *The Imitation of Christ* is arranged in four separate books, each with its own chapter V; but that's okay, we'll just sample them all. The four books are respectively titled: *The Spiritual Life, The Inner Life,*

Consolation, and *The Sacrament of the Altar.* Since I don't read Latin that well, I'm dependent on an English translation by the Reverend William Benham (1831-1910) which I've modernized a bit. You may be thinking 'oh no; theology,' but the book is actually pretty practical and down to earth.

Read scripture in the proper spirit, seeking for the spiritually useful, not subtlety in debate... profit by reading humbly, simply, honestly, and don't desire a reputation for learning.
BOOK I

The message is simple: scripture should be read in a spirit of humility. Those who assume pedantic airs or otherwise act like a big know-it-all will totally miss the point. I mean, you could argue with someone that a mature brontosaurus couple wouldn't fit in the Ark's coach class and maybe feel quite proud of your supposed erudition. But wait; maybe Mrs. Noah (she goes unnamed in Genesis) bid a tearful goodbye to the parents explaining that there was only room for two baby brontosauri, or maybe she just packed some dinosaur eggs in a wooden crate lined with straw. Or maybe Brontosaurus is extinct precisely because they missed the boat.

You could waste a lot of time on such discussions, calculated primarily to show off your 'intelligence'. Next you'll be arguing that those thousands of angels dancing on the head of a pin must keep at it for at least 10,000 hours in order to achieve the level of mastery of a Fred Astaire or Michael Jackson.

That, however, isn't going to help the tens of thousands of poverty stricken orphans in this world who cry themselves to sleep every night, anxious about where their next meal is coming from, or afraid even for their own personal safety. One simple act of kindness to alleviate a human being's suffering, or one creative act to make the world a more beautiful place is worth more than all that combined erudite talk, and great musical artists like Mozart, Beethoven and Liszt got that. Other smart people back then got it too.

A morning-glory at my window satisfies me more than the metaphysics of books.
WALT WHITMAN

A lot of pointless self-centered talk, especially about religion, is not going to accomplish very much in life. It's more about what you constructively do. And nowhere is this more applicable than in music.

The question is not "what do you know?" but "what can you do?" You'll find it put to you in every profession. A pupil who goes to the teacher finds that the first question is not "how many études have you studied?" but "play me something." The audience doesn't ask "who was your teacher, how long do you practice every day, or what method have you been taught?" but "play a solo for us."
CÉCILE CHAMINADE

Knowing is not enough; we must apply. Willing is not enough; we must do.
GOETHE

Well, it would be nice if people were really like that. Today they actually do seem to be asking a lot about teachers, hours, or methods. Tell somebody you play the piano and they usually ask you where you studied, or where you play, not what you play, and there's always that "can you make a living at that?" – a bit rude, don't you think? and likely a psychological projection of their own insecurities. General bar-raising is urgently needed today for both performers and music-lovers.

I'd rather be on the lowest step of Art's ladder than on the highest pinnacle of dilettantism.
BETTINA WALKER

In Book II of *The Imitation of Christ* we find this:

We find and criticize little faults in others and pass over great ones in ourselves. We're quick to dwell on what we endure at the hands of others, but don't reflect on how much others bear from us. Don't judge severely of others… rather, take full heed of your own.
BOOK II

… common sense stuff that can be summarized in the vernacular as: quit pointing fingers and mind your own business. We are advised to grow up, and become responsible adults.

Positive Piano

To continue, Book *III*:

Love is great and can make every heavy burden light, equalize every inequality. Strong love knows all things are possible; it creates success, and without it we fail. Embrace willingly, and humbly, all hard and bitter things for the beloved's sake.
BOOK III

More inspirational wisdom - do what you love, be prepared to make sacrifices for it. Let's do the Mozart quote again.

Neither a lofty degree of intelligence nor imagination nor both together go to the making of genius. Love, love, love, that is the soul of genius.
MOZART

And finally, from Book *IV*:

Priests - approach your work with fear and reverence, perform before God faithfully and devoutly, and show yourself to be blameless. You are bound to higher standards of discipline and holiness, and must set an example.
BOOK IV

If ever there was a high priest of Musical Art it was Franz Liszt; and viewed metaphorically these excerpts offer insights into his philosophy of art - just substitute 'artist' for 'priest'. If you want to be a real leader - start acting like one. Live your life according to the highest standards, both technical and moral. Authentic artists are bound to a higher standard.

Liszt devoured literary heavyweights like Dante and Goethe. We have the Dante symphony and the piano *Fantasy quasi Sonata 'après une lecture de Dante'*. Then there's Liszt's *Faust* symphony, and it really gets me that the composer of the *Mephisto* waltzes and polka was actually a card-carrying exorcist. Yes, later in life Liszt studied for, and was initiated into, the four minor orders of the Catholic Church: acolyte, exorcist, lector and porter.

The darkest places in hell are reserved for those who maintain their neutrality in times of moral crisis.
DANTE

310

Another of Liszt's favorite authors was Marcus Aurelius, Emperor of Rome. Considered one of the few 'good' emperors, he acquired a reputation for justice in his administration and contributed to the literature of philosophy with his *Meditations*.

As for Marcus Aurelius, I willingly put his bust among my household gods.
LISZT

Marcus Aurelius died in 180 AD at the age of fifty-nine, and in accordance with Roman law and religion was officially deified. I came across a 19th century translation of the *Meditations* by the English classics scholar George Long, educated at Trinity College, Cambridge. In the introduction he remarks that Roman citizens who could afford it kept a small statue or bust of the emperor among their 'Dei Penates' or household deities. That Liszt used the same expression indicates a more than superficial acquaintance with ancient history. You probably won't be surprised to learn that I own a plaster bust of Liszt and have placed it at the forefront of my own Dei Penates.

Before us all Leschetizky knelt at the bust of Chopin one evening and exclaimed "Oh Chopin, forgive us for what we have done to thy music in this room!"
ETHEL NEWCOMB

I love what turns up in the course of research. George Long (1800-1879) was a contemporary of Liszt (1811-1886). One of his first jobs, at age 24, was professor of ancient languages at my alma mater, the brand new University of Virginia founded by Thomas Jefferson in 1819. Long taught there from 1824 to 1828 and since Jefferson lived till July 4th 1826, it's likely that they met.

Marcus Aurelius benefited early in life from a whole bunch of very wise teachers and mentors, one of whom was Sextus of Chaeroneia, a grandson of Beethoven's beloved Plutarch. Written primarily as an exercise in journaling of sorts, the *Meditations* have inspired many throughout the ages.

Perform every act of your life as if it were the last, lay aside all carelessness and passionate aversion to the command of reason, and all hypocrisy, and

self-love, and discontent with your lot. See how few are the things you can truly lay hold of, in order to live a life which flows quietly, and is like the existence of the gods.
MARCUS AURELIUS

Always bear in mind, what is the nature of the whole, and what is your nature, and how this is related to the whole.
MARCUS AURELIUS

The best way of avenging thyself is not to become like the wrong-doer.
MARCUS AURELIUS

I never practice revenge. When I must antagonize others I do no more than is necessary to protect myself against them, or prevent them from doing further evil.
BEETHOVEN

Right up front the emperor acknowledged that much of his wisdom was acquired from his parents and mentors, and he identifies: "good morals, the government of my temper, modesty, manly character, piety and beneficence, consistency and undeviating steadiness, love of work and perseverance, abstinence, not only from evil deeds, but even from evil thoughts, giving to others readily and cherishing good hopes, and simplicity in my way of living, far removed from the habits of the rich" – this from a Roman emperor, but one who truly learned the fine art of appreciating the material without getting attached to it. He also liked to 'tell it like it is'.

With my brother Severus, I observed no concealment of his opinions with respect to those whom he critiqued, and that his friends had no need to conjecture what he did or did not wish, for it was quite plain.
MARCUS AURELIUS

Authenticity and sincerity should automatically manifest in whatever we do. Being straightforward and honest about things is always the best policy. Music critic and composer Alexander Serov once asked Liszt to read through his latest opera *Judith*. The response he got was perhaps not exactly what he wanted to hear.

This opera does not please me, it is not sufficiently interesting … and it's only to my friends that I say exactly what I think, owing them that privilege, at minimum; I don't pretend with friends.
LISZT

… an instance of the *Meditations* having influenced Liszt's character? During the exchange Liszt offered Serov specific suggestions to improve the drama, or lack thereof, in the libretto, and orchestration tips, like scoring of the harps, for example; all valuable input, coming as it did from a master. However, Liszt later had to write to another friend:

Serov is quite displeased with me, due to my sincere critique of his opera Judith, to which I suggested he do what Judith did to Holofernes.
LISZT

As recounted in the Biblical Book of Judith, she lopped off the head of the invading Assyrian general. Although it's no longer performed, Serov's opera Judith was moderately successful when it came out in the early 1860s; maybe some of Liszt's suggestions got incorporated after all.

Here's a very curious coincidence that turned up in the course of research. I wonder if Liszt was aware of this minor historical detail? In general, scholars agree that Marcus Aurelius adopted a relatively lenient attitude towards emerging Christianity. Now the Roman empire in 180 AD represented a sizeable chunk of real estate, and travel and communications were no doubt snail-paced … an emperor couldn't possibly be expected to be on top of everything, right? I mean, look - your average corporate manager doesn't know what his employees are doing, even in the same building.

We cannot be sure of the dates, but it appears that a certain Christian woman named Cecilia was martyred in Sicily in the closing days of the reign of Emperor Marcus Aurelius. Of course she wouldn't become the patron saint of music for at least another 300 years.

It doesn't really matter what religion you are, or aren't; everyone can benefit from wisdom literature, and the exposure will strengthen your natural predilection for open-mindedness, tolerance, and humility - or hopefully inspire these traits if you're a bit deficient.

But simply reading about character will only take you so far.

If you want a quality, act as if you already had it.
WILLIAM JAMES

You can design a set of personal experiences to develop some character. If you're not sure how, you can't go wrong by helping somebody else. Come up with a way to tangibly benefit someone or some cause in your community, not with the explicit goal of 'developing yourself' but to genuinely help. It can be as simple as reflecting on a person's challenges in life and calling them up to offer encouragement. Or give up some of your superfluous material amusements and transform them into basic necessities for someone else.

He who, at twenty, goes from pleasure to pleasure with the heart not absolutely closed to good, must now and then, at some turning in the road, become aware that there are hungry folk who could live a month on what he spends in a few hours on frivolity.
PAUL SABATIER The Road to Assisi

If you lack material assets, offer your music - the 'character' is in the act of giving.

When I give, I give of myself.
WALT WHITMAN

You've left an impression here which you'll leave in every country—that of a man of heart, talent, tact, and intellect. One of these qualities alone is enough to distinguish a man from the vulgar herd; but if you're so fortunate as to possess a quartet of them, it's absolutely necessary that an active will be added in order to bring out their best fruits, and this I'm sure you'll not be slow to do.
LISZT

Character begins with a mindset. If you envision and then act, your character takes care of itself. You can't build it in a vacuum; it's developed through social inter-action. So step out of your egocentric shell, get out of your own thinking, mingle and collaborate with living, breathing people, and try to see things from their perspective - walk a mile or two in their flip-flops.

Great artists possess a special quality, which for lack of a better word we call presence - and it's more than just personality or charisma. We enjoy the company of personable people, but don't necessarily feel that we're in the presence of someone uniquely special. Presence is power emanating from character.

We convince by our presence.
WALT WHITMAN

Presence, like 'success,' isn't something you work at directly; it's a byproduct of, and an outward manifestation of, the process of character development. Presence impresses in a way that mere talk never will. Though difficult to quantify, you'll know it when you see it, or rather, experience it.

Two pianists both possess the same amazing level of mechanical dexterity and memory ability. One plays beautifully and inspirationally, the other is a crashing bore. Think about it.

Authenticity, integrity, courage, commitment, and discipline – these are qualities that enable you to apply yourself and develop an overwhelming technical mastery to serve your higher artistic vision. And people will respond *overwhelmingly* – we're starving for it.

Leschetizky attached the greatest importance to a clear understanding of his pupil's character. "I talk with them during their lessons and twenty minutes speech will often be worth an hour's tuition. ...When I hear that such and such pianist pleases one more than he did a month ago, I know that his powers of reflection are asserting themselves".
LOUIS C. ELSON

Another thought about character: go about your daily tasks with a positive can-do attitude – no whining!

A noble unselfish soul, of sublime sentiment and resolution, best expresses itself with simplicity. Tears are acceptable only on those rare (thank God!) solemn occasions. Whimpering just parodies authentic tears, and I cannot tolerate it. Crying about trifles irritates me.
LISZT

PERSEVERANCE

Positive Piano

It takes discipline to accomplish worthwhile things; some days just getting out of bed can be a challenge. Continually keeping at it and maintaining commitment in the face of adversity is a long-term proposition requiring perseverance. It's about staying power, and hanging in there for the duration. Einstein claimed he really wasn't that smart (he was, relatively), but achieved because he kept pursuing solutions longer than most people.

The ingenious and elaborate works of the great masters offer you exquisite enjoyment, if you have the patience to overcome the difficulties generally inseparable from them.
CZERNY

Unconquerable, unyielding perseverance was the fundamental quality in Liszt's character.
ARTHUR FRIEDHEIM

There's no need to give up in discouragement; it's possible for every person to improve themselves.
SUZUKI

The power of sticking to a thing is mental; it's called 'will power', and few students have it. Thousands of them start in with the determination to do their best but very, very few "stick to it." They get good advice, they know what to do, but they won't do it.
HENRY THEOPHILUS FINCK

The path of a pianist, particularly when he is blazing a trail, is beset with difficulties, to put it mildly. ... Life was a stern, grim business then – nothing really mattered but work. The career was being built step by step in slow painful stages.
PADEREWSKI

You must attentively and assiduously persevere in the practice of this embellishment. ... it shall be more than sufficient if your zeal is equal to my wishes for your improvement.
JOSEF TARTINI

My old proverb: It will get done somehow.
CHOPIN

316

Every failure and sign of mediocrity I regard quite calmly as an experience, and continue undisturbed on my way.
BRAHMS

It's only the middle of the roaders who are discouraged by setbacks; the others derive new strength from them and go on to find their true identity.
CLAUDE DEBUSSY

The majority of those who wish to become musicians have no idea of the difficulties they will have to surmount, the moral tortures they will be called upon to endure, the disillusions they will experience, before they win recognition. Ambitious young musicians habitually fail to realize that it takes years and years of unremitting toil; that they must be well taught; that they must be well supplied with the tools of their craft; that they must have good health and great patience, in order to surmount the obstacles with which nature—and often man as well—will obstruct the road. ... The history of music, and of the great musicians, offers endless examples to corroborate what I say.
LEOPOLD AUER

I haven't yet succeeded in constructing the edifice to shelter my ambitions, but am not short of material or even the land to build it on. Doing the work, raising the walls will cause me difficulty and anxiety, until I can lay down the different floors according to my fancy. Please don't get impatient and lose confidence in me! Be sure that my serious and unshakeable determination, plus an original talent strengthened and developed by study and experience, will achieve much.
LISZT

Liszt wrote those words to his mother when he was thirty-five years old. By that time he had developed into the world's greatest pianist and interpretive musician, and had already composed masterpieces. One marvels at the incredible scope of his vast artistic imagination and that he could envision even greater things to accomplish in the future.

Rapid fortune is not lasting, Che vá piano, vá sano e vá lontano (slow and steady wins the race).
MOZART

Positive Piano

After one of Henselt's most brilliant concert triumphs, I went backstage with Count Wielhorski and found him surrounded by the flood tide of concert-goers, busy with his dumb keyboard! ... it was the artist's confession of faith, of giving himself up entirely to his art to the exclusion of everything else. I've often regretted it for his sake but understood it as a rare faithfulness to conviction, as an extreme of duty to his life-work for art – as a proof of endurance and strength of character... a longing of Henselt's to grasp with his hands the ever receding horizon of ideal perfection.
WILHELM von LENZ

Confronted with a high mountain, one cannot reach the summit in one stride, but must climb step by step to achieve the goal. There will be difficulties and hardships but neither disappointment nor despair if one follows the path steadily. ... Never forget that a person who fails at five hundred times can succeed at five thousand times.
SUZUKI

Fall down seven times, get up eight.
JAPANESE PROVERB

One can sooner attain eminence with industry and less talent than with much talent without industry. Unremitting industry will help over many a hard place, and enable its possessor to attain at least a respectable eminence in music; but talent without industry runs to seed. In fact, the arduous summit of Parnassus can be conquered only behind the double-team: industry and talent.
MALWINE BRÉE

Time and patience are in the habit of bringing many a thing to a good end. .... Having talent is not enough. In addition, and above all, one has to push oneself forward.
LISZT

(A lady related)... I've known Sgambati to begin practicing some passage which he thought wanted improvement in a Mendelssohn concerto, and there he would sit, from the closing in of a winter afternoon until near midnight, patient, absorbed, and untiring; nor would he leave off even then, had I not begged him to consider that the other lodgers in the palazzo might complain if he went on any longer.
BETTINA WALKER

318

But please, let's be reasonable ...

Practice should not be persisted in at times unpleasing to other people, no matter how much the enthusiast may desire to play scales at 5 a.m. or polish show pieces with midnight oil.
ANNIE W. PATTERSON

For the greater part of practice I recommend playing with restrained power. And, incidentally, your neighbors will thank you for it too.
JOSEF HOFMANN

Leschetizky had a psychotherapist's knack for understanding exactly what a particular student required for their unique self-development.

I have this morning found a new talent. His is an interesting but complex personality; young, oversensitive, believes in himself, expects everything of me. If only he can take the rebuffs that will come in life.
LESCHETIZKY

Actually he was a lot more perceptive and helpful than your average run of the mill therapist today. Leschetizky told Paderewski that he was already too old for a big career (in his twenties) and that he'd never make it. I guess that triggered something because look what happened. On the other hand, he insisted on telling Mark Hambourg he was great, because for some reason that's what he needed to hear. To a Jewish student he publicly said "You, above all, should work harder, given the immense musical contributions of your people".

Imagination creates reality...(but)....achievements, seldom credited to their source, are the result of unspeakable drudgery and worries.
WAGNER

Definition of genius: a transcendent capacity of taking trouble.
THOMAS CARLYLE

Having once decided to achieve a certain task, achieve it at all costs of tedium and distaste. The gain in self-confidence of having accomplished a

tiresome labor is immense.
ARNOLD BENNETT

One must achieve the understanding of a musical work through exhaustive study, and the more profound the work, the harder it is, and the more study it requires.
GUSTAV MAHLER

I see the full extent of the difficulties with which all composers have had to contend, but notwithstanding, I feel able to overcome these difficulties as well as another. … Now more than ever – I can never abandon my resolve.
MOZART

Keep right on; I tell you that you have the ability to succeed. Do not let yourself be deterred.
LISZT

Czerny, on whom I had already called, humbly as always, asked me what I'd studied industriously.
CHOPIN

I urge you to still greater diligence ... Consider the matter as if you were for a time compelled to wend your way among somewhat tangled and thorny bushes in order to arrive at last at a beautiful prospect, and a spot always blooming in vernal beauty.
CZERNY

Always be assured that ultimate success will ensue, if you work for it. Success may be deferred, but it will come at last.
ERNST PAUER

If a thing cannot be done in one way, it must be done in another. Through work directed by constant thought and by intelligence, study out the way your hand can do it best. The very necessity of having to study out the 'how' to do things makes every subsequent effort easier.
EDOUARD ZELDEN

Always come to your lesson with honest goodwill, and with a sincere desire to advance and improve. A good composition is worthy of good practice.
ERNST PAUER

Ill luck seemed to have dogged my opera so far, but I had spent more than five years on it and wasn't ready to yield. ... I resolved to force a third production which would be decisive.
ARTHUR FRIEDHEIM

Often when I was wrestling with obstacles of every kind, and my physical and mental strength were at a low ebb and it was hard for me to persevere in my chosen path, a secret feeling in me whispered "there are so few happy and contented people here below, sorrow and anxiety pursue them all, perhaps your work may someday become a spring from which the careworn may draw a few moments rest and refreshment". And that was a powerful motivation to press onwards.
JOSEPH HAYDN

I'm very much afraid that Schumann will have a struggle with the difficulties and delays which usually occur in trying to get any lofty work performed. One would say that a bad fairy, in order sometimes to counterbalance the works of genius, gives a magic success to the most vulgar works and presides over the propagation of them, favoring those whom inspiration has disdained, in order to push its elect into the shade. That is no reason for discouragement, for what matters the sooner or the later?
LISZT

Find your guide, press on without thinking of failure, and the way to success may be found before you know it.
SIGISMUND STOJOWSKI

All things come to those who can wait. But it's important to seize the right moment, and that you must decide. Don't fret passing disturbances and hold your ground with quiet, deliberate courage. Retreat belongs to the enemy. For us it is "Gradatim vincimus - Gradually we overcome".
LISZT

When you are doing something you believe in, you've got to stick to it. It isn't always easy.
LIBERACE

Wow; let's take five. I hope that last section gets you jazzed and encouraged to keep at it.

321

If there's a deadline, I work late.
DAVE BRUBECK

I will tell you this, quite truthfully: those last couple of pages helped me, over the course of years, to finish writing this book.

COPING WITH ADVERSITY

Life isn't always smooth sailing. There's no utopia; the word literally means 'nowhere'. We all experience adversity at one time or another, and often it's these temporary setbacks that teach us the most valuable lessons about life. The great ones persevered; they learned the lessons inherent in the experience and became more humble and stronger. They moved on.

The devil take the poets who dare to sing the pleasures of an artist's life.
L. M. GOTTSCHALK

Difficulties are necessary, so that they can be overcome.
LISZT

The education of life makes the artist to a great extent. Adversity helps make the artist and form his character; you have to struggle and to suffer in order to develop.
EDOUARD ZELDEN

You will get there, have no doubts about that, but even so; look around you and see how, for everyone, there has to be a large measure of suffering and patience.
GABRIEL FAURÉ

Sorrow and suffering, if they are really deeply felt, are factors which often form the greatest inspiration in Art.
LESCHETIZKY

Neurosis is always a substitute for legitimate suffering.
CARL JUNG

The reality is that life is challenging. And yes, there will always be floods, earthquakes, tsunamis and plane crashes; and frankly, these terrible things can be difficult to rationalize philosophically.

But many of our problems in life stem from the daily challenges of simply growing up, and the choices we make. Reading about the ups and downs of great artists can help put ours in perspective. Some of these anecdotes are light-hearted and entertaining, and incidentally illustrate that in some ways our modern times have actually become more sedate and conservative. Others are genuinely tragic, and give pause for serious reflection: in comparison, our own personal situation probably isn't that bad after all.

Since the best man could not be obtained, a mediocre one had to be accepted.
MAYOR OF LEIPZIG 1723 (on hiring J.S Bach)

The duties are by far not as agreeable as described to me originally, many of the bonuses attached to the position have been withdrawn, the cost of living is very high here, the authorities are curiously hostile to music, envy prevails, vexations are numerous, and I have to live in a state of almost constant struggle.
J.S. BACH

When it was my turn to perform, I signaled to the orchestra to begin playing with me my "Souvenirs of Ireland". Straight away, during the somewhat somber introduction to the piece, the louts in the third gallery started whistling, hissing, and yelling out things like "are you comfortable Jack?" and aiming whole salvos of sucked-out orange peel. I was barely able to conceal my fury, but stiffened my resolve not to give in to it.
IGNAZ MOSCHELES

"Now listen," Mottl said, "we can't do your concerto full justice with just one rehearsal. …we may as well be prepared for the worst." The showy, brilliant introduction sounded impressive and held the audience's attention momentarily … but signs of increasing restlessness were plain enough. The second movement called forth approval but the Scherzo, which needed a great deal of rehearsal, was downright grotesque; the audience was obviously displeased. And when the military drum made its entry with a prolonged, deafening roll, a stentorian voice from the gallery shouted "Fire! Fire!"
The house rocked with laughter. From that moment on every shred of decorum was cast aside in a wild chorus of catcalls, brayings, hurrahs, vivas, snatches

of student songs, shrill whistling and a deafening stamping of feet, while the orchestra, now playing an unrestrained fortissimo, reinforced by an equally loud piano, swept vigorously into the concluding march. The hubbub lasted for many minutes after the music was finished.
ARTHUR FRIEDHEIM

Greymuller told Chopin all in one breath: "that he was pleased to make his acquaintance, but wouldn't advise giving a performance since there were so many other good pianists in Vienna that a great reputation was required before it was possible to earn any money, adding that he personally couldn't be of any assistance to an artist newly arrived in the capital – because times were hard." Chopin, to use his own words "stared at him in blank amazement."
ALFRED CORTOT

Every day greater difficulties seem to arise. There's been an uninterrupted flow of concerts given by pianists, resulting in a surfeited public on whose interest it would be impossible to rely ... As for the potpourri on Polish themes, in my opinion it failed to come off. They applauded in the spirit of: "let him go away knowing we weren't bored".
CHOPIN

The man has not been born who can please everyone.
CHOPIN

That sentiment, incidentally, applies to authors as well.

Poverty may well be the worst thing that can happen to a person because it cuts you off completely from human society. I'm beginning to understand this.
ROBERT SCHUMANN

To repeat: that sentiment, incidentally, applies to authors as well.

You probably already heard that it was a complete frost (premier of the D minor Piano Concerto 1859). At the rehearsals it met with total silence, and at the performance, where hardly three people raised their hands to clap, it was regularly hissed.
BRAHMS

When we got to London there were more difficulties to overcome than in Paris. One reason was that we arrived too late and the season was accordingly far advanced and the soirées arranged. Another is that the artists who are here – Ries, however, was an honorable exception – did nothing at all for us, Kalkbrenner in particular. Yet as you know, good material does not remain suppressed for long, and victory is all the more glorious.

ADAM LISZT

PLYMOUTH: Franz Liszt played a concert here on 26 August 1840. A projected concert on the 27th was cancelled when only seven people bought tickets.
CORK: On January 2, 1841 Liszt returned intending to take part in a concert at the court house, but not a single ticket was sold. Liszt therefore invited a few music lovers to his hotel where he and the other members of his concert party went through their entire concert program.
DARLINGTON. Liszt took part in a concert here on 27 January 1841, during the course of which an inebriate offered him a sovereign to play "Rule Britannia".
AYR. A great deal of snow had fallen and it was bitterly cold. After taking some nourishment at the King's Arms tavern, Liszt departed at 11 AM in an open third-class train carrying cattle and pigs, and arrived in Glasgow at 2 PM.

A MUSICAL GAZETTEER, Plymouth 1841

On a more serious note....

During the night of October 17, 1833, I suddenly had the most frightening thought a human being can possibly conceive, the most terrible that Heaven could inflict: that I might lose my reason. It took possession of me with such violence that all comfort, all prayer vanished as if it were idle mockery. ... Anyone who has been once crushed like that knows no worse suffering, or illness, or despair that could possibly happen to him.

ROBERT SCHUMANN

Today Johannes (Brahms) set the stone over my dear one's grave. My whole soul went with him.

CLARA SCHUMANN

Every night when I go to bed, I hope that I may never wake again, and every

morning renews my grief.
FRANZ SCHUBERT

The experience (of deafness) almost made me despair, and I was at the point of putting an end to my life. The only thing that held me back was my Art.
BEETHOVEN

I'm puzzled, I'm melancholy, I don't know what to do with myself, I wish I weren't alone.
CHOPIN

In the early spring of this year, Moscheles was deeply moved by domestic sorrow and anxiety. His eldest boy died on the 23rd of March, and the only remaining child was in delicate health during the whole winter. "The poor mother" he says in his diary, "knows nothing but anxiety, sorrow, and sleepless nights. One of our darlings is in his grave; with God's help she will be spared her one remaining treasure. As a man I have a load of sorrow to bear, as an artist I belong to the public."
CHARLOTTE MOSCHELES

The older, 19th century biographies of famous pianists and composers present the artists as human beings with failures as well as successes. These days, with the incessant hype and self-glorification of modern publicity, the endless identical resumes of 'prestigious' teachers, together with awards and lists of professional engagements say virtually nothing about the artist's humanity, and become dull and stultifying.

As a young mother, Teresa Carreño found herself in the agonizing situation of having to put her child up for adoption for financial reasons. Those who haven't faced the same situation can't possibly understand the intense suffering. Years later, a successful concert artist and now mother of two more children, Teresa wrote to the adoptive mother, Mrs. Bischoff, asking permission to see her first daughter.

I earnestly beg of you to allow me to see my daughter for a few minutes. In all these years there's been a painful silence, in which I've longed with such a heavy heart, to hear something of my child without in any way causing you or her any pain.... In the name of the love you now bear her and once bore

me, I appeal to your heart to let me have the comfort of seeing her.
TERESA CARREÑO

Carreño's biographer Marta Milanowski explains that over the years Teresa had been disparaged to the child and now that she was an internationally lauded artist, Mrs. Bischoff perhaps felt threatened. Instead of responding, she had her lawyer draft a reply which some might see as a model of heartless cruelty but probably was just business as usual from his perspective. In so many words it basically said 'get lost'. What Teresa felt when she received the reply we can only imagine, but she had no choice except to steel her determination and continue with her professional engagements. In fact, she played a concert the very next evening.

A long life is going to have plenty of those ups and downs. Like most of us, Teresa had plenty of relationship challenges over the years; études and concertos were a piece of cake in comparison. During her particularly painful divorce from Eugen d'Albert she wrote: *"may God help me to bear my suffering. Only He knows what I suffer!!!"*

One can never marry too late or divorce too soon.
TERESA CARREÑO

Come quickly! Your children and my children are quarreling with our children.
EUGEN d'ALBERT to TERESA CARREÑO

Yesterday Ms. Carreño played for the first time the second concerto of her third husband in the fourth philharmonic concert.
NEWSPAPER, BERLIN, 1893

There's a story about a worried father of eight daughters seeking advice as to what he should do with them when they were grown. Moszkowski suggested training some as stenographers or governesses and marrying the rest off to Eugen d'Albert.
HENRY THEOPHILUS FINCK

A good marriage would be between a blind wife and a deaf husband.
MONTAIGNE

Positive Piano

(A second marriage) … Alas! another instance of the triumph of hope over experience.

DR. SAMUEL JOHNSON

Moritz Moszkowski's wife (a sister of Cecil Chaminade) ran off with another man. Moszkowski then lost all his German bond investments in World War I. Lots of things happen in life; we must cope, learn from the experience, and hopefully become stronger for a better tomorrow. Moszkowski's admiring colleagues banded together for a benefit concert to bail him out.

One of the most amazing pianists of the late 19th century also experienced some of the greatest tragedy. Earlier, after Liszt revised his monumental set of twelve *Transcendental Études,* he apparently lost interest in mechanical technique *per se* and turned to other endeavors saying *"I expected that someday a pianist would appear who would make this subject his specialty, and would accomplish difficulties that were seemingly impossible to perform".*

That pianist was to be Leopold Godowsky. Born in 1870, he was just sixteen years old when Liszt died in 1886, and as Godowsky described in his memoirs, he had hoped to study with Liszt, and was actually en route to Weimar when he heard of Liszt's death in Bayreuth.

Godowsky was a great musician and pianist possessed of a super analytical mind with which he acquired a phenomenal mechanical technique. His marvelous playing enchanted countless audiences and every professional pianist in his generation, including the likes of Busoni, Rachmaninoff, Hofmann, de Pachmann, and Lhévinne. Godowsky also taught extensively, and composed much interesting new music, including those incomparable 53 paraphrases on the Chopin *Études.*

A deeply personal letter starkly illustrates how terrible things can get (Berlin, 1932, to Isidor Phillipe).

You will understand and forgive my long silence when you see how much I suffered and how my sorrow was great and deep beyond human endurance. I lost all (material wealth) that I own … followed several months later by a still greater calamity: the ruin of my health … my wife became desperately ill … she had to be operated on without delay … diabetes, kidney trouble … the possibility of her losing her sight completely … you cannot imagine the intense heartache this gave me.

328

While I worried myself to death ... the last and most shocking thing happened to me: the suicide of my poor son. ... he wrote me a touching farewell note and then turned on the gas in his room. When he was discovered the next day he was already dead a number of hours. The terrible world economic depression had an effect on him ... my wife's grief is heartbreaking... I cannot play or walk well ... my doctor gives me injections of albumen with iodine alternating with strychnine ... I do not see any improvement ... I pay staggering sums to doctors and the sanitorium. The conditions in America are incredibly bad, while here the despicable Hitler regime makes life unbearable for decent people ... it is a frightful world, full of misery and hate, poverty and want, meanness and cruelty.
LEOPOLD GODOWSKY

Godowsky's wife died a year later of a heart attack.

Any pianist egotistical about his own supposed technical prowess would do well to humbly contemplate these words. Meditate on them when you go to perform a so-called virtuoso work, and if you can sincerely emote and relate to the above, your artistic interpretation will unquestionably become deeper.

Godowsky once commented that the best book on piano playing that he had ever read was Adolph Kullak's *The Aesthetics of Pianoforte-Playing*. Of course I had to get a copy and read it; I see the value but it's not my style. Ask me what I think is the most inspirational music book and I'll name one written by a violinist: *Nurtured by Love* by Shin'ichi Suzuki.

Suzuki offered inspiration, encouragement, love, and good will to thousands of young violin students. But life was harsh and cruel for the people of Japan in 1945. Their military and political leaders had deceived them, ruthlessly engaging in a pointless and unwinnable war with the United States. In the final months, it was the civilian population that suffered the most.

Suzuki tells of extreme famine, with people scouring the countryside for anything half-way edible, even moss and algae in the streams. They would boil it in a pot of water with a little salt to make a thin soup. His European wife, interred in a prison camp for foreigners, was once able to smuggle an apple out to him.

I still remember vividly the precious apple my wife gave me on a visit, saved for me from her rations. But I felt it was too precious for me to enjoy, and

saved it, without telling her, for the children in Kiso-Fukushima.
SUZUKI

I'm guessing that for most of you reading this book, your problems are pretty trivial relative to the millions of poor and hopeless on this planet. Count your blessings if you've been spared the torment that many must endure. Work all the harder to contribute something positive in this life, and help others. Read *Nurtured by Love*; it will provide perspective ... and hope.

You're going to need it for what's coming up next. I know the first word in my title is *Positive*, but in this world, part of the definition of positive is recognizing injustice ... and standing up for justice. The next three or four pages are going to get pretty intense. If you're not up to it, you might want to skip forward to the next chapter.

Now that I know everybody will keep reading, let's proceed. I offer these observations once again in the form of an Intermezzo ... in a minor key.

INTERMEZZO

SERIOUSLY...

Besides my love of music and the piano, I've always had a deep interest in history. Admittedly somewhat of an artificial construct, it still can be entertaining and educational. The world, with its animal inhabitants, natural resources, and our civilization of Man all combined has from day one experienced a plethora of highs and lows; those good times and bad ones. This creation has been amazingly resilient and has always managed to come through. But as I reflect on what's happening around me in my lifetime, I'm dismayed to think that the very survival of so many beautiful things in life is now in question.

Rather than harvested logically and sustainably for the common good, the planet has been repeatedly raped of its natural resources, mainly to the overall benefit of a not elite, but infamous few. What's left has become dangerously polluted to a perilous tipping point, even our majestic oceans. It's been building for some time. Rachel Carson wrote *Silent Spring* back in the 1960s.

Once conducted in noble harmony with nature, the ancient art of agriculture arguably started man out on his course of civilization. Now, apart from dwindling numbers of big-minded small farmers who still revere their crops and livestock and remain true to Nature, most of agriculture has become a nightmarish industrial chemical and genetically-engineered parody that is wreaking havoc on the system.

The wonderful wild animals with whom we share this planet are being ruthlessly decimated; the extinction rate of species has accelerated to an alarming degree. Elephants have stepped on land mines; whales have been hit by depth charges. Some dentist just shot and killed a magnificent old lion, the pet mascot of a game sanctuary in Zimbabwe; and that animal was being monitored for a conservation study. It's just been announced that there are only four white rhinos left on the planet. Maybe they'll be gone forever by the time you read this.

That kind of hunting isn't like bringing venison home for the family dinner table. Hunting is not a sport but a revered tradition of sharing in the abundant gifts of creation. Legitimate hunters ought to be up in arms against those illegitimate ones giving them a bad rap. 'Trophy' hunting is an obsolete sick mindset that ought to be legally banned worldwide. Real marksmen (the best) compete in the Olympics where they shoot at targets.

I was joking earlier about Noah's Ark. Some people scoff at that story thinking it physically impossible. It wouldn't occur to them to study Carl Jung or Joseph Campbell, either. Well, the way we know-it-all humans are going, pretty soon two of all remaining animal species will fit in a medium-sized rowboat or crew shell.

I wish that Edward Bernays had just stayed with the concert impresario business; then it would have been only the performing arts scene that gradually declined. It would be sad, but not a tragedy if our main problem was just artists' big egos, and whether or not musical art made any progress.

But the first virtuoso spin-doc and author of *Crystallizing Public Opinion, Engineering Consent,* and *Propaganda* also was instrumental in bringing toxic fluorine to your drinking water supply, 'persuading' millions of women to smoke cigarettes, and sweeping under the carpet a massacre of underpaid striking workers by hired thugs. In *One Hundred Years of Solitude,* Nobel Laureate Gabriel Garcia Marquez makes reference to one such event in Central America perpetrated by the American Fruit Company, a major client of Bernays.

In the last decades of the 19th century Franz Liszt presided over a marvelous assembly of young musical talent in the old cultural capital of Weimar, Germany; a town once home to artistic luminaries Bach, Hummel, Goethe, and Schiller. I just had a conversation about it with a friend and she asked if any city today could be compared to Weimar at its peak. Frankly, I drew a blank. I don't believe there is one.

In his final years Liszt poured all his remaining energies into helping the next generation move forward. Barely fifty years after Liszt's passing, and less than ten miles from Weimar in the small village of Buchenwald, the Nazis meticulously unrolled long coils of barbed wire and proceeded to construct a death camp. Buchenwald is a relatively unknown such camp – because there were so many of them. We mentioned Viktor Frankl, a psychiatrist who survived internment in one.

I've visited Weimar three times now; Buchenwald once.

Where am I going with this? The most shocking application of the new technology of propaganda occurred in Germany during World War II. Edward Bernays' memoirs came out after the war, when full knowledge of war crime atrocities had been revealed to the world. Despite the fact that he was Jewish, Bernays seemed to take pride in the fact that chief Nazi propaganda minister Joseph Goebbels publicly praised his books as the absolute best and most useful in the genre.

Bernays was a sociopath who once bragged about dining with clients on oysters and champagne, this in the midst of the great depression when millions of people were unemployed; but he was not evil. Joseph Goebbels, on the other hand, was a psychopath who helped murder millions; then he and his wife murdered their own children and committed suicide. An integral paragraph in one of the most heinous chapters in history was the new virtual mind control originating with psychological techniques for selling consumer products, and ... so very sad and strange to say ... the promotion of performing artists.

A small group of thugs led by the most fanatic of all psychopaths wrested power from a nation of millions, one with a cultural heritage that included Bach, Mozart, and Beethoven. How did they do it? Besides slick propaganda, the basic approach is plainly articulated in their evil boss's own book: *tell people the crudest and most stupid things; success determines right or wrong; and the first essential for that success is perpetual employment of violence.*

'Success' does not define morality. To make the right moral choice is to succeed. What would Liszt have thought of the death camp just nine miles from his beloved Weimar which is now a UNESCO World Heritage site celebrating the brilliant culture it once fostered? What would Beethoven have thought? They both would have been horrified and then outraged. And I know they would have put a stop to the violence, even if it meant dying for the cause.

After the war, during the Nuremberg trials, the U.S. Army brought in psychiatrists to interview and diagnose the imprisoned war criminals. The government wanted to know if these men were aberrant monsters or, could anybody become just like them? Captain Douglas M. Kelley was one of the doctors and his conclusion is as shocking as anything else in this whole drama. Kelley concluded that no, although evil, these Nazi war criminals were not insane; it could happen all over again at any time, in any place. He then stated that the way the higher-ups in the Nazi chain of command conducted 'business' actually reminded him very much of the typical American CEO. Other thinkers have described the out of control elements in the corporate world as psychopathic; Noam Chomsky, for example.

After the trials, Dr. Kelley returned to civilian life in California, his marriage disintegrated and he then took his own life. This tragic tale is recounted in *The Nazi and the Psychiatrist* by Jack El-Hai (PublicAffairs Books).

When questioning why these things happen - besides hatred, arrogance, and lust for power - if you follow the money it leads you to ... the money. In addition to world domination (as if that wasn't enough) those Nazis had their eyes on gold.

We're back to Chapter 2 – Purpose. For an artist with a purpose, money is not enough. For a lost soul without a purpose, there will never be enough money. This is older than Art, it goes back to the beginning of 'civilization'.

Although I remain an eternal optimist, our world now faces challenges more severe than ever in history. Unlike the result of our predominantly processed food diet, that 'veneer of civilization' gets thinner with every passing day. We're skating on thin ice, only with global warming it's now even more precarious. When something seems highly unlikely, they used to say that you had 'a snowball's chance in hell'. Well, now the glaciers are melting. If we don't mend our ways this planet is going down and Dante's concentric circles of Hell are going to run out of IP addresses.

Wilhelm Reich abandoned one-on-one psychotherapy because dealing with symptoms was an impossible task; there were hopelessly more patients than doctors. His alternative approach: build a healthy society from the ground up by creating a nurturing and empowering environment, through enlightened education. His books on sexuality, by the way, focused not so much on 'sex' as on making love - the ultimate creative act that results in new life.

Reich also came to realize that the more a person is abused and damaged, the more controllable he becomes. For the fascist agenda, that fact dovetailed nicely with another: excessive materialism erodes spiritual identity and engenders a powerful existential anxiety. 'Consumers' are more easily controlled politically because they don't think for themselves and basically exist in a spiritual void.

Fascist psychopaths began to implement delicately crafted, yet heavily repressive policies and propaganda as a means to control humanity. Goebbels' implementation of Bernays' methods is a horrible confirmation of the hypothesis. One hundred million human beings perished in the wars of the 20th century.

When music and morality are better understood and appreciated, there will be no war.
CONFUCIUS

Edward Bernays' uncle Sigmund Freud was doing the real research in psychology. He soon became a wanted man. After he fled to England his books were burned by the Nazis. Freud managed a weak joke about how we've come a ways since medieval times when they would have burned him at the stake instead of just his books. Wilhelm Reich was also targeted by both Nazis and Communists. He escaped to Norway thinking he'd be safe there. I would have thought so too because the Norwegians are pretty nice people, although they can be kind of tough on whales. Reich was asked to leave and he made it to the safe haven that is the United States … or so you might think.

Reich began writing books like *Listen, Little Man* in which he exposed the psychological tools of fascism, warning that democratic principles were in severe jeopardy worldwide. The U.S. Food and Drug Administration arrested Reich, convicted him on a vague charge of practicing medicine without a license, and then locked him up for two years in a federal penitentiary. Meanwhile, the FDA actually collected all his books they could find and burned them - this in the United States of America in the 1950s. One week before he was to be released from prison, Reich was found dead in his cell, officially of a 'heart attack', some say under 'mysterious' circumstances.

One of the most fascinating and surreal books I've ever read is Thomas Carlyle's *The French Revolution*. It's a magnificent post-spectacle wrap-up; a 20-20 hindsight analysis of another terrible time that shocked everyone; and yet some saw it coming. In the first chapter, Carlyle quotes Lord Chesterfield speaking over a decade earlier:

In short, all the symptoms which I have ever met within History previous to great changes and revolutions in governments, now exist, and daily increase in France ...
LORD CHESTERFIELD

That was one country at the end of the 18th century. This is the 21st and we've gone global. Let's not repeat that kind of history.

And which well-known artists or writers today are trying to teach, to inspire, to conduce to virtue? Which of them could even use this word "virtue" without gagging? Upon which of them can an "idealistic" young man model himself?
ABRAHAM MASLOW

We all must ratchet up our moral courage; our artists can lead the way.

The next chapter is most pertinent to those who play a musical instrument. But just as musicians can benefit from knowledge of business, the business world can benefit from more exposure to the creative process.

Business people often see as lazy the artist who cannot organize his affairs. Artists haven't yet invented the term to describe a business man incapable of understanding a work of art.
NICOLAS MEDTNER

The intellectual drill which the study of music gives the child is of great educational value - nothing can compare. In addition, the actual study of music results in almost limitless gratification later in life in the understanding of great musical masterpieces.
PADEREWSKI

I'm not comparing business men and women to children (their loss), but learning a bit more about music isn't going to hurt you.

Chapter 10

......

MAKING MUSIC

Works of music differ from all other Arts in that until translated into living tone, they are dead.

—CARL KREBS

Quarter, eighth, sixteenth notes, and so on are not rhythm but simply notation; an after-the-fact attempt to represent or codify the fundamental pulse of music, and of life. Musical rhythm originates in the great cycles of nature – ocean tides, the wind in the trees, the heartbeats of all living creatures relentlessly throbbing together as the planet and the whole cosmos rhythmically rotate.

In the beginning was rhythm.
HANS von BÜLOW

We probably derive all our basic rhythms and themes from Nature, which offers them to us, pregnant with meaning in every animal noise.
GUSTAV MAHLER

Among the artistic hierarchy, birds are probably the greatest musicians to inhabit the planet.
OLIVIER MESSIAEN

The dolphin is a creature fond of both Man and musical Art. It is charmed by harmonious melody.
PLINY THE ELDER

A genuine musical creation is like the pulse of a living human being which possesses its own determined, regular beat, though at times pulsating faster or slower under the occasional influence of a passing emotion.
LOUIS KÖHLER

Rhythm in music and dance must be mentally imagined and physically generated by the performer. Especially in the case of solo piano, there is no following, only leading.

People begin to play and don't get into swing until they have played one or two bars. The motto, the beat of the piece, ought to have begun in the mind, in the feeling of the performer, before he puts a finger on the keyboard.
STERNDALE BENNETT

We confuse measure with cadence; measure encompasses the number and duration of mechanical beats and cadence is the soul and spirit that must be added to it.
FRANÇOIS COUPERIN

Music has a rhythm whose secret force shapes the development.
CLAUDE DEBUSSY

Rhythm is organically independent from meter. Meter is a conventional means of measuring the relative values of rhythm by comparison with an even standard or measure. Rhythm is an element of life itself like respiration. Its genesis is found in the cosmos, but can be considered first in the human body, then in the act of dance.
E. ROBERT SCHMITZ

Rhythm is spirit in music, the most human thing in music. Make your rhythms live and your playing will be beautifully alive.
JOSEF LHÉVINNE

At a performance by King Frederick the Great:
AUDIENCE MEMBER: *"What rhythm!"*

Positive Piano

C.P.E. BACH: *"What rhythms!"*

It is rhythm that sways the audience.
ERNEST SCHELLING

Play in time. The playing of many a virtuoso is like the gait of a drunken man; do not model it.
ROBERT SCHUMANN

The most important qualification for the musician is a sense of rhythm. Together with the sense of hearing, it is a sine qua non for everyone who wishes successfully to devote himself to music.
LEOPOLD AUER

Even the uncultured members of an audience feel the effect of rhythm, or its absence. When the rhythm is strong, they are impressed by the fact that the piece is alive, but when the rhythm is lax, or irregular they feel that it's "dead as a door nail"; even though quite unaware of the cause of their comfort or discomfort. Indeed, so strong is this rhythmical need of the public, that when rhythmical grip is lacking in a performer no other attractions offered by him can save the piece.
TOBIAS MATTHAY

"Preserve rhythmic clearness," was another of Liszt's precepts. To a young lady who blurred the rhythm in his 'Gnomenreigen' he said: "There! you're mixing salad again." To another, who played similar passages devoid of rhythm or phrasing: "That's too much as if you were beating an omelet."
CARL LACHMUND

Mechanical technique - rapid scales, arpeggios, and octaves - are mere trifles beside rhythm and color. Of the two, probably rhythm is more difficult to achieve than color. Indeed many pianists never develop their rhythmic side, and are able to play no more than a very few pieces with the proper effect. Rhythm is the life of music; color is its flesh and blood. Without either, all interpretive art is dead.
IGNAZ FRIEDMAN

What would the orchestra do if you came in with such an uncertain beat?
ADOLPH HENSELT

It is a sadly noticeable thing when the orchestra plays better than the soloist.
LESCHETIZKY

In studying a work for piano and orchestra, I must not only know my own part, but all the other parts – what each instrument is doing. I always study a concerto with the orchestral score so I can see it all before me.
WILHELM BACHAUS

No performer can convey the true sense of music without a comprehension of rhythm giving proportion and meaning. The player should not be content only to play correct notes in a given time but should aim at giving a reading both intelligible and musical. … it's possible to play strictly in time and yet quite un-rhythmically.
LILIAS MACKINNON

One is inclined to regard rhythm as a kind of sacred gift. Whatever it may be, it's certainly difficult to acquire, or better, absorb. A good rhythm indicates a finely balanced musician, with perfect self-control. All the book study in the world won't develop it. It's a knack that seems to come intuitively or 'all at once'. My meaning is clear to anyone who has struggled to play two notes against three, for at times it seems impossible and then in a twinkling of an eye the conflicting rhythms apparently jump into place, and thereafter the pianist has little difficulty with them. Rhythmic 'swing' - the impelling force – is different from rhythm and tempo, but allied to them. The pianist must have played many pieces to develop this swing.
KATHARINE GOODSON

It don't mean a thing if it ain't got that swing.
DUKE ELLINGTON

Visit the zoo, where you can learn much about legato and staccato from the kangaroos.
HANS von BÜLOW

Gottschalk first made his mark by arranging rhythmically well-defined Creole melodies, and he played them with absolute rhythmic accuracy. This interpretive clarity contributed more than anything else to the fascination he always exerted over his audience.
WILLIAM MASON

Positive Piano

Make the drummer sound good.
THELONIUS MONK

TEMPO

Tempo is the relative speed of music. Just like an espresso drink today, there are plenty of fancy Italian words to describe it, e.g. *largo, adagio, andante, allegro, presto*. One difference is that these tempo designations actually hint at the character or personality of the music, but with the coffee it's still basically small, medium, large, and now gigantic.

Such terms as Adagio, Allegro, etc., are not designations of speed but, primarily, of mood.
CONSTANTIN von STERNBERG

Debussy didn't want 'cheerfully' and 'with life' turned into 'quickly'.
NINON VALIN

Every melodious composition has at least one phrase from which you can determine a suitable overall tempo. If all the information in the score is followed, the phrase is virtually forced into the right tempo, still; this all presupposes much experience in the performer. End a piece in the same tempo you begin it, don't speed up.
LEOPOLD MOZART

A piece played too fast or too slow becomes quite disfigured and loses all its effect. Where the tempo is not marked according to the metronome, the player must look to the Italian words which indicate the degree of movement (allegro, moderato, presto, etc.) and likewise the character of the composition, and gradually learn by experience to know their real significance. One of the worst faults is carrying to excess the ritardando and accelerando, so that we are often several minutes without knowing whether the piece is written in triple or in common time. This produces nearly the same effect as if someone were addressing us in a strange and unintelligible language.
CZERNY

All my music is mangled; they play so fast. 'Apanhei-te, Cavaquinho' is a disaster. It's nice and slow, the left hand playing arpeggio giving the

impression of a cavaquinho - (little guitar).
ERNESTO NAZARETH

Every time you change the tempo, your listener has to start afresh with you, and readjust to the new tempo. This engenders a complete disorganization and if this varying of the tempo is persisted in, not only does it lead to discomfort, but to positive irritation, although the listener may remain unaware of the actual cause of his troubles.
TOBIAS MATTHAY

The tempo of a piece is determined not only by the directions of the composer, but also by its harmonic and polyphonic content, by the hall in which it is played, and by the principle of utmost clarity.
MAX REGER

Honor scrupulously all tempo indications. Refrain from gratuitous fast playing; steady tempi, accuracy and expression demand and display greater ability, Hold notes for their full values; slow, careful practice of fugues will develop this.
THALBERG

THE METRONOME

A mechanical device for setting and regulating tempo was invented by Dietrich Winkel in Amsterdam in 1814. In England, Johann Maelzel improved on it and patented a version in 1815, branding it with his own name as Maelzel's Metronome. He probably coined the word as a compound of the Greek *metron* for measure and *nomos* for regulation. Beethoven took an interest in the new gadget and began to use it to indicate the tempos of his compositions.

The metronome has value as a practice tool, for example, guiding multiple repetitions with subsequent incremental increase in speed. The metronome cannot, at least musically and artistically, be used as a substitute for you creating your own rhythm.

I certainly approve of the metronome, and it's amusing sometimes to see how different the mechanical idea of rhythm is from the true sense and feeling for it. We can also use the metronome for working up velocity.
PERCY GRAINGER

343

I approve of the metronome to cultivate a sense of rhythm in those who are lacking in this particular sense. I sometimes use it myself, just to see the difference between the mechanical rhythm and the musical rhythm — for they are not always the same by any means.

WILHELM BACHAUS

A metronome cannot serve as a time-teacher. The pupil has to learn to play to a pulse-throb of his own making all the while; it is therefore of very little use learning to pay obedience to an outside, machine-made pulse-throb. And in any case, a metronome is apt to kill the finer time-sense implied by rubato.

TOBIAS MATTHAY

When I "go into training", the best means to attain velocity is to work with the metronome. One can't jump at once into the necessary agility and the metronome is a great help in bringing one up to the right level.

ERNEST SCHELLING

No great pianist has played with the metronome, but this device has importance in technical work, and is recommended to grade progress in velocity.

RAPHAEL JOSEFFY

On metronomes: I don't approve of continual practice with them. The most mechanical playing imaginable can proceed from those who make themselves slaves to this little musical clock, which was never intended to stand like a ruler over every minute of the student's practice time.

RACHMANINOFF

There's a stage in the development of every piece or étude where it's useful to play it with the metronome. If the time is found to be correct and the music can be played up to the proper speed, the metronome should not be used further with that selection, as it's now ready to be played in that flexible style which is demanded by the laws of expression and emotional delivery. To practice with the metronome while studying expression is, of course, a misuse of the little machine. Expressive playing constantly varies more or less in speed. In such playing the metronome is not to be used.

EDWARD M. BOWMAN

Although many compositions have metronome markings, the player's judgment must be requisitioned; discretion is advisable. One can't follow

tempo marks blindly, but it's not safe to stray too far from these important musical sign-posts.
RACHMANINOFF

Which brings up a very important point: we should be careful to differentiate between metronome settings specified by composers, and those recommended by editors.

This is a good place to discuss a composer's intentions concerning tempo in one particularly important historical example. Composed in 1817-1818, Beethoven's *Hammerklavier* Opus 106 is the only one of his published piano sonatas in which he specifically indicated the tempo by metronome markings, and the tempo for the grand first movement is set at half note = 138. The fact that it's notated in cut time is a clue that Beethoven had a brisk tempo in mind.

Beethoven once told me during a walk: "I'm now writing a sonata which is going to be my greatest".
(Opus 106, around 1818). CZERNY

Czerny cultivated a close relationship with Beethoven for more than two decades, eventually studying and playing virtually all his compositions, including that monumental Opus 106. Czerny corroborates that particular tempo indication. He also used metronome markings to indicate relative tempos in many of his own pieces.

We have everywhere endeavored to indicate the exact time, both by Mälzel's Metronome and by words; and the observance of the same is certainly of the greatest importance, as the whole character of the piece is disfigured by a wrong degree of movement.
CZERNY

In his youth, Liszt received several years of thorough instruction from Czerny. The *Hammerklavier* became a signature piece for Liszt, and his playing of it surpassed that of all other pianists in his generation (and ours, as well). In fact, more than any other individual, Liszt was responsible for elucidating this great work and firmly establishing it in the general consciousness.

In 1836, at age 25, Liszt was already the pre-eminent performer of genius in the world. Berlioz writes:

Beethoven's sublime poem of a Sonata (Opus 106) has been until now the riddle of the Sphinx for almost every pianist. Liszt, a new Oedipus, has solved it in a matter which would have made the composer, had he heard it in his grave, thrill with pride and joy. Not a note was omitted, not one added (I followed the score in hand), not a single alteration was made to what was indicated in the text, not an inflexion or an idea weakened or changed from its true meaning. In the Adagio, above all, he retained always the composers inspiration. ... by such a rendition of a work totally misunderstood until now, Liszt has proven that he is the pianist of the future.
HECTOR BERLIOZ

Yet almost two hundred years later, some 'professional' concert pianists still question Beethoven's metronome marking for the tempo of the opening movement. In an internet blog one pianist (let's protect the guilty with anonymity) calls the tempo 'ludicrous' and claims either Beethoven's virtual deafness or a faulty mechanical function of the metronome is to blame. He thinks the piece must be played slower, mainly because it's too difficult to successfully perform at the designated tempo. That says more about that particular pianist than Beethoven, I think.

(1) Inner rhythmic pulse is felt, not heard; a deaf individual can imagine musical rhythm, a deaf dancer can dance.

(2) the 'defective metronome' theory is purely speculative and flies in the face of performances by masters like Czerny and Liszt. Consider this anecdote from the memoirs of William Mason.

One evening Liszt said to us: "Boys, there's a young man coming here tomorrow who says he can play Beethoven's 'Sonata in B Flat, Op. 106.' I want you all three to be here." We were there at the appointed hour. The pianist proved to be a Hungarian, whose name I have forgotten. He sat down and began to play in a conveniently slow tempo the bold chords with which the sonata opens. He had not progressed more than half a page when Liszt stopped him, and seating himself at the piano, played in the correct tempo, which was much faster, to show him how the work should be interpreted.
"It's nonsense for you to go through this sonata in that fashion," said Liszt, as he rose from the piano and left the room. The pianist, of course, was very much disconcerted. Finally he said, as if to console himself: "Well, he can't play it through like that, and that's why he stopped after half a page." This sonata is the only one which the composer himself metronomized,

and his direction is half note = 138.
WILLIAM MASON

Another anecdote: in 1908 at Whitworth Hall, Manchester, Egon Petri (1881-1962) performed a series of four Beethoven piano sonata recitals. The pianist would have been about 27 years old. A critic present noted that for Opus 106: *"The tempo for the first movement was played according to Czerny/Beethoven designations: 1) half = 138, 2) dotted half = 80, 3) eighth = 92, 4) quarter = 144"* (ed. omitting the also-specified *Largo tempo marking).*

This famous *Hammerklavier* tempo marking is a starting point, of sorts, for analysis and comparison of recorded interpretations. Example: as fascinating as some of his J.S. Bach conceptions are, Glen Gould's recording of Beethoven's Opus 106 begins way too slowly; the composer (and Liszt) would not have approved.

Beethoven knew what he was doing; play as if you understood him.
LESCHETIZKY

The moral of the story: the great masters, in this case the greatest, really did know what they were doing; respect their intentions as best you can. Don't make yourself look silly by ignorantly second-guessing a master.

RUBATO

Rubato, like success and character, is not something to be consciously striven for, but again an 'after-the-fact' explanation of the rhythmic nuance employed by artists in interpreting music. The word derives from the Italian *robare* (to rob or steal) and in music means flexibility or pliability, where the overall rhythmic stream is slightly distorted, being pulled this way or that, to express musical nuance. A common misconception is that what's 'robbed' must later be returned in kind to maintain continuity. Often mentioned in reference to the music of Chopin, the concept is much older.

Rubato was known as early as Frescobaldi. Even if he didn't invent it, he said expressly that freedom in the measure, for the purpose of giving

347

meaning and expression to the words, is customary in madrigal singing.
CARL KREBS

Inequality is permissible in the case of melodies that increase in elegance when played freely.
FRANÇOIS COUPERIN

Tempo rubato means playing more or less notes than are found in standard bar divisions, but they must be given a consistent value across the distortion, so to speak. One hand appears to play against the bar lines while the other plays with them. … The effect works best for slow, dissonant, or meditative and sad melodies. This requires great discernment and sensitivity. It takes more than mere mechanical practice; sensitivity is paramount.
C.P.E. BACH

A thoughtful accompanist must yield to a virtuoso soloist, or he'll spoil his rubato. The 'stolen tempo' is easier demonstrated by example than described in words.
LEOPOLD MOZART

What these people cannot grasp is that in 'tempo rubato' in an adagio, the left hand should go on playing in strict time. With them, the left hand always wrongly follows suit.
(WOLFGANG) MOZART

In the variation and fluctuation of the tempo, Chopin was magnificent. Every single note was played with the highest degree of taste.
WILHELM von LENZ

So, far from implying any rhythmic weakness, rubato-playing on the contrary demands a particularly strongly cultivated feeling for pulse, in fact, one so full of vitality, that it enables us to feel a pulse (or beat) unwaveringly. To hear a Chopin nocturne for instance, or a more modern work, played without it is indeed (for anyone at all musically sensitive) a horrible experience. We know from Mozart's own letters that he used rubato greatly, and much to the astonishment, mystification, and probable confusion of his contemporaries. Rubato should be subtle. It must never become noticeable as such … Remember Chopin's illustration to his pupil; he first blew gently upon the candle in front of him, making it flicker, and

remarked: 'See, that is my rubato'; he then blew the candle out, adding: 'and that is your rubato!'
TOBIAS MATTHAY

Rubato means 'robbed,' which is misleading because it says nothing of giving.
LEOPOLD GODOWSKY

Liszt affirmed that anything in music, literature and life resembling melodrama inspired Chopin with a profound aversion. If his pupils are to be believed, his rubato had little in common with that of the modern virtuosi and their "Tempo Epileptic" (the mot is de Willy's), who play the figurations and arabesques with exaggerated emphasis. The rubato Chopin wanted was a fine nonchalance, and not disorder; the left hand ought to keep time, while the right hand moves in sympathy with the idea. He used to say: "The left hand is the Kappelmeister."
WANDA LANDOWSKA

Pianists should not heed the ridiculous but oft-repeated assertion that if you increase the speed for a few bars you must slow up for a few bars subsequently, so that the whole piece will last just as many seconds as if you had made no change in the pace. What would an actor say if he were told that if he spoke a few words in one line more slowly, he must make up for it by speaking a few words in the next line faster?
HENRY THEOPHILUS FINCK

To maintain a strict rhythm in each individual bar in certain passages will counteract the sense of expression and understanding.
ARTHUR FREIDHEIM

Flexibility of rhythm is and always has been a logical means of interpretation, provided always that it be dictated by artistic sense, and not by caprice.
ERNEST HUTCHESON

See that tree swaying in the wind; the twigs and leaves dance freely, the trunk is steady; let that be your tempo rubato. ... The dead letter of the music cannot convey the vivacity with which the gypsy virtuoso executes it, or the incessant mobility of its rhythms, the fiery eloquence of its phrases, the expressive accent of its declamation.
LISZT

An absolute essential in the rendering of Beethoven's compositions is rhythmic freedom...freedom, not uniformity of rhythm, is a natural law. It roots in the undulating nature of the temperament. Beethoven's own rendering was animated throughout by this freedom.
ADOLPH KULLAK

Leschetizky learned Beethoven's E-flat Concerto (Opus 73) with Czerny, a pupil of Beethoven. The copy he used for study had many marks on it in Beethoven's own handwriting. Over some heavy chords and some passages in the middle of the first movement Beethoven had written the word 'free'.
ETHEL NEWCOMB

When making music, the best place to start is always ...

THE SCORE

As you grow older, converse more frequently with scores than with virtuosos.
ROBERT SCHUMANN

Until the student has acquired skill in the ready understanding of what confronts him on the puzzling pages of his musical score, or as Berlioz says, "he divines music before he has read it", he cannot hope to take silent pleasure from reading it to himself, much less give pleasure by translating it into the vibrations of a singing voice or of the strings of a piano. The musical artist must somehow get the music into his soul before he can bring it to the tips of his fingers.
MARY VENABLE

In many compositions, the expression marks are so exactly indicated by the composer, that the performer can never be in doubt when to play loud or soft, increasing or decreasing as to tone, connected or detached, hurrying onwards in the time, or holding it back.
CZERNY

The score: now here's a subject where we can make use of some religious studies terminology. Let's even the score.

Exegesis means using your critical reasoning powers to understand or elucidate. With a religious text, for example, your intellect comes into play in your overall understanding of language, both your own native one and perhaps some long dead ancient ones like Syriac, Coptic, or Phoenician. Also important in your thinking process is your acquired knowledge of relevant disciplines like history, psychology, philosophy, sociology, and art.

Everything has broad cultural context. And pretty much your total life experience comes into play when trying to understand it. Since everybody's different, then there's the question of interpretation, or *hermeneutics*.

With a music score, the lowest common intellectual denominator is knowledge of music notation - note pitches, relative rhythmic values, and dynamic markings. Basic notes and rhythm have been explicitly defined on paper for centuries. Attempts to convey additional interpretative clues in the form of phrasing and dynamics increased from the end of the 18th century and into the 19th, especially in the case of Beethoven.

When studying a work by a composer, exposure to many (or all) of his/her works is going to help tremendously. Similarly, study of the works of many composers, and different styles across generations, will make you a much more capable and interesting musician, as will general study, again, of culture - people, art, and thought.

In the performance of classical compositions, especially Beethoven's, much depends on the individuality of the player (who is presupposed to possess a certain degree of virtuosity, for a stumbler cannot have an intellectual conception)... There are however, important conditions upon which everything else depends, namely: 1) the right time, 2) the accurate observance of all the marks of expression which Beethoven, particularly in his later works, has very carefully indicated, and 3) the thorough mastery of all difficulties, and the cultivation of good execution in all respects, which must have previously been acquired by the study of other excellent composers.
CZERNY

Von Bülow required of his students the same qualities so patent in his own playing. Clearness of touch, exactness in phrasing and fingering were the first requirements; the delivery of the composer's idea must be just as he had indicated it - no liberties with the text were ever permitted.
HARRIETTE BROWER

The author of several fascinating books about pianists and singers,

Ms. Brower attended the 'master classes' of Hans von Bülow in Frankfurt during the summers of 1884 to 1886. Two other attendees, Theodor Pfeiffer and José Vianna de Motta, also wrote reminiscences of their experience. These have been translated into English by Richard L. Zimdars (*The Piano Master Classes of Hans von Bülow, Two Participants Accounts*, Indiana University Press). Needless to say these books are must reads for pianists and music history buffs.

Pay attention to all the signs marked by the composer. Don't play by heart before knowing the piece fundamentally, so that not one of the signs may be neglected. You ought to enter deeply into the work, try to guess at the deepest feelings of the composer.
ANTON RUBINSTEIN

But music expressed in written notation, and religious and philosophical thought expressed in language are never going to be 100% satisfactory. The deepest spiritual truths are inherently ineffable and take on full meaning only when internalized, and realized in moral action. The spirit encapsulated in the words is the real truth, not the words themselves. It takes a human being to manifest spirit; otherwise it's just ink on paper.

Liszt used to say "There is more rhythm between the notes than in the notes themselves."
LESCHETIZKY

The music is not the notes.
PABLO CASALS

Although the notes, rhythm, and relative dynamics are conceived intellectually, the message or spirit behind those notes must be intuited by the individual performing artist and will reflect his/her life experience. The best we can do intellectually is to remain absolutely true to the score; personality and character will automatically do the rest. That's why performances or recordings of the same work may be considerably different when separated by a number of years. With the passage of time, the artist has matured (hopefully).

The related term *eisegesis* means interpreting a text in a way that introduces bias or an 'agenda', either willfully or unconsciously,

352

due to some intellectual prejudice or shortcoming. It's colloquially expressed as 'reading into', and can result in you imposing your own perhaps fanciful interpretation onto a text.

Be careful of the printed matter: you may not read it as it is written down.
F.M. ALEXANDER

When reading this treatise, consider that mental and physical perception, because connected, are subject to similar conditions.
MOSES MAIMONIDES

When I asked why so few people were able to read his music Debussy replied, after some reflection ... "because they try to impose themselves upon the music."
GEORGE COPELAND

How often do we think we've learned a score, only to discover years later that we were actually executing some detail quite differently than indicated in that score. Stick to the score. Research the manuscripts and first printed editions. Read first hand accounts of the composing process and initial performances.

In the early 19th century much new music often circulated in manuscript. Years often elapsed between initial composition and eventual formal publication. In the meantime, if musicians wanted to study and play the music, they would copy out the score by hand. This is one of those 'secrets' of how and why music-making back then was actually at a higher level than today.

Copying out a manuscript by hand, not to mention composing one from scratch, will make you intimately familiar with every detail of it in a way that you can never achieve by simply reading a printed score.

If you don't believe it, try it. Physically copying by hand forces you to notice every detail because you are in essence recreating it. You might be surprised to find that the way you've been playing the notes for years is not necessarily what's indicated in the score. Your memory will also be much strengthened by this exercise.

ACCURACY AND CLARITY

Playing the right notes is an absolute minimal requirement for artistic interpretation of music. Playing the right notes sequentially with clarity relative to each other is the next challenge.

Keyboard players are often found whose ready fingers serve them well in loud runs, but desert them, through lack of control, in the soft ones thereby making for indistinctness.
C.P.E. BACH

I don't understand Chopin's music, but he plays beautifully and correctly – oh so correctly! He does not allow himself to become careless like so many other young people.
JOHN CRAMER

The great concert-going public has no use for a player with a slovenly technique.
EMIL SAUER

Wrong notes disturbed Leschetizky greatly. "Is there anyone in this room who can play without striking wrong notes?" he called out one evening. Then turning to a row of long-haired young men standing at the back of the room, he said "come up here one of you, and see if your long hair will help you do it any better."
ETHEL NEWCOMB

In these days of keen competition, the student must look upon inaccuracies as unpardonable. Why so much inaccurate playing? - largely because of mental uncertainty. ... One of the chief offenders in the matter of inaccuracy is the left hand. The left hand gives quality and character to playing. Practice its parts as if you had no right ... your playing will improve one hundred percent.
JOSEF LHÉVINNE

Though accuracy alone may not lead to a good interpretation, accuracy is certainly at the base of the best interpretation.
LILIAS MACKINNON

Clearness, clearness, clearness, that is the first thing. Every line, every measure must be thoroughly analyzed for touch, tone, content and expression.

. ... When a new theme enters you must make it plain to the listener; every aspect must be organically illustrated. ... Brilliancy depends on clarity, not velocity. What is not clear cannot sparkle and scintillate.
HANS von BÜLOW

I have yet to discover whether you (a piano student) will ever be able to combine sureness with freedom. I'd like to think that you can, for accuracy without expression isn't worth "that" (snapping his fingers).
LESCHETIZKY

It may not be totally realistic because we're human, but we should still strive for nothing less than perfection in accuracy and clarity of execution. Yes, machines can now 'play' music flawlessly, but they can't sing from the heart, because they don't have one.

With today's high standards established by two generations of note-perfect (edited) recordings, you have to be a pretty amazing pianist these days to get away with anything less.

I would rather listen to (Anton Rubinstein's) wrong notes than my own correct playing.
HANS von BÜLOW

"May the Lord forgive me for the false notes I dropped!" was Anton Rubinstein's reply, and although he spoke in a half quizzical way, it was evident he took himself seriously to task for any blemishes in his work.
AUBERTINE WOODWARD MOORE

When the performer finds that same joy that the composer found in writing it, then something new and different comes into his playing. It seems to be stimulated and invigorated in a manner altogether marvelous. The audience realizes this instantly, and may even forgive technical imperfections if the performance is inspired.
RACHMANINOFF

Henselt all at once flung himself into Der Freischütz, and it was at the same time orchestra and piano – grand, exciting, mysterious, and sweet. Someone present said, 'One forgives everything to anyone who can play like that!'
BETTINA WALKER

PHRASING AND ACCENTUATION

Much more than just a structural building block, a musical phrase is the single most important manifestation of organic structure and spirit. It provides the relativistic framework for melody, harmony, and rhythm to jointly express meaning. In fact, the phrase can be considered the lowest common denominator of musical meaning.

An artistic interpretation is not possible if one doesn't know the laws underlying the very important subject of phrasing. Bach used phrase marks sparingly; it wasn't necessary to mark them because every musician who counted himself one could determine the phrases as he played. Knowledge of the phrase is not enough, executive skill is just as important ... real musical feeling must exist in the mind.
RACHMANINOFF

A player must be intelligent enough to discriminate between what is a real phrase and what is merely a mark to indicate smooth playing or for a sequence. ... No two pianists will feel even a single phrase in quite the same way, and this is as it should be, for the personality of the player should stamp itself on everything he does. There is no fixed interpretation of any piece.
LILIAS MACKINNON

You may be able to play that technically difficult composition and still not be able to play the piano. From a Bach Prelude or a Mendelssohn Song Without Words I can tell right away how much of a musician you are.
RAPHAEL JOSEFFY

To neglect phrasing would be about as sensible as it would be for the great actor to neglect the proper thought division in the interpretation of his lines in a great masterpiece of dramatic literature. ... In the study of accentuation and phrasing there's nothing more instructive than the works of J. S. Bach. They compel one to study details, forcing the student to think.
FERRUCCIO BUSONI

The master pianist gets his outlook on phrasing by being as familiar with the laws of composing as the composer himself.
RUDOLPH GANZ

A phrase may be defined as: a growth, or progression of notes towards a cadence or some clearly defined destination, revealed through tone and rubato inflections. ...Such directional movement is the vitalizing spark which turns mere notes into living music. Some teachers have tried to explain music as consisting of chunks or solid segments of accented or unaccented bars, thus wrongly implying that music consists of dead, disconnected bits of sound-stone or brick, instead of a living mass, a continuous swing and swirl of growth.
TOBIAS MATTHAY

Music is full of nuances and accents of greater or less intensity, critical for rhythmic expression - to which pupils hardly ever give any attention. They correspond to vocal accents in reading aloud, or in declamation. ... Liszt was very fond of strong accents in order to mark off periods and phrases, and he talked so much about strong accentuation that one might have supposed that he would abuse it, but he never did. When he wrote to me later about my own piano method, he expressed the strongest approval of the exercises on accentuation.
WILLIAM MASON

I don't play according to measure. Measure is in a musical sense what rhythm is in verse – not a heavy cadence that falls like a burden on the caesura. Music must not be subject to a uniformity; it must be kindled, or slowed down with judgment according to the meaning it carries. Don't conceive expression narrowly within one measure, but covering phrases of two or more measures, and it will be on broader lines.
LISZT

Music should be studied by phrases, not measures. To see the composer's message as a whole, rather than in small segments, is the key to artistic playing.
MAX PAUER

Clearly and readily seeing the phrases (both melodic and metric) by which a composition is built wonderfully simplifies interpretation of a new piece.
KATHARINE GOODSON

Analyze every note of a phrase, or no intelligent rendering of it can be expected. It is an accepted fact that music is a language, you must know where the sentences begin and end, where to place the stress and accent, or how can you give a musical speech? ... Just as you would do in reading

or speaking, you must know where the crescendos and climaxes should occur, the diminuendos and ritardandos. All these things make the playing expressive, but must not be used haphazardly.
HARRIETTE BROWER

The most serious faults: bad phrasing, and a failure to listen to one's playing so as to judge the relationship of one tone to another.
LESCHETIZKY

Laws of interpretation: never lay stress on a concord, but rather on a dissonance; the stronger the dissonance, the heavier the stress put upon it.
LEOPOLD GODOWSKY

In general, play dissonances strongly and consonances softly, since the former rouses our emotions and the latter quiets them.
C.P.E. BACH

The fairest harmony springs from discord.
HERACLITUS

To produce harmony, music must know discord.
PLUTARCH

PARALLELS WITH SINGING

If the abstract musical phrase seems difficult to grasp at first, don't think so much; try singing. Vocalize your phrase of piano notes and you'll immediately begin to get a much better idea of how it's 'supposed to go'.

Above all, lose no opportunity to hear artistic singing... think in terms of song. Indeed, it's beneficial to sing instrumental melodies to understand their correct performance. ... It's a better way to learn than books or lectures.
C.P.E. BACH

The nearer the piano comes to the singing voice, the better.
FRIEDRICH WEICK

An essential requirement of an instrumental virtuoso is that he

understand how to breathe – and how to allow his audience to take a breath. By this I mean a well-chosen incision, a lingering ("letting the air in" Tausig aptly calls it) which in no way impairs rhythm and time, but rather brings them into stronger relief, something that our music notation cannot adequately express.
WILHELM von LENZ

What cannot be sung in one breath cannot be played in one breath.
HANS von BÜLOW

Take long breaths, you will relax the muscles better then. Anton Rubinstein used to take long breaths at the beginning of long phrases, and what repose he had, and what dramatic pauses.
LESCHETIZKY

The habit of breathing freely and easily while playing cannot be cultivated too early.
HARRIETTE BROWER

The emotions have a direct and immediate effect upon the breathing, and as the brain registers new emotional impressions they are first observed in the breathing - joy, anger, love, tranquility, and grief – all are characterized by different modes of breathing, and trained actors must carefully study this. The pianist breathes his phrases. A phrase that is purely contemplative in character is breathed in a tranquil fashion without any suggestion of nervous agitation. If we go through the scale of expression, starting with contemplative tranquility, to the climax of dramatic intensity, the breath will be emitted progressively quicker. If a perfectly tranquil phrase is given out in a succession of short breaths, indicating, as they would, agitation, it would be a contradiction, just as it would be perfectly inhuman to suppose that in expressing dramatic intensity it would be possible to breathe slowly.
HAROLD BAUER

Can you think of a melody, and sing exactly what you have thought, then write it down, and play it in all keys?
HARRIET SEYMOUR

Few pianists allow music to 'breathe' sufficiently.
LILIAS MACKINNON

Study vocal technique and repertoire; listen to fine singers at every opportunity. ... The art of singing well applies to all instruments. No concession should be made to the particular mechanism of any instrument; the executant must subject it to the will of his art. As the piano cannot prolong sounds - we must, by dint of skill and art, overcome this defect, and succeed not only in producing the illusion of sustained and prolonged notes, but also of swelling notes. One of the first conditions for obtaining breadth of execution, pleasing sonority and great variety of sound production, is to avoid all stiffness. The player must possess as much suppleness and as many inflexions in the forearm, the wrist, and the fingers, as a skillful singer possesses in his voice. In broad, noble, and dramatic song we must sing from the chest. Similarly we must require a great deal from the piano, and draw from it all the sound it can emit, not by striking the keys, but by playing on them from a very short distance; by pushing them down, by pressing them with vigor, energy, and warmth. In simple, sweet, and graceful melodies, we must 'knead' the piano; tread it with a boneless hand, and fingers of velvet: in this case the keys ought to be felt rather than struck.
THALBERG

In earlier times, in the 17th and the beginning of the 18th century, the study of singing was pursued with the persistence and earnestness of which we today have little idea. An education in music lasted ten to fifteen years; three hours a day were given to singing alone. Keyboard and theory were diligently studied, and choral singing as well.
CARL KREBS

TOUCH AND TONE

The neuroscientist Wilder Penfield (1891-1976) came up with the sensory homunculus, a relativistic depiction of the concentration of nerve endings in the body. The tongue, lips and fingertips are the most sensitive, nerve-laden areas. Apparently, humans are ideally suited for playing musical instruments and sexual foreplay.

The hands are the instruments of man's intelligence. ... The human hand allows the mind to reveal itself.
MARIA MONTESSORI

With regard to tone production, virtually infinite granularity of coloring and shading is literally at your fingertips - if your mind can first imagine it.

Apart from the interpretive concept itself, after vibrant rhythm, tone quality is probably the second most important aspect defining an artist. Get ready for lots of quotes on this subject.

You can conquer the world with rhythm and beautiful tones.
LESCHETIZKY

When Ignaz Moscheles heard pianist John Field in 1831 he noted his *'enchanting legato, tenderness, elegance and beautiful touch'*. Field had a part-time job demonstrating pianos at Muzio Clementi's factory. Parents brought in their sons and daughters and after listening in amazement to the beautiful tone of the instruments immediately ordered one for the household. A number returned in a few days complaining that the piano didn't sound as good when played at home.

It's sad to what extent pianists concern themselves with empty artifice and misconceived technique, and forget the study of tone and interpretation.
FRIEDRICH WIECK

Herr Weick might just as well have been commenting on today's piano scene. There's still way too much emphasis on mechanical execution and remarkably scant awareness of the significance of tone in both today's lower echelons, and the supposed upper ones.

In today's consumer-oriented world, when people speak of tone they are usually referring to the instrument itself; this or that brand of piano has an 'awesome' tone. Contrary to what piano salesmen would have you believe, tone production is not simply a function of the instrument itself, but also of the extent of your musical mastery.

PLAYER-PIANO SALESMAN: *Our model can record 16 dynamic levels.*
ARTUR SCHNABEL: *I have 17.*

The potential for beautiful tone may exist in the instrument, but it takes a human being to manifest it or draw it out. When somebody boasts to you about their piano's wonderful tone, take it with several grains of NaCl.

Let's talk about violins for a minute. It's a bit more credible to speak of an instrument's supreme tone when referring to the famous ones made by Amati and Stradivarius. These wonderful string instruments had their origins in an age that placed great value on art and craftsmanship.

Our age sadly appears to value the antiques primarily for their ... supreme value. They've become items for investment and command huge premiums. Their chief 'selling point' today is how much they sell for on the auction block, along with bragging rights they 'afford' in press releases.

Prince Carl Lichnowsky, a great patron and friend of Beethoven, once made him a present of a quartet of stringed instruments including two violins, (Guarnerius 1721, Amati 1667) a viola, (Ruger 1690) and a cello (Guarnerius 1721). This magnanimous gesture was lobbied for by the famous quartet player Schuppanzigh, who also deserves some credit. The instruments were already quite valuable in the early 19th century.

The gift wasn't to celebrate Beethoven's birthday or anything but to ensure that a master creating musical masterpieces had at his disposal the best tools possible. Those who knew him often remarked on Beethoven's 'indifference to luxury'. What he did next corroborates that observation to some extent. Tired of his servants constantly pilfering the silverware, Beethoven took a penknife and scratched a letter 'B' on the back of each one. Nobody recalled him ever commenting on their monetary value, but playing those instruments brought him a great deal of pleasure; and he composed ... well you know all about that. The instruments are preserved in the Bonn Beethoven-Haus Museum.

Now, if you're an aspiring concert violinist who just won the lottery and you want to immediately run out and buy yourself a nice Strad ... hold on just a second.

The question of tone production, we might as well acknowledge at once, is not primarily a matter of the hairs on the stick, of rosin, of change of bow on the strings, nor of change of position by means of the fingers of the left hand. All these really signify nothing, absolutely nothing, when it comes to the production of a pure crystalline and transparent violin tone. To achieve that, the student must not only expect to sacrifice whatever time may be necessary, but he must be willing to bring to bear on the problem all the

intelligence and mental and spiritual concentration of which he is capable. And for guidance in this he must rely upon the precepts of the great masters of the past, and the example of the great violinists of the present day.
LEOPOLD AUER

A great instrument is a wonderful thing but it can't play itself. Needless to say, a master on a lesser instrument will always trump a mediocre player on a fine instrument.

Notwithstanding his tired condition and the oppressive heat...Liszt sat at the piano and began the beautiful étude (Chopin Opus 10.11 E-Flat major) which he played from memory, played as none present had ever heard it before, as only Liszt could play it. ...He seemed to have everything at memory's command, even to the smallest detail. What a wondrous tone he produced! ... and this from a modest upright piano.
CARL LACHMUND

In the 19th century, when most people spoke of tone they referred to the artist. I say most, because every now and then you'd encounter someone who didn't get it.

A critic once declared that the effect of Gottschalk's playing was doubtless due to the superiority of the instrument. His simple reply? "That's a nice thing for Chickering's pianos, and I'm glad of it, for they are grand and inspire me. Now, where's my cigar-case?"
OCTAVIA HENSEL

Tone production is the result of collaboration between artist and instrument, of pianist and piano. It's really the man or woman who extracts tone from the instrument. Quality instruments are great, the higher the better; but they only contain varying potential for tone – artists must literally create the tone out of their imagination.

Pianos are sensitive, and their tone is affected by the physical expression of the player's mood. If one regards it as an anvil to be hammered on, musical results will not be secured. Treat a piano badly and it will sulkily lock up its treasures of tone. Treat it with love and respect and the piano is one of the most responsive of instruments.
MAX PAUER

Positive Piano

From every musical instrument we may produce either a fine tone or a detestable one, according to how we handle it. If we merely bang the keys, the best instrument will sound hard and unpleasant. On the other hand, if we employ too little force, or do not know how to use this power in a proper manner, the tone will be poor and dull, and the performance unintelligible, and without soul or expression.
CZERNY

The piano is a lovely instrument! You must fall in love with the sound of it, and then try to be tender to it in order to make it sweeter to you. In it lies divine beauty, which can only be called forth by the player, who must be inspired by this divine beauty!
ANTON RUBINSTEIN

When you study five years to get one tone as you want it, and still cannot always be sure of playing it that way, then you know how difficult it is to become a pianist.
LESCHETIZKY

Henselt had hardly seated himself at the piano, scarcely played a few bars, before it was clear to me that I was in the presence of one who united in himself all the rarest excellences of a musician and a virtuoso of the highest order…His touch was deep, and yet he seemed to have the power of creating, whenever he chose to do so, a pianissimo of timbre which was at once most penetrating and yet most exquisitely delicate. Professor Zschocher told me… "now that you are with Henselt, try if you can to get at the secret of his wonderful touch, that touch that Liszt has so often spoken to me of, saying no one can imitate it."
BETTINA WALKER

So glorious and fragrant a touch as Henselt's I have never heard, nor will I myself achieve.
CLARA SCHUMANN

I too could have had velvet paws like Henselt if I had wanted to.
LISZT

It wasn't easy to impress Liszt or Clara Schumann. Imagine what Henselt's unique tone must have been like.

To speak of this wonderful touch, to convey any idea of what it was like to those who have heard him, (now alas, will never hear him) is a hopeless, almost absurd task, and yet I shall try. ... Henselt's touch suggested a shelling, a peeling off of every particle of fibrous or barky rind; the unveiling of a fine, inner, crystalline, and yet most sensitive and most vitally elastic pith. With this, it suggested a dipping deep down into a sea of beauty, and bringing up a pearl of flawless beauty and purity; something else, there was this exhalation of an essence – so concentrated, so intense, that the whole being of the man seemed to have passed for the moment into his fingertips, from which the sound seemed to well out, just as some sweet and pungent aroma from the chalice of a rare flower.
BETTINA WALKER

When was the last time somebody emphatically commented on your tone (in other than pejorative terms)? We don't often read about tone in concert reviews these days. Maybe it was just an aspect of that dusty old "poetic" 19th century, but that's exactly the point. Tone, like poetry, requires vision and imagination.
A simple formula:

imaginative vision + rational means + hard work + listening
= manifestation of aesthetic beauty

Beautiful tone is an important hallmark of a great artist. Why is it relatively rare these days? The answer may lie in the wholistic concept of earlier ages that the end result of whatever we attempt ultimately depends upon our total personality and character. Earlier we quoted Liszt:

Technique should create itself from spirit, not mechanics.
LISZT

He also used to say ...

All technique originates in the art of touch and returns to it.
LISZT

Everything originates with that inner spirit, imagination, and individual character; there are some fascinating statements from the 19th century to that effect.

Above all let kindness and goodness control you; if you are filled with kindness your tone will be beautiful.
RAOUL PUGNO

Most every artist has a strong consciousness that there's a very manifest relation between his emotional and mental conditions and his tactile sense, or highly developed sensitivity of the fingertips on the keyboard. However the phenomena may be explained from the viewpoint of psychology, it's nevertheless true that feelings of longing, yearning, hope, or soulful anticipation, for instance, induce a totally different kind of touch from that of anger, resentment, or hate.
LEOPOLD GODOWSKY

There is no modulation in your tone because there is none in your mind, or heart either...the only excuse you have for playing any instrument is that you have a heart, and that your heart inspires you to express yourself in beautiful tones.
LESCHETIZKY

Liszt sat down to the piano, and played a long piece - a concert study of his own. He thrilled even more than he astonished me by his sweet, penetrative tone, and the tender pathetic ring that pervaded the whole. The winter afternoon sunlight streamed in and lighted up the silvery hair that fell down to his shoulders; and as I listened and looked, I realized that he was aged, and therefore could not be with us very long, and that I would gladly give up my life just to add it to his precious existence.
BETTINA WALKER

Touch is certainly a wonderful and subtle thing, and reveals the whole personality of the musician in a most mysterious way.
AMY FAY

Remember Clara Schumann's impression of Anton Rubinstein's character?

... He must be a most good-natured creature, free from any trace of jealousy, and he is the only person here who is perfectly sincere...

Artists and audiences alike marveled at the beautiful tone that Anton Rubinstein produced at the piano.

(Anton Rubinstein's tone) "A golden French horn."
RAFAEL JOSEFFY

With sufficient careful study and attention, every player can produce a beautiful tone. Without this, the pianist will find it impossible to make charm or poetry of expression emanate from his instrument. Anton Rubinstein, that master of touch, who was undoubtedly one of the greatest exponents of 'how to sing on the piano' said he acquired his knowledge from listening to the singing of the great tenor Rubini. Happening to hear him one day, he was so impressed by the wonderful quality of sound-production that ever afterwards his ideal remained to reproduce something of the tone of Rubini's voice upon the piano.
MARK HAMBOURG

Strength with lightness, that is one secret of my touch ... I have sat hours trying to imitate the timbre of Rubini's voice in my playing.
ANTON RUBINSTEIN

Much as the strong personality of Anton Rubinstein's playing was admired— his noble, though utterly subjective imagination, his gigantic memory, and all that—no one acquainted with his playing ever failed to comment rapturously upon the wonderful beauty of his tone. Many an auditor quite unable to follow the soaring of Rubinstein's fancy, was none the less grateful for this extraordinary and unparalleled aural treat.
CONSTANTIN von STERNBERG

Anton Rubinstein's tone was strikingly full and deep. With him the piano sounded like a whole orchestra, not only as far as the power of sound was concerned but in the variety of timbres. With him, the piano sang as Patti and Rubini sang.
MATVEY PRESSMAN

Touch is the distinguishing characteristic which makes one player's music sound different from another's, for touch dominates the player's means of producing dynamic shading or tone quality... No matter how rapidly and accurately one can play passages of extraordinary difficulty, it's

quite worthless without control over touch enabling interpretation of the composer's work with proper artistic shading. A fine mechanical technique without the requisite touch to liberate the performer's artistic intelligence and 'soul' is like a gorgeous chandelier without the lights. Until the lights are ignited all its beauty is obscured in darkness.
OSSIP GABRILOWITSCH

Every pianist who aspires to acquire a beautiful tone must have a mental concept of what a beautiful tone is. You're lucky if you have this, but don't despair if you don't, because through hard work and by listening to pianists who have beautiful tone, you may develop it. I've seen it accomplished many times by persistent efforts.
JOSEF LHÉVINNE

All who have heard (CPE) Bach play the clavichord are struck by the endless nuance of light and shadow that he casts over his performance.
JOHANN CRAMER

The subject of tone generation can get as deep as an individual player wants to take it. There's plenty of practical advice we can consciously experiment with and apply, but a 'stretch of the imagination' is required to get you to your next, higher level.

Listen to your own playing every moment when at the piano. Study scales, chords and other technical points with every variety of shading. Make your own experiments. Anton Rubinstein would sit at the piano, working ceaselessly over single tones or bits of melody, until he secured the quality or effect he sought. It is a case of seeking and finding. The wonderful tone colorings are there, hidden in the "cold white keys," waiting to be brought out by patient mental effort.
HARRIETTE BROWER

The arm plays a vital role in mastering piano tone. Naturally, the fingers must be well-trained, but in playing they don't need to be lifted high. In fact, the nearer they are held to the keys - provided strength and elasticity have been developed – the better the tone. It takes strength to play softly...fingers must be very strong and held close to the keys for pianissimo effects.
LEO ORNSTEIN

Softness of touch depends on keeping the fingers as close as possible to the keys.

FRANÇOIS COUPERIN

Liszt considers perfect equality in tone production to be supremely important; and expects it. His ear can catch the slightest discrepancy. All of the notes must be round, full, equal-sounding and never abrupt or uneven, betraying the thumb or some other finger. The weak fourth finger and the sometimes too strong third occasionally show this weakness.

Mme. AUGUSTE BOISSIER

Tone on the piano can only be beautiful in the right place, that is, in relation to other tones. A beautiful tone may result when two or more notes are played successively, through their difference of intensity. ... Variety is life. We see this fact exemplified in the speaking voice, if one speaks or reads in an even tone it is deadly monotonous.

HAROLD BAUER

A few lessons under a really good teacher and a few tickets to high-class piano recitals will often give the feeling and "knack" of producing a good touch, for which many strive in vain at the keyboard for years.

FRANZ XAVER SCHWARENKA

When ten years old I was taken to hear Thalberg (1812-1871) and though I never heard him again, the enchanting effect of his tone and touch still lives in my memory. Of his qualities as a musician I could at that time not judge, of course, but I know that I never heard such "singing" on the piano again until it came from the fingertips of Henselt and - better still, of Rubinstein. Scales, like strings of pearls, immaculate arpeggios, nice distinction between melody and by-work, and shallow effects crossing both sides of the melody, with the aforesaid singing melody touch et voila tout! ... He resorted to paraphrasing popular operatic melodies, which, of course, assured him of a friendly welcome. Liszt, too, has done some of this, but, oh the difference! Learn this lesson from Thalberg: the purely tonal side of piano playing ought to be a matter of very serious consideration; ... since the modern piano admits of so much of it, tonal beauty is the element in piano music which carries dignified musical thoughts, beyond hearing and intellect, into the hearts of auditors. Admiration cannot be coerced; it must ever be coaxed out of an audience, and it is the tone and touch which do

the coaxing, and persuade the erstwhile unwilling auditor to listen with attention to worthy musical messages.
CONSTANTIN von STERNBERG

Observe great moderation in the movements of body, and great repose of the arms and hands; never hold the hands too high above the keyboard. Eliminate all tension, especially in the forearms. Avoid striking the keys; rather, depress them as an extension of arm and body movement. ... Play close to the keys. Always listen when playing, and subject yourself to severe self-criticism. Learn to judge your own performance.
THALBERG

Thalberg's technique seemed to be confined mainly to the finger, hand, wrist, and lower-arm muscles, but these he used in such a deft manner as to draw from his instrument the loveliest tones. He was altogether opposed to the high-raised finger of some of the modern schools, and in his work 'L'Art du Chant applique au Piano' he cautions students against this habit. The same advice had been previously given by Carl Czerny in his 'Letters on the Art of Playing the Pianoforte', namely: "do not strike the keys from too great a height, as in this case a thud will accompany the tone."
WILLIAM MASON

Think of the instruments of the orchestra and their different qualities of tone, and try to imitate them on the piano. Think of every octave on the piano as having a different color; then shade and color your playing.
HANS von BÜLOW

Music is the art of the ear, and the first consideration of the pianist should be beautiful, varied, and expressive tone. No matter how carefully one may have attended to all the outward technical directions regarding hand position, fingers, etc., if the tone is not right, his whole technique is faulty.
ERNEST HUTCHESON

It's like flying in the face of nature to attempt to acquire equality of strength in the fingers. Instead acquire the ability to produce finely graded qualities of sound. ... Since each finger is formed differently, better to develop their special characteristics rather than attempt to destroy their individuality. The strength of each finger is relative to its shape.
CHOPIN

I assure you, no matter how beautifully we play any piece, the minute Liszt plays it you would scarcely recognize it! His touch and his peculiar use of the pedal are two secrets of his playing, and then he seems to dive down into the most hidden thoughts of the composer, and fetch them up to the surface so that they can gleam out at you one by one, like stars!
AMY FAY

Do not play on the sides of the finger or with a sideways stroke, for then the touch will be weak and uncertain.
HANS von BÜLOW

The main things in piano playing are tone and sentiment.
WILLIAM MASON

(On Paderewski's Carnegie Hall debut 1891) Here was one who could create beautiful, soulful, warm vibrant tone, and in all degrees of quality, from the most airy pianissimo to thundering fortissimo, yet without harshness. People listened almost breathlessly – as they do only when a great master performs. ...It was doubtless Paderewski's wonderful piano tone, so full of variety and color, so vital with numberless gradations of light and shade that charmed and enthralled his listeners.
HARRIETTE BROWER

Touch, more than anything else, gives individuality to the playing of the virtuosos and makes their efforts so different from the playing of machines. It's near impossible to show how certain touches produce certain effects, but the ear hears these effects and if the student has the right kind of persistence he will work and work until able to reproduce the tones he has heard.
KATHARINE GOODSON

Busoni is the only one of the modern pianists who has introduced new tone values. He has not a touch, he has 'touches'. He realized that there's no expression in touch per se, but the expression comes from regulating tonal values in a series of notes. The manner of each note struck depends upon the relation of that tone to the whole.
RUDOLPH GANZ

Questions to ask oneself when striving for delicacy and singing tone: "Is my arm floating? Am I pressing each note to key bottom? Am I keeping my

371

fingers on the surface of the keys?" ... It's next to impossible to produce a singing tone with a stiff wrist; the wrist must always be flexible.
JOSEF LHÉVINNE

One cannot make his sense of touch too sensitive. ... The arm should feel as if it is floating, and should never be tense.
OSSIP GABRILOWITSCH

As to tonal color, (Paderewski) requires all possible variety in tone production. He likes strong contrasts, which are brought out, not only by variety of touch, but by skillful use of the pedals.
ANTOINETTE SZUMOWSKA

Quality of tone and variety of tonal gradations are special qualities of Paderewski's playing. These must be acquired by aid of the ear, which tests and judges each shade and quality of tone. He counsels the student to listen to each tone he produces, for quality and variety.
SIGISMOND STOJOWSKI

The artist working day in and day out at the keyboard discovers subtle touch effects which he will associate with a certain passage. He may have no logical reason for doing this other than it appeals to his artistic sense, in all probability following no law but that of his own musical taste and sense of hearing.
KATHARINE GOODSON

The pianist shouldn't think of the muscles and nerves in his arm, nor of the ivory and ebony keys, nor of the hammers and strings in the interior of the instrument, but first and always of the kind of tone he is eliciting from the instrument, and whether it's the most appropriate tonal quality for the proper interpretation of the piece he's playing. If the ideal touch is presented to his mind through the medium of the ear, he'll be much more successful in attaining the required artistic ends. He must realize clearly what is good and what is bad, and his aural sense must be continually educated in this respect.
OSSIP GABRILOWITSCH

It makes no difference whether the individual note is struck by a child or Paderewski – it has in itself no expressive value. In the case of the violin, voice, and many other instruments, the individual note may be modified after it is emitted, offering the possibility of a whole world of emotional

372

expression. Our sole means of expression in piano playing lies in the relation of one note to the others in a series, or in a chord. ... It's the principal subject for intelligent and careful study, yet few appear to understand it. The charm of the piano lies in the command which the player has over many voices singing together. But until the pianist has regard for the individual voice in relation to the ensemble, he cannot make his work really beautiful.
HAROLD BAUER

Henselt said "imagine you're sinking your fingers in dough." This is but one instance of his abhorrence of anything inelastic. He once said "An ass can give the notes a knock like that that!" Another time ..."You just come in there with the tramp of a trooper."
BETTINA WALKER

The moment a pianist touches the keyboard you're either attracted or repelled. He has only to play a few measures to show whether he'll speak to you from the inner depths, or only glide superficially over the keys, strike the notes harshly and monotonously, or charm you by his infinite variety of tone. ... A musical touch is gained from doing the right thing in each hour of practice and study. It results from laying a thorough foundation, and a correct understanding of technical principles, and therefore can be acquired through intelligent study. I make this statement without hesitation, for I have seen its fulfilment over and over again.
HARRIETTE BROWER

I saw Liszt's countenance assume that agony of expression, mingled with radiant smiles of joy which I never saw in any other human face except in the painting of Our Saviour by some of the early masters; his hands rushed over the keys, the floor shook like a wire, the whole audience was wrapped in sound.
HENRY REEVES

When tone awareness so infuses the human body that perfect cooperation becomes possible between the performing artist and his instrument, then body and spirit mingle in song in a wonderful unity, defying analysis.
CARL KREBS

Liszt, compared to Thalberg, was incontestably the more artistic, the more vibrant, the more electric.
ERNEST LEGOUVE

Positive Piano

*I am electrical in my nature, I must interrupt the flow of my ineffable wisdom
or I might neglect to practice or develop it.*
BEETHOVEN

I sing the body electric.
WALT WHITMAN

INTERPRETATION

The 19th century was a superbly creative and vibrant music scene.
Many of the great compositional masterpieces from that era still
dominate the current repertoire. They survive not just because they
are finely crafted, but because they express great humanity. The men
and women who publicly performed these works had big conceptions
of life. If we are to achieve similar greatness, we must elevate our
standards, and continually work at improving and upgrading all the
important aspects of our lives – just like they did.

*If Beethoven's playing was notable for its tremendous power, character,
unheard-of bravura and facility, Hummel's performance, on the other hand,
was a model of clarity and distinctness, of the most charming elegance
and delicacy, and its difficulties were invariably calculated to produce the
greatest, most astonishing effects, since he combined Mozart's manner with
the Clementi school so wisely adapted to the instrument.*
CZERNY

In the 1820s, as a child prodigy, Liszt had amazed audiences with
his rendition of the Hummel Piano Concerto in B minor. In Weimar,
in 1844, at the height of his concert career, he once again turned to
that old warhorse. Hummel's widow was present and commented
"My husband played it well, but not like this".

Poetry and music are just two modes of communication and
expression. When seeking to praise Chopin in the highest possible
terms people called him a poet of the piano. If you find yourself
feeling uninspired and blocked, if you're unproductively spinning
your wheels in an oxymoronic creative rut, if you feel stonewalled,
stymied, and stagnant ... you need an attitude adjustment. In every
generation, artists have resorted to two sides of the same coin for
inspiration – nature and poetry.

You will ask me whence I take my ideas? That I cannot say with any degree of certainty; they come to me uninvited, directly or indirectly. I could almost grasp them in my hands out in Nature's open, in the woods, during my promenades in the silence of the night at earliest dawn. They are roused by moods which in the poet's case are transmuted into words, and in mine into tones that sound, roar and storm until at last they take shape for me as notes.
BEETHOVEN

Beethoven and I were taking a walk and we lost our way so completely that we didn't get home until eight o'clock. Throughout our walk he had hummed and howled up and down the scale as we went along, without singing any individual notes. When I asked him what it was he replied: "The theme for the final allegro of the Sonata (Opus 57) has occurred to me." When we arrived at his rooms he ran to the piano without taking off his hat.
FERDINAND RIES

The examples of great composers being inspired by poetry are so numerous that even in miniscule font they would easily quadruple the size of this book.

The world is not going to end if you take off one afternoon and go for a hike with a picnic lunch and an anthology of great poetry. Let go of your worrisome thoughts for a few hours, get some exercise and fresh air, and let those two timeless soul-elixirs work their rejuvenation magic ... and see how your work, and your attitude, improve the next time you go at it.

Poetry feeds the mind with beautiful and picturesque images of thought, and familiarity with its treasures aids the instrumentalist in playing poetically. MacDowell often prefaced his works with a poem or verse. While in Europe he read all he could of legendary lore; the results are seen in his compositions. This kind of knowledge fires the imagination, stimulates the fancy, and enables a player to think, feel and play poetically and expressively.
HARRIETTE BROWER

ORNAMENTS

Regard ornaments as spices too much of which can ruin a good dish, or as gaudy architectural elements that can deface an otherwise well-proportioned building. If speakers were to embellish every word with accent, all would be

375

similar and unclear. ... Practice ornaments to acquire skill, but ornaments that cannot be executed with charm are best omitted entirely.
C.P.E. BACH

Never discard any embellishment which serves to accentuate the melodic curve, or adds to its declamatory character. A well-educated taste assisted by experience will be a fairly reliable guide, however; it's hardly advisable for amateurs with limited training to attempt any home-editing of this kind. C.P.E. Bach spent years on the proper exposition of embellishment.
JOSEF HOFMANN

Mechanical execution is still driven by the mental conception – especially in the case of delicate ornaments.

To trill quickly we must think quickly; for if we trill only with the fingers they will soon stick, lose their rhythmic succession, and finish in cramped condition.
JOSEF HOFMANN

Independent thinking, discernment and creativity are the tools, so to speak, of moving projects forward beyond the ordinary. Most people routinely try to get away with only the minimum amount of those; they're content to follow the crowd, to conform to what everyone else is doing or has done, partly due to a lack of real enthusiasm for their projects - which often means they don't dig in deeply enough.

The way to secure results is to go deep into things. Pearls lie at the bottom of the sea. Most pupils seem to expect them floating on the surface of the water. They don't float, and he who would have his playing shine with the beauty of splendid gems must first dive deep for those gems.
VLADIMIR de PACHMANN

A second reason results from the first; people lack real confidence because they don't have real experience. Here's an example of the confidence that arises from experience and authenticity. A late 19th century New York performance of the Bach triple concerto in D Minor brought together Anton Rubinstein, William Mason and Sebastian Mills, with Theodore Thomas conducting.

Mason was concerned about authentic renderings of ornaments.

Knowing that Anton Rubinstein was 'not precise in historical methods', Mason showed him a copy of Marpurg's *Anleitung zum Klavierspielen* (1765) that explained correct execution.

Ignoring historical evidence, Rubinstein exclaimed: "All wrong; here's how I play it," and demonstrated on the piano. The other two pianists followed Rubinstein's example without argument. The newspaper praised their sense of ensemble and believed that most listeners were relieved that the piece was not "dry and uninteresting" as they had assumed it would be, but was "bright, cheerful, and not oppressive."
WILLIAM MASON

Perhaps Chopin had little strength, but nobody could approach him in grace and elegance, and when he embellished, it was always the apotheosis of good taste.
WILHELM von LENZ

Embellishments ought always to be played more delicately than the passage which they are intended to adorn. In modern music the ornaments are generally written in smaller notes, thus implying that the tone, like the print, ought to be diminished.
ERNST PAUER

I'm fond of long trills. ... Really trill, so that it dawns on the public why they had to pay twice the admission price.
LISZT

That comment was made to a room full of young, aspiring concert pianists, about twenty years after Liszt had retired from the field. It's intended, of course, to be humorous, not egotistical.

Double thirds trill exercises are purely mental, and with care and slow practice, can be accomplished.... By playing the trill exercises in every key, and on various combinations of black and white notes, much greater facility may be secured. "Begin the trill slowly" was Chopin's advice, and those who have heard him, testify that this was his custom in playing them. ... The trill is one of the chief effects of our best song birds. Listen to your canary, as he raises his little head, ruffles his throat feathers, and pours out his song. How he practices those trills, over and over; how brilliant, even, and rapid they are. Surely he is a good model for the singer, who does well to copy his

Positive Piano

tones and effects, as well as his industry. The pianist should also learn from
both bird and singer, and endeavor to model his trills after theirs.
HARRIETTE BROWER

We could go on forever with advice on preparation, but at some
point you've got to just get out there and perform.

Chapter 11

......

PERFORMANCE

The mind is not a vessel to be filled but a fire to be kindled.

—*PLUTARCH*

Music should strike fire from a man.

—*BEETHOVEN*

Mechanical music has been around for a long time. Ctesibius, a Greek inventor living in 3rd century BC Egypt, experimented with compressed air and hydraulic pumps and invented a self-playing musical water organ. The 17th century had its musical snuff box, which used a pin-studded revolving metal drum brushing against a steel comb to crank out popular tunes all by itself. European clock-makers and bell ringers had created similar devices even earlier.

In 1737 the French engineer Jacques de Vaucanson built a robotic flute player. In his 1754 treatise *Musico-Theologia* Johann Michel Schmidt comments on that novelty and reminds us that machines can't think, not to mention compose meaningful music. A machine, he says, will never create or interpret as did the great J.S. Bach.

The invention in the 19th century of the pianola or player-piano basically made human pianists obsolete, at least as far as mechanical dexterity and accuracy are concerned. It also intensified the debate about whether or not a machine could replace a human artist. The pianola could 'play' piano music more accurately than any human (like 100% error-free), and it wasn't even cutting-edge technology out of NASA or Silicon Valley. Pianolas were built from simple wooden parts and a bellows mechanism forcing air pressure through holes in a perforated roll of paper which encoded the relative pitches and rhythms. Their interpretive sensitivity was amazing, but they were just faithfully reproducing the human artist's input.

Wonderful as the mechanical inventions are, there is always something lacking.
KATHARINE GOODSON

Increasingly sophisticated computer technology is capable of significant dynamic and rhythmic finesse; but the 'performance' is still just a lifeless regurgitation of sorts, with software mindlessly executing the input received. The computer will play the 'music' exactly the same, every time (unless you direct it differently) and fulfill that arbitrary criterion for judging mastery suggested by Ericsson.

The essence of music is, of course, the spirit of the human being behind it; and that's something that machines will never be capable of because they aren't human and never will be.

The divine spark! The French call it "the holy fire" (le feu sacré), which expresses better the resplendent heavenward blazing, illuming flame of genius which was the gift of heaven to Liszt and Anton Rubinstein.
CONSTANTIN von STERNBERG

Music is a kind of spiritual language capable of conveying deep insights into the universal human condition.

There's a theory that music is the faint reminiscence of a language we used, either in a previous and immaterial existence, or in some earlier stage of our development, the meaning of which we have lost. I'm not saying that I believe this, but it may not be very far from the truth.
GIOVANNI SGAMBATI

Music is in some measure a species of language, by which may be expressed those passions and feelings with which the mind is burdened or affected.

Expression, feeling, and sensibility are its soul, as in every other art.
CZERNY

The best works of literary, plastic, and musical art give us more than mere pleasure; they furnish us with information about the nature of the world.
ALDOUS HUXLEY

He who would be a poet must command poetry.
GOETHE

The greatest composers don't just notate pitches; they express their magnificent vision of life through music. The greatness of a composition will be a combined function of the composer's: (1) personal character, life experience and vision; and (2) musical aesthetic, knowledge and craftsmanship. Lesser composers may have the craftsmanship, but it's their smaller vision that makes them lesser.

Performers also need knowledge and craftsmanship, usually called 'technique'. But even more importantly, they need their own deep life experience and vision to be able to interpret the musical message. Performing someone else's good music is always a deeply psychological, collaborative effort. You must somehow empathetically bond with the composer's spirit embodied in the notes (and rests) of the score.

In the art of musical interpretation, Franz Liszt set a pretty high standard, to say the least. It's seriously doubtful that if you assembled in one room today those great musical artists who personally knew him - Chopin, Robert and Clara Schumann, Brahms, Mendelssohn, Berlioz, Wagner, and even Beethoven, and many others not so famous – that any adult pianist today would even summon the courage to perform these master's works before them.

I deliberately specified adult, because a child would take a shot at it; little kids are faultless – and fearless. Even if a confident adult pianist were to hazard it, how likely is that every one of those masters would unanimously declare the performance the most moving, exhilarating, meaningful and insightful interpretation of their work conceivable - possibly exceeding their own conception? Yet that is exactly what Liszt repeatedly did.

So if machines can outplay us mechanically, and Liszt was the ultimate interpreter, what does that leave us today? Let's remain positive and look at it as a huge opportunity. Machines will never interpret as humans can and the playing of Liszt is now a memory, albeit a huge one. Life moves on … Ol' Man River keeps flowing along.

You cannot step twice into the same river.
HERACLITUS

Character develops itself in the stream of life.
GOETHE

Today we live in a much larger world, both in terms of people and material advantage. Our challenges may seem greater today, but so are the opportunities.

The advance in the demands upon all who play the piano has been so enormous that the student has to work to-day almost four times as hard as when Liszt held his master classes at Weimar. But the student to-day, by means of better methods, is able to accomplish so much more.
MORIZ ROSENTHAL

One thing unfortunately hasn't changed much – the human propensity for self-absorption and thinking small, as opposed to acting magnanimously, with the welfare of others at heart. Hopefully one thing is beginning to sink in: it's a huge factor in the difference between mediocre and great.

The mechanical skill of piano-playing has of late been so systematized, and the methods of acquiring it so improved, that the possession of mere technical facility is a foregone conclusion, and has in a great degree lost its interest unless combined with a discriminative and poetical conception and a true musical interpretation. Of two pianists possessing equal technical equipment, it is the one whose personality is the most intense, and at the same time lovable, who will be sure to delight and interest.
WILLIAM MASON

Bland and self-centered does not make for an ingratiating or interesting personality. Nurturing and expressing gifts with humility and genuine enthusiasm is what Art is fundamentally all about.

Every man has some personal characteristics which mark him from his fellows and some lines of endeavor into which they are impelled. When following out these lines and developing these characteristics a man is happiest and most likely to be of service to his fellow-men.
HUBERT PARRY

Music becomes really beautiful when lovingly offered to the community. If it ends up being solely about your relatively undeveloped and unsophisticated super-sized ego, then between the player-piano and the historical precedent of Liszt you're out of luck.

Public performance is not just a test of accomplishment but an opportunity to inspire. But anybody who's tried it knows that it's a totally different animal compared to playing in the relative privacy of your own home. An audience exclusively focused on you has a way of magnifying any weakness in your state of preparation, and of generating significant levels of stress that weren't present back home. (Actually, you are generating your own stress).

Concerns about successful performance basically fall into one of two categories, at significant remove from each other. At the lowest level the performer is concerned with just getting through the ordeal, so to speak. He or she wants to remember all the notes and play them accurately.

The inexperienced pianist with tendencies towards nervousness fears missing notes or forgetting some complicated passage. He does not seem concerned, however, over the equally important subject of whether his tone will be uniformly fine or whether his touch will be beautiful, whether the dynamic treatment will prove effective and within the canons of well-poised aesthetic judgment, whether the pedals are well employed, whether his playing will show a clear distribution or outline as regards the proper distinction of phrases, sections, periods, episodes, also of contrasts and climaxes. Yet were he to give serious, conscientious thought to all this while playing, he would in all probability not have time nor inclination to fret about accuracy or memory.
ALBERTO JONÁS

You shouldn't even be sitting for this exam if you haven't already completed your homework assignments.

Before you hit the stage, your fundamental technical ability should already have been developed, securely ready to be now drawn forth as needed in the service of the interpretation. Otherwise, you may find yourself in a very uncomfortable situation ...

There is nothing more terrible than to meet a good success for which one is not ready or ripe. It is an agony.
PADEREWSKI

There is no higher satisfaction than in being able to distinguish oneself before a large company, and in receiving an honorable acknowledgment of one's diligence and talent. But we must be thoroughly sure of our business, for want of success is vexatious, tormenting, and disgraceful.
Above all, you must select for this purpose such compositions as are fully within your powers, and respecting the good effect of which you can entertain no doubt. Every difficult piece becomes doubly difficult when we play it before others, because the natural diffidence of the performer impedes the free development of his abilities.
CZERNY

Study as difficult pieces as you can, but when you perform always choose one of your easier compositions. If you play what is too hard, you will learn nothing, you will be wearied, disgusted; whereas if you perform something which to you presents no technical embarrassment, you can give yourself wholly to the art with which you render it; you will have grace and charm.
CÉCILE CHAMINADE

There's also the 'danger' of a drone-like state where the overly self-conscious pianist plays as if on automatic pilot, too preoccupied with execution to be actually aware of what he or she is playing. It's kind of like driving home from work where sometimes you 'arrive' not really even remembering the details of the drive because your thoughts were who knows where. (Hopefully you weren't texting ... please don't do that).

Acts very frequently performed become so mechanical that they can be repeated without conscious awareness. The pianist, after constant rehearsal, will perform the most intricate passage while his attention is engaged with

an entirely unrelated subject – although when the performance of music falls temporarily into such an automatic repetition, the connoisseur will instantly recognize the loss of emotional quality.
F.M. ALEXANDER

Beyond mechanical execution, in performance one must consciously shape the interpretation at all times.

Through diligent practice, physical execution becomes mechanical, and reaches a stage where attention may be focused on more important expression.
C.P.E. BACH

What transforms the whole concept of public performance is a paradigm shift away from ego-satisfaction to one of service to both the audience and also the abstract concept of Art. When your ego takes a back seat (or no seat) and you put these higher concerns first, an extraordinary experience becomes possible.

But it's not like some kind of light switch that you can deliberately turn on at performance time. Interpretation mirrors your internal personality and character, and your total life experience measured by all of your birthdays.

No matter how excellent the training and acquired mastery of mechanical technique, by itself, it's not enough in the naked and exposed atmosphere of the public platform, where magnetism, personality and power of concentration are the means by which the pianist may hope to convince his hearers. ... It's imperative to throw oneself so completely into his work while on stage as to become oblivious of one's surroundings, and thus be transformed into a complete medium, a vehicle of transmission, between the composer's ideas and the audience. But you can't do that if the underlying character is not already present in your personality.
MARK HAMBOURG

There can be nothing exclusive about substantial art. It comes directly out of the heart of the experience of life and thinking about life and living life.
CHARLES IVES

There's a big difference between the auto-pilot zone-out of self-absorption, and the genuine conscious expression of emotional drama embedded in the music.

One must not absorb, one must express.
BRAHMS

Let's see how we can deal first with the anxiety. But please remember; you're in this for the long haul - continual implementation of everything in Chapters 1-10 so far is what's going to give you the strength you'll need.

Anticipating public performance through visualization can help. Then rehearsing in front of small groups ramps up the pressure, inducing a good kind of stress that helps you find the weak spots in your playing and stimulates you to higher levels of performance.

We talked about Dale Carnegie back in the chapter on social skills. Like most of us, in the beginning he was terrified at the thought of speaking in public. He decided to practice by giving speeches to stuffed animals, imagining that they constituted a real live critical audience. It worked; he gained confidence. You can start by performing a recital for your teddy-bears. Visualize, act, record, analyze.

It's said that Demosthenes spent hours haranguing the waves by the seashore. He completely overcame a nervous tremor and inclination to stutter, and prepared himself to face the commotions of a vast assemblage.
LOUIS CHARLES ELSON

Eloquent speeches aside, the imagining and doing of a thing, not talking about it, is what brings artistic growth.

Playing before others has the great advantage that it compels one to study with unusual zeal. For the idea that we must play before an audience spurs us on to a much greater measure of diligence than if we play only to ourselves, or to the four senseless walls.
CZERNY

By 'suffering' through a few trial runs we gain experience, and become stronger. We can now go back each time with a slightly deeper perspective and rework the problem areas. We basically revisit our previously established best practice methodology, only with every repetitive cycle, the new real-world practical experience gained enables us to fine tune that methodology, continuously adapting it to our individual challenges.

Another common concern of performers (both lower and higher tier) is whether or not the audience will clap, or preferably cheer and bestow a standing ovation. If one gets through the performance without a wrong note and the audience cheers, it's considered a big success; and if the box-office draw is good, so much the better. But of course there's more to it; big applause is not necessarily the proper standard to judge your own continuing development as an artist.

I've had a triumph with the connoisseur as well as with the music-lover, and the press will have something to talk about. When I finished, there was so much applause that I had to appear a second time to make my bow.
CHOPIN

A sentence (above) that should give present-day virtuosi, accustomed to being recalled dozens of times and to receive ovations as if by right, food for thought.
ALFRED CORTOT

He who praises everybody, praises nobody.
DR. SAMUEL JOHNSON

Especially in the larger cities, 19th century audiences were for the most part more exacting and demanding than they are today, reflecting the past greater emphasis on arts in education and relatively greater numbers of musical amateurs in the population. Ovations were not just indiscriminately bestowed on every performer. And audiences would also let you know if they were displeased.

I'm aware of at least one of today's piano 'superstars' who programs Chopin and then promptly boasts in publicity material about the number of encores received (or maybe that was the manager). Most of us maintain a humble reverence for Chopin and his art don't we? We wouldn't presume to play his music 'better' than he could himself, simply measured by modern audience approbation ... at least I hope not.

I wasn't deceived by the flattery of well-meaning but incapable critics, who

387

were quite willing to convince me that my playing was as perfect as it could possibly be. I knew better than anyone else there were certain deficiencies in my playing that I could not afford to neglect. Every seeker of artistic truth is more widely awake to his deficiencies than any of his critics could possibly be.
FERRUCCIO BUSONI

The brilliant reception given to the public performance of Mendelssohn's Midsummer Night's Dream Overture did not dazzle him. "I must do better in everything" was his motto; and to my praises he merely answered: "Do you like it? Well, I am glad of that."
IGNAZ MOSCHELES

The second, higher level issue for the performing artist is grasp of the music's meaning and the desire to sincerely share it with others in an uplifting and enlightening mutual artistic experience.

The artist has such a beautiful calling, a glorious message – to educate people to see the beauty and grandeur of his art, of the ideal.
TERESA CARREÑO

In a small town of magnificent scenic beauty about twelve hours from Vancouver, I was the first internationally known pianist to give a recital. Afterwards, my host confided to me that he had never been able to understand or appreciate music of the heavier type, but that he had enjoyed my recital because I had unfolded the beauty and meaning of the compositions on my program, particularly the Beethoven sonata, so clearly, that he had fully grasped the message of the music. Such words mean more to the artist than columns of praise from the experts.
ARTHUR FRIEDHEIM

Good, the more communicated, more abundant grows.
MILTON

Real masters always seek to expand their vision of what's possible and strive to elevate standards of excellence; that's part of the definition of master. It's still what separates the ordinary from the extraordinary today.

When all adverse elements are reconciled and he can lose himself in his

interpretation, secure that the mind of the public is with him, then the general collective public mass can be galvanized into becoming like one single vibrating nerve, responding instantaneously to every variation of color, rhythm and passion.
MARK HAMBOURG

It's annoying that virtuoso singers and instrumentalists often act as if they were simple reciters. Virtuosity is not a passive slave. It can resuscitate all the charm of a composition or make it banal; effectively destroying it …
'virtuoso' derives from 'virtue', and should not be falsified or misapplied.
LISZT

Artistic expression is … exactly that. There has to be something 'artistic' to express inside. All the potential aesthetic beauty embedded in the score remains *outside* unless you grok it. All that technique was acquired to be used as a tool, but at the core must be a vision. And the relative value of its expression is somehow mysteriously linked to the moral character and philosophical insight of both performer and composer.

Music is a moral agent, reviving man's memory, exciting his imagination, developing his sentiment … it is one of the most powerful means for ennobling the mind, elevating the morals, and above all, refining the manners.
L. M. GOTTSCHALK

Since all things of permanent value in music have proceeded from a fervid artistic imagination, they should be interpreted with the continual employment of the performer's imagination.
SIGISMUND STOJOWSKI

When Liszt played Beethoven, it was 'Beethoven' as Beethoven would have written if he had known the tonal and mechanical perfection of the modern piano. Whether it was Bach or Beethoven, Liszt's conception remained true to the composers' time and style, plus all the newer means of extolling their thoughts.
CONSTANTIN von STERNBERG

Eight bars from the adagio of Beethoven's Opus 106 played by Liszt was an absolute revelation. If you did not hear it, you'll never know what penetration, what speech a piano tone is capable of; it really cried out in

389

pain. It was as if two great souls greeted each other sorrowfully: the souls of Beethoven and his wonderful re-creator Liszt.
JOSÉ VIANNA DA MOTTA

In the pathetic and slow movements, whenever he had a long note to express, (C.P.E. Bach) contrived to produce a cry of sorrow and complaint as can only be effected on this instrument, and perhaps by himself.
DR. CHARLES BURNEY

Let music suggest to you what to do as the piece unfolds; then you'll use your imagination as well as your reason. When the music commands you, eventually your subconscious faculties come into play. In practice don't try to 'do', but learn to 'see'; during performance you may then be able to see music, its shape, feeling, and rhythmic unity, while you compel your fingers to give all this.
TOBIAS MATTHAY

If you consciously implement superficial effects, that is, ones not in service of the musical interpretation but calculated simply to impress your audience, the mental effort will distract you and the result will ultimately annoy the audience. We mentioned Liszt's fondness for the meditations of Marcus Aurelius. Many of the Emperor's aphorisms could almost be interpreted in a performance context.

Labor willingly, with due consideration and regard to the common interest… let not studied ornament distract thy thoughts … let the deity inside you be the guardian of a living being - manly, mature, and engaged.
MARCUS AURELIUS

All means of expression must always be applied, never for their own sake, but solely to express music, something beautiful we perceive in that moment. No means of expression (whatever their nature) must ever be applied so coarsely as to become obvious to the listener, and force themselves upon the attention.
TOBIAS MATTHAY

Only when the player has control of the means does he have the true freedom to clearly and adequately express himself. Then his interpretation takes on the nature of an improvisation. … To bring out the spiritual side of piano playing depends on absolute freedom, both mentally and physically. This

freedom of interpretation presupposes the artist's mind and taste to be so well trained as to warrant him in relying on the inspiration of the moment. But back of it all must be his logical plan of action.
JOSEF HOFMANN

The ideal interpreter is one who, keeping before him the ideal, has first thought out every effect and nuance he wishes to make, yet leaves himself mentally untrammeled, to be moved by the inspiration which may come to him in performance.
LEOPOLD GODOWSKY

It's beautifully apparent when an individual authentically comes into his own, starts thinking independently, and becomes fully accountable for his actions. The reverse is painfully obvious. Authenticity in music means having your own concept - something really interesting to audiences, by the way.

My husband had a theory that the pupil should use his own innate musical and rhythmic feeling to get at the meaning of a piece. He sometimes gave one of his compositions to several pupils at the same time, to see how they would work it out. He preferred they express their own individuality, if it didn't offend against some musical law.
MARIAN MACDOWELL

I cannot indicate to my pupils the way to play emotionally, that is impossible. They must be emotional themselves. If you have to ask me that question, you will never play emotionally ... Don't ask me what the music means – the music means what it says to you.
LESCHETIZKY

(On the question "What is Jazz"...) if you have to ask, you'll never know.
LOUIS ARMSTRONG

An artist's individual worth is very closely allied with his personality, his whole extrinsic attitude towards the world about him. Personality is the virtuoso's one great unassailable stronghold. It makes us want to hear a half-dozen different renderings of a single Beethoven sonata by a half-dozen different pianists. Each has the charm and flavor of the interpreter.
JAMES FRANCIS COOKE

Liszt's method, hard to describe, is an expression of his unparalleled pianistic technique, and it would be a mistake to suppose that anyone could ever approach such individuality, no matter how thoroughly he might overcome the difficulties of his piano writing. ... Let all pianists come together and attack the E flat piano concerto of Beethoven. Liszt's first chord would betray the fact that it is he, and no other! His imagination, his conception, his fantasy is imponderable. All other pianists are lost in the shadow cast by Liszt.
WILHEM von LENZ

"Natural abandoned passion" is Liszt's motto. His playing is never pretentious or mundane but independently reflects every thought of his proud, wild, and fiery soul. The sole purpose of all is to draw forth his noble imagination. The effect caused by his music is incredible, drawing us into a dream world which simultaneously depresses and magnificently elevates our spirit.
Mme. AUGUSTE BOISSIER

We must give ourselves to a musical composition before we can reproduce it, give it once again that life and pulsation which it lost when crystallized into mere notes and passages on a page.
ANNA STEINECKE

In Joseffy's performance (Rubinstein D minor Concerto) his tone was so enormous and there was such a broad sweep to his playing that it seemed like a veritable reincarnation of Rubinstein himself.
WILHELM GERICKE

What makes the playing of the greatest artists a tantalizing force is: to be at once self-contained and impassioned, firmly balanced and yet floating midway between earth and heaven.
BETTINA WALKER

The feeling of intensity shows itself not merely by quickening the time but by means much less obvious, much deeper-lying than this. There is more gain than loss in taking a movement somewhat slowly ... It must be done by the tone, the turn of the phrase. Think well over this.
STERNDALE BENNETT

Two great factors in interpretation are logic and proportion; they must

dominate the thought of the interpreter, he must express them in his work. In just the degree that he lacks them will his performance fall short of beauty and expressiveness. ...If you examine a Greek statue you will find it perfect in classic form and line. Among the composers the most perfect examples of proportion are Beethoven and Brahms. They are the Greeks of musical art.
LEOPOLD GODOWSKY

Study a work closely and carefully, gain knowledge of the musical laws underlying its structure and the necessary keyboard technique to express it. Study the composer's life environment, investigate the historical background of the period in which he worked, learn of his joys and sufferings, cultivate a deep and heartfelt sympathy for his ideals, and be scrupulous in the constant evolution of your own ideals and conceptions of standards by which masterpieces may be judged.
SIGISMUND STOJOWSKY

Nothing is more important to the virtuoso than a profound understanding of the tone-poet whom he undertakes to interpret.
WILHELM von LENZ

In this increasingly noisy world, we're losing the ability to appreciate silence. There's virtually continuous background noise from automobiles, airplanes, sirens and jackhammers (especially if you live in the Big Apple). Thumping subwoofers have become as invasive as medical testing (almost) and the die-hard television is like the pesky cockroach, difficult to stamp out, its mindless talking heads and virtual-reality stars accosting you in every airport lounge. Internally our minds are often a jumble of 'noisy' thoughts, and most of us find the simple act of peaceful meditation not simple at all, but in fact almost impossible to attain.

Don't give up on the meditation; as with most things it comes with mindful 'practice'. I promise that it gets easier in less than 10,000 hours. An advanced degree of mental composure and 'quiet' is necessary to understand perhaps the most contextually expressive aspect of music – the rest.

Rests are just as important as notes. Music is painted upon a canvas of silence. Mozart used to say "silence is the greatest effect in music."
JOSEF LHÉVINNE

Positive Piano

Rests, not just notes, must be given their full value, to avoid a sense of vagueness.
C.P.E. BACH

The essential nature of musical art is the rest and the hold. Consummate players, and improvisers, know how to employ these means of expression in lofty and ample measure. The tense silence between two movements, in itself music in this environment, leaves wider scope for divination than the more determinate, but therefore less elastic, sound.
FERRUCCIO BUSONI

Don't fill rest spaces with sound – how many players sin in this way; either by not observing rests, or by filling up the place of silence with tones prolonged by pedal. Silence should not be interfered with.
LEOPOLD GODOWSKY

The notes I handle no better than many pianists. But the pauses between the notes - ah, that is where the art resides.
ARTUR SCHNABEL

A rest in music means silence. One has to listen to appreciate it. Audiences can take part in this process as well.

A painter paints his pictures on canvas. Musicians paint their pictures on silence. We provide the music, you provide the silence.
LEOPOLD STOWKOWSKI

The more we hear great artists on interpretation, the more we understand how intimately it involves our total being. Playing the notes on the instrument is just the beginning.

Traditions of interpretation should not mean the dry academic formulas of schools and conservatories that simply conserve old ideas, (for that's the meaning of the word). Real tradition in piano playing originates with great artists who have discovered and evolved certain effects through intuition. When these intuitions stand the test and measure up to the highest standards of art, they become traditions.
LEOPOLD GODOWSKY

The aim is, or ought to be, to reproduce, in all the glow of life and pulsation of the moment first breathed into being, those exquisite tone poems in which those master-spirits of the divine art have embodied some of the subtlest thoughts, the most weird and wonderful fancies, some of the most impassioned yearnings of the human soul.
BETTINA WALKER

Metaphor is effective for communicating artistic wisdom because it stimulates the imagination. The great pianists often expressed themselves poetically when articulating musical ideas, or even when talking about each other.

The mere mechanical attainments of piano technique meant very little to Liszt. Speed, pure and simple, of which so much is made by today's pianists, he held in contempt. I remember a pianist performing Chopin's Polonaise in A flat with great gusto. When he came to the celebrated octave passage in the left hand, Liszt interrupted him by saying: "I don't want to listen to how fast you can play octaves. What I wish to hear is the canter of the horses of the Polish cavalry before they gather force and destroy the enemy."
FREDERIC LAMOND

The virtuoso isn't just a mason dutifully chiseling stone according to the architect's plan ... and adding nothing of himself. He's not a reader of books without margins for his own personal notes. Spirited musical works are actually emotionally dramatic settings. The virtuoso must sigh, weep, and sing to mentally resuscitate the work. He also creates, as did the composer himself, and must live the passions he'll bring to light in all their brilliance. He breathes life into the score, gives it a pulse, charm, grace, or lights it on fire. He gives life to the lifeless, infusing it as with the spark Prometheus snatched from Jupiter.
LISZT

When Liszt played he seemed to be devoured by an inner flame, and he projected himself into music like a comet into space. He simply threw himself headlong into it, and gave all there was in him.
AMY FAY

In everything that he played, Sgambati far exceeded all I could have anticipated. His lovely elastic touch, the weight and yet the softness of his wrist-staccato, the rhythmic swing, the rich coloring, exquisitely delicate, and over all the atmosphere of grace, warmth, charm and repose which perfect mastery alone can give.

His tone was always rich and full … his pianissimi were so subtle and delicate, and the nuances, the touches of beauty, were fraught with a sighing, lingering, quite inimitable sweetness, which one could compare to the many hues where sky and ocean seemed to melt and blend in a dream of tender ecstasy along the coast-line between Baia and Naples. What wonder then, if I was at once captivated by the Liszt school in Sgambati.

BETTINA WALKER

To make an effective accelerando you must glide into rapidity as steadily as a train increases its speed when steaming out of a station.

Teach yourself to make a rallentando evenly by watching the drops of water cease as you turn off a tap.

A player with an unbalanced rhythm reminds me of an intoxicated man who can't walk straight.

LESCHETIZKY

Playing Chopin is not like driving a coach over the Weimar cobblestones.

LISZT

You seem to be a Christian pianist – you do not let your left hand know what the right doeth.

LISZT

The unmusical artist is like the man who takes you canoeing and does not know the river. You may paddle over it easily enough, but the one with whom you feel safe is the one who knows all the peculiarities, difficulties, and danger points.

LESCHETIZKY

Liszt and his instrument seem to have grown together; a piano-centaur.

GREGOROVIUS

When a student rushed from one section to another without artistic pause, Liszt remarked: "No, don't rush headlong there; hesitate a bit, as if to glance back over the road you have come, and to decide which direction to go." When the student hesitated at difficult spot he cried: "Too much; that's like a

guest stopping to read the house-number before entering."
CARL LACHMUND

That part should be played piously. Do you know what it means to be pious?
LESCHETIZKY

Can't you read? The score demands 'con amore' and what are you doing? You're playing it like old married men.
ARTURO TOSCANINI

Our personal quest for the metaphorical holy grail of self-actualization is a lifetime proposition. We're always imagining ways to manifest our ever expanding vision and Ideal – or should be.

In all effort and quest there is joy and pain; because we can never attain to our ideal. Indeed, we advance only to realize that there are fresh vistas opening in every direction around us; and when the shadows fall, we seem only to have reached the true starting point. But the spell does not lose its power. Henselt at the age of seventy-six was still wrestling with 'the flesh' (his name for technique) in order to render it ever a fitter medium for embodying his ideal aspirations.
BETTINA WALKER

How I would have enjoyed witnessing Chopin's ecstasy, could he have heard Henselt thunder, whisper, and lighten through his "Winter Wind", the A minor Étude. Henselt's rendering is so poetic, so indescribably grand, so infinitely idealized, as if touched by the wand of Oberon, that I can find no words to adequately describe it. The ineffable tones produced in the right hand to the herculean strokes of the left are like the twinkling of stars – the unknown language of the heights. Taken all in all, this performance of Henselt's is one of the grandest that it has ever been my privilege to hear. From the depths of his soul the artist loves this poem; for years he has fostered and tended it, and warmed it on his breast. When Henselt plays the A minor Étude, he plays it not once but over and over again, for he cannot satiate himself with the euphony with whose atmosphere he surrounds himself! If there is any one performance in which the artist's consuming impulse for absolute perfection is realized, I believe it is this – and my opinion is formed by the result of many years of observation.
WILHELM von LENZ

Wilhelm von Lenz heard both Chopin and Liszt in person, so that statement constitutes remarkable praise for Adolph Henselt. Now fast forward to the early 20th century for an enlightening anecdote: Artur Rubinstein (not 'Anton' – I got those two mixed up all the time when I was kid) recalled in his memoirs a problematical concert where his audience was just not responding. They appeared indifferent to his Brahms intermezzo so he decided to substitute for the beautiful but not particularly showy first two Chopin *études* of Opus 25, the much more impressive *Winter Wind*, number eleven, though still far from being mastered.

Rubinstein banged out the piece as loud and fast as he could, trying to make it as flashy as possible and covering up all the mistakes with the pedal. The crowd jumped up and enthusiastically yelled 'bravo'. He learned that night that poor musical performances of virtuoso numbers can often get rave reviews from the less sophisticated members of the audience, and even admitted to exploiting that bit of intelligence in subsequent recitals.

Well, credit Artur Rubinstein with honesty; and besides being an overall remarkably fine pianist and elegant man, he was an engaging raconteur; both *My Young Years* and *My Many Years* (Alfred Knopf 1973, 1980) make great reading.

But the point of the story is that an earlier age maintained a higher standard.

An audience can have a great effect on the sensibilities of the artist. I can feel at once if any of my listeners are sympathetic, if they're with me and appreciate what I'm doing. This mentality in the audience is a tremendous help to an artist and urges him to do his best. A cold or unsympathetic audience naturally has the opposite effect, and no one is so quick to notice this atmosphere as the player himself.
ALEXANDER BRAILOWSKY

In performance, an adjustment in tempo, tone, and even general interpretation may be called for to suit the temper of the audience or the acoustic conditions. I don't recommend changing the actual numbers of the program though, that would be in bad taste.
LESCHETIZKY

The real truth is perhaps, that the abuse of the pedal is only a means of hiding

a lack of technique, also, a means of making a lot of noise in order to cover up the music which is being butchered.
CLAUDE DEBUSSY

Nuance in piano playing rules. The reign of noise is past.
JAMES HUNEKER (in 1899)

Difficulty shouldn't be estimated by technical complications. To play a Mozart concerto well is a colossally difficult undertaking. The pianist who has worked for hours to get such a composition as near as possible to his conception of perfection is never given the credit for his work, except by a few connoisseurs, some of whom have been through a similarly exacting experience. ... The opposite is also true. A little show of bravura, possible in a passage which has not cost the pianist more than ten minutes of frivolous practice, will turn many of the unthinking auditors into a roaring mob. This is, of course, very distressing to the sincere artist who strives to establish himself by his real worth.
WILHELM BACHAUS

Never attempt to play in public a piece you have just finished studying and have not thoroughly mastered. Put it away for a time, digest it, then repeat the learning process a second, and a third time; and the piece will become a part of yourself.
FANNY BLOOMFIELD-ZEISLER

Never attempt to go beyond what you can reasonably control in public performance, where it can be challenging to maintain composure. Gauge the limits of your command of a piece by what is most rapid and difficult to execute, to minimize the potential of breaking down in performance. ... Postpone public performance of compositions with passages which are yet troublesome in private. Thus you mitigate anxiety, which, far from garnering sympathy, will annoy the audience.
C.P.E. BACH

Exacting attention to detail, persistent application, progressive evolution of aesthetic sense stimulated by a broad outlook and involvement in all the arts - and life - inevitably results in higher standards, and superior results.

Skill can enhance the value of material forces, even double them, but it has its limitations.
LISZT

The key word that keeps coming up repeatedly is 'heart'.

Keyboard players whose chief asset is mechanical technique are clearly at a disadvantage. Their fingers may be agile and yet the effect is less than a more pleasing player. They overwhelm hearing and mind without moving them, playing the notes, but not succeeding like those that gently move the heart rather than the ear.
C.P.E. BACH

Coming from the heart should in turn find its way into the hearts of others.
BEETHOVEN

Once I heard the great Tausig say that one does not play upon the strings of the piano, but upon the heartstrings of the audience.
RAPHAEL JOSEFFY

Louis Moreau Gottschalk captivated our senses by speaking to our hearts .... scintillante, animato, and brilliante awoke us to consciousness of heart-life.
OCTAVIA HENSEL

How many of those men who devote hours and hours a day to mechanism can be accounted for when the hour for artistic demonstration arrives! They disappear. Without heart people come to nothing.
EDOUARD ZELDEN

Genuine art comes from the inside out. To sound like a real artist you must be a real artist. It can't be faked or manufactured.

Exhibition of sentimentality invariably invoked Liszt's sarcasm. A young Swiss lady, who had once been very successful with Chopin's Spianato Polonaise came to grief with Beethoven's Variations in C minor. She started the sturdy theme in a sentimental manner, and as she proceeded, this grew from bad to worse. I expected an outburst of anger but the Master was in a philosophical mood and took it merely as a joke. Audibly he soliloquized: "Aha! A sentimental lover's proposal." Then a moment later: "Now we have a funeral." At the next

exhibition of dolefulness: "Here we see the hearse." Finally, in distress he left the piano, exclaiming: "Gracious! Now the sexton himself is being buried."
CARL LACHMUND

All exaggeration in feeling leads to caricature, and repeated application of the same mode of expression to different subjects deteriorates into mannerism.
ERNST PAUER

The deepest feeling needs the fewest words and gestures.
FERRUCCIO BUSONI

Moscheles was especially great as a Bach-player, and it was a delight to hear him. I was enchanted with the finish, repose, and musicianship of his preludes and fugues from the Well-tempered Clavier, which was without fuss or show... I vividly recall the similarity of Paderewski's interpretation to that of Moscheles, both being characterized by perfect repose in action, yet, at the same time, an intensity of expression. ... In Paderewski's conception and performance, like that of Moscheles, each and all of the voices received careful and reverent attention, and were brought out with due regard to their relative, as well as to their individual, importance. Nuances were never neglected, neither were they in excess. Thus the musical requirements of polyphonic interpretation were artistically fulfilled. Head and heart were united in skillful combination and loving response.
WILLIAM MASON

There's a vital spark in great piano playing that makes each interpretation of a masterwork seem like a living thing. It exists only for the moment and cannot be explained. Two pianists of equal technical ability may play the same piece; one is dull, lifeless, and sapless; with the other there is something indescribably wonderful, the playing seems fairly to quiver with life. What is this vital spark that brings life to mere notes? It may be called the intense artistic interest of the player, that astonishing thing known as inspiration.
RACHMANINOFF

The more energetic the metrical figure, the greater the force required. Great fullness of tone is required for discords and chromatic chords, also in passages in too distant a key from the one just quitted. Such chords and passages require, so to speak, to be forced upon the ear.
M. MATHIS LUSSY

There was much of the heroic in Liszt's nature. In fact, in almost every one of his compositions you find a climactic outburst at which one might exclaim: "See, the conquering hero comes!" Once, when a young man was interpreting a typical melody of this sort in a rather maidenly way, he cried: "Why, that is one of those melodies, each note of which should be fairly rammed into the ears of the listener".
CARL LACHMUND

Some students sit down before the keyboard to 'play' the piano as though they were going to play a game of cards. They've learned certain rules governing the game, which they dare not disobey, being preoccupied with them rather than the ultimate result – the music itself. The Italians don't say 'I play the piano' but rather 'I sound the piano.' (Suono il pianoforte.) If we had a little more 'sounding' of the piano, that is, producing real musical effects, and a little less playing on ivory keys, the playing of our students would be more interesting. .... Imagine a composition as it could be played upon one of many different instruments besides the piano, yet still interpret it primarily as music, irrespective of the instrument.
HAROLD BAUER

Dreyschock spoke of Chopin's extremely delicate and exquisite playing, but said that he lacked the physical strength to produce contrasting forte effects in accordance with his own ideas. This is illustrated by another anecdote I heard years later from Korbay. A young and robust student broke a string while playing Chopin's 'Polonaise Militaire' to him. When, in confusion, he began to apologize, Chopin said, "young man, if I had your strength and played that polonaise as it should be played, there wouldn't be a sound string left in the instrument by the time I got through."
WILLIAM MASON

All the details are important. ... it's often perfection in little things which distinguishes the performance of the great pianist from that of the novice, who usually manages to get the so-called main points, but does not work for the little niceties of interpretation which are almost invariably the defining characteristic of the interpretations of the real artist – that is, the performer who has formed the habit of stopping at nothing short of his highest ideal of perfection.
FERRUCCIO BUSONI

For public playing the heart must be in the right spot, and there must be

'nuances' in the fingers. Tone and diction are everything. The pianist who knows how to tell a story in his playing is the one who holds the public. One must be constantly looking to discover new and unexpected effects—whether they are beautiful or not they will always captivate an audience. Better it is, of course, when they are beautiful!
LESCHETIZKY

Every individual note in a composition is important, but just as important is the soul. After all, the vital spark is the soul, the source of that higher expression in music which cannot be represented in dynamic marks. It feels the need for crescendos and diminuendos intuitively. Every note must awaken a kind of musical consciousness of one's real artistic mission. Resorting exclusively to mechanical rules results in soulless playing.
RACHMANINOFF

Music expresses the eternal, infinite and ideal; it does not express the passion, love, or longing of such-and-such an individual on any particular occasion; but passion, love or longing in itself - and this it presents in unlimited variety exclusively characteristic of music, inexpressible in any other language.
RICHARD WAGNER

The nobility and absolute "selflessness" of Liszt's playing had to be heard to be understood. There was something about his tone that made you weep, it was so apart from earth and so ethereal!
AMY FAY

Gottschalk is one of a very small number who possess all the different elements of a consummate pianist, all the faculties that surround him with an irresistible prestige, and give him a sovereign power ... his success before an audience of musical cultivation is immense.
HECTOR BERLIOZ

The question as to whether the performer must have experienced every emotion he interprets is as old as antiquity. In Plato's Dialogues, Socrates was discussing whether an actor must have felt every emotion he portrayed in order to be a true artist. ... The final argument was: if the true artist had to live through every experience in order to portray it faithfully; then, to act a death scene he would have to die first in order to picture it with adequate facility.
HAROLD BAUER

Positive Piano

You don't have to have died to convincingly play Chopin's funeral march from the B flat minor sonata; but your life experience certainly shapes your interpretation. Consider the experience of the funeral of a loved one, especially a parent, spouse, sibling, close friend, even a pet, or perhaps most tragically, that of your own child. Confronting our human mortality is one of the deepest experiences in life. Our emotion finds expression in our art.

Marcus Aurelius' philosophy tutor recommended he meditate on the death of his mother (before the fact) to emotionally strengthen him for the day that the event would eventually come to pass. Though that example may sound extreme, it can be an interesting exercise to explore emotion in your imagination.

Cultivate a very definite mental attitude as to what you really desire to accomplish. Do you wish to make music? If so, think music, and nothing but music, all the time, down to the smallest detail even in technique.
HAROLD BAUER

If we were to play a piece of music with exactly the same degree of forte or piano throughout, it would sound as ridiculous as if we were to recite a beautiful poem in the same monotonous tone with which we're accustomed to repeat the multiplication table.
CZERNY

No masterpiece will result if the black charcoal sketch the artist outlines upon a canvas shows through the colors of the finished painting. Really artistic piano playing remains an impossibility until the outlines of technique have been erased to make way for true interpretation in the highest sense of the word.
JOSEF HOFMANN

Some painters transform the sun into a yellow spot while others, through art and intelligence, transform a yellow spot into the sun.
PABLO PICASSO

What do I mix my paints with? I mix them with my brains, Sir.
JOHN OPIE

Music has this over painting: it can bring together all variations of color and light.
CLAUDE DEBUSSY

404

The pianist draws from many sources the experience, the feeling, and emotion with which he strives to inspire the tones he evokes from his instrument. The keener his perceptions, the more he labors, suffers, and lives, the more he will be able to express.

HARRIETTE BROWER

The performer's duty is not simply to play mere notes and dynamic marks, but to make an artistic estimate of the composer's intention, and to feel and simulate the natural psychological conditions which affected the composer during the actual process of composition. In this way the composition becomes a living entity, a tangible resurrection of the composer's soul. Without such penetrative genius a pianist is no more than a mere machine, but with it he may develop into an artist of the highest caliber.

ALFRED REISENAUER

Don't ever forget what I'm going to tell you: Beethoven's music must not be studied, it must be reincarnated.

ANTON RUBINSTEIN

My Chopin study in sixths was encored, though I took the tempo too fast. Frau Excellency von X said she had heard it from Henselt, but that "I played it just as well as he did". That's absurd of course, though not bad considered as a compliment. They all said "what a pity Henselt wasn't here!" I said to myself "what a blessing he wasn't!" - though I would give much to see him, as he is the greatest piano virtuoso in the world after Liszt.

AMY FAY

I shall never forget the extraordinary impression Henselt made when he played his F sharp major étude "Si j'etais Oiseau." It was like an Aeolian harp hidden beneath garlands of the sweetest flowers! An intoxicating perfume was crushed from the blossoms under his hand - soft, like falling rose leaves, the alternating sixths, which in one and the same octave pursued, teased, embraced, and enraptured. Such a charming rich fullness of tone in his pianissimo had never before been heard on the piano. After this most delicate whisper in the principal theme, the 'minore' entered energetically, gathering force from one degree to the next, and taking the instrument by storm – only to lose itself in a magic dialogue in sixths. Thirty-two years have passed since that performance, but the enchanting picture still lives fresh in the memory.

WILHELM von LENZ

Positive Piano

Stage actors and singers routinely consider projection of the voice. For the audience to hear, it must be addressed. Few solo instrumentalists consider that their sound and tone must be projected out to the audience and that it's a question of both physical sound and the psychological conversation. Great pianists attended to every conceivable issue and detail, large or small.

Don't play for the people sitting in the front rows who usually have free tickets, but play for those in the gallery that pay ten pfennigs for a ticket. They should not only see but hear.
LISZT

In the final stages of preparation for public performance, my father (Theodor Kullak) used to choose a point on the opposite side of the hall, as distant as possible from the piano, for the purpose of regulating the conception of it as an entirety, and of prescribing the different shades of tone.
FRANZ KULLAK

Anton Rubinstein's playing gripped my whole imagination and had a marked influence on my ambition as a pianist. It wasn't so much his magnificent technique that held one spellbound as the profound, spiritually refined musicianship, which spoke from every note and every bar he played and singled him out as the most original and unequalled pianist in the world.
Once he repeated the whole finale of Chopin's Sonata in B minor, perhaps he hadn't succeeded in the crescendo at the end as he would have wished. One listened entranced, and could have heard the passage over and over again, so unique was the beauty of tone.... I've never heard the virtuoso piece Islamey by Balakirev, as Rubinstein played it, and his interpretation of Schumann's little fantasy The Bird as Prophet was inimitable in poetic refinement: to describe the diminuendo of the pianissimo at the end of the "fluttering away of the little bird" would be hopelessly inadequate. Inimitable, too, was the soul-stirring imagery in the Kreisleriana, the last (G minor) passage of which I have never heard anyone play in the same manner.
RACHMANINOFF

I observed that Anton Rubinstein had played Islamey at his last historical concert in Berlin and that he used comparatively little pedal. Liszt said: "There he was right. I thought it a wonderful performance."
FREDERIC LAMOND

My orphan child, (Rondo for two pianos Opus 73 post.) is capable of producing effect ... but the two pianos were not perfectly in tune with each other, the delicacy of feeling was not always present nor were all those other trifles which tinge everything with their light and shade.
CHOPIN

It was these trifles that gave to Chopin's playing an inexpressible note of inspired improvisation. Those who witnessed it despaired of ever hearing anyone else attain it.
ALFRED CORTOT

Trifles make perfection, and perfection is no trifle.
MICHELANGELO

The day has arrived ...

It's true that on the day of a recital, I practice for hours – all day perhaps – but I don't touch the pieces I am to give for my program. Instead I practice many other things, often Bach. In this way the program seems to me much fresher than if I had delved on it up to the last moment.
LEO ORNSTEIN

Personally I find it a bad plan to practice a piece on the day I play it in public. One or two days before a concert it's alright to practice it, but not later. Then, when you come before the audience your mind is fresh, and the interpretation will consequently be better.
JOSEF HOFMANN

"Do you practice on the day of the concert?" I asked Chopin. "It's a terrible time for me", he replied. "I don't like the publicity, but it's a duty I owe to my position. For two weeks I shut myself up and play Bach. That's my preparation. I don't practice my own compositions".
WILHELM von LENZ

I followed your advice (Clara Schumann's) and practiced last night in the hall itself. It was exceptionally good.
BRAHMS

Leschetizky used to describe Liszt's manner of approaching the piano at concerts. His appearance was electric and his walk toward the piano, seating himself at the keyboard, and the first chord all seemed simultaneous. But when his improvisation was over, he brought about a dramatic silence before the piece began.

ETHEL NEWCOMB

To play with freedom and inspiration, strike out boldly and don't hold back in timidity and bashfulness. We see people who fear to make a faux pas so they hold back stiffly and bore everybody, besides being very uncomfortable themselves. Cast fear to the winds and risk everything…be an absolutely free and open avenue for expressing the emotional and spiritual meaning of the music.

JOSEF HOFMANN

Fantasy is the key, and fantasy means absence of rule. Play from the heart and use your mind for your study, which is way behind you when you come to perform. The music is the emotion itself.

LESCHETIZKY

You're finally up there on stage. One detail often overlooked at this point is the very first note. Confidently plunging into a composition (or anything in life) with a pre-conceptualized tempo and vibrant rhythm sounds obvious, but many players don't begin well. Like most 'problems' it's an issue of awareness, of getting really tuned in to the goal and how to achieve it, rather than hurrying into any old solution because you are eager to achieve 'something'. You should actually begin before the beginning, by visualizing your beginning.

For an Olympic sprinter or crew team, a good clean start is often the difference between winning and losing. The flawless start is very important even when practicing the piano at home because it establishes good habits. It's especially critical when performing in front of a crowd – because that's your big chance.

Get disciplined, get poised, and pay attention to how you work. In concert, it's absolutely necessary to compose yourself prior to launch. Remember those exciting Apollo rocket lift-offs? Hundreds of brilliant men and women were totally focused on the countdown.

With solo musicians, all too often the focus gets misplaced. It's not on the imminent benefit to the audience, but on me, me, me … my ego, my reputation, my nervousness, or whatever. Get over it. Get the Art going in your head and get your whole self in synch with it. Then go for it with all the confidence you've got.

Once I played a Liszt rhapsody pretty badly. After a bit, (Anton) Rubinstein said, "The way you play this piece would be all right for auntie or mama." ... I began again, but had not played more than a few measures when Rubinstein said loudly, "Have you begun?" "Yes, Master, I certainly have." "Oh," said Rubinstein vaguely, "I didn't notice."
JOSEF HOFMANN

Henselt expected one to begin a piece in a very decided manner, and to come in with the greatest exactness in the middle or end of a bar before which there had been a rest or a pause. Everything that he ever said on these points remained indelibly impressed on my mind because he was so severe in his manner of pointing out the delinquency.
BETTINA WALKER

Never begin a piece quicker than you can with certainty go on with it to the very end.
CZERNY

Be beyond what you are doing; it is the only way to attain perfection. It is only by being beyond your piece that you can produce an effect.
CECIL CHAMINADE

The performer who's more concerned about the technical claims of a composition than its musical interpretation can only hope to give an uninteresting, uninspired, and stilted performance that should rightly drive all intelligent hearers from the hall.
OSSIP GABRILOWITSCH

The difference between Liszt's playing and that of others was the difference between creative genius and interpretation. His genius flashed through every pianistic phrase, it illuminated a composition to its innermost recesses.
WILLIAM MASON

Interpreting a Chopin ballade is quite different from a Scarlatti capriccio. There's really little in common between a Beethoven sonata and a Liszt rhapsody. Consequently, one must seek to give each piece a different

character. Each must stand apart by its individual conception; if one fails to convey this to his audience, he is little better than some machine. … Josef Hofmann has the ability of investing each composition with an individual and characteristic charm that has always been very delightful to me.
RACHMANINOFF

In two separate letters of 1894/95, Edward Grieg (Norwegian) listed four pianists he considered "suitable as soloist for my piano concerto": Raoul Pugno (French), Arthur de Greef (Belgian), Teresa Carreño (Venezuelan), and Ferruccio Busoni (Italian).

Including the composer - that's five different nationalities.

The first condition when it comes to choosing a performing artist is that they have an understanding of my music. With respect to the artists listed above, with whom I am personally acquainted, I know that this is the case.
EDWARD GRIEG

Art has no fatherland; all that is beautiful should be prized by us no matter what clime or region has produced it.
CARL MARIA von WEBER

… so much for theories about nationalistic prerequisites in interpretation. At least musically, we're all simply human beings sharing one world. It's our differences as individuals that matter, not where we come from or what we look like. Let's face it - we're all indigenous to this planet; some of us just need to act more like it.

Let observation with extensive view,
Survey mankind from China to Peru.
DR SAMUEL JOHNSON

But seeing how we're 'human', things don't always work out 'perfectly'. We shouldn't go overboard with interpretation and lose our artistic objectivity.

Damn these virtuosos with their Bessermachen ('improvements' on what the composer wrote). In the first part of the concerto Mrs. Carreño decided to play slower in the brilliant passages, thus disrupting the flow; and in the Finale she took the second theme much slower…. and the worst part

of it was that she bragged about doing it. There should be punishment for things like that. I told her what I thought, adding 'at least Chopin is dead so he didn't suffer this!'
EDWARD GRIEG

Regard it as an abomination to meddle with the pieces of good composers, either by alteration, omission, or by the introduction of ornaments. This is the greatest indignity you can inflict on Art.
ROBERT SCHUMANN

When Bach, Beethoven, Chopin, and Brahms put their thoughts down on paper, they left a record in ink which must be born again every time it is brought to the minds of men and women. This rebirth is the very essence of all that is best in interpretative skill. New life enters the composition at the very moment it passes through the soul of the master performer. A great truth in music, more than any other art, is "the letter kills and the spirit vivifies". The interpreter must master the "letter" and seek to give "rebirth" to the spirit. One who can do this will attain the greatest in interpretive ability.
SIGISMUND STOJOWSKI

Tausig's most distinguishing characteristic was that he never played simply for effect, but was always completely absorbed in the piece itself and its artistic interpretation.
WILHELM von LENZ

The most astonishing thing about Tausig was his great humility.
MORIZ ROSENTHAL

The artist incapable of communicating his emotions to the keyboard or who must depend upon artifice to stimulate emotions rarely electrifies his audiences.
LEOPOLD GODOWSKY

Bach can be played in so inhumanly boring a fashion, in such a consciously correct style that it becomes lethal. In my opinion Bach was no cold formalist, but a man of flesh and blood, full of vitality and strength.
MAX REGER

We've all been to a concert expecting to hear something really good when heavyweight composers like Bach, Beethoven or Liszt appear on the program. And then, astonishingly, you suddenly find yourself bored stiff. What's up with that?

Much playing of music (such as Bach) sounds meaningless to the listener because the pianist is merely playing so many notes in a given time without any regard for their musical sequence. Until each phrase is made to sound in every sense moving, a combination of parts can never be truly musical.
LILIAS MACKINNON

Interpretation is a matter of individuality. Take five great pianists... in the matter of detail they are entirely different. Each sees from his own point of view, and who is right or wrong it's impossible to say. The best judge is the cultivated public. Conservatism in performing Beethoven is the curse of the pianist. Beethoven is not dead parchment but a great personality, with passion, intelligence, and imagination. The public loves individuality in the performance of Beethoven. Intelligent persons never object to five great artists playing Hamlet according to their own individuality. Then why should we always play the Shakespeare of music the same? Music is a language in which to express your own feelings. Why not play Beethoven so that he can be understood as Shakespeare is when he is acted?
MARK HAMBOURG

I still feel the power to move the Vienna public, so intelligent and so thoroughly appreciative - a public which I've always considered the best judge of a pianist.
LISZT

When Liszt plays, one no longer thinks of difficulty overcome; the piano vanishes and music appears.
HEINRICH HEINE

These composers' beautiful creations have resonated with humanity for centuries. The problem is not with the music but with the performer's attitude and interpretation, and the audience's relative understanding of music and its history. With the performers, you can't blame it on inadequate preparation; we now take for granted the mechanically note-perfect renderings. But soulless performance will still leave us cold. Critics and audience members in the know who love music may become disappointed.

Sometime in 1917 Debussy went to hear the suite Pour le Piano played by a famous pianist. "How was it" I asked. "Dreadful, he didn't miss a note." "But you ought to be satisfied, you who insist on the infallible precision of every note." "Oh, not like that" he said, then emphatically "not like that."
MARGUERITE LONG

Driven by tireless importunity and publicity, audiences attend concerts and hear dozens of young pianists. One plays like the other with more or less faulty technique, and for all their slamming and banging are unable to draw a decent tone from the instrument. They play with a hypocritical show of emotion signifying nothing. These meddlers have so soured the discriminating public on piano playing that it no longer wishes to hear even the good, sensible, and sensitive artist who, as a gentleman, cannot raise an audience from people on the street.
You meddlers who have condemned this lovely art to the pillory, I say get out! Leave off this wood chopping and look for work in a factory or on the railroad, where you might be able to make yourself useful. ... Let me whisper in your ear ... simple naturalness, tenderness, intimacy of feeling, gratifying refinement, poetry, inspiration, true noble passion.
FRIEDRICH WIECK

Love people, love nature. But if you hate people and hate nature, go be a woodchopper (not an artist).
LESCHETIZKY

Woodman spare that tree! Touch not a single bough.
In youth it sheltered me, and I'll protect it now.
GEORGE P. MORRIS The Oak

Notation and keyboards are simply symbols of music, cages in which the beautiful bird is caught.
ALFRED REISENAUER

An unimaginative interpretation limits itself to forte, piano, crescendo, and diminuendo; however, the art of expression begins at the point where one reads 'between the lines' where the unexpressed is brought to light.
MAX REGER

Positive Piano

Anton Rubinstein never made any generalization of the interpretation of Chopin during my study with him, for the reason that Chopin is different in every single one of his compositions. You cannot speak of him as appearing in them as the same individual, for in each thing that he has given out he is different.
JOSEF HOFMANN

In listening to Rubinstein or Liszt, one forgot all idea of technique, and it must be so with all great artists; to be absorbed by the sheer beauty of the musical message, and expression of musical self.
MAX PAUER

Chopin, listening to an interpretation that was at variance with his own feeling for the work but was emotionally convincing said, "that isn't how I would play it, but perhaps your version is better."
ALFRED CORTOT

Music that has no underlying meaning is false.
CHOPIN

(Contemporary music composers, listen up: this applies to both composition and performance).

Unfortunately music is not exactly like painting and poetry: body and soul alone are not enough to make it comprehensible; it has to be performed, and very well too, to be understood and felt.
LISZT

Superior performance consists of the ability to make people conscious of a work's deep emotional content. The tools are the relative loudness or softness of tones, the touch, the legato and staccato execution, arpeggiation, the retard and acceleration. ... Lack of, or inept use of these results in a poor performance. ... Learn from accomplished musicians.
C.P.E. BACH

The real secret to success in public appearance is thorough preparation. Genuine worth is the great essential, and thorough preparation leads to genuine worth. That technical finish is the underlying essence goes without saying. It's indispensable to a creditable performance, and the consciousness of possessing it creates confidence in the player, without which he cannot

hope to make an impression on the public.
FANNY BLOOMFIELD-ZEISLER

Even though the performer may possess the most highly perfected mechanism and technical mastery that allows him to play the great masterpieces effectively; if he does not possess the emotional insight, his performances will lack a peculiar subtlety and artistic power that will deprive him of becoming a truly great pianist. .... one must develop the artistic and emotional phase of playing the piano largely through his own inborn artistic sense and his cultivated powers of observation of the playing of master pianists. It is the sacred fire communicated from one art generation to the next and modified by the individual emotions of the performer himself.
LEOPOLD GODOWSKY

For too many people, the thought of performing in public remains associated with fear and stress, a daunting experience to be avoided at all costs. 'Stage-fright' is, of course, common with actors, musicians, dancers, public speakers - pretty much anyone who must appear before a group. Think back to your bar mitzvah, that first school play, or the first time you had to give a presentation at work.

It should be just the opposite: an experience that's eagerly anticipated and welcomed for its great potential opportunity for self-expression, self-improvement, and adding value to the lives of others. Live performance offers a unique opportunity to deeply connect and bond with other human beings.

Materia medica contains no remedy for either seasickness or stage fright.
JAMES H. ROGERS

I've read many articles about musician stage fright and it's astonishing that almost all are totally ignorant of the work of F. M. Alexander.

FM noted that when the head and neck retracted down and back (among other posture/movement abnormalities) it simultaneously produced a negative mental state; a lack of confidence and feeling of depression or even anxiety and outright fear. (Fear and stress are reasons why the neck and spine retracted in the first place). By consciously willing a mechanical re-adjustment of his body into a physical configuration expressive of power and confidence (head forward and up, spine lengthened, shoulders widened etc.), and maintaining it dynamically through a series of motions, the fear disappeared. In fact, fear was not possible – as long as the naturally confident 'physical or mechanical' configuration was maintained.

Piano playing in itself does not promote nervousness, evidenced by the well-known performers. Most of the virtuosos I have known are exceptionally strong persons, with hearty appetites and good nerves; they would never be able to stand the strain otherwise. Nervousness comes to those who have not yet learned how to control themselves mentally and physically.
ALBERTO JONÁS

Reminder: it took FM months of rigorous, scientific self-analysis to attain this; however, FM claimed that anyone with sufficient discipline could do it as well. Once, just for fun, he trained a group of novices to act in a Shakespeare play, and not one of them experienced stage fright during the public performance. So don't discount the theory just because you can't do it yourself in a few minutes. Seek out a qualified instructor and get the live experience, then get disciplined and work on it.

Adolph Henselt presents a particularly vivid example of 'nerves'. One of history's greatest piano virtuosos was apparently terrified of performing publicly.

Dreyschock called on Henselt one morning, and heard the loveliest tones of the pianoforte imaginable. Fascinated, he sat down at the top of the landing and listened for a long time. Henselt was repeating the same composition, his playing specially characterized by a warm emotional touch and a delicious legato, causing the tones to melt one into the other, and this, without any confusion or lack of clearness.
Finally, for lack of time, Dreyschock was obliged to announce himself, although he could have listened for hours. He entered the room, and after the usual friendly greeting asked what the piece was. Henselt replied it was a new composition in progress. Expressing his admiration of it, Dreyschock begged him to play it again. After prolonged urging, Henselt sat down to the piano and resumed, but, alas! his performance was stiff, inaccurate, and even clumsy, and all of the exquisite poetry and unconsciousness of his style completely disappeared. Dreyschock said that it was quite impossible

to describe the difference; simply the result of diffidence and nervousness, which, as it appeared, were entirely out of the player's power to control. Pianists frequently experience this state of things. The only remedy is freedom from self-consciousness, which can best be achieved by earnest and persistent mental concentration.
WILIAM MASON

Once again, the issue must be addressed from a wholistic perspective encompassing your total being: mental and physical health, confidence, attitude, character, knowledge, awareness, and spirituality.

It also will help to consider these experiences of the great pianists.

Stagefright: the one lucid moment in the life of the virtuoso.
MORIZ ROSENTHAL

Nervousness is a matter of poise and self-consciousness. Be sincere and genuine, and you will realize that the world is not going to stand or fall because of the manner in which you play a certain piece … Nervousness is often nothing more than self-consciousness unduly magnified over the real significance of the player's artistic message.
Mastery is wonderful insurance against nervousness. Not to say that anyone who has mastered a piece cannot be nervous, but mastery brings an indescribable confidence. Where a pianist knows that he can play a work accurately, safely, and also beautifully, he should not fret. If he does fret, he should look to the piece quite as much as to his own nerves.
ALBERTO JONÁS

What might we have been forced to endure, had not a merciful Providence invented "stage-fright"? True, the genuine artist finds it a stumbling-block which can be done away with only by dint of study and by much playing in public, whereby he gains a feeling of confidence. Let him do like the hero in Schiller's 'Fight with the Dragon' who accustomed his horse to a painted dragon before introducing him to the real one, and take the edge off his dread of the public by much playing to others. Knock at every door and request a kindly hearing, play before fellow-artists. If you can meet their criticism, it's proof against the dragon himself.
MALWINE BRÉE

The habit of listening to one's own playing is an antidote for nervousness.

Positive Piano

If you are hearing the sounds, telling the story, painting the picture in tones, you have no time or room for fear or stage fright, for you are wholly concentrated on the matter in hand.
HARRIETTE BROWER

The experience of frequent playing in public is essential if one would get rid of stage fright or undue nervousness and would gain that repose and self-confidence without which success is impossible.
FANNY BLOOMFIELD-ZEISLER

To be cautious and afraid of failing will only chill one musically, and thus cause one to fail. Fear of failure does not constitute a care for Music at all; on the contrary, it's a form of selfishness, and as such must therefore cause failure. To succeed in art as in anything else we must be 'unselfish' - so far as that is possible to us humans - we must throw our self overboard, and really caring for Art, wish to do well because Art is so beautiful, so worthy. Thus we shall indeed take trouble, we shall be as keenly alert as lies within our power, not for the sake of our own aggrandizement, but for the sake of making the Beautiful attain to its highest possible perfection; and our 'carefulness' will thus, so far from chilling us, stimulate us musically to ever increasingly effective efforts.
TOBIAS MATTHAY

Before a performance a student said: "Professor, it's so difficult, I'm afraid." I said - what are you afraid of? ... you're not showing off for the audience. Stop thinking like that, play for the spirit of the composer, the wonderful poetry, heart, and inspiration. Play it together with your own, then there's nothing to be afraid of. That night she played really wonderfully. I was moved to tears when I went up to the stage to shake her hand.
SUZUKI

Search deeper into the psychological aspects of nervousness and you'll often find a wrong and frankly ignoble attitude. The performer is afraid because he consciously or unconsciously craves the applause and flattery of the listener. This should not be so and indeed is never the case with the true artist. He is, of course, glad if the audience understands him, and of success and all the good it may bring him. But should the audience fail to respond ... then he should quietly investigate if he accomplished what he set out to do, or whether the selections he played were too deep, abstract, or new for the

418

average audience to understand.

Approach your task of playing for others without fear or trepidation, but rather with that spirit of sincere investigation.
ALBERTO JONÁS

We're all human; if you slip up, try to maintain your poise.

The pianist must learn to control himself in the emergency of memory loss - one of the most agonizing experiences one can undergo in public. But if he can keep his presence of mind, he can often extricate himself from his predicament with the aid of his musical instinct, and sometimes so cleverly, that his lapse will pass unnoticed by any save the most knowing amongst the audience. This needs great command of nerve on the part of the performer, but as in every public career emergencies do arise occasionally, it is an essential part of the professional artist's equipment that he should know how to meet them.
MARK HAMBOURG

Liszt was rolling up the piano in arpeggios in a very grand manner indeed, when he struck a semi-tone short of the high note upon which he had intended to end. I caught my breath and wondered whether he was going to leave us like that, in mid-air, as it were, and the harmony unresolved; or whether he would be reduced to the humiliation of correcting himself like ordinary mortals, and taking the correct chord. A half-smile came over his face, as much to say "Don't fancy that this little thing disturbs me" and he instantly went meandering down the keyboard in harmony with the false note he had struck, and then rolled deliberately up in a second grand sweep, this time striking true. I never saw a more delicious piece of cleverness. It was so quick-witted and so characteristic of Liszt. Instead of giving you a chance to say "He has made a mistake," he forced you to say "He has shown how to get out of a mistake."
AMY FAY

Educated audiences will give you credit for all kinds of things that other audiences will not, and how everyone loves beautiful tones and stirring rhythms! But you must not break down before an audience under any circumstances. They will always be nervous over you afterwards.
LESCHETIZKY

Positive Piano

The next best thing to having played a passage well is to go on and betray no immediate consciousness of having done it badly.
STERNDALE BENNETT

Actually performing the music you've lavished so much love and attention on is the culmination of a long, hard-won process of preparation. Performing is not practicing, or even playing; it is a unique activity in itself that must also be 'practiced'. Learn to enjoy it!

No pressure, no diamonds.
THOMAS CARLYLE

Realize the necessity of getting accustomed to playing before people. Always an ordeal at first, it must be studied like anything else ... but is invaluable. Before a concert, the wise one will gather his friends and even his enemies together, and try to please them. Make them listen to you whether they want to or not. You may think you have a piece learned but you never know until you have tried it in public. If you had enough imagination this would be unnecessary. You might fancy yourself before an audience at home, come out and bow to it, and then see how nervous you would be. Even then, you never know what kind of audience you might have, and how it will affect you.
LESCHETIZKY

You'll never cease studying and learning new things from real masters of the instrument, but the time has come for you to play. What you want is more audiences. The impressions you receive when you're playing alone in your room or in the studio before your teacher, may be quite different from those you experience when you play before audiences. The reason is very simple. When you go before an audience you become a different individual. Your nervous system is under a great strain and you do things that you never imagined you could do. All pianists know this, and many, myself included, have come to dread the experience of going before an audience. Some never recover from this experience. There is only one remedy for those who are willing to take it, and that is, more and more audiences.
RAPHAEL JOSEFFY

You're so worried over what you must do next - throw all that away. It only hinders your free fantasy. Get down to the real meaning of the music and put warmth into every tone. The tones are the story and the musical form is the

420

plot. What more do you need if the music is good?
LESCHETIZKY

In the hands of a master, the piano will reveal varied and manifold beauties, showing that it has a soul, a life, and a warmth which cannot fail to strike a sympathetic chord in the performer, and through him, the listener.
ERNST PAUER

Each pianist reveals a certain mental type through his performance; one is a poet, another is a philosopher, the third an orator or even a stump orator, and so on. Some express what they feel; others are more reticent, and not given to showing emotion; they rather repress it and seem to stand aloof. Some are ready to reveal everything; they are the ones who are popular with the public and never fail to please. Rather than 'descend to the public,' they merely work out their natural temperament; and are one with the public.
LEOPOLD GODOWSKY

Frequent playing before others is an absolute necessity; nothing can take its place. The only way to learn to play in public is – to play. Pupils who play their pieces correctly for me (privately) will make shocking mistakes and go all to pieces through sheer nervousness, if playing for the first time in a musicale. They soon get used to it however. Even three or four performances during the season will be of great benefit.
ERNST HUTCHESON

The longer you know a piece before you play it in public, the more you have thought it out and fixed it in your mind, the better will be your performance. You must get it settled in your mind; it must become part of you. But, after all, the playing of a piece in public is what makes it fireproof. That is the pre-eminent source of its development and finish; therefore, the more often you play a piece in public, the better will be your development of it.
JOSEF HOFMANN

When you have played it several times in concert, the necessary verve will also come to you.
LISZT

The absolute best way to grow is doing your thing in public, sharing it with a real live audience.

Positive Piano

To be sure, in the matter of absolute technique one man may not be as great a virtuoso as another, but that does not prevent his giving pleasure through his performances if his mind shines in them.
MARK HAMBOURG

There are many circumstances that influence the artist's interpretation which he must take into account when performing in concert – his prevailing mood at the moment, the piano, the mental quality of the audience, the acoustics of the space, and so on. I play very differently in the concert hall than I do at home in my study. If I am to fill Carnegie Hall, my scale of dynamics is quite different from the one I use in a smaller space. There must likewise be corresponding differences in touch and tone color.
JOSEF HOFMANN

The words 'opportunity to excel' have become something of a trite sarcasm in the business world, usually translating as something like: 'you just got saddled with a particularly onerous task everyone else is avoiding like the plague'. Of course, interpreting those three words literally, in a positive sense, is a much more powerful proposition.

That Theodore Thomas had entire confidence in himself was shown in the outset of his career. One evening, as he came home tired out from work, and after dinner had settled himself in a comfortable place for a good rest, a message came to him from the Academy of Music, about two blocks away from his house on East Twelfth Street. An opera was in progress. The orchestra was in its place, and the audience seated, when word was received that Anschütz, the conductor, was ill. The management had not provided against that contingency, and was in a position of much embarrassment. Would Thomas come to the rescue? He had never conducted opera, and the work for the evening's performance was an opera with which he was unfamiliar. Here was a life's opportunity, and Thomas was equal to the occasion. He thought for a moment, then said, "I will." He rose quickly, got himself into his dress-suit, hurried to the Academy of Music, and conducted the opera as if it were a common experience. He was not a man to say, "Give me time until next week." He was always ready for every opportunity.
WILLIAM MASON

At a concert given by any famous player, the audience has been well-schooled in anticipation. The artist always appears under a halo his reputation has made for

him. This very reputation makes his conquest far easier than that of the novice who has to prove his ability before he can win the sympathy of the audience.
JAMES FRANCIS COOKE

When the artist appears in public, he leaves part of his security at home; it follows, that he can never have enough of it. The prospective concert-player must, therefore, make it a point from the very start to play a piece faultlessly from beginning to end the first time. It is of no avail, to play it right only on repetition. Should you break down in practice, or make a mistake, stop playing, and begin again after a considerable pause, making it, as it were, another "first time." Also observe this method while learning études and pieces, or their several phrases and divisions, and finally, when practicing compositions already memorized.
MALWINE BRÉE

I've played so much and am always so sure of what I am going to play that nervousness is out of the question. Of course, I'm anxious about the way the audience will receive my playing, I want to please them so much. If I cannot bring pleasure to them I do not deserve to be before the public.
PEPITO ARRIOLA

You say one of two things as you stand before an audience: either, 'I love you all so much that I will enjoy myself and be free,' or, 'I despise you all so much that I don't care at all what I do.' There is no middle ground unless you're satisfied with not distinguishing yourself.
Playing in public is a larger field than the salon; more strength is needed, more breadth of effect required. It's as though ten persons came to a dinner where only six were expected. In the cookbook one finds nothing to help one out of the dilemma, but a good cook must know how to get around the difficulty.
LESCHETIZKY

The greatest gratification to me is the satisfaction of my audience.
EDOUARD ZELDEN

You must surprise rather than disappoint. Never disappoint an audience ...
Remember, before an audience the chance for the second time never comes.
LESCHETIZKY

Surely one of the most enviable possessions of the successful pianist is

magnetism, which is nothing more than earnestness and sincerity, coupled with insight, sympathy, patience and tact. These essentials cannot be bought or taught, they are dyed with the 'red ripe of the heart'.
HYPNOTIC THERAPEUTICS

We all possess what is known as magnetism. Some, like Liszt, have it in an unusual degree. ... Among virtuosos, Paderewski is peculiarly forceful in the personal spell he casts over his audience. His command of the audience is at once imperial...his art and his striking personality (apart from his appearance) soon made him the greatest concert attraction in the music world. Anyone who has conversed with him for more than a few moments realizes what the meaning of the word magnetism is. His entire bearing, his lofty attitude of mind, his personal dignity all contribute to the inexplicable attraction that Mesmer first described as animal attraction.
JAMES FRANCIS COOKE

THE PROGRAM (the 'script')

The object of a concert is not merely to show off the skill of the performer, but to instruct, elevate, and entertain the audience. The program must look well (interesting), must sound well in rendition, and should be chosen from a variety of compositions of merit, with contrasting character and tone. Avoid anti-climaxes. Study the program selection of established artists.
FANNY BLOOMFIELD-ZEISLER

Offer a certain number of familiar works the public wants to hear, a variety of keys and modes, and a variety of forms. ... Never play down to an audience. By this I mean, never play second-rate music to a certain class of public on the plea that they are not sufficiently educated to appreciate the best; that's the greatest possible fallacy. I've played all over the world to every class of people, and I've always found that they respect and are interested in one's art even when they don't quite understand it all; they appreciate and desire the best a man can do. Always stimulate your public up to the highest kind of music and never sink to clap-trap in order to entice their passing fancy. Otherwise, though they may enjoy themselves for the moment, they will associate you with the level of what they've heard.
MARK HAMBOURG

Why seek difficulty when there is so much that is quite as beautiful and yet

not difficult? Why try to make a bouquet of oak trees when the ground is covered with exquisite flowers?
WILHELM BACHAUS

Only two compositions were regularly rejected (at Liszt's Weimar master classes), Chopin's B flat minor Scherzo, which he called the "Governess Scherzo" because 'every governess plays it', and his own second Hungarian Rhapsody. Both works were heard too much he said. Everything else of Chopin found permanent favor with Liszt, particularly the Preludes.
ARTHUR FRIEDHEIM

Programs are many times entirely too long and too stereotyped. Let us hear more of the new things! What great pianist is there who plays the works of living composers? They are all afraid of the critics. Even Paderewski doesn't have the courage to play more than a few of his own compositions.
LESCHETIZKY

Today, this is the piece that every ass of an up-to-date pianist plays! (Bach-Tausig Toccata and Fugue in D minor transcribed for piano). This season I have heard this piece at least a dozen times. Pianists are like sheep. Whenever one jumps in all the others jump in after him.
LISZT

In the case of reasonably short instrumental works of serious content, given for the first time in public, I seriously plead for the adoption of the custom of an immediate repetition; such works should be performed at least twice in immediate succession. This would give worthy new music a far better chance of being accepted forthwith. The old masters unconsciously felt this, when, in their sonata movements, they insisted on repeating all the subject-matter, before proceeding to its amplification.
TOBIAS MATTHAY

Constant exertion at maximum capacity is simply not sustainable, and also is contrary to basic dramatic theory. A good suspense story mixes up the level of tension, and gradually builds to a climax. If you give it all away at the beginning, how can you keep the reader's attention afterwards? Also, operating at maximum capacity can give the impression that maybe things could get out of control or break down at any moment. A consummate master holds back power until the score demands it, or a particularly vivid artistic interpretive impulse arises.

Practice wise economy in the use of force and display of feeling.
JOSEF HOFMANN

Take for example the Chopin *Étude* in C minor Opus 10.12, the so-called *"Revolutionary"*. This dramatic concert piece starts with a bang, marked forte or strong, the dominant seventh chord is struck with the right hand and the left cascades downwards in modified arpeggios. Too many players over-do this beginning, and continue trying to exert maximum power. Where do you go from there if you begin with all you've got?

Just three minutes later the piece ends at fortissimo, that's "ff" to the single 'f' at the start. A genuine artist intuits the inherent drama in the piece and begins strong, gradually building drama through the course of the short but taxing composition and magnificently ending twice as strong (at least) as it began.

The first movement of Beethoven's *Hammerklavier* Sonata Opus 106 begins fortissimo 'ff' and ends with a super 'fortissimo-issimo', 'fff' – and the movement runs about ten minutes, more than three times the length of the Chopin étude. Think of the planning, the insight, and the reserve required to perform that titanic Beethoven movement.

If I admired the spiritual passion, the fire and the life in Liszt's rendering of the first movement (Carl Maria von Weber Sonata in A-flat), in the second part I was even more astounded by his confident repose and certainty, by the way in which he held himself back so as to reserve his strength for the last attack. So young and so wise!
WILHEM von LENZ

Though Liszt usually only played a few bars of the pieces brought to him by aspiring pianists, he was a dazzling radiant sun before which all the younger talents paled in significance. He seemed to possess an almost terrible mastery over every conceivable aspect of technique – especially in wide, leaping intervals, where playing securely and at ease is almost as impossible as being in two different places at the same time. I've heard him ... and a cold shiver went right through me, not so much at what he actually bestowed on us, as at what he suggested as having still in reserve.
BETTINA WALKER

The player should never urge his force to the limit; he must always keep something in reserve. If tone production is at its utmost capacity it will sound hard, there must always be some reserve power back of it. (Anton) Rubinstein was capable of immense power, for he had a very heavy arm and hand. His fifth finger was as thick as my thumb – think of it! Then his fingers were square on the ends, with cushions on them. It was a wonderful hand, and very large besides. Yet with all his power, one felt he had more in reserve.
JOSEF HOFMANN

There is a need for more reserve and sensitivity in piano playing, so that the pianistic values may be better observed.
RUDOLPH GANZ

Never be carried away by temperament, for that dissipates strength, and where it occurs there will always be a blemish, like a stain which can never be washed out of a garment.
FERRUCCIO BUSONI

Many pianists think that they ought to display all their powers during a performance. It is not so. Their rendering should be only in accordance with the character of the music; impassioned or simple as called for.
LOUIS PLAIDY

After you're finished with your piece ....

It's a mistake to wish for anything from the public that's not given spontaneously. Accept with good grace whatever comes to you. The public is on the whole a very good judge and one can learn a great deal by putting oneself before it.
LESCHETIZKY

I had to come back to take a bow – Brandt having taught me how, I did it this time more like a human being.
CHOPIN

Don't neglect the all-important issue of graciously, and gratefully accepting praise; and that goes for anytime in life, not just when you're on stage. Look into the person's eyes and give a sincere 'thank you'; it can work wonders. Don't spoil a great performance with a clumsy bow, or a gloomy look on your face. Practice bowing in front of a mirror, try smiling a bit more.

Don't be discouraged if you fail with one audience, or with a dozen audiences. The time will come when you will adjust yourself to them. This does not mean that you should lower your art ideals. It merely means that by more and more exposure to public opinion you gradually get better control of yourself, lose your self-consciousness and say what you really have in your mind and in your heart.
RAPHAEL JOSEFFY

And now - another Intermezzo in this way too long chapter, as my editor likes to say; but this one's more like a *Scherzo*, a musical form originating in the Italian word for 'joke'.

There's a strange phenomenon found in all walks in life, and I'm dismayed that it's by far most prevalent in the piano world ... just make sure this joke's not on you.

INTERMEZZO

MANNERISMS

In *Ends and Means*, Aldous Huxley comments on a passage from the medieval philosophy text *The Cloud of Unknowing*. The anonymous author observed that attainment of higher states of consciousness can be hampered by uncontrolled fidgeting, nervous laughing, odd gestures and grimaces. In fact, these are symptoms of underlying 'physical maladjustment and strain', which Huxley realized could be ameliorated through F. M. Alexander's methodology.

When listening, some men cock their heads on one side quaintly and with chin raised gape open-mouthed as if hearing that way instead of with their ears. Some can neither sit, stand, nor lie still unless they wag their feet or do something else with their hands. Some row with their arms while speaking, as if swimming over a great water, and some smile or laugh at every

word they speak. I say not that all these unseemly practices be great sins in themselves, but if these un-ordained practices govern, insomuch as they cannot be left off at will, I say they be curious tokens of pride and vanity, and of unstableness of heart and un-restfulness of mind, and especially lacking of the work of attaining higher consciousness.
THE CLOUD OF UNKNOWING Anonymous, 14th Century

That sounds a lot like a number of pianists I've seen in concert. Truly accomplished pianists have always performed naturally and effortlessly, because conservation of energy and freedom from excess vanity is what enables and empowers superior playing. Mannerisms are a symptom of underlying unease and tension. If rooted in vanity, it means that the mind is distracted by the ego and not absorbed with the music as it should be. Both are clear indications that the mastery isn't quite there yet; and you can't fake it.

A hallmark of great artists is that they enjoy helping others, and they would like to help you with this problem. Here's some expert coaching and advice on the subject.

Oh, your head! Why do you nod your head in company to your music? (And when the pupil repeated the passage without nodding). You see, it goes nicely without the head!
ANTON RUBINSTEIN

Don't continuously imitate the metronome with your head. At the present time that is terribly popular with ladies and gentlemen and I can't endure it.
LISZT

It is better and more sensible not to beat time with the head, the body, or the feet. Assume an easy manner at the keyboard and avoid staring fixedly at any object or looking too vague; look at the audience as if you were occupied by nothing else. This advice is for those who play from memory.
FRANÇOIS COUPERIN

Anyone who sees and hears the playing of Maria Ann Stein and can keep from laughing must, like her father, be made of stone. Instead of sitting in the middle of the clavier, she sits right of the treble as it gives her more opportunity to flop about and make grimaces. She rolls her eyes and smirks.... When playing a passage she must raise her arm as high as possible, stressing passage notes with the arm in a clumsy and heavy manner. But the best joke of all is that in passages where it should flow like oil, she just leaves out notes, raises her arm, and begins anew; a method by which she is all the more likely to strike a wrong note, and produces a curious effect ... She has talent but will never make significant progress.

I don't make grimaces and yet play with an expression that Herr Stein admits no one else can match. They are amazed that I can simply play in strict time! Count Wolfegg and several other passionate admirers of Beecke publicly admitted at a concert the other day that I had wiped the floor with him. The Count kept running about the hall saying "I've never heard anything like this in my life".

MOZART

Some players display the peculiarity of making extraordinary faces during performances, from a desire to express the maximum of emotion, or sometimes provoked by a perceived physical exertion required for some technical feat. This is a very absurd fault, and too often becomes a habit terribly hard to get rid of, because it's done quite unconsciously as a rule.

MARK HAMBOURG

We can play with great power without excessive exertion, and without using any unnecessary and ridiculous movements of the hands, arms, shoulders, or head. Unhappily, many even very good pianists are guilty of these and similar contortions and grimaces; against which I must warn you.

CZERNY

Some common faults and bad habits to be strictly guarded against: shrugging the shoulders, swaying the body back and

forth, or from side to side, protruding the elbows, contortions of the face, such as frowning, raising the eyebrows, and grimacing, crossing the legs, shaking the head, etc. All such habits should be studiously avoided until an easy, graceful and unconstrained position at the piano becomes habitual.
H. R. PALMER

Assume a free and unembarrassed position … Avoid all unnecessary movements of the body, such as shaking the head, shrugging the shoulders, crossing the legs, or clinging to the seat with the feet.
LOUIS PLAIDY

Overcome the obnoxious habit of grimacing while playing.
PADEREWSKI

Deppe disapproved of pianists who "saw the air with their hands, and who move their elbows after a fashion which calls up visions of a cobbler at work on his bench." Nothing caused him greater nervous irritation than to see and hear a pianist in whose performance one sought in vain for a sweet and mellow tone, or beautiful, natural motion. The fusion of these two things was to him a law of primary importance in the art of music.
ELISABETH CALAND

'Posing' is not to be approved. The poseur's usual method is to lean back with an air of being inspired, and to play with the head waving about and the eyes cast upwards in rapt gaze. Then there's the careless pose of disdainful ease; or the pianist buries his head in the keys, raising it in pauses to give the audience a questioning smile. Such procedure makes a more or less comic effect, and will detract from the impression of the best performance. Real feeling in the pianist's art is not expressed by emotional faces or poses; it manifests naturally through one's playing.
MALWINE BRÉE

Pianists are not the only guilty ones; a few conductors have been caught 'posing' …

Nowadays people go to see a conductor direct the orchestra just as they go to hear a tenor, and they arrogate to themselves the right to judge the conductors as they do the tenors. But what a fine sport it is! The qualities of an orchestra conductor which the public appreciates are his elegance, his gestures, his precision, and the expressiveness of his mimicry, all of which are more often directed at the audience than at the orchestra.

If such an important detail as the author's meaning is obscured and slighted, if a work is disfigured by absurd movements and by an expression which is entirely different from what the author wanted, the public may be dazzled and an execrable conductor, provided his poses are good, may fascinate his audience and be praised to the skies. Formerly the conductor never saluted his audience. The understanding was that the work and not the conductor was applauded. The Italians and Germans changed all that. Lamoureux was the first to introduce this exotic custom in France. The public was a little surprised at first, but they soon got used to it. In Italy the conductor comes on the stage with the artists to salute the audience. There is nothing more laughable than to see him, as the last note of an opera dies away, jump down from his stand and run like mad to reach the stage in time.

CAMILLE SAINT-SAËNS

And the name of that town is Vanity; and at that town there is a fair kept, called Vanity Fair.

JOHN BUNYAN Pilgrim's Progress

Back to the pianists ...

Strive for naturalness. Avoid ostentatious movements in your playing. Let your playing be as quiet as possible. Ease in playing is always admirable.

EMIL SAUER

Some endeavor to manifest their feelings by widely jerking out their elbows; or they mark the commencement of every bar by making a low bow with their head and chest, as if they were desirous of showing reverence to their own playing. Some,

after every short note, suddenly take up their hands far from the keys, as if they had touched a red hot iron. Many, while playing, put on a fierce and crabbed countenance; others assume a perpetual simper, etc. In the zeal of practice, we may accustom ourselves to all these faults without knowing it; and when to our mortification we are made to observe them, it is often too late wholly to leave them off.
CZERNY

One cannot, and need not, always be oohing and ahhing in dealing with music.
BRAHMS

You must not make grimaces and bite your lips while playing.
ANTON RUBINSTEIN

All tendency to facial contortions, grimacing, raising the eyebrows, frowning, shaking the head, or any other tricks should be carefully avoided. The same may be said of the habit of swaying the body sideways, backwards and forwards, or shrugging the shoulders. A natural, unaffected, and graceful appearance will greatly aid the effect produced by an intelligent, expressive performance.
ERNST PAUER

There's some video footage on YouTube of Vladimir Horowitz, at age 85, being interviewed by Mike Wallace of CBS 60 Minutes. On the subject of pretentious facial expressions Horowitz says *"I don't do those things"* and then playfully mimics pompous pianists who do. He smiles gently and adds, *"that you will not see it...I cannot do it"*. Horowitz's playing was always marked by total absorption in making music - without the silly faces.

Liszt opposes all affected and contorted expressions. His goal, above all, is musical truth ... he detests affectation, wants only to hear beautiful sounds... When he plays, nothing stands between his heart and the listener's, it's just pure passion, unpretentious. And if some passages are amazingly brilliant,

it's only a means to an end. In his expansive adagios he always communicates grace and ease; the crescendos and decrescendos serve the music, not like the affectations of others that in reality express nothing, yet often inspire fools to cry 'bravo!'
Mme. AUGUSTE BOISSIER

I warn pianists and other performers against any showy and unsuitable display. Why should you wish to attract attention, and to create an effect by foppishness and all sorts of grimaces, or by curious and marvelous exhibitions of virtuoso-ship? You have only to play musically and beautifully, and to deport yourselves with modesty and propriety. Direct your whole attention to the business in hand, that is, to your performance. Don't devote yourself exclusively to pieces calculated to show the skill of the performer. Why desire always to show off your power in octave passages, your trills, your facility in skips, your unprecedented stretches, or other fantastic feats? You only produce weariness, satiety, and disgust; making yourselves ridiculous.
FRIEDRICH WIECK

Many people make the mistake of thinking that if they are only sufficiently worked up themselves they will work up other people; the reverse is nearer the truth. The feeling can only be expressed through the medium of sound.
LILIAS MACKINNON

One thing that always struck me was Clara Schumann's look of absolute absorption in her work. I don't think I ever saw any artist more completely wrapped up in her art. She never thought of herself, but only of the composition she happened to be playing, her whole soul steeped in the work she was rendering. In her playing there was never the smallest suspicion of self-display ... she was the classical pianist par excellence.
OSCAR BERINGER

Now, for all of you audience members out there; you can't just blame the performers, this applies to you as well.

I had just started playing Chopin's Scherzo in B minor, when my eye was caught by a lady at the farther end of the piano, who was evidently badly afflicted with St. Vitus' dance; at any rate, the poor creature was making the most fearful grimaces. Good heavens! I thought, I mustn't look at her, or my memory will go. But do you think I could get away from that face? Not for a moment! It seemed to exert a hypnotic fascination upon me, so that my eyes returned again and again to it, in spite of all I could do to resist the fatal influence. How I got through without a breakdown I don't know, but get through I did, though in a cold perspiration and with shattered nerves.

OSCAR BERINGER

Heinrich Neuhaus believed that pianists incapable of expressing themselves without 'hysterics or cramps' will inevitably have imperfect mechanical technique, with 'perverted and distorted' rhythm and tone. He maintained that the Latin maxim *Men's Sana in Corpore Sano* (a sound mind in a sound body) is distinctly applicable because the physical and mental effort behind grimaces and mannerisms detracts from focus on the music and wastes valuable energy. And incidentally, you run the risk of accidentally being perceived as some kind of vain, pretentious jerk, if you know what I mean.

I never wonder at seeing men wickedly vain, but I often wonder to see them not ashamed.

JONATHAN SWIFT

I sincerely hope that this particular shoe doesn't fit. But who knows? ... maybe there are two or three of those vain and pretentious jerks out there. Would you few individuals please at least take a hint from the masters whose music you're trying to play? The world will be more harmonious if you exercise a bit of humility and respect. Think in terms of making a positive contribution, and not making a display of your insecurity.

Beethoven's bearing while playing was masterfully quiet, noble, and beautiful, without the slightest grimace.
CZERNY

Beethoven made a point of plying without effort.
COUNTESS GIULIETTA GUICCIARDI

Thalberg's total freedom from ceremony and affectation totally charmed me.
CARLO MINASI

In Henselt's dignified, simple carriage, in his self-poised manner combined with the sincerest modesty, he never is or will be satisfied with his achievement. – a fact that the keen observer easily recognizes.
WILHELM von LENZ

Your art reflects your mental and physical health, and your character. You'll never attain your full potential as an artist unless you do so as a human being.

A man wrapped up in himself makes a small package.
ANONYMOUS

If the mannerisms are really an unconscious nervous issue, then get conscious about it and get some professional help; or look at yourself in the mirror, and work on eliminating them.

The only remedy for 'making faces' is to have a mirror hung in front of the culprit whenever he's practicing.
MARK HAMBOURG

As for facial grimaces, one can correct them by placing a mirror on the instrument.
FRANÇOIS COUPERIN

If it's not accidental, note that according to psychologists, vanity and arrogance are rooted in insecurity and immaturity, two traits pretty incompatible with big success.

Through pride we are ever deceiving ourselves. But deep down below the surface of the average conscience a still, small voice says to us, something is out of tune.
CARL JUNG

Vanity working on a weak head produces every sort of mischief.
JANE AUSTEN

Renounce all superficiality, convention, vanity, and delusion.
GUSTAV MAHLER

Pretentiousness may achieve a temporary measure of material success with the naïve and unenlightened, but unless you're even more naturally gifted and industrious than the greats, your success will be short-lived.

Those whom the gods would destroy they first make proud.
EURIPIDES

In ancient times the definition of pride was more subtle; it meant failure to recognize your place in the pantheon of gods. Don't step out of bounds when the referees are the likes of Beethoven and Liszt.

Now, nobody's saying that you should play like a marble statue. But motion in performance should be natural, relaxed, and unaffected. If you're playing sincerely, chances are you're enjoying it. A smile every now and then would be natural, and will endear you to your audience.

Don't suppose, however, that you're to sit at the piano as stiff and cold as a wooden doll. Some graceful movements are necessary while playing; it's the excess that must be avoided.
CZERNY

Ugly grimaces are, of course, inappropriate and harmful, but

subtle suitable expressions help the listener to understand our meaning.
C.P.E. BACH

Beware of your stage deportment. Do nothing at the keyboard that will emphasize any personal eccentricity. Remain sincere to your own nature, but try to make a pleasing impression.
FANNY BLOOMFIELD-ZEISLER

You must accept the truth from whatever source it comes.
MOSES MAIMONIDES

In this case, the masters have spoken. Let's take it to heart.

If you dwell too much on yourself, you miss out on all the potential growth that becomes possible when collaborating with others, as epitomized by the unending process of ...

Chapter 12

......

LEARNING

Education is not something which the teacher does, but a natural process which develops spontaneously in the human being.

—*MARIA MONTESSORI*

Maria Montessori (1870-1952) wasn't just another innovative 'teacher'. She ranks up there with Roger Bannister for breaking a four-minute mile barrier of sorts by becoming the first Italian woman in modern history to earn a Doctor of Medicine degree from the University of Rome. The 'good ole boy' network was so intent on stopping her that Pope Leo XIII supposedly had to intervene. Thanks Pope, for punching a hole in that stained-glass ceiling. She ended up being one of the top students in her class.

Incidentally, Maria's favorite hobby, when she made time for it? ... that's right; playing the piano.

If you're still thinking that the Montessori approach is maybe the difference between a B and a B+ for a six-year old, consider these graduates of the program: the tech world is represented by Jeff Bezos of Amazon and Larry Page and Sergei Brin of Google; creative types are exemplified by the much more impressive novelist Gabriel Garcia Marquez, and many others as well. The Montessori Method may even make you better looking - George Clooney also attended.

Montessori devoted her life to helping children learn. The difference in wording may seem subtle but the paradigm is poles apart. With education, just as with motivation, you can't do it for or to somebody. 'Teaching' is a process of facilitating learning.

We can't teach anyone anything, in the sense of our being able directly to lodge any knowledge of ours in another mind. All we can really do is to stimulate another mind to wish to learn, and suggestively place things before them. That other mind must make the effort to apprehend. Good teaching consists not in trying to make the pupil do things, but in encouraging him to think ... don't try to turn the pupil into an automaton, prompt him to grow into a living, intelligent being.
TOBIAS MATTHAY

Anton Rubinstein did not so much instruct me, merely he let me learn from him ... If a student, by his own study and mental force finally comprehended the master's wizardry, he gained reliance in his own strength, knowing he would always find that point again even though he should lose his way once or twice, as everyone with an honest aspiration is liable to do.
JOSEF HOFMANN

I try not to burden the child's memory with my own wisdom but rather seek to stimulate him spiritually, to let him develop in his own way, and avoid reducing him to a wooden machine.
FRIEDRICH WIECK

When you begin to see teaching as learning you realize that it can't be forced on anybody. Artificial external rewards don't really get results either.

Knowledge acquired under compulsion obtains no hold on the mind.
PLATO

Perhaps putting a stop to all publicity and prizes would set things and people straight and remind them of a forgotten path ... art is entirely its own reward.
CLAUDE DEBUSSY

Prizes and punishments incentivize forced effort, and we certainly cannot speak of the natural development of the child in connection with them. Education is a natural process carried out by the child and is not acquired by listening to words but by experiences in a dynamic environment, one arranged and directed by an adult who is prepared for the mission.
MARIA MONTESSORI

Grading and ranking produce artificial scarcity. Only a few students get high grades, only a few employees get high ratings. This is wrong; there's no scarcity of good students or employees.
W. EDWARDS DEMING

I could never see the use of grading pieces. Pupils vary so greatly in comprehension and mentality that the same piece might be difficult for one and very simple for another, both having studied for about the same length of time.
ERNEST HUTCHESON

Learning about everything that exists in this big universe is the most interesting and fascinating part of life. Sometimes we just need to get out of the way and let it happen.

The main duty in all elementary work is to make piano study interesting, and the teacher must choose the course most likely to arouse interest in the particular pupil.
JOSEF LHÉVINNE

The trouble with music appreciation in general is that people are taught to have too much respect for music, they should be taught to love it instead.
STRAVINSKY

In praise of the Almighty's will, and for my neighbor's greater skill.
J.S. BACH epigraph to Little Organ Book, 1717

Don't forget that it's a two-way street. You'll learn from your students; if you're humble and open-minded you can often learn more from them than they learn from you.

One learns from every new pupil, the untalented as well as the talented.

441

Sometimes the pupil who seems slow and unpromising in the beginning becomes an interesting student under good training. Often the talented ones find simple things difficult, so every day I learn something new.
LESCHETIZKY

If you set out to help somebody learn something, it's a really good idea to know something about your subject.

There was only one goal with Leschetiszky: good piano playing; and he did not believe that one could be a good piano teacher who could not play himself.
ETHEL NEWCOMB

No teacher is worthy of the name unless he, himself, is also an artist - and a finely perceptive one, too! ... you must possess (or at least have possessed) a technique sufficiently ample to enable due expression to the artistic feeling which you have cultivated in yourself. Besides, you may also be able to stir artistic fire and enthusiasm in others by actual example.
TOBIAS MATTHAY

Learn that you may teach.
TERESA CARREÑO

Maybe you're one of those teachers or professors (learning facilitators?) complaining that 'their' students (they aren't 'yours') are bored, unmotivated, don't work hard, or don't even show up. Maybe you're a librarian concerned that your library is empty. Well maybe, just maybe ... you're part of the problem; perhaps you're not setting much of an example. Great leaders inspire. If you're enthused about your subject, naturally that will be communicated to the student.

Can we not find men talking about art in a broader way, who can be older and wiser friends to the students, rather than stuffy old professors of aesthetics? They could point out, in a friendly fashion, not so much the way in which these young people ought to proceed, but rather the way in which the Great Masters proceeded - the masters of a past to which those who are preparing the future owe a responsibility. And lastly, these men could perhaps give the younger generation that love of Art of which nobody speaks any more, but of which in a confused and somewhat interested way they are aware.
CLAUDE DEBUSSY

442

From the zest with which Sterndale Bennett went into every special beauty of the composition being studied, he seemed to be entering a new and enchanting region, instead of (as was the case) walking over well-trodden, old, familiar ground. And his sense of enjoyment communicated itself to the pupil, and gave life and charm to all one learned of him.
BETTINA WALKER

The teacher cannot hope to stimulate his pupils to do real, honest work, unless he himself shows that the work matters to him, that it's a matter of life-and-death to him whether his pupil succeeds or not.
TOBIAS MATTHAY

A teacher tired of music and unable to conceal his fatigue imparts to the pupil both music and the fatigue. A yawn in Art is a pestilence to be placed in strict quarantine.
NICOLAS MEDTNER

That example that you set for others is going to be really powerful ... or not.

You heard Liszt do something and you wanted to do it, too. Of course, you couldn't, but it developed you a good deal to try. ... He presents an idea to you and it takes fast hold of your mind and sticks there.
AMY FAY

Such a great artist as Liszt undoubtedly did have an overwhelming influence musically on all who came into contact with him. He was not a real 'teacher' at all in the strict sense in which the term is used, although he was truly a great seer. Indeed, I doubt very much whether he ever gave a single real 'lesson' in his life. What Liszt often did, with his overwhelming enthusiasm and wonderful personality, was to stimulate an incipient, latent, and perhaps lukewarm enthusiasm into a blazing flame.
TOBIAS MATTHAY

If he is to provide proper guidance, an adult must always be calm and act slowly so that the child who is watching him can clearly see his actions in all their particulars.
MARIA MONTESSORI

The teacher must control himself if he would teach control; he must master himself if he would help those who come to him to attain self-mastery. ... An impatient, excitable and irascible teacher will never foster control in his pupils and is likely to unnerve all but the most stolid.
HARRIETTE BROWER

A dad hurling F-bombs at the referee or two soccer moms in a cat-fight is not going to set a good example.

Also, it's helpful to be able to verbally articulate the how and why.

Example is most helpful when given in conjunction with explanation. ... you point out to the pupil where he's wrong and what the right effects should be, the cause, the why and wherefore of all faults, and hence, the means of their immediate correction. Thus you stimulate him to use his own judgment.

... When a slow movement is wrongly played too slowly, instead of saying "play quicker"; ask the pupil to think the music in longer phrases. Again, if a quick movement is played too fast, instead of "slow down", draw attention to the sub-divisions of the beats, and the result is immediately attained, and with certainty.

The teacher must also "really listen" all the while. Not listening, but merely hearing a performance, is just as useless in teaching as it is when practicing, and we must always analyze all we hear, including the pupil's mental attitude in making the fault, and the reasons why, so that the fault-making may be corrected at its very root.

Insist that all corrections be made strictly subservient to the musical effects required at the moment; else we shall only provoke self-consciousness in place of the desired correction. For instance, a muscular fault must never be corrected as such, but its musical bearing pointed out, with reasons and causes always made clear.
TOBIAS MATTHAY

The 'teacher' is bound to encounter some challenges.

Many a man of genius perishes because he had to gain his bread by teaching instead of devoting himself to study.
JOSEPH HAYDN

It must have had something to do with one of Haydn's unruly pupils.

444

Though I had some instruction from Haydn, I never learned anything from him.
BEETHOVEN

The 'learning-facilitator' serves as friend, mentor, and guru ... you give your all.

Sterndale Bennett more than once said that it was not a mere lesson he gave, but an hour of his life, in the fullest sense of the word. Although he gave from ten to twelve one-hour lessons a day when the season was at its height, I've never caught him looking either jaded or absent, and he has given me more than once the last hour of his long day's work ... it was impossible to gather from his manner which was the most or the least clever pupil, so thoroughly did he interest himself in each individual.
BETTINA WALKER

The teacher's greatest mission is to raise the consciousness of the pupil until he can appreciate his own powers for developing an idea.
MAX PAUER

We should always encourage independent thinking - tough to do when your 'teaching' grant is coming from the government or a corporation. (Notice they don't call them 'learning' grants).

Teachers err when they fail to encourage their pupils to form their own opinions. I abominate machine teaching. Instead of leading the pupil to seek results for himself, they lay down laws and see that these laws are obeyed like gendarmes. ... It seems brutal and inartistic. The best teacher is the one who incites his pupil to penetrate deeper and learn new beauties by himself.
VLADIMIR de PACHMANN

Henselt stimulated his pupils to strive and aim for virtuosity, yet the special tendency of his teaching, one that should be the true end of all earnest study, was to awaken and intensify in his students a perception and appreciation of an excellence lying beyond their reach – something more important to its possessors than any degree of personal attainment.
BETTINA WALKER

Ask the (advanced) student: "What is your feeling about this passage? In the light of what you know, how do you think it ought to be interpreted?" In

almost every case this will effect more positive results than if the teacher lays down ironclad rules and insists upon their observance.
RUDOLPH GANZ

The student is cautioned not to mistake rules for laws.
CONSTANTIN von STERNBERG

Experience is the best teacher. He who wishes to advance in his art must apply what he is told by others.
FRESCOBALDI fiori musical 1635

Be aware of two signal faults in teaching methods: The student is told 1. to play the piano, and 2. to play like me. The teacher says in the first instance: 'Here is the music, now play it and at the next lesson I will criticise you.' Criticism means pointing out to the student this and that thing which does not please the teacher. The poor pupil is therefore blamed for errors which he makes out of his own ignorance. It never seems to occur to the teacher that it is his duty to make the pupil understand how to play before he permits him to play, to understand certain principles which must be mastered before his brain can work correctly and profitably, without the waste of the time of both the teacher and the student.

The second error comes from encouraging the student to imitate. Imitation may be 'the sincerest flattery,' but mere imitation without original creative thinking is liable to be destructive to the pupil's initiative and to the development of his own artistic sense, without which his playing becomes insufferable. The pupil cannot act without being told how, and may struggle through months of disappointment and never achieve anything.

Imitation is the lowest phase of education. It is the monkey stage, and requires the least brain action. Rather let the teacher provide the pupil with a definite reason for the principal kinds of action at the keyboard. Only in this way can the pupil acquire a technique that will include the mind, the muscles and the nerves. Piano playing is an art and not merely a few cheap tricks learned by empirical practice or by imitation. When one has mastered it, when one knows the science back of this art, one comes into possession of something of real tangible value, not an inconsequential nothing composed of a few clap-trap devices.
E. ROBERT SCHMITZ

We have it from Ruskin that all fatal artistic faults arise from three things:

either from the pretence to feel what we do not; the indolence in exercise necessary to obtain the power of expressing the Truth; or the presumptuous insistence upon, or indulgence in, our own powers and delights, with no care or wish that they should be useful to other people, so only they should be admired by them. These three fatal faults must be avoided, or conquered, by the person who would interpret music.
AUBERTINE WOODWARD MOORE

Teachers of real importance are those with the ability, gift, experience, and inclination to create a brand-new method for each pupil.
MAX PAUER

In the wider sense of the word the greatest artists are self-taught. In my own case I was fortunate in having years of training under renowned teachers. This is a great asset, but thousands of pupils have a similar asset advantage. What counts is what the individual artist is able to put into his playing as a result of his own cerebration, the conscious and unconscious action of his brain, developed through study. What the teacher does for the artist is just so much. What the artist adds creatively to what he has absorbed from his individual teacher is what makes him an individual. There are thousands of conservatory graduates every year who 'can play like streaks'. Most of them are very much alike; usually depending upon what they have been taught rather than what they have thought out for themselves.
To get a start as a virtuoso in these days, when concert platforms are literally flooded with artists, real and potential, one must reveal to the public some new and fresh aspect of art which can only come through your own brain, plus the best experience the world commands. To get the real kind of a start as a virtuoso you must do something genuinely artistic which will stand out from the crowd. Your natural talents combined with your introspective study of yourself, and the artistic works you elect to interpret, are therefore of vast importance.
MISCHA LEVITZKI

Referring to his different treatment of different pupils, I've been amused by hearing Henselt say 'I don't comb all my lambs with the same comb.'
BETTINA WALKER

Selection of teaching material should be technically appropriate, but should also excite and motivate the student.

447

Positive Piano

I protest against the folly of giving deadly-dull and unmusical pieces and studies to children. How can the child learn to love music by being soaked in non-music? No wonder so many look upon their practice-hour with loathing!
TOBIAS MATTHAY

You're never too young or too old to learn.

The proper age to start children is from six to seven years, not that this excludes persons of older age, but naturally, the sooner one begins, the better. At first, it's recommended that the child practice only in the presence of the instructor. Children are too easily distracted to discipline themselves to hold their hands in the prescribed position. ...One should begin to teach children notation only after they have a number of pieces in their fingers. Their fingers may get out of position and fumble if they have to look at notes. Besides, memory is developed in learning things by heart.
FRANÇOIS COUPERIN L'Art de Toucher le Clavecin

Sounds a bit like the Suzuki method, doesn't it? Basic principles are timeless, but often the strength of a particular school or method lies in the charismatic leadership of the founder.

Lessons in rhythmic gymnastics help children in their other lessons, for they develop the powers of observation, of analyzing, of understanding and of memory, thus making them more orderly and precise.
ÉMILE JAQUES-DALCROZE

Man is the product of his environment. Every child can be educated; it's only a matter of the methods used. Anyone can train himself; it is only a question of using the right kind of effect.
SUZUKI

If you're a student, remember (at least) two things: (one of them you already heard several times in this book)

No-one can do your work for you.
ALBERTO JONÁS

There are no good teachers, only good pupils.
LESCHETIZKY

448

If all good musicians required a great man as a teacher in order to be good musicians; there wouldn't be too many of them, I'm afraid.
ARTUR SCHNABEL

There is a certain type of person, you know, who always remains a student – always studying, but learning nothing.
PADEREWSKI

You repay a teacher badly if you remain nothing but a pupil.
FRIEDRICH NIETZSCHE

That said, some 'teachers' are better that others.

The selection of a good teacher is a serious issue but once you've found a good one and are progressing properly, don't think of changing just because someone suggests that you might do better elsewhere. A teacher is not a suit of clothes to be changed every day.
YOLANDA MERO

Have as good a teacher as you can possibly secure and afford. There is nothing that helps so much as to be really well taught from the very beginning. So many artists have had to go through irksome and irritating labor in later life, and lost much valuable time in having to undo the effects of bad tuition in student days.
MARK HAMBOURG

Great care should be taken in selecting a teacher, for with the wrong teacher not only is time wasted, but talent, energy, and sometimes that jewel in the crown of success – ambition.
FRANZ XAVER SCHWARENKA

It's so important to cultivate the 'teacher–student' relationship (or collaboration between two individuals seeking to learn together) because many things in music cannot even be verbalized, much less 'taught'.

We will suppose the teacher thoroughly competent, wise, and experienced; that her personality is winning and lovable, and that she's enthusiastic and devoted to her work. She will look upon the new pupil as a fresh opportunity to give the best that is in her for another's good. The pupil's good qualities will be noted as well as his defects. The aim will be not alone to develop some special gift, but to make him an all-around intelligent musician. If instruction on true principles is faithfully given in the first place, there will be nothing to undo later. The right way is really much simpler than the wrong, for the pupil. For the teacher, it involves complete grasp of the subject, much experience, and infinite patience and love.

HARRIETTE BROWER

Everybody knows Godowsky was a 'wizard of technique' (as dubbed unanimously by the world press). Numerous young pianists from all over the world flocked to him hoping to get his recipe for attaining virtuosity. Alas for them, Godowsky hardly ever said a word about technique in the sense they understood; all his comments during a lesson were aimed exclusively at music, at correcting musical defects in a performance, at achieving maximum logic, accurate hearing, clarity, plasticity, through scrupulous adherence and broad interpretation of the written score.

VLADIMIR de PACHMANN

Liszt believed in the group system of teaching implicitly; the teacher doesn't have to play the same piece over and over for different pupils and endlessly repeat suggestions for fingerings, phrasing, pedaling, and so on. If an auditor knows the work being played he has the same advantages as the performer, and if he does not know it, he becomes better prepared to study it later. Liszt knew that even the best teacher has his good and bad days, and the group system enables everyone to profit from the good ones. Its best aspect is the opportunity for pupils to play for critical listeners and so rid themselves of nervousness and gain confidence.

ARTHUR FRIEDHEIM

The so-called "Master Class" method of instruction has its origin in Liszt's now famous sessions in Weimar, initially in the 1850s at the Altenburg (villa), and later in the 1880s at the Hofgärtnerei (gardener's cottage). Notice that Liszt significantly downsized later in life. The material thing really isn't so much a plus as a minus; if we'd all downsize a bit we'd be richer for it.

These days just about anybody can preside over a 'master' class, significantly devaluing that title. It's been criticized by some as being merely a pretentious vehicle for the instructor's ego. A first step in the right direction might be to take Schumann's advice and imagine a real master sitting in on your session. If one was truly present, all involved would really perk up and get focused.

The study of music in our high schools, till now altogether neglected, is a requisite of higher general education. ... it would be an epoch-making gain and the source of the most beautiful enjoyment in art if we had reform along these lines in the schools.
RICHARD STRAUSS

And, of course, learning never ends. Why, besides vanity, do people keep asking pianists 'where did you study?' I forget now who said it (possibly Teresa Carreño) but the 'correct' answer to the wrong question is: "I'm still studying".

One can always learn. I learn every day of my life.
LESCHETIZKY

There's a 'critical' aspect of learning that's a type of art form in itself. Schumann, Berlioz, Debussy, and the likes of James Huneker, Henry Theophilus Finck and George Bernard Shaw have added much to the history of music through criticism.

INTERMEZZO

CRITICISM

If you're going to perform professionally, then be prepared for criticism. The critic's job is primarily to inform and entertain the public, and just like film or book reviews, ultimately add value and help the public get their money's worth. In principle, it's a good thing for the performer too because the prospect of it will keep you honest, and motivate you to polish and perfect your program well in advance of a public performance.

It is good practice to criticize if we do it with intelligence and without prejudice.
LESCHETIZKY

It becomes a problem if the above words go unheeded. The degree to which a critic should give actual advice to the performer is moot. In the 19th century most critics were themselves accomplished musicians who often knew every note of a piece because they played it too; or they brought along the score. Today, some critics are not as well prepared to offer advice to a performer on performing.

There's always been favoritism, cliques and claques, and downright *ad hominem* misanthropy; all, of course, highly unprofessional; but such is life, or rather - politics. But be thankful if a professional critic gives you their time at all. The best thing to do is to learn as much as you can from a review, and remain gracious whether it's favorable or not, fair or unfair.

One reason why performers may get caught off guard by critics is that they've spent too much time thinking about themselves, and not enough time thinking about the audience and those critics. Get tough on yourself before you go out on stage. Are your standards high enough? Have you met them? How does your playing compare with that of your peers? Do you offer something unique and exciting?

Honestly and sincerely criticize your performance with a view towards future improvement, and there will be no sterner and fairer judge than you.
ALBERTO JONÁS

As much as I love music, and like to support other musicians, I too have often been disappointed, and sometimes terribly bored - and who enjoys being bored? Critics are people too and they also can become bored by insipid and uninspired playing, even if it's mechanically note-perfect. They're dying to hear something special, something really outstanding – like a truly authentic and extraordinarily polished artistic interpretation from a unique personality. Performers: please give it to them.

There sits a critic who expects to see you obliged to play slower when you come to that difficult passage. Take your time with the phrases that come before so that you will be rested – then let go – and disappoint him!
LESCHETIZKY

After being a musical critic for nearly three decades, I confess that I'm deathly tired of concerts and operas, and recitals of all descriptions. I long for authentic expression, but seldom get it unless Seidl conducts, or a great pianist like Paderewski plays, or a Geraldine Farrar sings and acts. ... I hate these conservatory pianists with their finicky 'touch, methods, pearling scales, and technical abominations'. I detest those singers of the 'Italian school' whose one idea is to sing notes so loud, high, and shrill, that they'll be sure to arouse 'thunders of applause'.
HENRY THEOPHILUS FINCK

With every performance, take the attitude that you'll give critics that something special to write home about.

One bad review is not going to make or break you. But if you've been repeatedly beat up by the critics, there's probably a reason for it. Get over that personal rejection part of it and get working on improving yourself. Analyze why, be objective, take a good hard look at your art and then make it better. You're in this for the long haul; you must persevere, and always be increasing your personal standards of excellence. Everybody has had at least one poor review. If yours is unjust, shrug it off and work harder.

To the gentlemen critics I recommend a bit more foresight and shrewdness, particularly with respect to the products of younger authors, as many who might otherwise make progress, may be frightened off. I'm far from thinking myself perfect, and above criticism; yet initially the critical clamor was so debasing that I could scarcely discuss the matter when I compared myself with others, but had to remain quiet and think: they do not understand. I was the more able to remain quiet when I

recalled how men were praised who signify little among those who know, and who have almost disappeared despite their good points. Well, Pax Vobiscum, peace to them and me.
BEETHOVEN

Criticism is all too often no more than a brilliant set of variations on the theme of 'you didn't do it as I would, that's your mistake'; or even, 'you have talent, I have none, and that certainly cannot go on'.
CLAUDE DEBUSSY

We are aware that the official aim of its representatives (criticism) has always been to weaken the new generation whose tendencies seem to them dangerous.
MAURICE RAVEL

How long this critical comedy is to last I cannot tell. In any case I have made up my mind to pay no attention to these yells, but to proceed in my path undisturbed.
LISZT

Critics get a little carried away with what someone should have done, rather than what he did.
DUKE ELLINGTON

One critic suggested I apply for a teacher's position at the Institute for African Drum Languages. I didn't change my profession.
ARTUR SCHNABEL

Schnabel may have misinterpreted that remark as a jab, when it could have been intended as a helpful suggestion. I can think of a few pianists who might benefit from matriculating in such an Institute. You can't beat indigenous peoples for real rhythm and authentic musical interpretation. They have much to teach us in this respect.

Don't be flattered by unmerited praise either.

It is a singular sensation to see and hear one's self praised, and be conscious of one's own imperfections as I am. I always regard such occasions as admonitions to get nearer the unattainable goal set for us by art and nature, hard as it may be.
BEETHOVEN

I pay no attention whatever to anybody's praise or blame. I simply follow my own feelings.
MOZART

From my adoptive father, the Emperor Antoninus Pius I learned to have no vain-glory in those things which men call honors.
MARCUS AURELIUS

Don't be led astray by the applause which often greets the so-called virtuosos. More valuable to you is the approval of artists rather than that of the masses.
ROBERT SCHUMANN

Form the habit of determining things for yourself. Well-meaning advisers, if they have their way, may confuse you. It's one thing to give pleasure and receive appreciation for it, and the manner of expression and wording of a remark will reveal it as such. But caught in the morbid mania of hobnobbing with celebrities, more pianists of lesser character have been misled by blatant flattery than anything else. They become convinced that their efforts are comparable to those of the greatest artist, and their desire for improvement diminishes in direct ratio to the rate in which their opinion of themselves increases. The pianist should continually examine his own work with the same acuteness he would show when teaching another.
JOSEF HOFMANN

He only profits from praise who values criticism.
HEINRICH HEINE

An undeserved bad review is an injustice; but neither is there satisfaction in receiving a good one that's undeserved. ... It's impossible for any critic to ruin one's career with a scratch of

his pen. An artist may do himself justice at one time and not at another; in such event, and even if the adverse criticism is deserved, it cannot destroy his prospects. If I play badly one night I strive to make up for it the next. Real, true criticism doesn't knock a man down in one evening. When asked my own opinion, I give it with reserve; for I know how difficult it is to play the piano, and I know what's required to do it.
EDOUARD ZELDEN

Artists sometimes say that they never pay any attention to reviews, in fact never bother to read them - I find that hard to believe. I doubt if there are many performers who do not scan the leading newspapers as early as possible on the day following an appearance. If the reviews are friendly the day is that much brighter. If they are unfriendly, there is always the consolation that, after all, this particular review is merely one individual's opinion. Now and then one comes across a review of sufficient literary distinction to make one want to keep it, if for that reason alone.
ARTHUR FRIEDHEIM

Naturally the pupil must expect to work with a teacher who will (constructively) criticize his efforts with relentless severity if he expects his advanced work to be profitable. An aspiring virtuoso can progress more rapidly by playing a great deal for different people who are frank enough to speak their minds, and intelligent and experienced enough to give criticism of value.
MARK HAMBOURG

The critics don't always get it right ...

Chopin presents nothing but the most ridiculous and extravagant themes in his music. ... All his compositions have to offer the listener is a surface distorted by unintelligible overstatements and atrocious discords. And when he is not showing himself off in this guise, he is no more than a purveyor of the dullest waltzes.
E.W. DAVIDSON, LONDON TIMES 1848

Debussy has a too pronounced tendency toward an exploration of the strange. We strongly hope that he will guard against this strange impressionism, which is one of the most dangerous enemies of truth in works of art.
ACADÉMIE CRITIQUE (1887)

We hold that Wagner is not a musician at all. It's clear to us that with this excommunication of pure melody and utter contempt of time and rhythmic definition so notorious in his compositions (we were about to say his music) he wants to upset both opera and drama. He can build up nothing himself. He can destroy, but not re-construct; kill, but not give life. Lohengrin, that 'best piece', is rank poison; the overture to Der Fliegende Hollander is the most hideous and detestable of the whole. This preacher of the 'future' was born to feed spiders with flies, not to make happy the heart of man with beautiful melody and harmony.
THE MUSICAL WORLD 1850

Finally ... a few parting thoughts on critics.

If you have a good 'critique' you probably have a good certificate from the conservatory too.
LISZT

Liszt desired a game of whist, but Friedheim objected that he didn't know how to play, having little understanding of the game. "Well then," Liszt said, "you must be a critic".
ALEXANDER SILOTI

No one has ever erected a monument to a critic.
JEAN SIBELIUS

CODA

*Love for, and enjoyment in music deepens
rather than lessens as we advance in life... and
every beautiful thing we loved in our early
years returns in a host of memories.*

—STERNDALE BENNETT

Musical drama often intensifies when we arrive at the coda; we sense that we're in the home stretch as the music builds to a climax in anticipation of the end of the piece. But the coda is not the end, and although close, we're not quite finished with this book yet.

Thank you for reading *Positive Piano*, I sincerely hope you enjoyed it. In writing the book I've come to more fully appreciate the expression *"per aspera ad astra"*, especially the *per aspera* part; but it's been worth it. They say you should write about what you know; I see now that it's better to write about what you wish to learn. Researching hundreds of 19th century books by and about the greatest musical artists has been quite an education.

He that merely makes a book from books may be useful, but can scarcely be called great.
SAMUEL JOHNSON

I wanted *Positive Piano* simply to be useful; not only to performing artists, but to everyone engaged in the life's work of becoming who they're meant to be.

The most original authors are not so because they advance what is new, but simply because they say it as if it had never been said before.
GOETHE

I tried to give this valuable wisdom a unique context and create a constructive synthesis that would add value. Hopefully you're now a bit more motivated to renew your efforts on a grander scale, and work smarter and more enthusiastically to attain your enhanced goals in life. If you're a pianist, you've also picked up some valuable tips from the masters. And I'm also hoping you got a few laughs from my quirky humor, no offense intended.

He who joins the useful with the agreeable succeeds by delighting and at the same time instructing the reader.
HORACE

As a performing artist and someone who chose to study religion and philosophy in college I've given all this history more than a little thought. I love music and the memory of these great musical artists. I wrote this book to help pianists with their goals and also to promote the magnificent legacy of piano music to persons perhaps not as familiar with it.

True glory consists in doing what deserves to be written, in writing what deserves to be read, and in so living as to make the world happier and better for our living in it.
PLINY THE ELDER

Like all of you, I'm working on that last part about harmonious living.

Well, we're still in the Coda, not quite at the end. Another thing that's not quite finished yet, dear reader, is your life's work. For us human beings, as long as we're breathing and our heart is pumping, as long as we're alive, we'll never be 'done'.

A pupil once said to Anton Rubinstein regarding Beethoven's sonata Opus

53: "I don't need to practice it—I know it thoroughly; it's only a waste of time to practice it more." The saddest expression came over Rubinstein's face ... "Don't you?" he said slowly. "Well, you are eighteen and I am sixty. I have been half a century practicing that sonata, and I need still to practice it. I congratulate you." From that time on he took no further interest in that pupil.
ALEXANDER McARTHUR

There is no end to art; progress is all one can look forward to. The greatest living virtuoso is only great because he is on the way to some coveted goal. The moment he stops, or the moment he commences to retrograde, his greatness ceases. ... The joy is in going ahead, every day, every hour, every minute. If today you find yourself where you were last year, question why. Perhaps you do not deserve to go ahead. Perhaps you have merely been sitting passively by wondering why you do not progress and at the same time failing to do your level best at the work at hand. No matter what you may read, no one has ever succeeded without practice, careful practice, regular practice, intelligent practice, inspired practice, hard practice.
EMIL SAUER

Like learning a piano piece, human development and mutual interaction is never 'finished'. Our self-development trajectory must be inexorably forward and upwards. A classic metaphor remains appropriate: Mount Parnassus perpetually beckons, compelling us to climb not just to the basecamp and intermediate sites but to push for the summit where Orpheus, Apollo and the Muses await, symbolizing the promise of wisdom, joy, and fulfillment through self-actualization of the artist and human being within.

The greatest pianists and composers knew that the journey is un-ending, all-inclusive, and wholistic. Their simple secret is that they became great all-around human beings. An integral part of that process was to confront the great themes and variations of religious experience.

Whatever your own personal thoughts about God, all the greatest pianists and composers of our subject 19th century possessed a deep faith in a divinity and an underlying universal moral order. They believed that It's on our side, constantly advocating for each and every one of us; and they placed the highest value on becoming attuned to it.

This faith profoundly inspired, motivated, empowered, and

galvanized them to fully-actualize their tremendous potential.

The aim and final end of all music should be none other than the glory of God and the refreshment of the soul.
J.S. BACH

God must come first! From His hands we receive our temporal happiness; and at the same time we must think of our eternal salvation. Young people do not like to hear about these things, I know, for I was once young myself. But, thank God, in spite of all my youthful foolish pranks, I always pulled myself together. I avoid all dangers to my soul and ever kept God and my honor and the consequences - the very dangerous consequences - before my eyes.
LEOPOLD MOZART

I've always had God before my eyes, ... I know myself, and with my sense of religion I shall never do anything which I wouldn't do before the whole world; but I'm alarmed at the very thought of being in the society of people whose mode of thinking is so entirely different from mine (and from that of all good people). But of course they must do as they please. I have no heart to travel with them, nor could I enjoy one pleasant hour, nor know what to talk about; for, in short, I have no great confidence in them.
WOLFGANG A. MOZART

Guided by our faith, we hope for, and await salvation; yet as long as we are here on earth, we must perform our daily task.
LISZT

If order and beauty are reflected in the universe, then there is a God above... and without Him there is nothing ... There is no loftier mission than to approach the Divinity, and to disseminate the divine rays among mankind.
BEETHOVEN

Beethoven copied the above lines into his notebook ... from the Hindu *Upanishads*. A devout Catholic, he recognized that great spiritual truths are eternal and transcend all human categorization.

Of all the great pianists, the greatest was the most mystical. I know, that's a word that gets tossed around a lot these days but I'm using it in the religious studies sense of union with the divine; of separate identities merging into one.

Liszt entered into the minor orders of the Catholic Church and was an intimate of the Pope; or rather, the Pope was an intimate of Liszt. Of the hundred or even thousands of references to religion in his writings, I find one very short and cryptic one most fascinating: Liszt once remarked that he was gripped by an especially powerful religious experience ... in a Berlin synagogue.

I've treated many hundreds of patients. Among those in the second half of life - that is to say, over 35 - there has not been one whose problem in the last resort was not that of finding a religious outlook on life.
CARL JUNG

Rarely mentioned these days in the context of 'success', religious faith served to inspire every musical artist in this book to attain the height of their creative powers and also offered solace to sustain them in hard times.

Faith is much better than belief. Belief is when someone else does the thinking.
BUCKMINSTER FULLER

Whatever faith your parents brought you up in, whatever you as an adult choose to believe in; it's a major step forward in psychological self-actualization to humbly acknowledge that our needs as individuals aren't necessarily the most important thing in life. Now more than ever, we need to coexist in harmony, as a community of human beings on this beautiful planet.

Earlier we saw one definition of 'mastery'. This included education in terms of degrees granted, awards and prizes, reputation or celebrity, a capacity for mechanically identical repetition - all way off base for many reasons, but mainly because 'success' is viewed as a strictly individual accomplishment.

The distinguished violinist Leopold Auer, born in 1845, was inexplicably quoted in one of those studies, actually refuting a key premise of that tired idea that 10,000 hours alone will make you a master. Here's what Mr. Auer had to say about the definition of mastery.

Violin mastery represents the sum total of accomplishment on the part of those who live in the history of the Art. All those who may have died long since,

yet the memory of whose work and whose creations still lives, are the true masters of the violin, and its mastery is the record of their accomplishment.
LEOPOLD AUER

The greatest musical artists of the past knew full well that we are all in this life together; we succeed together ... or not at all.

However narrow may be our sphere of action, we should all bear our part in the progressive evolution of civilization. I'm proud to have contributed within the modest limits of my powers to the extension of knowledge of music throughout our country.
L.M. GOTTSCHALK

If we were all determined to play the first violin we should never have an ensemble. Therefore, respect every musician in his proper place.
ROBERT SCHUMANN

Success in the deepest sense is really about adding your unique individual contribution to the great legacy of human civilization. And don't forget those flowers and tomato plants ...

To leave the world a bit better, whether by a healthy child, a garden patch or a redeemed social condition ... this is to have succeeded.
ANON

Today, right now, we artists need to get involved in the big issues facing the world. We must not only perfect our own talents but somehow put them to good use in the service of society. If we strive for moral choices and just being our true selves, doing the absolute best we can - then the good life and the great Art it engenders will flourish once again. If we pool our resources and work together - we can do it.

And we desperately need real leaders. We need another Beethoven, or a Liszt or a Paderewski; we need dozens of them.

All musicians are potential band leaders.
THELONIUS MONK

A great artist must be capable of making significant independent decisions about what's right or wrong or how something should go;

and he or she must be able to set the tempo, and set an example...
and that's a hallmark of a great leader.

In this very moment, we've once again arrived at a new place, one
step further along in the unfolding life journey, confronted with more
choices, new decision points – as we are virtually every moment in
life, whether conscious of it or not.

What path shall we take?

Two roads diverged in a wood...
I took the one less traveled by, and that has made all the difference.
ROBERT FROST

There is no road, you make it as you walk
While walking, you create the road
ANTONIO MACHADO

Multiple pathways always stretch out before us. Admittedly,
most are paved and flat and covered with many faded footprints all
pointing the same way. Robert Frost hinted that the grassy, less worn
trails may hold more promise, but Antonio Machado really nailed it.
Create your very own road.

The best is always yet to come.

The strongest and sweetest songs yet remain to be sung.
WALT WHITMAN

And when you've done your best and have really lived up to your
potential, you'll have a lot to give - as Beethoven pointed out to the
boy Liszt:

"It will be your destiny to bring joy and delight to many people and that
is the greatest happiness one can achieve."

Our purpose in learning is to give pleasure, not only to ourselves, but also to
our beloved parents and worthy friends.
CZERNY

At the risk of you thinking me an absolute quote fanatic, I would
like to leave you with a few final thoughts ...

There is no denying the principle of creative power that governs life... Love, work, and knowledge are the wellsprings of our lives, they should also govern it.
WILHELM REICH

The barriers are not erected which can say to aspiring talents and industry, 'Thus far and no farther.'
BEETHOVEN

To be yourself in a world that is constantly trying to make you something else is the greatest accomplishment.
RALPH WALDO EMERSON

Our life always expresses the result of our dominant thoughts.
SØREN KIRKEGAARD

Create like a god, command like a king, work like a slave.
CONSTANTIN BRANCUSI

We are called to be the architects of the future, not its victims. If humanity does not opt for integrity, we are completely through. It's absolutely touch and go. Each one of us could make the difference.
BUCKMINSTER FULLER

Deus impossibilia ni iubet - God does not command the impossible.

Lord, grant me what you have made me want
Praise and thanks for this desire you've inspired.
St. ANSELM of CANTEBURY

May you successfully follow the noble career of an artist with industry, perseverance, resignation, modesty, and an unshaken faith in the Ideal.
LISZT

It seemed impossible that I should leave the world before I produced everything I felt within me.
BEETHOVEN

It's never too late to be what you might have been.
GEORGE ELIOT

Positive Piano

Create memories.
LISZT

Forward, forward. More energy!
LESCHETIZKY

Do not hurry, but do not wait.
SUZUKI

Most of those old books I read ended with 'Finis'.
I prefer to end *Positive Piano* with ...

Novum Initum
New Beginning

Godspeed and *Pax Vobiscum*

ACKNOWLEDGMENTS

Many thanks to those who provided moral support and/or graciously consented to review and comment on portions of the draft - Bridget, Carole, Chandi, Cheryl, Christine, Dick and Margaret, Jackie, Karen, Joanie, Linda, Laurie, Lori, Monica, Mike and Tammy, and Teri... I'm very blessed in my friends.

I'm eternally grateful to Jane and Maggie at Honest Knave Books for the constant encouragement and technical support - I couldn't have done it without you - and thank you Julian for the marvelous artwork. ... Looking forward to working with you again on future projects.